"A Sport at which Jews Excel": Jewish Basketball in American Society, 1900-1951

A Dissertation Presented

by

Arieh Sclar

to

The Graduate School

in Partial Fulfillment of the

Requirements

for the Degree of

Doctor of Philosophy

in

History

Stony Brook University

May 2008

UMI Number:

Copyright 2008 by

All rights reserved

INFORMATION TO USERS

The quality of this reproduction is dependent upon the quality of the copy submitted. Broken or indistinct print, colored or poor quality illustrations and photographs, print bleed-through, substandard margins, and improper alignment can adversely affect reproduction.

In the unlikely event that the author did not send a complete manuscript and there are missing pages, these will be noted. Also, if unauthorized copyright material had to be removed, a note will indicate the deletion.

UMI Microform
Copyright 2009 by ProQuest LLC
All rights reserved. This microform edition is protected against
unauthorized copying under Title 17, United States Code.

ProQuest LLC
789 East Eisenhower Parkway
P.O. Box 1346
Ann Arbor, MI 48106-1346

Copyright by
Arieh Sclar
2008

Stony Brook University

The Graduate School

Arieh Sclar

We, the dissertation committee for the above candidate for the

Doctor of Philosophy degree, hereby recommend

acceptance of this dissertation.

Shirley Jennifer Lim – Dissertation Advisor
Professor, History Department

Nancy Tomes – Chairperson of Defense
Professor, History Department

April Masten
Professor, History Department

Hasia Diner, Paul and Sylvia Steinberg Professor
American Jewish History, New York University

This dissertation is accepted by the Graduate School

Lawrence Martin
Dean of the Graduate School

Abstract of the Dissertation

"A Sport at which Jews Excel": Jewish Basketball in American Society,

1900-1951

by

Arieh Sclar

Doctor of Philosophy

in

History

Stony Brook University

2008

Between 1900 and 1951, Jews played an important role in the development of basketball in American society. A Jewish basketball culture emerged both from an 'Americanization' project intended to facilitate immigrant adjustment and from a Jewish project that sought to normalize Jewish masculinity through sport. Jewish basketball flourished within the public space of American society as an inter-connected network of local neighborhoods, independent clubs, Jewish centers, public schools, colleges, and professional basketball. As it grew, Jewish basketball confronted internal and external tensions, which complicated its role in American Jewish life. Due to a complex interplay of cultural and political factors that arose from the effort to unite a fragmented American Jewish community, the culture eventually diminished, but not before Jews had helped transform basketball from a marginal sport into a mass, commercialized spectacle.

During the interwar period, public recognition of Jewish basketball led both Jews and non-Jews to describe basketball as a uniquely 'Jewish game.' The 'Jewish game' existed not simply because of the prevalence of Jewish players, but also because Jews were considered inherently good at basketball. This led to the construction of a racialized 'basketball Jew,' whose small, but quick body and mental agility produced the ideal basketball player. By considering the connection between racial identity and athleticism, this study of Jewish basketball will help reveal the relationship between sport and American Jewish culture, which involved play on the court and the meanings associated with this play.

Jewish basketball reflected the experiences of American Jews during the first half of the twentieth century as they moved from being viewed as an 'alien' immigrant group to a relatively accepted minority within mainstream society. This dissertation will examine how the negotiations and power struggles involved in controlling the direction of, and the meanings associated with, Jewish basketball elucidate the complexities of a developing American Jewish community under the stress of integration.

Table of Contents

Acknowledgments..vi
Introduction...1
Chapter One: The Beginning of Jewish Basketball.....................................13
Chapter Two: The Emergence of Jewish Basketball...................................63
Chapter Three: From Caged to Court Jews..103
Chapter Four: "Mental Agility" not "Physical Strength".........................140
Chapter Five: "We Are Average Americans"..184
Chapter Six: The End of an Era...222
Epilogue..266
Bibliography..272

Acknowledgments

Throughout this process, I have received support and assistance from many individuals. First and foremost, I would like to thank my advisor Shirley Jennifer Lim, who provided sound theoretical and methodological advice throughout the writing process. Shirley guided me through difficult racial concepts and helped me gain invaluable insight into the theoretical tools which allowed me to see connections between race and sport that previously escaped my attention. I would also like to thank the other members of my committee. Nancy Tomes brought an enthusiasm to the project that renewed my own energy and vigor and her understanding of consumer society and cultural meanings attached to the physical body. April Masten provided critical structural and grammatical help, which was often needed more than I would have liked to admit. Finally, to Hasia Diner, who over the years has provided assistance beyond all expectations. I thank the entire committee for providing essential support and encouragement throughout the researching and writing process.

I am grateful for the help and support I received from the History Department at Stony Brook University, including Susan Grumet and Pat Klosowicz. I would also like to thank Robert Goldenberg for lending an ear from time to time. My fellow students have served as sounding boards to my enthusiastic ramblings about Jewish basketball. I would especially like to thank Greg Jackson, Lynn Rubin, James Nichols, and Eric Cimino.

Librarians and archivists at a number of institutions provided valuable assistance during the project. I would like to thank those at Joseph and Miriam Ratner Center for the Study of Conservative Judaism at the Jewish Theological Seminary, the University of Minnesota Social Welfare Archives, the Nathan and Theresa Berman Upper Midwest Jewish Archives, and the American Jewish Historical Society. In particular, I would like to thank a number of individuals whose assistance went above and beyond. The staff at the New York Public Library's Jewish Division was invaluable in helping locate materials. In particular, Eleanor Yadin provided personal and engaging assistance. I would also like to thanks Matt Zeysing of the Basketball Hall of Fame and Sydney van Nort at the City College of New York Archive. Steve Siegel's assistance at the 92nd Street Y was essential in providing assistance and guidance in wading through the archive's expansive and diverse holdings.

I would like to thank Cynthia Allen, Meir Ribalow, Michael Feldberg, and George Blumenthal for all contributing to the Jews in Sports web site, without which I would not have started this project. In addition, I would like to thank Ari Kelman for his encouragement, Linda Borish and Jeffrey Gurock for their support.

Most importantly, I would like to thank my family. My parents, Abe and Nancy Sclar provided a love of learning at an early age and encouraged my intellectual and academic growth. My brother David Sclar, who helped me think clearly and readings various drafts. My brother-in-law Ken Gold helped me work through some difficult spots and provided assistance in navigating graduate school and the dissertation process. To Avital, my wonderful and beautiful daughter, whose mere presence inspired me to complete this dissertation. Finally, I dedicate this work to my amazing wife Rachael. Her love, support, patience, and willingness to listen to my infinite theories and ideas gave me the inspiration to work through the difficult stages and charge ahead to the finish.

Introduction

Between 1900 and 1951, Jews played an important role in the development of basketball in American society. A Jewish basketball culture emerged from both an 'Americanization' project intended to facilitate immigrant adjustment and from a Jewish project that sought to normalize Jewish masculinity through sport. Jewish basketball flourished within the public space of American society as an inter-connected network of local neighborhoods, independent clubs, Jewish centers, public schools, colleges, and professional basketball. As it grew, Jewish basketball confronted internal and external tensions, which complicated its role in American Jewish life. Due to a complex interplay of cultural and political factors that arose from the effort to unite a fragmented American Jewish community, the culture eventually diminished, but not before Jews had helped transform basketball from a marginal sport into a mass, commercialized spectacle. This study examines the role of both individual Jews and Jewish basketball culture in the development of basketball. It will ask how the evolution of Jewish basketball reflected the experiences of American Jews during the first half of the twentieth century as they moved from being an 'alien' immigrant group to an accepted minority within mainstream society.

Basketball emerged from an American sport culture constructed in the late nineteenth century. Not until after the Civil War did middle class and elite Americans begin to believe that competitive sport could develop character, manhood, and moral behavior. The closing of the frontier, mass immigration, urbanization, and industrialization transformed American society. Many people, especially the northeastern elite, looked for new ways to develop masculine Americans and argued that team sports such as football taught physical and moral courage, teamwork, and fair play, and thus produced "healthy, moral, and strong"

Americans. Sport also became connected to Anglo-Saxon racial superiority as Americans began to idealize the physically imposing and undeniably masculine athlete who symbolized the strength and vitality of the American nation in his body. Proponents believed the modern athlete would save bourgeois culture even as American sport shook free of its anti-modern foundation to become an end in itself.[1]

In the midst of this transformation, Dr. James Naismith invented basketball or basket ball, as commentators wrote it in its early years, in 1891 at the Young Men's Christian Association (YMCA) Training School in Springfield, Massachusetts. Naismith did so under the auspices of a movement called 'muscular Christianity,' which helped legitimize competitive sport among elite and middle class Americans. Progressive reformers also encouraged the acceptance of competitive sport and believed its wholesome influence would transform the children of immigrants, both Jews and non-Jews, into productive Americans by teaching them traditional American values.[2] Basketball became a

---

[1] For information on the rise of the 'strenuous life' in the late nineteenth century, see T.J. Jackson Lears, *No Place of Grace: Antimodernism and the Transformation of American Culture, 1880-1920* (New York: Pantheon Books, 1981), 98-137. On the rise of sport and physical activity in the late nineteenth century, see Roberta Park, "Healthy, Moral, and Strong: Educational Views of Exercise and Athletic in 19th Century America," in *Fitness in American Culture: Images of Health, Sport, and Body, 1840-1930*, ed. Kathryn Grover (Amherst: University of Massachusetts Press, 1989), 123-160. On America in the late nineteenth century, see Alan Trachtenberg, *The Incorporation of America: Culture and Society in the Gilded Age* (New York: Hill and Wang, 1982); Ronald Takaki, *Iron Cages: Race and Culture in Nineteenth-Century America* (New York: Knopf, 1979); Robert H. Wiebe, *The Search for Order* (New York: Hill and Wang, 1967). During the Gilded Age, sport served primarily as a male activity, though some women played golf or tennis at exclusive country clubs.

[2] On muscular Christianity, see Clifford Putney, *Muscular Christianity: Manhood and Sports in Protestant America, 1880-1920* (Cambridge: Harvard University Press, 2001). On the mass immigration of eastern and southern Europeans, see Thomas Archdeacon, *Becoming American: An Ethnic History* (New York: Free Press, 1983); Roger Daniels, *Coming to America: A History of Immigration and Ethnicity in American Life* (New York: Perennial, 2002); John Higham, *Send These To Me: Immigrants in Urban America* (Baltimore: Johns Hopkins University Press, 1984); Ronald T. Takaki, *A Different Mirror: A History of Multicultural America* (Boston: Little, Brown, and Co., 1993). For works on the struggles, negotiation, and accommodation within the construction of the American Jewish identity, see Andrew Heinze, *Adapting to Abundance: Jewish Immigrants, Mass Consumption, and the Search for American Identity* (New York: Columbia University Press, 1990); John Bodnar, *The Transplanted: A History of Immigrants in Urban America* (Bloomington: Indiana University Press, 1985). For general studies of the Progressive movement, see Peter G. Filene, "The Progressive Movement" *American Quarterly* 22 (Spring

popular sport among Jewish youth because unlike other popular team sports such as football or baseball, it could be played anywhere, under almost any conditions. It also provided an open space in which to participate in mainstream society.

As reformers attempted to 'Americanize' immigrants, Jews became "ambivalent symbols" of a modern, urban life that many Americans believed caused the degeneration of individuals and society. Immigration restrictionists, especially eugenicists in the 1910s, believed that the Jew would negatively impact American society. Immigration opponents combined notions of the economically successful western Jew with the ghettoized eastern Jew to produce a racialized stereotype of the intellectual, crafty, physically small, and weak Jew.[3] The athletic world contained a stereotype of the *non-athletic*, weak Jew which served

---

1970): 20-34; Daniel T. Rodgers, "In Search of Progressivism" *Reviews in American History* 10 (December 1982): 113-132; Steven J. Diner, *A Very Different Age: Americans of the Progressive Age* (New York: Hill and Wang, 1998); Michael McGerr, *A Fierce Discontent: The Rise and Fall of the Progressive Movement in America, 1870-1920* (New York: Oxford University Press, 2005); Allen F. Davis, *Spearheads for Reform: The Social Settlements and the Progressive Movement, 1890-1914* (New York: Oxford University Press, 1967); Richard Hofstadter, *The Age of Reform: From Bryan to FDR* (New York: Knopf, 1956); Wiebe, *The Search for Order*; Mina J. Carson, *Settlement Folk: Social Thought and the American Settlement Movement, 1885-1930* (Chicago: University of Chicago Press, 1990).

[3] On the Jews as "ambivalent symbol," see Eric L. Goldstein, "The Unstable Other: Locating the Jew in Progressive-Era American Racial Discourse," *American Jewish History* 89, no. 4 (2002): 389-393; Higham, *Send These To Me*, 155. John Higham explained that American ambivalence toward modernity manifested in anti-Semitism; For Americans' attitude toward urban life, see Trachtenberg, *The Incorporation of America*, 102-139; For information on anti-modernism in late nineteenth century American life, see Lears, *No Place of Grace*. For examples of studies on Jewish physicality prior to 1890, see "Ethnology, or the Science of the Races," *Edinburgh Review* reprinted in *The Eclectic Magazine of Foreign Literature*, January 1849, 55-87; Josiah Nott, "The Physical History of the Jewish Race," *Southern Quarterly* 1 (July 1850); "Biostalic Immunities of the Jewish Race in Europe" *Medical News* 27, no. 20 (August 1869): 124-125; J.C. McCoan, "The Races of Asiatic Turkey," *The Eclectic Magazine of Foreign Literature*, October 1878, 452-462; P. Kirkpatrick Picard, "The Health and Longevity of the Jews" *The Eclectic Magazine of Foreign Literature*, April 1885, 540-545; William Z. Ripley, *The Races of Europe: A Sociological Study* (New York: D. Appleton and Company, 1899). Ripley did not discuss Jewish athleticism or even an aversion to physical labor, but rather discussed Jews' lack of size and apparent physical degeneracy due to the ghetto existence. He explained that environmental factors contributed to the adaptability of Jewish physical size. For an additional example, see "Culture and Physique," *Current Literature* 5, no. 3 (September 1890): 175-176. The author explained Jews as the "race…most susceptible to culture."

as an example of physical degeneration that resulted from an absence of athletic activity.[4]

Acceptance by both Jews and non-Jews regarding the perceived distance between Jewishness and sport led to a culture of Jewish basketball. American Jews who accepted the notion of the degenerative Jewish body argued that sport would allow Jews to become equal to an American ideal informed by the Anglo-Saxon racial elite. Jewish leaders initially focused their efforts toward immigrant youth, but the Jewish body implied a disjunction between Jewish culture and American society.[5] American Jews hoped athletic participation would normalize Jews' supposed degenerative bodies and allow for full integration into mainstream society. Jewish basketball thus developed at Jewish communal institutions, especially Young Men's Hebrew Associations (YMHA) and Jewish Community Centers (JCC), as a way for young Jews to engage with mainstream society without losing their Jewish identity. This environment thrived during the interwar period until after World War II when Jewish basketball became primarily a recreational sport.

During the early years of Jewish basketball, many American Jews began to believe that only the communal development of 'champion' athletes would guarantee the group's acceptance and integration. In the 1910s, Jewish leaders constructed a 'champion' model to prove that athletic success equaled normal physicality, not in relation to size and strength but in ability and achievement. This athletic model expanded American Jews' use of basketball beyond the initial Progressive project. Irish, Italians, and Polish immigrants, as well as others, also found basketball success within the socializing organizations established by reformers and constructed their own athletic subcultures during the interwar

---

[4] On the movement for immigration restriction, see Roger Daniels, *Guarding the Golden Door: American Immigrant Policy and Immigrants Since 1882* (New York: Hill and Wang, 2004); John Higham, *Strangers in the Land: Patterns of American Nativism* (New Brunswick, N.J.: Rutgers University Press, 1988); Dale T. Knobel, *"America for Americans": The Nativist Movement in the United States* (New York: Twayne Publishers, 1996); Lears, *No Place of Grace*.

[5] Edmund J. James and others, *The Immigrant Jew in America*, (New York: B.F. Buck and Company, 1906), 315-316. The text was issued by the National Liberal Immigration League.

period. However, no group other than Jews produced an athletic model intended to promote elite athletes over mass participation.[6] This model laid the groundwork for a basketball culture that provided young Jewish men with an arena in which they might succeed in mainstream society.

During the first half of the twentieth century, the dominant conception of Jewish athleticism existed as the public performance of modern, integrated Jewish men in competitive sport. Although they existed as important parts of American Jewish life, recreational, non-competitive, non-public, or female athletic activity did not prove Jewish ability, normality, or productivity. This occurred because, as sociologist Michael Messner has explained, American sport historically constructed a dominant masculinity as bodily superiority over feminine or non-athletic masculinity. Historian George Eisen argued that the absence of a traditional athletic culture meant that Jews organized their sporting activities around the accepted culture of their 'host' country.[7] Thus, the champion model reflected the American sport culture's pressure on immigrant groups to conform to the standards of the dominant society. The Jewish press contributed to this idea

---

[6] All ethnic and racial groups advocated some form of competitive or recreational sport, but the limited historiography on ethnic sport indicates that no group encouraged the widespread development of elite athletes to compete in mainstream society. Other groups did produce elite athletes in a variety of sport and Catholic leagues frequently encouraged the development of elite athletes, but the general nature of these leagues were to provide athletic opportunities. Groups often supported athletes in their individual endeavors, but no champion model appears to have existed among other groups. On studies of other immigrant groups and sport, see George Eisen and David K. Wiggins, eds., *Ethnicity and Sport in North American History and Culture* (Westport, CT: Greenwood Press, 1994); Michael Oriard, *King Football: Sport and Spectacle in the Golden Age of Radio and Newsreels, Movies and Magazines, the Weekly and the Daily Press* (Chapel Hill: University of North Carolina Press, 2001); Gary Ross Mormino, "The Playing Fields of St. Louis: Italian Immigrants and Sport," *Journal of Sport History* 9 (Summer 1982): 5-16.

[7] Michael Messner, *Taking the Field: Men, Women, and Sports* (Minneapolis, University of Minnesota Press, 2002), 20-22. See George Eisen, "Jewish History and the Ideology of Modern Sport: Approaches and Interpretations." *Journal of Sport History* 25, no. 3 (1998): 505. Also see Jack Kugelmass, "Why Sports" in Jack Kugelmass, ed. *Jews, Sports, and the Rites of Citizenship* (Urbana: University of Illinois Press, 2007); Jeffrey S. Gurock, *Judaism's Encounter with American Sports* (Bloomington: Indiana University Press, 2005), preface. For a discussion on the idealized male in rabbinic Judaism, see Daniel Boyarin, *Unheroic Conduct: The Rise of Heterosexuality and the Invention of the Jewish Man* (Berkeley: University of California Press, 1997). For an alternative analysis, see Hillel J. Kieval, "Imagining 'Masculinity' in the Jewish Fin de Siecle,' in *Jews and Gender: The Challenge to Hierarchy*, ed. Jonathan Frankel (New York: Oxford University Press, 2000), 142-152.

as columnists and writers magnified the power of the male champion by directly connecting athletic success to the destruction of the stereotype of the weak Jew, social acceptance, and integration.

Competitive sport involved tensions generally absent from physical education and/or recreational sport. Athletes, fans, and coaches often became more interested in winning than in the physical, moral, and mental development of the players. Throughout the first half of the twentieth century, middle class proponents of an amateur ideal attempted to keep professionalism and commercialism from 'corrupting' the sports world. They ultimately failed, but the belief that competitive sport could be harmful led some American Jews to try to remove competitive sport from organized Jewish athleticism. The re-conceptualization of Jewish athleticism as a recreational activity inevitably impacted Jewish basketball even as Jewish players continued to succeed in mainstream basketball into the 1940s.

During the interwar period, public recognition of Jewish basketball led both Jews and non-Jews to describe basketball as a uniquely 'Jewish game.' The 'Jewish game' existed not simply because of the prevalence of Jewish players, but also because Jews were considered inherently good at basketball. This belief led to the construction of a racialized 'basketball Jew,' whose small but quick body and mental agility produced the ideal basketball player. Sander Gilman has illustrated how the idea of superior Jewish intelligence became essential to the stereotypical notion of Jewish physical weakness.[8] The use of intelligence to explain Jewish athletic success implied that the Jewish body was abnormal since other Americans celebrated athletes for their brawn, not brains. Yet, American Jews also used the 'basketball Jew' to invert the negative stereotype of the non-athletic, weak Jew into a positive expression of racial identity. The fact that the generalized, or stereotyped, identity of the short, smart, and quick 'basketball

---

[8] Sander L. Gilman, *Smart Jews: The Construction of the Image of Jewish Superior Intelligence* (Lincoln: University of Nebraska Press, 1996); Robert Singerman, "The Jew as Racial Alien: The Genetic Component of American Anti-Semitism," in *Anti-Semitism in American History*, ed. David A. Gerber (Urbana: University of Illinois Press, 1986), 103-119.

Jew' barely changed during a four decade span does not minimize its importance to the project of Jewish athleticism. American Jews internalized the notion of Jewish intellectual ability, transformed it into a racial characteristic that could produce athletic success, and maintained it to prove their difference from white society.

Race is a useful analytical tool for interpreting Jewish basketball. Historian Peter Levine noted how, in the 1930s, Jewish sportswriter Stanley Frank and non-Jewish sportswriter Paul Gallico constructed versions of the 'basketball Jew' by providing "slightly different spins on the same biological deterministic ball" to explain Jewish success in basketball. He argued that they "offer no more satisfactory explanations of Jewish involvement in basketball half a century ago than similar arguments sometimes offered to explain black domination of the game today."[9] To dismiss racial language misses its cultural importance. Levine examined Jews as an ethnic, not racial, group, and did not explore either the cause or the impact of this biological determinism, which leads to an incomplete examination of Jewish basketball. Then, as now, race often defined and explained athletic success. By considering the connection between racial identity and athleticism, this study of Jewish basketball will help reveal the relationship between sport and American Jewish culture, which involved play on the court and the meanings associated with this play.

Sport can serve as a window to the complicated and political framework of multiculturalism that celebrates diversity and encourages the identification of 'difference.'[10] Internal conflicts occur when people within diverse groups attempt

---

[9] Peter Levine, *Ellis Island to Ebbets Field: Sport and the American-Jewish Experience* (New York: Oxford University Press, 1992), 27.

[10] Historians Michael Oriard and Eliot Gorn have argued that sport history has been banished from cultural studies and thus has not informed notions of power or hegemony and theories of race, gender, and culture. See Elliot J. Gorn and Michael Oriard, "Taking Sports Seriously," *Chronicle of Higher Education*, March 24, 1995. For an example of sport's absence in a general history work, see Diner, *A Very Different Age*. Sport is also barely discussed in readers in cultural studies. For the exception, see Pierre Bourdier, "How Can One Be a Sports Fan?" in *The Cultural Studies Reader*, ed. Simon During (New York: Routledge, 1991). Also see John Storey, *Cultural Theory and Popular Culture: An Introduction* 4th ed. (Athens, GA: University of Georgia Press, 2006);

to control the process and outcome of identity construction. Historian Lon Kurashige explained that these complex negotiations indicate that ethnic identity must not be viewed from the "false dichotomy between assimilation and ethnic retention." Likewise, historian George Sanchez explained in his study of Mexican Americans that ethnicity does not contain "a fixed set of customs," but is rather "a collective identity that emerged from daily experience."[11] These ethnic studies provide a framework in which to explore Jewish basketball as a reflection of the cultural adjustment involved in the construction of an American Jewish identity.

The historiographies of American sport and immigration/ethnic studies have rarely converged. This has limited understandings of how racial identity influenced conceptions of immigrant groups' athleticism. In his study of college football, historian Michael Oriard examined how the racial discourse of immigration restriction impacted conceptions of athleticism during the interwar period. Using Matthew Jacobson's idea of 'reconsolidated' whiteness, Oriard found that ethnic groups, including American Jews, became normalized as whites in comparison to African-Americans during the interwar period.[12] According to

---

Meenakashi Gigi Durham and Douglas M. Kellner, *Media and Cultural Studies: Keyworks*, Rev. ed. (Malden, MA: Blackwell Publishing, 2006).

[11] Lon Kurashige, *Japanese Americans Celebration and Conflict: A History of Ethnic Identity and Festival, 1934-1990* (Berkeley: University of California Press, 1994), xiii; George Sanchez, *Becoming Mexican American: Ethnicity, Culture, and Identity in Chicano Los Angeles, 1900-1945* (New York: Oxford University Press, 1993), 11; Also see David. K. Yoo, *Growing Up Nisei: Race, Generation, and Culture among Japanese Americans of California, 1924-49* (Urbana: University of Chicago Press, 2000). For information on racial formation, see Michael Omi and Howard Winant, 2nd ed., *Racial Formation in the United States: From the 1960s to the 1980s* (New York: Routledge, 1994). On ethnicity, see David A. Hollinger, *Postethnic America: Beyond Multiculturalism* (New York: Basic Books, 1995); Werner Sollors, *Beyond Ethnicity: Consent and Descent in American Culture* (New York: Oxford University Press, 1986); Richard D. Alba, *Ethnic Identity: The Transformation of White America* (New Haven: Yale University Press, 1990).

[12] Matthew Frye Jacobson, *Whiteness of a Different Color: European Immigrants and the Alchemy of Race* (Cambridge: Harvard University Press, 1998); Michael Oriard, *King Football: Sport and Spectacle in the Golden Age of Radio and Newsreels, Movies and Magazines, the Weekly and the Daily Press* (Chapel Hill: University of North Carolina Press, 2001). There are few studies on ethnic groups' involvement in sport. See Levine, *Ellis Island to Ebbet's Field*; George Eisen and David K. Wiggins, *Ethnicity and Sport in North American History and Culture* (Westport, CT: Greenwood Press, 1994); Gary Ross Mormino, "The Playing Fields of St. Louis: Italian Immigrants and Sport," *Journal of Sport History* 9 (Summer 1982): 5-16. Kathleen Susan Yep,

Jacobson, immigration restriction in 1924 began the "reconsolidation" of whiteness and the dynamic transformation of immigrants' racial identities as the nation's conceptions of race, ethnic identity, and citizenship became structured around a black-white paradigm.[13] As historian Eric Goldstein recently illustrated, however, Jewish racial identity remained outside a black-white paradigm than had been thought by historians. Although they accepted the privileges of white identity, American Jews also realized whiteness demanded conformity to external values. This internal discomfort with dominant notions of whiteness accompanied the qualification of Jewish players as Jews within the broader athletic world.[14]

In recent years, the complex meanings of sport have become a more central part of American Jewish historiography. Although no single conception of physicality existed within Judaism or Jewish culture, John Hoberman asserted that sport had a negative impact on religious or cultural Jewish values that were constructed to distance Jews from Gentile society. Jeffrey Gurock recently examined sport's impact on Jewish religious practices and indicated that Jews often had to choose between Jewishness and sport.[15] Other historians have

---

"They Got Game: The Racial and Gender Politics of Basketball in San Francisco's Chinatown, 1932-1949" (Ph.D. diss: University of California, Berkeley, 2002). For an Asian-American study that expands the racial discourse beyond the black-white paradigm, see Shirley Jennifer Lim, *A Feeling of Belonging: Asian American Women's Public Culture, 1930-1960* (New York: New York University Press, 2006).

[13] Jacobson, *Whiteness of a Different Color;*. For the importance of Immigration Restriction on American conceptions of race, also see Mae Ngai, *Impossible Subjects: Illegal Aliens and the Making of Modern America* (Princeton: Princeton University Press, 2004); David Roediger, *Working toward Whiteness: How America's Immigrants Became White: The Strange Journey from Ellis Island to the Suburbs* (New York: Basic Books, 2005); Michael Rogin, *Blackface, White Noise: Jewish Immigrants in the Hollywood Melting Pot* (Berkeley: University of California Press, 1996); Karen Brodkin, *How Jews Became White Folks and What That Says About Race in America* (New Brunswick, NJ: Rutgers University Press, 1998).

[14] Eric L. Goldstein, *The Price of Whiteness: Jews, Race, and American Identity* (Princeton: Princeton University Press, 2006), introduction.

[15] John Hoberman, "Why Jews Play Sports: Do Sport and Jewish Values Conflict?" *Moment* (April 1991). Jeffrey S. Gurock, *Judaism's Encounter with American Sports* (Bloomington: Indiana University Press, 2005), preface, 2-7. Gurock claimed that sport is always in opposition to tradition Judaism and becomes an "alternative religion." He illustrated that American sport ignored the importance of the Jewish Sabbath, thus placing Jews at a distinct disadvantage and

examined sport's role in the construction of an American Jewish ethnic identity. Linda Borish's works on Jewish women have provided important analysis regarding the function of sport in community building.[16] Perhaps most influentially, Peter Levine argued in his seminal work, *Ellis Island to Ebbet's Field* that sport served as a "middle ground" for the children of Jewish immigrants, who made "sport their own." According to Levine, this middle ground became less important as those children joined the white middle class and migrated away from their urban neighborhoods after World War II.[17] Yet, American Jews had neither total freedom to determine the meanings surrounding Jewish athleticism nor an easy time using sport to gain acceptance and facilitate integration into American society. This study will examine how the negotiations and power struggles involved in controlling the direction of, and the meanings associated with, Jewish basketball elucidate the complexities of a developing American Jewish community under the stress of integration.

---

forcing competitors to choose between sport and Judaism. Irving Howe's depiction of inherent Jewish ambivalence toward physicality has been used as the root of sport's impact on American Jewish life. Irving Howe, *The World of Our Fathers: The Journey of the East European Jews in American and the Life They Found and Made* (New York: Harcourt Brace Jovanovich, 1976).

[16] Linda J. Borish, "'Athletic Activities of Various Kinds': Physical Health and Sports Programs for Jewish-American Women." *Journal of Sport History* 21 (Summer 1995): 241-250; Linda J. Borish, "'An Interest in Physical Well-Being Among the Female Membership': Sporting Activities for Women the Young Men's and Young Women's Hebrew Associations." *American Jewish History* 87 (March 1999): 61-93.

[17] Levine, *Ellis Island to Ebbets Field*, 3-86, passim; Gerald Gems, "Sport and the Forging of a Jewish-American Culture: The Chicago Hebrew Institute," *American Jewish History* 83, no. 1 (March 1995): 15-26; As opposed to America, many European Jewish communities were instrumental in popularizing sport even as it remained connected to national projects. On the importance of Jews to European sport, see Eisen, "Jewish History and the Ideology of Modern Sport," 512-513; Steven A. Riess, "Sports and the American Jew: An Introduction," in *Sports and the American Jew*, ed. Steven A. Riess (Syracuse: Syracuse University Press, 1995), 8-9; Jack Kugelmass, ed. *Jews, Sports, and the Rites of Citizenship* (Urbana: University of Illinois Press, 2007). Deborah Dash Moore, *At Home in America: Second Generation New York Jews* (New York: Columbia University Press, 1981). Moore's study was groundbreaking in American Jewish history because she discredited the belief that the second generation was marginalized and disenchanted with their Jewish identity. Moore explained that there were "many ways to be a Jew," and illustrated that their synthesis of the moral community constructed by their immigrant parents influenced the emergence of a new American Jewishness.

During the first half of the twentieth century, religious Jews, Zionists, and socialists allowed those who acquiesced to the America's dominant notions of athleticism to define Jewish athleticism as proof of Jewish normality and masculinity. The pressure for Jews to change their cultural identities in order to become American perpetuated the idea that athleticism, or physical activity, was absent from traditional Jewish culture.[18] Thus, the experiences of players within Jewish basketball cannot be isolated from the tensions involved in American Jewish integration. Players may have simply wanted to play, but communal leaders wanted to control this play and the Jewish press wanted to attach meanings to it. The opportunities and freedom of American society allowed Jews to enter into an athletic world neither created by them nor intended for them. This participation allowed existing fissures within organized Jewish life to infiltrate Jewish basketball. It also resulted in a rich historical record of Jewish achievement in American society.

My study draws from cultural studies that will help reveal the complexities surrounding the culture of Jewish basketball.[19] Historian Steven Riess explained that cultural baggage, class, and access to facilities influenced immigrant groups' experiences in sport.[20] Communal institutions provided athletic opportunities to young Jewish boys and men which counterbalanced the perception of Jews' lack of athletic tradition. Thus, the focus is on Jewish men

---

[18] George Eisen discussed the uses of sport by integrationists, Zionists, and socialists, as well as the lack of sporting culture within traditional Judaism. See Eisen, "Jewish History and the Ideology of Modern Sport."

[19] Laurence J. Silberstein, "Others Within and Others Without: Rethinking Jewish Identity and Culture," in *The Other in Jewish Thought and History: Construction of Jewish Culture and Identity*, ed. Silberstein and Robert L. Cohn (New York: New York University Press, 1994), 1-34. Also see David Theo Goldberg and Michael Krausz, eds., *Jewish Identity* (Philadelphia: Temple University Press, 1993); Jonathan Boyarin and Daniel Boyarin, eds., *Jews and Other Differences: The New Jewish Cultural Studies* (Minneapolis: University of Minnesota Press, 1997); David Biale, Michael Galchinsky and Susan Heschel, eds., *Insider/Outsider: American Jewish and Multiculturalism* (Berkeley: University of California Press, 1998); Goldstein, *The Price of Whiteness*.

[20] Steven A. Riess, *City Games: The Evolution of American Urban Society and Rise of Sports* (Urbana and Chicago: University of Illinois Press, 1989), 93-109.

because of the opportunities and meanings connected to male athleticism. The dissertation also focuses on New York's Jewish basketball. The city's large Jewish population provided an athletic infrastructure that produced Jewish champions who played an important role in both college and professional basketball. New York, in many ways, became the center of the college basketball world in the 1930s and 1940s, and the city provided far greater opportunity for mainstream success than other cities. Within this environment, Jewish basketball gained its greatest recognition and the Jewish press focused on New York Jews as the predominant representation of Jewish basketball.[21]

The first two chapters focus on Jewish basketball during the Progressive era. Chapter one examines the beginning of Jewish basketball in a Progressive environment and its expansion into the organized American Jewish world. The chapter asks why, in the 1890s and 1900s, Jews and non-Jews alike conceived of Jewish athleticism as a rejection of traditional Jewish culture, and how the 'basketball Jew' reflected American Jews' desire for athletic success that would not diminish a distinctive identity. Chapter two explores how Jewish basketball existed in both Jewish life and mainstream society. In the 1910s, young Jews left the Progressive environment of the lower East Side and emerged into college and professional basketball. At the same time, the development of a champion model at YMHA's and community centers expanded the cultural imprint of Jewish basketball. The chapter also shows how the model marginalized Jewish girls and women and led to conflicts between athletes and communal leaders.

Chapter three asks why the growing recognition of Jewish basketball within mainstream society strengthened acceptance of the 'basketball Jew' among both Jews and non-Jews. Jewish basketball had its greatest direct impact on

---

[21] I have examined the Jewish press in a number of cities, including Minneapolis, Detroit, Philadelphia, and Baltimore, and found consistency in this area. Some sport historians have argued that media representations of sporting events do not solely consist of 'facts,' and are cultural texts that need to be deconstructed in order to recognize the complicated meanings tied to such events. Specifically, see Jeffrey Hill, "Anecdotal Evidence: Sport, the Newspaper Press, and History" in *Deconstructing Sport History: A Postmodern Analysis*, ed. Murray G. Phillips (Albany: SUNY Press, 2006), 117-131; Michael Oriard, *Reading Football: How the Popular Press Created an American Spectacle* (Chapel Hill: University of North Carolina Press, 1993).

mainstream basketball during the interwar period. Sport after World War I reflected changes in broader society. The rejection of Progressive reform allowed competitive sport to become a mass, commercialized spectacle. In the 1920s, the Jewish press constructed a discourse of Jewish athleticism that celebrated athletic 'champions' as symbols of Jewish ability and racial identity. Chapter four focuses on Jewish basketball's importance to a new model of college basketball in the 1930s, which produced a commercialized spectacle. It explains why, despite the strengthening of a black-white racial paradigm, Jewish racial identity continued to inform athletic ability.

Chapter five focuses on basketball at the communal level as Jewish community centers, Jewish socialists and Zionists used the sport to attract native-born Jews to their organizations. Immigration restriction transformed American Jewish life and even as some American Jews celebrated Jewish athleticism, communal leaders began to question the value of competitive sport in relation to Jewish values. This chapter explains why American Jewish leaders sought to avoid competitive sport and how a different concept of Jewish athleticism impacted the communal use of basketball.

The effective removal of the champion model from organized Jewish life changed Jewish basketball. Into the late 1940s, Jews remained an important presence in New York college basketball even as American Jewish socio-economic mobility and migration to the suburbs reflected the emergence of a post-war consumer society that encouraged the development of a new basketball culture. African-Americans made their initial forays into this new culture as the Jewish presence steadily declined. The final appearance of the basketball Jew occurs in chapter six, which asks how important changes within basketball and American Jews life contributed to the decline of Jewish basketball.

Jewish basketball evolved between 1900 and 1951, but the basketball 'Jew' retained a constancy that is both surprising and important. The history of Jewish basketball and the basketball Jew serves as a window into the dynamic relationship between race and athleticism and the struggles of American Jews to maintain a distinct identity as they integrated into American society.

Chapter One

The Beginning of Jewish Basketball:

American Sport, Weak Jews, and Progressive Reform

In March 1882, the *New York Times* reported on a group of Jewish "refugees" who had fled Czarist Russia and arrived at Ward's Island. At a time when approximately 250,000 Jews lived in the United States, the article described the "educated outcasts" as having faced discrimination by Russian authorities. It noted their "Oriental" characteristics, and claimed that, "the coarser features of the Jewish type are singularly lacking." It especially noted that "the disagreeable peculiarities of the Shylock mask, [and] the corkscrew curls…are entirely absent." Notably, the article described a number of the men as "splendidly equipped, both intellectually and physically," who "are devoid of national as well as religious prejudice, [and] make no objection to intermarriage with Christians." They had "emigrated solely for the purpose of founding an agricultural colony in the West." The reporter concluded: "when the [American] public once realizes the intrinsic value and special claims of these refugees, more practical means will surely be taken to promote on a large and generous scale the grand movement for their immigration and colonization."[1]

The *New York Times'* optimistic tone regarding the refugees' ability to seamlessly assimilate as frontier farmers stood in stark contrast to a later text from sociologist E.A. Ross. Ross, who wrote during a different time in American history, after the frontier had "closed," based his analysis of Jewish immigrants on a different set of criteria. In 1914, he stated:

---

[1] "Among the Russian Jews," *New York Times*, March 26, 1882, 12.

> On the physical side, the Hebrews are the polar opposite of our pioneer breed. Not only are they undersized and weak-muscled, but they shun bodily activity and are exceedingly sensitive to pain. …Natural selection, frontier life, and the example of the red man produced in America a type of great physical self-control, gritty, uncomplaining, merciless to the body through fear of becoming 'soft.' To this roaming, hunting, exploring, adventurous breed what greater contrast is there than the denizens of the Ghetto?

Ross believed that "by blending with the American the Jew will gain in physique and this with its attendant participation in normal labor, sports, athletics [track and field], outdoor life and the like." Assimilation would be neither easy nor quick, however. "It will be long before they produce the stoical type who blithely fares forth into the wilderness…for 'fun' or 'to keep hard.'"[2]

Ross's treatise reflected a number of important changes regarding sport's place in American society. By the 1900s, many people believed that sport, defined as structured, supervised, and organized games, had replaced the frontier as a way for Americans to prove themselves as worthy successors to the "pioneer breed." Sport served an additional purpose since many Americans believed immigrants had "lost the knowledge of how to play."[3] This led Progressive, mostly Protestant, reformers who believed that all people instinctually and spontaneously played, to direct the play instincts of immigrant youth toward positive expressions of Americanism. Ross recognized sport's role in the assimilation process, but he viewed "the Jew" as antithetical to America's

---

[2] Edward Alsworth Ross, *The Old World in the New: The Significance of Past and Present Immigration to the American People* (New York: The Century Company, 1914), 157-164, 289-290. For information on Ross' racism, see Thomas F. Gossett, *Race: The History of an Idea in America* (Dallas: Southern Methodist University Press, 1963), 168-171, 292-293. Gossett also explained that Ross was an advocate of the "strenuous life."

[3] On the frontier thesis, see Frederick Jackson Turner, *The Frontier in American History* (New York: H. Holt and Company, 1920). Alan Trachtenberg, *The Incorporation of America: Culture and Society in the Gilded Age* (New York: Hill and Wang, 1982). Frederic L. Paxson, "The Rise of Sport" *Mississippi Valley Historical Review* 4, no. 2 (September 1917): 143-186. On the influence Turner's frontier thesis on Paxson's 'safety valve' thesis, see Donald Mrozek, *Sport and the American Mentality, 1880-1910* (Knoxville: University of Tennessee Press, 1983). Quote from George W. Wingate, "The Public Schools Athletic League," *Outing* 52:2 (May 1908): 166.

"pioneer breed." His denigration of Jewish immigrants conflated a lack of physical stature with their unwillingness to partake in "bodily activity" and produced an imagined category of the weak "Jew." This Jew, who represented both 'American' and 'immigrant' Jews, possessed physical deficiencies and intellectual acumen which indicated to immigration restrictionists that Jews were racially inferior outsiders who would irrevocably, and negatively, change the country.[4]

Jewish basketball began as a project to transform 'new' immigrant boys, both Jews and non-Jews into masculine, productive American citizens. Proponents of basketball did not initially intend to use the sport to educate immigrant youth. Progressive basketball came to serve this purpose for some immigrants and provided them with the opportunity to explore American society. American Jews began their own project in response to the stereotype of the weak Jew, which had separated Jews from other 'new' immigrants. Jewish leaders promoted sport as a means to improve the Jewish body and disprove theories of non-athleticism. Some American Jews believed that athletic participation would not change an essential Jewishness. Whereas Ross denigrated Jews for an inability to measure up to the 'pioneer breed,' American Jews sought to retain positive expressions of racial Jewishness as they participated in a sport culture constructed in racial and national terms.

Before the Civil War, middle class Americans opposed sport as a morally suspect activity that served as a negative counterpart to an American work ethic. Some mid-century Victorian reformers promoted gymnastics and calisthenics as part of the era's interest in health reform and medical science increasingly

---

[4] Ross, who coined the term "race suicide" famously used by Theodore Roosevelt, joined other prominent Americans such as Madison Grant, Henry Cabot Lodge, and Owen Wister to argue that only immigration restriction would save America. Although they did not agree on the exact impact that immigrants would have on American society, restrictionists feared that 'new' immigrants would destroy America. Also see Madison Grant, *The Passing of the Great Race; or, The Racial Basis of European History* (New York: C. Scribner's Sons, 1916); Charles Davenport, *Heredity in Relation to Eugenics* (New York: H. Holt and Company, 1911).

endorsed the need for physical health.⁵ In the same vein, reformers opposed sports that encouraged unrestrained emotional outbursts since Victorian culture emphasized self-control, a strong work ethic, and an evangelical spirit of improvement. Sport thus generally existed as an informal and local pastime, confined to the elite and subcultures among the working class.⁶

Changing notions of masculinity spurred on the growing acceptance of physical education, if not sport. In 1858, Oliver Wendell Holmes revealed the growing anxiety that weak men would be unable to meet the challenges of a changing society. "I am satisfied that such a set of … stiff-jointed, soft-muscled, paste-complexioned youth as we [Americans] can boast in our Atlantic cities never before sprang from the loins of Anglo-Saxon lineage." 'Brahmins' like Holmes feared the 'feminization' of Christian men, but Victorian culture did not fully incorporate sport into its spirit of self-improvement until after the Civil War.⁷

---

⁵ 'Rational' recreation that refreshed the mind and body could conform to the work ethic if it allowed the individual to return to work stronger and more alert. Elliot J. Gorn and Warren Goldstein, *A Brief History of American Sports* (New York: Hill and Wang, 1993), 82-86; Linda J. Borish, "The Robust Woman and Muscular Christian: Catharine Beecher, Thomas Higginson, and Their Vision of American Society, Health, and Physical Activities," *International Journal of Sport History* 4, no. 2 (1987): 139-154. For information on 'rational recreation' in late nineteenth century England, see Catriona M. Parratt, "Making Leisure Work: Women's Rational Recreation in Late Victorian and Edwardian England," *Journal of Sport History* 26, no. 3 (1999): 471-487.

⁶ Steven A. Riess, *Sport in Industrial America, 1850-1920* (Wheeling, IL: Harlan Davidson, 1995), 4; Benjamin G. Rader, *American Sports: From the Age of Folk Games to the Age of Television Sport* (New Jersey: Prentice Hall, 1999), 20-23; Goldstein and Gorn, *American Sports*, 63. The elite sometimes produced spectacular horse or boat races that attracted thousands. For information on harness racing as the first 'modern' sport, see Melvin L. Adelman, *A Sporting Time: New York City and the Rise of Modern Athletics, 1820-1870* (Urbana: University of Illinois Press, 1986).

⁷ Oliver Wendell Holmes, "The Autocrat at the Breakfast Table," *Atlantic Monthly* 1 (1858): 881. In the 1860s, a number of published articles called forth to 'muscular Christians' to take their rightful place in society. See Thomas Wentworth Higginson, "Saints and their Bodies" *Atlantic Monthly* 1 (1858): 585-586; Moses Coit Tyler, "Muscular Christianity" *Herald of Health* 8, no. 3 (September 1866): 97-99; Clifford Putney, *Muscular Christianity: Manhood and Sports in Protestant America, 1880-1920* (Cambridge: Harvard University Press, 2001), 11-23. On American manhood in the early and middle of the nineteenth century, in particular, Self-Made Manhood, see E. Anthony Rotundo, *American Manhood: Transformation in Masculinity from the Revolution to the Modern Era* (New York: Basic Books, 1993), 18-25; Michael S. Kimmel, *Manhood in America: A Cultural History* (New York: Free Press, 1996), 55-70.

Beginning in the 1870s, the excitement and dynamism of sports such as baseball attracted 'gentlemen,' young businessmen, clerks, and the working class as both players and fans.[8] Educators attempted to construct an American gymnastic system that would produce balanced and orderly bodies and used sport to aid in muscular development. They feared that reliance on one sport would develop abnormal bodies, but sport's popularity overwhelmed physical culture activities such as gymnastics and calisthenics.[9] The broader capitalist society encouraged the development of professional sport as a commodity for consumers to purchase and in the 1870s, began to lead to excessive competition, gambling, and commercialism in college and amateur sport. The 'evils' associated with competitive sport did not prevent some Americans from believing that sport contained an inherent goodness that produced moral development.[10]

Social and cultural changes in the late nineteenth century strengthened the acceptance of sport among the elite and middle class. The *need* for sport intensified due to rising concerns over the potential impact of urbanization, industrialization, and immigration. Many of sport's most fervent supporters emerged in the northeast.[11] Elite and middle class Americans constructed a

---

[8] For information on baseball, see Riess, *Sport in Industrial America*, 153-176. Since immigrant groups often participated in their own physical activities, sports such as baseball encouraged the children of immigrants to join the American mainstream. On German players in the late nineteenth century, see Larry R. Gerlach, "German Americans in Major League Baseball: Sport and Acculturation," in *The American Game: Baseball and Ethnicity*, eds. Lawrence Baldassaro and Richard Johnson (Carbondale: Southern Illinois University Press, 2000), 27-54. Supporters of German *turnverein* (nationalistic gymnastic clubs) generally opposed English sport due to strong ethnic and nationalistic impulses.

[9] On gymnastic movements, especially the German 'turner' movement, see Allen Guttmann, *Games and Empires: Modern Sports and Cultural Imperialism* (New York: Columbia University Press, 1994), 141-155. On Dr. Dudley Sargent and other early physical educators, see Mrozek, *Sport and American Mentality*, 36-41, 219.

[10] Richard Butsch "Introduction: Leisure and Hegemony in America," in *For Fun or Profit: The Transformation of Leisure into Consumption*, ed. Richard Butsch (Philadelphia: Temple University Press, 1990), 13; Lawrence D. Glickman, ed. *Consumer Society in American History: A Reader* (Ithaca: Cornell University Press, 1999); Mrozek, *Sport and the American Mentality*, preface.

[11] See Park, "Healthy, Moral, and Strong," 123-160; Lears, *No Place of Grace*, 102-110; Mrozek, *Sport and American Mentality*, 22-28.

national sporting ideology that connected sport's physical and moral characteristics to national strength. In 1899, Theodore Roosevelt spoke on the merits of living a "strenuous life" that would provide character and manliness to the "American boy." The Spanish-American War provided a brief opportunity for Americans to prove their manhood on the battlefield. Otherwise, elite and middle class Americans viewed sport, especially football, as an excellent substitute for war.[12] The athlete symbolized American masculinity and served as the worthy successor of the sturdy and strong yeoman farmer. Much like the cowboy, the athlete became a modern symbol of a strong and glorious nation.[13]

Sport's acceptance occurred as a sense of moral, intellectual, and physical superiority among white, or Anglo-Saxon, Americans emerged. Lamarckian theories of inherited characteristics and social Darwinian thinking encouraged the development of a racial hierarchy in which civilized Anglo-Saxons would dominate the world.[14] Only white men could attain the highest levels of

---

[12] Theodore Roosevelt, "The American Boy," in *The Strenuous Life: Essays and Addresses* (New York: The Century Co., 1900). Gail Bederman explained that the masculine ideal proposed by Theodore Roosevelt and other physical culturalists was aggressive and passionate. Nonetheless, the ultimate expression of such an ideal in the twentieth century was something Roosevelt would have abhorred. See Gail Bederman, *Manliness and Civilization: A Cultural History of Gender and Race in the US, 1880-1917* (Chicago: University of Chicago Press, 1995), 215. For spectatorship's role in sport's popularity, see Michael Oriard, *Reading Football: How the Popular Press Created an American Spectacle* (Chapel Hill: University of North Carolina Press, 1993). Also see Amy Kaplan, *The Anarchy of Empire in the Making of U.S. Culture* (Cambridge: Harvard University Press, 2002), 113-115. Kaplan's treatment of a unified 'sport' ignores the important differences between sports at the end of the nineteenth century.

[13] Rotundo, *American Manhood*, 239-244, 259. Michael Kimmel discussed Owen Wister's celebration of rugged masculinity as exemplified by the cowboy, see Kimmel, *Manhood in America*, 148-155. Theodore Greene found that size and strength became emphasized as positive traits in magazine articles in the 1890s. See Theodore P. Greene, *America's Heroes: The Changing Models of Success in American Magazines* (New York: Oxford University Press, 1970), 127-131, 258-262.

[14] Richard Hofstadter, *Social Darwinism in American Thought*, Rev. ed. (Boston: Beacon Press, 1992). On the expansion of racial thinking and Anglo-Saxon superiority in relation to American imperialism, see Gossett, *Race*, 144-174, 310-336. Ronald Takaki explained that advocates of Anglo-Saxon racial superiority believed the perfection of the body had social, moral, and spiritual significance; see Takaki, *Iron Cages*, 260-263. For information on Anglo-Saxon culture's dependence on 'physicality,' see Higham, *Send These to Me*, 45-46; Matthew Frye Jacobson, *Special Sorrows The Diasporic Imagination of Irish, Polish, and Jewish Immigrants in the United States* (Cambridge: Harvard University Press, 1995), 178-181, 195-196.

civilization, but this achievement potentially drained them of their racial vitality. Some Americans began to fear that 'overcivilization' would produce 'neurasthenia,' defined as exhaustion of nervous energy.

As a solution to this problem, G. Stanley Hall proposed his "recapitulation" theory. A psychologist, Hall helped spread the belief that due to inherited characteristics, individuals repeated the experiences of their race, from savagery to civilization, through childhood into adulthood. Hall feared that overcivilization endangered American manhood due to the inadequacies of the Victorian ideology of self-control. Allowing children to experience the stages of evolutionary development would help overcome the negative effects of civilization and produce strong men.[15]

Hall constructed his evolutionary framework on the belief of 'white' supremacy and attributed the ability to organize, the desire for teamwork, and the power of individual strength to the Anglo-Saxon race. Many physical educators built their ideologies around Hall's ideas and believed that sport served as the highest form of a play instinct that needed to be harnessed and controlled for the sake of the individual and society. Luther Gulick, an influential promoter of basketball and a disciple of Hall's, stated in 1901: "Games demanding team-play are played by the Anglo-Saxons peoples, and by these peoples alone, and may thus be said to be a differentiating characteristic of the Anglo-Saxon adolescent male."[16] Gulick did not specify how other European racial groups differentiated

---

[15] For an examination of race and civilization and a discussion of Hall's recapitulation theory, see Bederman, *Manliness and Civilization*, 77-120. On 'neurasthenia,' see Roberta Park, "Physiology and Anatomy are Destiny!?: Brains, Bodies, and Exercise in 19th Century American Thought," *Journal of Sport History* 18, no. 1 (Spring 1991): 40. On Hall's impact on conceptions of adolescence, see Joseph F. Kett, *Rites of Passage: Adolescence in America, 1790 to the present* (New York: Basic Books, 1977); Jeffrey T. Moran, *Teaching Sex: The Shaping of Adolescence in the 20th Century* (Boston: Harvard University Press, 2002). According to Hall and his followers, all children had a play instinct, though it was more developed in some races than others.

[16] Luther Gulick, "Games and Gangs," *Lippincott's Monthly Magazine*, July 1911. An earlier article that defined sport as distinctly Anglo-Saxon was C. Turner, "The Progress of Athleticism," *Outing: An Illustrated Monthly Magazine of Recreation*, November 1888. On the synonymous use of Anglo-Saxon with American, see J. Parmly Paret, "Basket Ball" *Outing* 31 (December 1897): 224. On racial science and sport, see Mrozek, *Sport and American Mentality*, 28-34. Quote from Luther Gulick, *Line Basket-Ball or Basket-Ball for Women* (New York: American Sports Publishing Co., 1901), 12.

from the Anglo-Saxon ideal. At the time of his comments, Jews increasingly became viewed as the polar opposite of Anglo-Saxons.

In the mid to late nineteenth century, American Jews faced exclusion due to religious, economic, and racial reasons. They resisted efforts to be converted to Christianity amid familiar "demonic images" of the Jewish Christ-killer, and found themselves socially excluded by the non-Jewish "new" rich who deflected attacks on their own capitalistic activities onto negative characteristics associated with Jews. An economic depression in the 1870s led to criticism that Jews' mercantile behavior contrasted unfavorably to the activities of yeoman farmers, and thus to traditional American values.[17] In the 1880s, the rise of racial science led to notions that Jewish difference was not just religious, but inherent and possibly fixed. Both immigrant and American Jews found themselves depicted as inferior to Anglo-Saxons within the dominant racial hierarchy. Jews often used racial language as a form of self-defense and as positive expressions of Jewishness, but racial identity remained rooted in a sense of difference from a normative American identity.[18]

In 1890, Jewish difference served as the focus of a U.S. government study. Dr. John Billings examined Jews' health and vitality and found that American Jews had lower birth and death rates than other groups. He differentiated assimilated Jews from immigrants, who according to Billings, had a higher death rate. Overall, however, Jews "have shown that they can resist adversity" because

---

[17] David A. Gerber, "Cutting Out the Shylock: Elite Anti-Semitism and the Quest for Moral Order in the Mid-Nineteenth Century American Marketplace," in *Anti-Semitism in American History*, ed. David A. Gerber (Urbana: University of Illinois Press, 1986), 202-225; Higham, *Send These To Me*, 95-114, 117-150; Leonard Dinnerstein, *Antisemitism in America* (New York: Oxford University Press, 1994), 35-57. Hasia R. Diner, *A Time for Gathering: The Second Migration, 1820-1880* (Baltimore: Johns Hopkins University Press, 1992), 166-191; Robert Rockaway and Arnon Gutfeld, "Demonic Images of the Jew in the 19th Century United States," *American Jewish History* 89, no. 4 (December 2001): 355-381. Rockaway and Gutfeld illustrated that by the 1890s, Christian images of the "demonic" Jew had become common and stereotypes of Jewish desire for money and status had risen to the forefront of public imagination.

[18] Jacobson, *Whiteness of a Different Color*, 174-180; Goldstein, *The Price of Whiteness*, 15-22.

of their "temperance, their system of female hygiene, and their occupations."[19] Between 1890 and World War I, sociologists, economists, and other academics frequently cited the Billings Report as an important study that captured "race factors in social studies."[20]

Billings did not focus on Jewish physical ability or appearance, but social science studies highlighted Jews' lack of stature, narrow chests, weak lungs, flat feet, and other physical abnormalities. Both supporters and opponents of Jewish immigration agreed that the Jewish 'tradition' of city dwelling had caused unique mannerisms, stunted physical development, and encouraged their prevalence in certain professions, especially trade and commerce. Jewish 'overcivilization' had led to neurasthenia, which became seen as a common Jewish malady. The general consensus among social scientists regarding immigrants' lack of physical size did not disallow notions of Jewish vitality. Some scientists and commentators believed Jewish survival in unhealthy urban areas proved strength rather than weakness. Such ideas provoked fears among immigration opponents that Jews would survive and even thrive in unnatural and corrupt urban environments where E.A. Ross's "pioneer breed" could not.[21]

---

[19] John S. Billings, "Vital Statistics of the Jews," *North American Review* 152 (January 1891): 70-84.

[20] *American Economic Association Publications* (May 1903), preface.

[21] Ripley, *The Races of Europe*; Joseph Jacobs, *Studies in Jewish Statistics: Social, Vital, and Anthropometric* (London: D. Nutt, 1891). Jacobs studied European Jews, but was influential on American though in this regard. Sidney Schwab "Neurasthenia among Garment Workers" *American Economic Association Publication* (April 1911): 265-270. Schwab stated that the "Russian Jew...[is] primarily a trader and not a maker of things." Florence Kiper "The Jewish Problem in America," *Forum* (August 1913): 145-152. Kiper compared Jews and women and their commonality as "victims" of neurasthenia and hysteria. Kiper also explained that the Jewish physiognomy was "psychic...stigma of the Ghetto experience." Also see Daniel E. Bender, *Sweated Work, Weak Bodies: Anti-Sweatshop Campaigns and Languages of Labor* (New Brunswick: Rutgers University Press, 2004), 36-40. On other studies, see Alan M. Kraut, *Silent Travelers: Germs, Genes, and the "Immigrant Menace"* (New York: Basic Books, 1994), 138-149. For information on the effects of urbanization on the degeneracy of Americans, see Mrozek, *Sport and the American Mentality*, 24-30; Jacobson, *Whiteness of a Different Color*, 175-185. For information on late nineteenth century medicine, see Nancy Tomes, *The Gospel of Germs: Men, Women, and the Microbe in American Life* (Cambridge: Harvard University Press, 1998).

As the movement for immigration restriction intensified its ties to racial science, the Jewish body transmitted the notion of racial difference to many Americans. Historian Daniel Bender explained that the supposed physical and moral degradation of lower East Side inhabitants served as a material example of racial decline.[22] American Jews often attempted to deflect charges of physical weakness onto immigrants, but even defensive studies conflated 'immigrant' and 'American' Jews into a single physical image that "appears to be inferior to the Anglo-Saxons."[23] The perception of Jewish physical inferiority influenced notions within an athletic world informed by Anglo-Saxon superiority and American Jews became viewed as a nation apart in physical and racial terms.

As sport's widening popularity in the 1890s led to comparisons of the athletic abilities of different nations, some commentators noted Jews' absence from the annals of sport history. In 1892, author George Alfred Townsend argued in *The Chatauquan*: "the law of Moses, omitting social and athletic amusements…weakened his [the "Hebrew"] moral influence while making him commercially eminent and superior."[24] Three years later, the *North American*

---

[22] Goldstein, *The Price of Whiteness*, introduction; Jacobson, *Whiteness of a Different Color*, 225-242; Gossett, *Race*, 329-336; Julius Ullman, "The Racial Factor in Hysteria," *Medical News*, August 31, 1901, 328-332. Ullman explained that "hysteria is almost unknown in the savage and barbarous states," though modern Jews, even in America, "shows the stigma of this disease because of the suffering of their ancestors." Jacob Riis' investigations into ghetto life shocked middle class Americans and helped popularize and expand the parks and playground movement of the early twentieth century. See Jacob Riis, *How the Other Half Lives: Studies among the Tenements of New York* (New York: Charles Scribner's Sons, 1890). New York's lower East Side became a national symbol of Jewish immigrant life. See Bender, *Sweated Work, Weak Bodies*, 25-41. Some investigative journalists probed the East Side and found a vibrant life. Others reported on a crowded, filthy, and 'foreign' neighborhood filled with strange languages, customs, and people. See Burton J. Hendrick, "The Skulls of our Immigrants," *McClure's* 35 (May 1910): 36-50; "The Children of the Ghetto," *Physical Culture* 12 (August 1904).

[23] James and others, *The Immigrant Jew in America*, 282 On the racial aspect of the immigration restriction movement, see Knobel, *"America for Americans,"* 190-195. Also see Higham, *Strangers in the Land*; Daniels, *Guarding the Golden Door*; Jacobson, *Whiteness of a Different Color*; Roediger, *Working toward Whiteness*, 58-72. Religion was often at the root of the anti-immigration movement in the middle of the nineteenth century, but race certainly played a role. See David R. Roediger, *The Wages of Whiteness: Race and the Making of the American Working Class* (New York: Verso, 1991); Noel Ignatiev, *How the Irish Became White* (New York: Routledge, 1995).

[24] George Alfred Townsend, "Recreations of Eminent Men" *The Chatauquan* 15 (August 1892): 582-588.

Review celebrated Anglo-Saxon physical superiority in comparison to other "civilized nations" and charged: "The Jews, who alone refuse active exertion, either as a means of livelihood, or as a source of amusement, are perhaps the sole instance of a successful people…who explicitly or implicitly reject the duty of exercise; this no doubt is a survival of the oriental feeling that the burden of labor should fall on slaves." Similar in tone, though with less denunciatory rhetoric, the elite sporting magazine *Outing* noted in 1899 that, "the Jews in all nations and times have produced…their share of leaders in art, in drama, in music, in literature, and in law; in fact, in all those walks of life in which intellectual acumen and close application to books, and to the study of mankind, is the main force; but they have hitherto, as a people, shown little aptitude for, or application to, the sports of the field and of sustained interest in outdoor recreation."[25]

In these articles, one can see the construction of the "Jews" as a group with intellectual and commercial abilities that compensated for their moral degradation and a lack of physical activity.[26] *Outing*'s isolation of Jewish "intellectual acumen" had the element of praise, but also the implication that traditional Jewish culture simply did not contain physical activity. None of the commentators explicitly discussed immigrant Jews or their supposed lack of size, and *Outing* praised members of an elite Jewish country club who had "somewhat broken away from tradition" due to the "more settled conditions resulting from their civic and religious freedom in America."[27] *Outing* indicated that American

---

[25] Oliver S. Jones, "Morality in College Athletics" *North American Review* 160 (May 1895): 639-640; Charles Turner, "Golf in Gotham," *Outing* 34 (August 1899): 443-457. It would be easy to overstate the commonality of articles in popular magazines regarding the non-athleticism of Jews. These articles were quite rare, but their presence nonetheless indicates a general sentiment shared by elite Americans.

[26] Gilman, *Smart Jews*, 6-7, 22-25. On the intellectual-physical dichotomy in late nineteenth American society, see Park, "Physiology and Anatomy are Destiny!?," 41-42. Action became seen as a way to form character. See Mrozek, *Sport and American Mentality*, 226-227; Rotundo, *American Manhood*, 225-228.

[27] On the establishment of country clubs among acculturated Jews, see Peter Levine, "Our Crowd At Play: The Elite Country Clubs in the 1920s" in Riess, *Sports and the American Jew*, 160-181. The country clubs formed by Jews, while they contained elite sports like golf and tennis, served more as social institutions than athletic. The establishment of the country club is intimately connected to the increased social discrimination that acculturated Jews faced in the late nineteenth

freedom allowed Jews to overcome perceived negative cultural components that had opposed "outdoor recreation." The perception that "the Jews" had failed to become sportsmen ignored Jewish participation in America's growing athletic culture during the late nineteenth century.[28] Yet, even as individual Jews such as runner Lon Myers and football star Phil King found fame and success, American Jews remained only marginally committed to providing competitive athletic opportunities on the communal level.

In the late nineteenth century, New York's Young Men's Hebrew Association (YMHA) served as an example of Jewish communal athleticism. Founded in 1874, the YMHA included an extensive program of literary, social, educational, and religious classes and clubs. During its first decade, it established a gymnasium, hired a paid instructor, and confronted a controversy over the use of the gymnasium on Friday nights.[29] Physical work, however, remained only a minimal part of the broader program and in May 1890, YMHA director H. Pereira Mendes addressed "our failure to provide attraction for our young men." The YMHA could not compete with organizations such as the "German Halle near our institution," which offered "gymnastic instruction and that active exercise in which all healthy men take delight."[30] Mendes believed that sport and recreation

---

century. On social discrimination and immigration, see Higham, *Send These To Me*, 123-136. On anti-Semitism in American sports, see Frederic Cople Jaher, "Antisemitism in American Athletics," *Shofar* 20, no. 1 (Fall 2001): 61-73. The most famous example of individual Jews' participation in secular athletic clubs was Daniel Stern's involvement in the founding of the famous New York Athletic Club. The NYAC, however, became notorious for its exclusion of Jews.

[28] Michele Helane Pavin, "Sports and Leisure of the American Jewish Community, 1848 to 1976," (PhD diss.: The Ohio State University, 1981).

[29] Benjamin Rabinowitz, *The Young Men's Hebrew Association, 1854-1913* (New York: National Jewish Welfare Board, 1948), 51. Diner, *A Time for Gathering*, 108-109; Gurock, *Judaism's Encounter with American Sports*, 38-39. The 92nd Street YMHA presents a unique opportunity to examine Jewish athleticism in the early twentieth century due to a vast source of archival material. The breadth of opportunities offered at the 92nd Street YMHA provides a unique glimpse into an environment in the forefront of a burgeoning American Jewish athletic culture.

[30] H. Pereira Mendes to "the President and Directors of the YMHA," May 24, 1890, YMHA Board of Directors minute book, Young Men's Hebrew Association Records, 92nd Street Y Archives, New York. The New York YMHA did not have a permanent building in the late nineteenth century and moved on a number of occasions.

needed to become a more prominent component of the Association and would function as a means to attract Jewish 'young men.'

Mendes' plea generated limited activities in the 1890s. The YMHA briefly established a Committee on Physical Culture and offered billiards, checkers, and chess to its membership. In 1897, officials suggested "forming of a baseball or bicycle club for the summer to attract the Jewish young men of the neighborhood."[31] Some 'young men' who wanted a more formal athletic environment formed the YMHA Athletic Club in 1898 as a member-controlled but subordinate organization within the larger YMHA. Within weeks of the club's founding, the superintendent suspended a prominent member "for boisterous conduct in the Gym," and for "refusing to stop his tomfoolery."[32] Association officials still recognized the club's importance since it "promotes good-fellowship among the Gymnasium members and helps maintain the grade of work."[33] The club focused exclusively on gymnastics during its early years as YMHA officials encouraged proper behavior rather than developing individual athletes. The YMHA's hesitancy to participate in competitive sport can be

---

[31] Minutes of the YMHA Board of Directors, June 1893–January 1898, Young Men's Hebrew Association records, 92nd Street Y archives, New York. The Committee on Physical Culture was established in 1893 and purchased a 'barge' for newly formed boat club that year. The Committee was not included among official YMHA committees in 1895. In addition, inclusion of bicycling in the midst of a nationwide bicycle craze indicates the middle class nature of YMHA members. For information on the bicycle craze, see Riess, *City Games*, 63-65.

[32] William Mitchell Journal, September 21, 1898, Young Men's Hebrew Association records, 92nd Street Y archives, New York. The following year, Mitchell recorded in his journal that he arrived to a chaotic situation in the gymnasium and "in order to quell the spirit of boisterous fun had to suspend one of them for the evening. This took all the fun out of the matter and things quieted down." William Mitchell Journal, March 22, 1899, Young Men's Hebrew Association records, 92nd Street Y archives, New York.

[33] For the formation of the athletic club, also see William Mitchell Journal, September 3, 1898, Young Men's Hebrew Association records, 92nd Street Y archives, New York. In the late 1890s, institutional leaders initiated an annual fee for gymnasium members and hired a permanent gymnasium instructor. On the gymnasium, see the New York Young Men's Hebrew Association, *Twenty-Fifth Annual Report, 1899* (New York: 1900). Also see the Minutes of the YMHA Board of Directors, January – October 1898, Young Men's Hebrew Association records, 92nd Street Y archives, New York. Among the moves made by the directors was the addition of gymnastic apparatus, such as a horizontal bar and a medicine ball. The instructor organized physical culture classes and gymnastic exhibitions in 1898.

understood since sport included tensions that complicated its inclusion within an America adjusting to mass immigration, urbanization, and industrialization. Some Americans worked to increase sport's acceptance as a vital part of America's changing society.

In the late nineteenth century, influential physical educator Luther Gulick promoted physical education as a legitimate profession. Gulick began his career within the 'muscular Christianity' movement, which believed that a complete Christian man needed physical activity and development as much, if not more, than spiritual and moral development. Gulick, who frequently discussed the importance of action over study or meditation, took his belief in sport outside the 'muscular Christian' realm. He played a prominent role in both the American Association for the Advancement of Physical Education (AAAPE) and the American Physical Education Association (APEA), which brought him into contact with a wide range of individuals concerned with the moral and physical condition of Americans. He, like many other educators, believed that the developing industrial society had the potential to destroy traditional American values and sap Anglo-Saxon strength through the overcivilizing effects of urban life.[34]

Gulick as well as other physical educators wanted to direct the play instincts of children toward positive activities in order to prepare them for the demands of citizenship. Gulick believed motor behavior served as the primary agency of shaping moral reflexes and that repetitive use of certain muscles would aid in the moral development of children. Instructional sport would educate participants and produce positive social ends. Since the play instinct could result in either wholesome or wicked reflexes, Gulick and other play reformers concluded that only strict supervision would teach children correct moral

---

[34] Marc Horger, "Play By The Rules: The Creation of Basketball and the Progressive Era, 1891-1917," (Ph.D. Diss., Ohio State University, 2001) 85-88. Gulick never abandoned his work as a 'muscular Christian,' but this move represented a shift toward a more practical and Progressive ideology. Gulick's "conversion" to the calling of physical education occurred after his failed attempt to become a minister. His father was a prominent missionary in Hawaii. He consistently used the language of 'science' and 'efficiency' in describing the work of physical education.

behavior.[35] Supervision proved vital for all sports, but none more so than basketball, which contained all the tensions involved in American sport in the late nineteenth century.

In 1891, Gulick served as head of the physical education department at the YMCA Training School. He asked fellow 'muscular Christian,' James Naismith, to invent a winter sport to occupy a disgruntled class of future YMCA directors, which resulted in basketball. Naismith later explained that, "basket ball is not a game intended merely for amusement, but is the attempted solution of a problem which has been pressing physical educators. Most of the games which are played out of doors are unsuitable for indoors, and consequently whenever the season closes, the game, together with all the benefits to be derived therefrom, is dropped."[36]

Naismith invented basketball as a sport that would be physically active but not overly rough. He attempted to modify a number of outdoor games before taking a rational approach toward the problem. As he later stated, basketball "is a modern synthetic product of the office. The conditions were recognized, the requirements met, and the rules formulated and put in typewritten form before any attempt was made to test its value." Naismith elevated the goals, originally peach baskets, in order to lend a degree of difficulty, skill, and 'science' to the game. His original 13 rules also included a restriction against carrying the ball. Players could only pass with the ball, which he expected would limit physical contact and eliminate roughness. Naismith believed the game would teach "the right kind of manhood."[37]

---

[35] Benjamin Rader, "The Recapitulation Theory of Play," in *Manliness and Morality: Middle-Class Morality in Britain and America, 1800-1940*, ed. J.A. Mangan, and James Walvin (Manchester: Manchester University Press, 1987), 123-129. Also see Dominick Cavallo, *Muscles and Morals: Organized Playgrounds and Urban Reform, 1880-1920* (Philadelphia: University of Pennsylvania Press, 1981), 88-106.

[36] James Naismith, *Rules for Basket Ball* (Springfield, MA: Springfield Printing and Binding Company, 1892), 3. For a reprint of the quote, see "Popularity in Basketball," *Current Literature* 16, no. 1 (July 1894): 58.

[37] James Naismith, "Basket Ball," *American Physical Education Review* 19, no. 5 (May 1914): 339. Naismith attempted to alter outdoor sports, but found them unsuitable because of excessive

Basketball's inclusion in any institution required a number of conditions. First, officials had to believe basketball would provide a valuable experience for the institution's target audience. Second, the intended participants needed to want to play basketball. Third, the institution would need a gymnasium large enough to arrange a full game. And finally, the institution would willingly have to concede the gymnasium to basketball for a certain amount of time. The final requirement meant only a specialized few could play and would thus monopolize the gymnasium. This situation led some YMCA officials to ban the game at their Associations in the 1890s. Even with these requirements met, however, basketball remained a relatively marginalized sport in mainstream society since indoor sports generally received less broad support than outdoor sports such as baseball, track, and football.[38]

Naismith's intentions regarding the new game differed from how 'muscular Christians' at YMCA's played. Innovative players discovered that dribbling did not violate the original rules. Players quickly acquired more skill in dribbling, which led the game to become rougher as defenders began to guard the

---

violence, lack of space, damage to the gymnasium, or harm to the participants. Also see Allen Guttmann, *A Whole New Ballgame: An Interpretation of American Sports* (Chapel Hill: University of North Carolina Press, 1988), 70-79. Guttmann has argued that Naismith took a rational, scientific approach to inventing basketball. The YMCA helped legitimate sport among the Christian public by serving as the symbolic and material site of 'muscular Christianity.' On muscular Christianity and the YMCA, see Putney, *Muscular Christianity*, 64-71; Charles H. Hopkins, *The History of the YMCA in North America* (New York: Associated Press, 1951). The YMCA taught a 'restrained' and self-controlled Christian conception of manhood, which was symbolized by the 'Triangle' of mind, body, and spirit.

[38] "Athletics in Winter," *Washington Post*, December 17, 1894. An instructor at the YMCA opposed basketball because "it interferes with other Athletic work." For examples of early media attention to local basketball tournaments, see "Seven Teams Entered for Next Friday's Event," *Brooklyn Daily Eagle*, April 22, 1896; "Dispute About Reed Cup," *New York Times*, April 14, 1896; "Basket Ball League Organized," *Washington Post*, January 4, 1895; "Basket Ball Tournament," *Los Angeles Times*, July 29, 1893. Newspapers from around the country often mentioned basketball's initial appearance in respective cities. See "A New Game of Ball," *New York Times*, April 26, 1892; "A Novel Sport to be Instituted," *Washington Post*, May 6, 1893; "Basket Ball," *Atlanta Constitution*, March 23, 1893; "Novelties in Sports," *Brooklyn Daily Eagle*, September 28, 1893. All these articles mentioned that the sport was being played exclusively at YMCA's, and often gave a brief description of the games. Allen Guttmann has discussed the wide dispersal of the game, especially in Asia, due to the missionary work of those who learned the game at the YMCA. See Guttmann, *Games and Empires*, 101-104.

man not the ball. Gulick and Naismith had not initially opposed dribbling, but they watched its development carefully because they believed roughness polluted a 'pure' game that could improve society. Yet, dribbling added excitement to basketball, which by the mid-1890s, had become popular among athletic clubs, military organizations, schools, and sport enthusiasts.[39] Basketball's departure from the YMCA, however, hindered the ability of 'muscular Christians' to regulate the sport's form and function.

Although Naismith invented basketball, Gulick took more responsibility in directing basketball's broadening popularity. Until his death in 1918, Gulick struggled to keep basketball a 'clean' sport. Gulick and his allies in the APEA conducted symposiums on how to maintain order in basketball and struggled to develop rules that would successfully exclude roughness and immoral behavior.[40] As early as the mid-1890s, glimpses of a losing battle could be seen in Hartford and Philadelphia, where YMCA's participated in competitive leagues and participants transformed the game's ends. Gulick and other 'muscular Christians' did not find competition in itself objectionable. One YMCA official stated: "Competitive sports have a place in meeting the need of modern conditions of living by providing opportunity for physical strength and physical conflict."[41] Nevertheless, roughness, violent rivalry, unruly spectators, and excessive competitiveness led the YMCA to eliminate the league in Philadelphia. The players formed a new league outside YMCA control, kept the gate money, and

---

[39] Horger, "Play By The Rules," 24-34. Dribbling first occurred when players at the YMCA realized that the original 13 rules did not forbid losing control of the basketball and then re-gaining possession. Players could drop the ball ahead of them and move down the court in the process. Eventually, skilled players learned how to dribble the ball while running. An additional attempt to 'dribble' the ball in the air while running was forbidden.

[40] "A Symposium on Basket Ball, collected and arranged by Luther Gulick," *American Physical Education Review* 14, no. 6 (June 1909): 376-387.

[41] George J. Fisher, "Athletics Outside Educational Institutions," *American Physical Education Review* 12, no. 2 (June 1907): 119.

created what would become the bane of Progressive basketball: the professional player.[42]

Gulick believed professionalism changed not only why one played, but also how. Middle class and elite proponents of sport idealized the notion of amateurism as the correct way to produce proper moral, physical, and spiritual development. In the nineteenth century, the amateur ethic in Great Britain held that sport should serve as a leisure pursuit for 'gentlemen.' In America's society, middle class and elite proponents of amateurism differentiated the status of amateur and professional sport.[43] If basketball became professionalized, players would be more concerned with winning and attracting paying customers than improving their social behavior. According to Gulick, professionalism "has ruined every branch of athletics to which it has come. When men commence to make money out of sport, it degenerates with most tremendous speed, so that those who love sport have come to set their faces like a flint against every tendency toward professionalism in athletics. It has in the past inevitably resulted in men of lower character going into the game, for, on the average, men of serious purposes in life do not care to go into that kind of thing."[44]

Basketball's novelty meant it had to avoid condemnations often associated with competitive sport. By the late 1890s, even the wholesome and revitalizing sport of football had become associated with the harmful effects of professionalism. Capitalism intruded on sport's purity and a 'win-at-all-costs'

---

[42] Horger, "Play By The Rules," 32-38; Robert Peterson, *Cages to Jump Shots: Pro Basketball's Early Years* (New York: Oxford University Press, 1990), 32-37.

[43] Ronald A. Smith, *Sports and Freedom: The Rise of Big-Time College Athletics* (New York: Oxford University Press, 1988), 165-167. Elite journals often mimicked English notions of sport that defined English amateurism as the natural successor to the ancient Greeks. Smith explained that the English sought legitimacy to their claims of superiority through successorship to Greek athleticism, though they conveniently ignored the fact that the Greeks did not place any sort of moral differentiation between the amateur and professional, and in fact, did not even conceptually define athletic participation along such a dichotomy. Also see S.W. Pope, *Patriotic Games: Sporting Traditions in the American Imagination, 1876-1926* (New York: Oxford University Press, 1997).

[44] Quoted in Horger, "Play By the Rules," 38; Peterson, *Cages to Jump Shots*, 46-47.

mentality overwhelmed 'character-building' manhood. Colleges hired professional coaches whose job security required competitive and commercial success. Player recruitment, subsidies, and paid non-students known as 'tramp' athletes turned college football into big business. Proponents of the game such as Theodore Roosevelt continued to endorse the sport's inherent goodness, but an increasing number of deaths in college football into the 1900s led magazines such as the *Nation* to condemn competitive sport.[45]

Critiques of football served as a warning to basketball's promoters that they had to actively confront disreputable behavior. Gulick continued to endorse wholesome competitiveness, as did many other proponents of amateur sport. The elite sporting magazine *Outing*'s sole article on basketball read like a propaganda manual for the amateur ethos. It declared in 1897 that, "between these two evils – roughness of play and professionalism – the fate of basket-ball trembles in the balance." *Outing* quoted Gulick: "Basket-ball is a good game…but there is no game that offers greater opportunities for dirty work and roughness, and if it falls into the hands of these professional players, it is gone. …They play to win, merely, and roughness is more often the rule than the exception."[46]

Gulick's denunciations of professionalism did not prohibit him from commodifying amateur basketball through the sale of basketball guides. Gulick associated himself with Spalding, a sporting goods manufacturing company founded by former professional baseball player Albert Spalding. Spalding marketed "official" basketball guides that mixed entrepreneurship, promotion, and control by displaying 'proper' technique, rules, and of course equipment, which

---

[45] On the football crisis, see Smith, *Sports and Freedom*, 191-208; Oriard, *Reading Football*, 164-165, 170-171.

[46] Paret, "Basket Ball," 224-225. *Outing* published other articles on basketball that covered the women's game, and occasionally mentioned basketball in overviews of the athletic world, but this article was the only one that specifically examined basketball. According to Paret, Gulick, and others, basketball's characteristics led to both positive and negative experiences. The rapidity of the game, the small space, and the limited number of participants meant one player could dominate since individual skill often preempted teamwork. The small space meant physical contact was inevitable, though roughness depended on the players themselves. In contrast, the same characteristics made basketball a sport which players could cooperate and share in a competitive environment.

Spalding provided to the sporting public.[47] Spalding also promoted *amateur* athletic competition as a wholesome and civilized activity. The 1902-03 basketball guide repeated Gulick's earlier fear that, "few other games can give such thorough discipline of self-control. Few are so beneficial to the boy, when properly played, and few so disastrous to character when allowed to run wild, without regard to rules because of lack of control and direction."[48]

Gulick did not recognize how his promotion of basketball may have intensified the speed with which professional basketball took hold. *Spalding* guides promoted specialty equipment and endorsed the propagation of skills. With more people playing and watching the sport, consumption of basketball could take place in either the amateur form promoted by Spalding or the innovative professional game. The first professional basketball league formed in 1898 and lasted five years. By 1902, other leagues formed and proponents of 'clean' professional basketball, which they believed would be devoid of random violence and roughness, established a guide called *Reach*.[49] The end of *Spalding's* publishing monopoly seemed especially abhorrent to Gulick because some professional games took place in 'cages' made of chicken wire. Historian Marc Horger explained that professionals' manhood included public

---

[47] On Albert Spalding, see Peter Levine, *A.G. Spalding and the Rise of Baseball: The Promise of American Sport* (New York: Oxford University Press, 1985). On the 'nationalization' of sporting equipment, see Stephen H. Hardy, "'Adopted by All the Leading Clubs': Sporting Goods and the Shaping of Leisure, 1800-1900" in Butsch, *For Fun and Profit*, 71-101. On male consumer culture in the late nineteenth century, see Mark A. Swiencicki "Consuming Brotherhood: Men's Culture, Style, and Recreation as Consumer Culture, 1880-1930" in Glickman, *Consumer Society in American History*, 228-231.

[48] Horger, "Play By The Rules," 56-58. Quote in 1902-03 *Spalding Guide* from Horger, 58. Reformers believed 'character' was developed by experience and it was therefore important to ensure that experiences remained within their definitions of 'positive.'

[49] See Albert G. Applin, "From Muscular Christianity to the Marketplace: The History of Men's and Boys' Basketball in the United States, 1891-1957" (Ph.D. Diss.: University of Massachusetts, 1982), 53-57. According to Applin, the guides overwhelmingly helped basketball's quick dispersal. For information on the expansion of middle class magazines, see Christopher P. Wilson, "The Rhetoric of Consumption," in *The Culture of Consumption: Critical Essays in American History, 1880-1980*, ed. Richard Wrightman Fox and T.J. Jackson Lears (New York: Pantheon Books, 1983), 41-64. For a discussion on how magazines, the media, and advertising transformed people's experiences, see Trachtenberg, *The Incorporation of America*, 117-125, 135.

demonstrations of aggressive, violent and materialistic behavior. To Gulick and his supporters, the cages symbolized unrestrained primitiveness, which further led them to believe that professional basketball corrupted Naismith's pure game.[50] Among the growing number of proponents of the amateur ethos were Progressive reformers who believed sport could educate immigrants about America.

In the early 1900s, Gulick worked with Progressive reformers to expand the athletic opportunities of immigrant youth. They formed a number of socializing athletic organizations intended to provide access to competitive sport. As New York City's first director of physical education of public schools, Gulick proved instrumental in the formation of the Public School Athletic League (PSAL), the first athletic organization connected to public schools. The PSAL's mottos of "Duty, Thoughtfulness, Patriotism, Honor, and Obedience" reflected the belief that urban youth would be taught traditional American values through team sports. At the same time, New York City settlement houses established the Inter-Settlement Athletic Association and promoted competition through a hierarchical system so that "the weaker and younger members have always a higher object to strive for."[51]

---

[50] Peterson, *Cages to Jump Shots*, 26, 80-83. Horger, "Play By The Rules," 56-66. The cages were deemed necessary to separate and protect players and spectators from each other. In addition, Robert Peterson explained that backboards were initially used because of audience interference. The moral character of amateur sport provided the central focus of *Spalding* and its editors hoped to confine professional basketball to a separate sphere of the sport's universe. *Reach* guides, on the other hand, viewed rough play and professionalism as mutually exclusive and promoted a 'wholesome' version of professional basketball that would have eliminated the roughness and instability.

[51] On the development of the PSAL, see Riess, *City Games*, 161-167; Paula Fass, *Outside In: Minorities and the Transformation of American Education* (New York: Oxford University Press, 1989). The organization was financed by private corporations and individuals such as Andrew Carnegie, J.P, Morgan, and others. The schools and playgrounds were thought to be especially important socializing forces in changing immigrants. Schools had long been a middle class institution and were believed as a powerful location to stave off immigrant's cultural, racial, and religious traditions that may have otherwise hindered assimilation. *Official Handbook of the Inter-Settlement Athletic Association of Greater New York* (New York: A.G. Spalding & Bros., 1911). Occasionally, the exploits of immigrant participants advanced beyond mere description to the athletic events of the PSAL and the settlement leagues. See "Unique Athletic Event," *New York Times*, March 22, 1903 commented on the first track and field event of the Inter-Settlement League; "Amateur Athletics in the Settlements," *New York Times*, December 12, 1909. On the first activities of the PSAL at Madison Square Garden, see "Public School Athletic Triumph," *New York Times*, December 27, 1903; Wingate, "The Public Schools Athletic League."

The settlement league and PSAL, along with the national Playground Association of America (PAA), promoted and popularized Progressive education in the realm of sport. The same cultural and societal changes that caused elites such as Roosevelt to view sport as a means to revitalize the American nation also led reformers to use sport as a way to improve society. The racial, both biological and cultural, threat posed by southern and eastern European immigrants raised fears that inferior 'stocks' would destroy American values. Reformers provided parks, playgrounds, and recreation to residents of urban, and especially immigrant, neighborhoods and believed that the universal experience of play would help diminish ethnic, religious, and class differences. Teamwork, obedience, and efficiency became buzzwords of professional physical educators, play advocates, and bureaucrats who believed the power of wholesome sport would protect children, teach immigrants, and ensure the safety of society.[52]

Progressive reformers hoped to direct immigrants' leisure time toward wholesome activities. They believed sport would serve as an alternative to, in their opinion, the disreputable commercialized entertainment of dance halls, saloons, nickelodeons, and amusement parks prevalent in urban areas.[53] They also focused on getting immigrant youth off the streets. General George Wingate, president of the PSAL, explained in 1908 that the streets provided a "child about the same opportunity for exercise as it would have had in the space of a grave." The street had caused "miserable physical development," and deprived youth of

---

[52] PAA leaders included Luther Gulick, Theodore Roosevelt, Jacob Riis, G. Stanley Hall, and Sadie American of the National Council of Jewish Women (NCJW). On the play reformers and PAA, see Cavallo, *Muscles and Morals*, 38-48, 56-106, passim. On the Progressive use of sport, see Horger, "Play By The Rules"; Riess, *City Games*, 165-167. Ernest Poole, "Chicago's Public Playgrounds" *Outlook* 87 (December 7, 1907): 776-777. Poole explained that, "On one basketball team a German, a Jew, a Swede, a Pole, and an Irishman fought side by side for months. On inquiring I found that the Irishman was leader..."

[53] Carson, *Settlement Folk*, 173-176. On debates over the wholesomeness of social activities and the struggle to control these institutions, see David Nasaw, *Children of the City: At Work and At Play* (Garden City, NY: Anchor Press/Doubleday, 1985); Kathy L. Peiss, *Cheap Amusements: Working Women and Leisure in Turn-of-the-Century New York* (Philadelphia: Temple University Press, 1986); Roy Rosenzweig, *Eight Hours for What We Will: Workers and Leisure in an Industrial City, 1870-1920* (Cambridge: Cambridge University Press, 1983).

"an opportunity to even learn to play organized games." The lack of supervised, organized sports also meant that "the morals of the boys were deteriorating even more than their bodies. Having no opportunity of working off their superfluous energies by wholesome games, as nature intended that they should, and as boys do in the country, the boys of the street were led to join 'gangs.'"[54]

Reformers believed that Progressive sport needed to be a positive Americanizing force in the lives of immigrant youth. The formation of the PSAL and Inter-Settlement League occurred as neighborhood, ethnic, and employment-based athletic clubs democratized athletic activity in America's cities. These clubs often refused to conform to the amateur ethos, which intensified reformers' desires that sport remain wholesome and respectable.[55] Settlements provided "official" handbooks that specified rule and equipment requirements for participants, and also explained the importance of appropriate dress during athletic participation. "If the spectators see a man come on the athletic field with unkempt uniform, one is apt to go away with a rather poor opinion of athletes in general." The handbook noted "how careful actors are of their personal appearance and clothing, especially when on the stage. The athlete, to a certain extent, occupies a similar position when competing in athletic contests. All eyes are riveted upon him and to the public he is a sort of a hero." Athletes needed to "make it a point to have two suits of athletic apparel, one for competition and one for practice purposes. The clothing that some of our crack athletes wear in competition is a disgrace."[56]

---

[54] Wingate, "The Public Schools Athletic League," 166.

[55] On the athletic club movement in the United States, see Richard Wettan and Joe Willis, "Social Stratification in New York City's Athletic Clubs, 1865-1915," *Journal of Sport History* 3, no. 1 (1976): 45-62.

[56] *Official Handbook of the Inter-Settlement Athletic Association of Greater New York* (New York: A.G. Spalding & Bros., 1908). On different interpretations of reformer activity and success, see Cavallo, *Muscles and Morals*; Nasaw, *Children of the City*, 17-35; Cary Goodman, *Choosing Sides: Playground and Street Life On the Lower East Side* (New York: Schocken Books, 1979). Goodman concluded that social control and cultural hegemony destroyed the vivid street culture of the lower East Side as reformers determined that parks and playgrounds were necessary. Some historians have viewed sort of activity as inhibiting reformers' ability to reach the children of immigrants. Goodman argued that reformers destroyed an authentic immigrant street culture by

The handbook's instruction to purchase apparel, and even the handbook itself, indicated that amateur sport, much like leisure and recreation at large, had become commercialized by the turn of the century. Players needed some discretionary income since membership fees, uniforms, shoes, and laundering cost money. Basketball equipment cost virtually nothing compared to football or baseball, but as historian Mark Swiencicki explained, simply working out at a gymnasium "constituted a form of consumer activity."[57] Reformers most likely did not intend to encourage a consumer culture that symbolized modernity's disruption of a rural, production-based society. Progressive sport nonetheless constructed a sporting environment that provided young immigrants access to the mainstream culture.[58] American Jews provided further athletic opportunities to immigrant youth, which led to the expansion of Jewish participation in the emerging sport of basketball.

As reformers used sport to improve immigrant bodies and morals, American Jews, some of whom were also involved in reform movements, began to view the athletic world as invaluable to direct the assimilation process of the children of eastern European immigrants. This project took its cues from Progressive reformers, but Jewish leaders also promoted sport as a means to

---

developing unwanted parks and playgrounds. Some historians have criticized Goodman's methods since his evidence often came from the reformers themselves. They have also criticized his conclusions that children were coerced or duped into using playgrounds. See Stephen H. Hardy, review of *Choosing Sides: Playgrounds and Street Life on the Lower East Side*, by Cary Goodman, *Journal of Sport History* 8, no. 3 (Winter 1981): 85-87.

[57] Swiencicki, "Consuming Brotherhood," in Glickman, *Consumer Society in American History*, 201-203, 217-218. Swiencicki's quote was in reference to middle class men at YMCA's, but such an idea is valid in any environment. He explained that pre-Depression American men were not considered consumers for four reasons. First, they 'acquired' goods. Second, their consumption took place outside the home. Third, it was not in direct relation to services. Finally was the existence of the myth of the producing man and the consuming woman.

[58] On the emerging consumer society, see T.J. Jackson Lears, "From Salvation to Self-Realization," in *The Culture of Consumption: Critical Essays in American History, 1880-1980*, eds. Richard Wrightman Fox and T.J. Jackson Lears (New York: Pantheon Books, 1983), 3-30. On immigrant and consumer culture, see Heinze, *Adapting to Abundance*; and Jenna Weissman Joselit, *The Wonders of America: Reinventing Jewish Culture, 1880-1950* (New York: Hill and Wang, 1994). On the generational divide within Jewish sport, see Levine, *Ellis Island to Ebbet's Field*; Riess, "Introduction" in Riess, *Jews in American Sports*; Gurock, *Judaism's Encounter with American Sports*, 47-50.

counter charges of Jewish abnormality in relation to the American ideal.[59] A philosophy emerged that connected an immigrant's ability to overcome prejudice and discrimination with the ability to learn and appreciate the value of physical activity and work. Jewish leaders attached sport to a project of immigrant adjustment as early as 1893 when officials at the Jewish institution, the Educational Alliance, stated:

> The importance of physical training for our down-town brethren cannot be over-estimated. Our co-religionists are often charged with lack of physical courage and repugnance to physical work. Nothing will more effectually remove this than athletic training. Let a young man develop his body, and he will neither shrink from imaginary danger nor shirk manual work which falls to his lot.[60]

The statement did not attribute the immigrants' "repugnance to physical work" to any racially determined characteristic. Nor did Alliance officials define "athletic training," although they implied that they intended to use it as a means toward participation in mainstream society, not as a gateway toward broader athletic opportunities. Anxiety concerning Jews' place in society led Alliance officials to link sport with assumptions concerning manhood, labor, and physical development.[61] Jewish leaders embraced the belief that sport's goodness would

---

[59] See James and others, *The Immigrant Jew in America*, 282-333. Chapter 9 covered "health and sanitation." Also see George Dorsey, "New Race Strains Modify Jew Type," *Chicago Tribune*, October 24, 1910.

[60] Educational Alliance, *First Annual Report, 1893* (New York: 1894). Howe, *The World of Our Fathers*, 31-33. Howe explained that 'German' Jews were generally opposed to unrestricted immigration until 1891. On 'German' Jewish desire for rapid Americanization, see Gulie Ne'eman Arad, *America, its Jews, and the Rise of Nazism* (Bloomington: Indiana University Press, 2000), 46-51. On industrialization in relation to the body, see Carolyn de la Pena, *The Body Electric: How Strange Machines Built the Modern American* (New York: New York University Press, 2003).

[61] For brief analysis of the Alliance's statement, see Howe, *The World of Our Fathers*, 231; Riess, "Sports and the American Jew," in Riess, *Sports and the American Jew*, 18; Levine, *Ellis Island to Ebbet's Field*, 14; Butsch "Leisure and Hegemony in America" in Butsch, *For Fun and Profit*, 11-15; Marc Horger, "Play By The Rules: The Creation of Basketball and the Progressive Era, 1891-1917," (Ph.D. diss.: Ohio State University, 2001), 85-88; Bodnar, *The Transplanted*, 86-116. Bodnar argued that immigrants experienced industrial capitalism in Europe and had little difficulty adapting to industrial work rhythms. Bodnar countered the assertions of Oscar Handlin regarding the ability and willingness of immigrants to acculturate into American society. See Oscar

provide the necessary training and education to turn immigrants into productive citizens.

In the late 1890s, the Educational Alliance began to use sport to attract young Jews to the institution. The Alliance's 1897 annual report mentioned the formation of a "baseball nine," and contained the first official reference to basketball, only six years after the sport's invention. The brief citation merely indicated that the institution would provide "the principal part of one evening each week to basket ball, wrestling, and tumbling." The report did not make a value judgment of basketball, although it did encourage individuals to participate in "competitive trials of strength and skill."[62] By 1899, Alliance basketball monopolized the small gymnasium for one night a week. The following year, the growing popularity of the sport led officials to form a representative basketball team that "won seven-tenths of all the matches with their adversaries, some of whom were very strong teams, among others that of the YMCA."[63]

Basketball proved popular because it required little space or money, but the Alliance offered a wide variety of athletic activities. It used an athletic field on Long Island for track, baseball, and soccer. Between April 1901 and June 1902, the *Alliance Review* only mentioned basketball once while it extensively detailed soccer tournaments. Officials found, however, that "only a small minority of the members will take the trouble of regularly visiting grounds not within easy reach of their homes."[64] East Side youth at non-Jewish settlements

---

Handlin, *The Uprooted: The Epic Story of the Great Migrations That Made the American People* (New York: Grosset and Dunlap, 1957).

[62] Educational Alliance, *Fifth Annual Report, 1897* (New York: Educational Alliance, 1898).

[63] Educational Alliance, *Seventh Annual Report, 1899* (New York: 1900). In July 1898, David Blaustein became superintendent and instituted a different attitude toward the immigrant community surrounding the Alliance. On the Educational Alliance, see Adam Bellow, *The Educational Alliance: A Centennial Celebration* (New York: Educational Alliance, 1990).

[64] See *Alliance Review*, April 1901-June 1902. The field was located in Maspeth, Long Island. See Educational Alliance, *Eleventh Annual Report, 1903* (New York: Educational Alliance, 1904). Quote on the trouble of holding outdoor exercises, see Educational Alliance, *Eighth Annual Report, 1900* (New York: Educational Alliance, 1901).

experienced similar difficulties. Hall of Famer Barney Sedran, who played basketball at the University Settlement before becoming a famous professional, remembered that basketball "was the only sport I could play with little trouble. …It was difficult for an East Side youngster like myself to play baseball because there was no diamonds close by."[65]

In the 1900s, other Jewish institutions unevenly produced basketball teams. The Hebrew Educational Society of Brooklyn (HES) hoped to imitate the success of the Alliance in the Brownsville section of Brooklyn, but neither the 1903 or 1904 annual reports mentioned basketball. The sport first merited a brief listing as "basketball games" under the activities section in the 1905 report. An internal league formed two years later.[66] Annual reports from a number of Jewish orphan asylums indicated that they offered physical culture classes, but not sport. These institutions often commented on the underdeveloped state of the children under their care and advanced the notion that they needed corrective education, in both the physical and moral sense. It cannot be assumed that basketball did not exist at these institutions, but the lack of mention in the annual reports indicates that even if basketball was played, it remained a minor component and unworthy of official notice.[67]

---

[65] Bernard Postal, Jesse Silver, and Roy Silver, ed. *Encyclopedia of Jews in Sports* (New York: Bloch Publishing Company, 1965), 92. Historians often presume the supremacy of basketball due to the lack of space in urban neighborhoods. At the Alliance, the purchase of an athletic field belies the claim that young Jews *had* to play basketball because they did not have access to other sports. It is likely that basketball was the most accessible sport for the majority of Jewish youth on the lower East Side, but the availability of soccer and baseball at the Alliance indicates that if an individual had the desire, they could play those sports.

[66] Daniel Soyer, "Brownstones and Brownsville: Elite Philanthropists and Immigrant Constituents at the Hebrew Educational Society of Brooklyn, 1889-1929," *American Jewish History* 88, no. 2 (2000): 181-206. Also see the Hebrew Educational Society, *Annual Reports*, 1903-1907.

[67] The annual reports viewed were between 1895-1905 at the Cleveland Jewish Orphan Asylum, the Pacific Hebrew Orphan Asylum, and the Hebrew Orphan Asylum of New York. It is known that the HOA of New York did have basketball at the institution by the 1910s. The Hebrew Educational Society of Philadelphia did not mention a gymnasium, physical culture, or any sport in the annual reports from 1900, 1901, and 1905. On orphan asylums, see Gary E. Polster, *Inside Looking Out: The Cleveland Jewish Orphan Asylum, 1868-1924* (Kent, OH: Kent State University Press, 1990); Hyman Bogen, *The Luckiest Orphans: A History of the Hebrew Orphan Asylum of New York* (Urbana: University of Illinois Press, 1992); Reena S. Friedman, *These Are Our*

Due to the limited number of competitive basketball teams at Jewish institutions in the 1900s, the Educational Alliance primarily played against athletic clubs and non-Jewish settlement houses in mainstream competitions. In 1901, the *Alliance Review* noted that "rumors are afloat of the organization of a powerful Alliance Basket Ball team that will challenge all teams of the city."[68] The following year, the Alliance entered a team in the Inter-Settlement League, and in 1906, Alliance teams won the senior, middle, and junior class competitions in the league's second division. In 1905, however, officials had warned that, "a tendency toward professionalism has been noticed in some individual cases, especially in the indoor work. Of course, all such ideas have been repressed."[69] Participation in the settlement league brought the Alliance into a mainstream basketball culture that espoused a Progressive and amateur ethos. The New York YMHA participated in the same culture, but officials attempted to focus on the mass, not the elite athlete, within the physical education program.

In spring 1900, the New York YMHA moved into a permanent building on 92nd Street, which provided greater athletic opportunity and larger gymnasium facilities.[70] Members initiated the formation of a competitive basketball team, but officials wanted Jewish institutional basketball to exist within the context of a 'character-building' ideology. The first notice of an organized YMHA basketball

---

Children: Jewish Orphanages in the United States, 1880-1925 (Hanover, NH: University Press of New England, 1994).

[68] "Clubs and Classes," *Alliance Review* (November 1901).

[69] On the championship results of the settlement league, see "Basket Ball Records," *Official Handbook of the Inter-Settlement Athletic Association of Greater New York* (New York: A.G. Spalding & Bros., 1908). On the warning against professionalism, see Educational Alliance, *Thirteenth Annual Report, 1905* (New York: Educational Alliance, 1906).

[70] For changes at the YMHA, see Riess, *City Game*, 100; David Kaufman, *Shul with a Pool: The 'Synagogue Center' in American Jewish History* (Hanover, NH: University Press of New England, 1999), 52-60, 72. The development of the communal center represented the gradual transformation of American Jewish life that would take place over the next few decades as eastern European immigrants and their children eventually organized American Jewish life. For general information on the 92nd Street YMHA, see Rabinowitz, *The Young Men's Hebrew Association*, 56. In 1899, the total gymnasium attendance was 5,644. In 1901, the total attendance was 17,326 and only the library attracted more visitors. The physical department's income also increased, from $168.50 to $3,839.95. See Young Men's Hebrew Association records, 92nd Street Y archives, New York.

team occurred in the November 1900 issue of the *YMHA Bulletin*, and simply stated: "a basket-ball team is being formed." The following month, the *Bulletin* declared that the squad "appeared in their new uniforms, and the effect was dazzling," and in January 1901, it praised the YMHA's victory over "seven or eight outside teams." *The Bulletin* also stated that:

> Our men are beginning to realize the great possibilities for physical improvement to be derived from the game and are doing all in their power to make it clean, healthful, and sportsmanlike…[to] eliminate all rough playing and make the sport one in which players can win a victory with becoming modesty or accept a defeat without bitter feeling. It rests with the players to make the game all that it should be, and they can then depend upon the good will and active co-operation of the officials of the YMHA.[71]

The *Bulletin* passage warned that if basketball were to exist at the Association, players needed to ensure the "co-operation" of officials. Basketball had not gained the complete acceptance of YMHA officials who believed it taught correct values when played according to its original intentions and provided "physical improvement" within an environment devoid of improper behavior. The elimination of "all rough playing" would allow participants to attain the necessary moral education. Competition needed to be "clean" so that basketball could be used as a means to accomplish healthy and positive ends.

---

[71] For mention of basketball, see "Physical Department," *YMHA Bulletin*, November, December 1900. Quote from "Basket Ball," *YMHA Bulletin*, January 1901. Institutional members appear to have initiated the formation of a representative basketball team. See Minutes of the Board of Directors, October 1900, Young Men's Hebrew Association records, 92nd Street Y Archives, New York. The best source for information on the YMHA's daily operations in the early 1900s is the daily journal of William Mitchell, the superintendent from 1898-1912 (he resigned in 1912 to work for the United Hebrew Charities of Brooklyn). He noted in his journal that the Executive Committee agreed to "add a complete Basket Ball team outfit to the Gym." See William Mitchell Journal, October 21, 1900, Young Men's Hebrew Association records, 92nd Street Y Archives, New York. Mitchell often noted basketball games, though with little mention of the events beyond the final score. The need to petition the YMHA board indicates that athletics could not be organized on an informal basis. The 1900 Annual Report mentioned basketball, but did not mention the existence of competitive games outside the institution. The *Bulletin* began in the spring of 1900, just after the institution opened the 92nd Street building.

The YMHA experienced both success and problems during its first two basketball seasons. By February 1901, a second YMHA team had formed. The "first" team, made up of the YMHA's "brawniest members," opened its second season in October 1901 with high hopes since, "during the Summer months, [the players] practiced the rules of 1901 and are quite proficient in the game." A "regular second team" opened its season with a 44-5 victory over the Nordica Basketball Team in a "free and easy fashion." The YMHA also increased its admission charge to ten cents in order to decrease attendance.[72] The measure did not appear to have the desired effect. At the end of 1901 and YMHA officials banned basketball games with outside, or non-institutional, teams. The institution's 1902 annual report declared that "intense rivalry and limited quarters" influenced the decision.[73]

---

[72] For mention of the second team, see "Physical Department," *Y Bulletin* (February 1901). On the "brawniest" members, the opening victory and the admission charge, see "Physical Department," *Y Bulletin* (October 1901). While an admission charge successfully decreased attendance, it is unclear whom the YMHA was attempting to exclude. The *Bulletin* commented it was due to a "large number of outsiders" at games. Superintendent Mitchell wrote in his journal that the fee resulted in "much less crowding and the classes were not depleted of their pupils." See William Mitchell Journal, February 6, 1901, Young Men's Hebrew Association records, 92nd Street Y Archives, New York. The 1901 Annual Report simply mentioned that the charge was made to "avoid overcrowding of the track." See Young Men's Hebrew Association, *Twenty-Seventh Annual Report, 1901* (New York: 1902). In the 1890s, YMCAs charged admission in order to exclude unwanted guests. Luther Gulick believed spectators could learn as much from the instructional game as the players. If basketball was to serve instructional ends, it needed to exist as a respectable medium since the enforcement of certain standards of decorum would improve the public behavior – and thus morals – of working class spectators. While at the YMCA, Gulick believed this possible through two methods: charging admission and stopping games until unruly behavior ceased. Historian Marc Horger has connected charging admission to historian Lawrence Levine's description of a "cultural hierarchy" since some reformers hoped that sport could exist in a polite, and even silent, environment. Gulick believed that the audience needed to abide by cultural norms imposed by basketball's guardians. This conception fit into the standard pattern of cultural development described by Levine. See Horger, "Play By The Rules," 42-44; Lawrence Levine, *Highbrow, Lowbrow: Cultural Hierarchy: The Emergence of Cultural Hierarchy in America* (Cambridge: Harvard University Press, 1988).

[73] Young Men's Hebrew Association, *Twenty-Eighth Annual Report, 1902* (New York: 1903). The *Bulletin* explained that the final game occurred on December 18, 1901, because competition with outside teams, "interfere too much with the regular work of the gymnasium." See Physical Department, *YMHA Bulletin*, January 1902. Mitchell made no reference of interference, but he noted that two YMHA players were injured in the December 18th game and that during an October game, one of the players "struck his head against the wall." See William Mitchell Journal, October 23, 1901, Young Men's Hebrew Association records, 92nd Street Y Archives, New York.

The basketball ban reflected the ideology of YMHA physical education, which limited competitive opportunities. In January 1902, the *Bulletin* published an article entitled "Athletic 'Specialists.'" The article explained that members would "derive great benefit" from physical activities, but denounced the "small minority [of members] who seem to think that the gymnasium is a training ground for specialized work…we think that a young man ought to join a gymnasium for the purpose of rounding himself out physically, and not for the purpose of abnormally developing some particular muscle."[74] Attempts to minimize the importance of athletic specialization conflicted with some members' aspirations, especially those of the Atlas Athletic club, which had changed its name from the YMHA Athletic Club in order to function "without being interfered with by the YMHA." The club had been formed to encourage physical culture, but members primarily focused on competitive sport in the early 1900s.[75] They found the YMHA generally unwilling to cater to their desires. Officials initially kept their distance from the competitive basketball world as they encouraged mass education, not specialized athletics.

For example, the YMHA did not immediately join the Amateur Athletic Union (AAU), amateur basketball's ruling body, after forming its original

---

[74] "Athletic 'Specialists'," *Y Bulletin*, January 1902.

[75] Soon after the publication of "Athletic 'Specialists,'" the YMHA suspended the Atlas Athletic club. The following is derived from the Minutes of the Atlas Athletic Club, William Mitchell Journal, the *Y Bulletin*, Minutes of the Board of Directors and Minutes of the House Committee, Young Men's Hebrew Association records, 92nd Street Y Archives, New York. In February 1902, one of the club's founding members was suspended from the gymnasium. In response, the club expelled the YMHA's physical instructor, Charles Jardine, as an honorary member. In April, Jardine appealed to the Board of Directors for an assistant and suspended three more Atlas members for "insubordination and mischief breeding in the Gymnasium." At the club's meeting on May 5, 1902, which was held at the home of the one of the members due to the suspension, it was club decided: "Applicants for membership need not be member of YMHA gymnasium." Association officials demanded the club turn over their minute book, but they refused and in response, the YMHA suspended the entire club. After club representatives met with YMHA President Percival Menken, the club returned to the Association without further penalty. That summer, Jardine resigned and was replaced by a professional physical director, George Schoening. An examination of the Atlas minute book indicated no reason for YMHA officials to demand its appearance. No pages appear to have been removed. In the midst of the controversy, Atlas joined the AAU in April 1903, preceding the YMHA's AAU membership of November 1903. See Minutes of the Atlas Athletic Club, May 5, 1903, Young Men's Hebrew Association records, 92nd Street Y Archives, New York.

basketball team. The AAU took over control of basketball after YMCA leaders denounced basketball due to commercialism and professionalism. Led by Luther Gulick, the AAU Basketball Committee implemented a registration plan in the 1890s to combat the influence of professionalism in basketball and forbad AAU teams from playing even independent, or non-AAU, amateur teams.[76] The AAU realistically understood it could not eliminate professional basketball, but sought to contain it from spreading into 'pure' amateur competition by banning non-registered players and teams from all AAU competitions. During its initial foray into basketball, therefore, YMHA basketball had been on the outside of the official amateur structure.[77]

In November 1903, the YMHA joined the AAU and resumed basketball games against outside teams. Both developments brought the YMHA closer to the commercial and competitive culture of mainstream amateur sport. AAU membership meant emphasizing conformity to the amateur ideal. It also introduced new pressures. Competition necessitated practice, representative teams, and a hierarchical athletic structure. An admission charge to all games accompanied the resumption of outside competition. Unlike the initial admission fee established in 1901 to control attendance, the new admission charge served purely financial ends. Officials requested that "since the money is to go toward the vacation camp fund everybody ought to patronize them [basketball games]."[78]

---

[76] Some commentators praised the 'perfect' plan, but it proved ineffective since registration did not stop amateurs and professionals from playing against one another. See Horger, "Play By The Rules," 67-72; "AAU Controls Basket Ball," *New York Times*, November 13, 1907; Paret, "Basket Ball," 225.

[77] For the first mention of the YMHA's membership in the AAU, see Harry Sperling, "Gymnasium Notes," *Y Bulletin*, November 1903. The YMHA would not have been considered a renegade, but it is nonetheless surprising that YMHA officials did not immediately conform to governing amateur rules in order to avoid any pretense of controversy. Throughout the late 1890s and early 1900s, the AAU found itself in the midst of controversies involving the registration policy. Problems were often intensified when a non-registered team played a registered team, which made the registered team ineligible for AAU membership. If that team then played others, all the teams would be considered non-registered and so on. For information and controversies regarding AAU sport, the use of registration fees, and the AAU's connection to commercial consumption, see Horger, "Play By The Rules," 76-79.

[78] Harry Sperling, "Gymnasium Notes," *YMHA Bulletin*, December 1903.

Membership in the AAU made competitive sport more visible at the YMHA. After the YMHA's representative team went winless in five games at the 1904 Metropolitan AAU championship, including a 57-10 loss, the Association hosted the tournament in 1905.[79] YMHA officials publicly explained that they had offered the use of the gymnasium out of a "belief that all amateur sport should be put on a high plane and kept free from professionalism." More importantly, the tournament "attracted several thousands [spectators]...many of whom had never heard of the Association," and generated almost $150 from tournament receipts. Officials also claimed that the AAU tournament directly increased basketball's popularity at the YMHA.[80]

The tournament expanded the YMHA's role in New York's amateur basketball culture, but competitive *success* among young Jews first occurred in a Progressive environment. In the 1900s, New York Jewish youth dominated play at a number of non-Jewish settlements, most importantly, the University Settlement. Upon the formation of the Inter-Settlement League, University Settlement members organized an Athletic Association, which by the end of 1903, had "upwards of one hundred members, each paying monthly dues of fifteen cents and an initiation fee of twenty-five cents." Though the settlement had a "small and inadequate gymnasium," basketball became a popular sport. "The enthusiasm and skill developed" at the settlement resulted in the junior class winning the title during each of the Inter-Settlement League's first three years. In 1906, the settlement received $50,000 to expand the gymnasium facilities and brought in a

---

[79] "Metropolitan Basket Ball Championships, *Spalding's Official Basket Ball Guide, 1904-05* (New York: American Sports Publishing Co., 1904); "Championship Basket Ball Games," *New York Times*, April 14, 1904. See Gymnasium Notes, *YMHA Bulletin*, April 1904. An article in the 1906-07 *Spalding Guide* on the 1905 AAU championship written by William Mitchell did not comment on the importance of a Jewish institution hosting such a tournament. See William Mitchell, "Metropolitan Junior Championships," *Spalding's Official Basket Ball Guide, 1906-07* (New York: American Sports Publishing Co., 1906).

[80] Quote on professionalism from "The Recent Basketball Tournament," *Y Bulletin*, May 1905. Comment on publicity from Young Men's Hebrew Association, *Thirty-First Annual Report, 1905* (New York: 1906).

new coach for the youngest and smallest players, called the schoolboys or midgets.[81]

Harry Baum, a Jewish immigrant from Central Europe, had never played basketball when he began coaching at the University Settlement. He had, however, played one year of lacrosse in college and applied many of the lessons he learned in that sport to basketball. Lacrosse "taught him the value of passing and the folly of losing possession of the ball with long heaves," so he taught a style of constant movement, cutting to the basket, and quick passes. The spatial limitations of urban environments shaped how participants played basketball as cramped city gymnasiums restricted player movement. Yet, Baum applied his concepts to basketball not only because of limited space, but also because of the type of player at the settlement. His first team, made up exclusively of Jews and nicknamed the 'busy izzies,' consisted of "players [that] were so small," Baum developed "tactics based on speed and deception." He focused on developing a style that commentators later claimed had placed a "heavy emphasis on brains in the absence of brawn."[82]

Baum had tremendous success at the University Settlement, which dominated the schoolboy division during his five-year tenure. He became a "slave-driving coach" to Jewish youth "who wanted exactly that sort of thing. They were fearless and had an overwhelming ambition to make good…and [were] grateful for instruction in their main passion in life." His first team, consisting of future professionals Barney Sedran, Marty Friedman, and Ira Streusand, among others, won both the schoolboy division in the Inter-Settlement League and the

---

[81] On the settlement league, see "Basket Ball Records," *Official Handbook of the Inter-Settlement Athletic Association of Greater New York* (New York: A.G. Spalding & Bros., 1908). On information of the University Settlement's Athletic Association and gymnasium, see Settlement Athletics, *Seventeenth Annual Report* (New York: University Settlement, 1904 and 1905). On the donation, see Headworker's Report, *Twentieth Annual Report* (New York: University Settlement, 1906).

[82] Stanley Frank, "It Was Obvious – But Here is the First Man to See It," *New York Evening Post*, December 12, 1934. For a similar depiction of early black basketball, see Bob Kuska, *Hot Potato: How Washington and New York Gave Birth to Black Basketball and Changed America's Game Forever* (Charlottesville, VA.: University of Virginia Press, 2004).

Metropolitan Amateur Athletic Union (AAU) championship.[83] Their success reflected a broader athletic success of American Jews, which the mainstream press presented as a break from the Jewish past.

In 1905, *Physical Culture* magazine, a leading proponent of sport and physical education, published an article called "The Jew as an Athlete."[84] The non-Jewish former Olympian, Edward Bushnell, stated: "Even the casual observer of athletic development in America must have noted and marveled at the way in which the indefatigable Jew has been sweeping to the front in the world of outdoor games." Bushnell believed Judaism had opposed sport in Biblical days while persecution in "later times," had "destroyed their desires to measure athletic prowess with the Gentiles." In America, however, Jews experienced freedom "from both religious and political oppression," which allowed them to "become the physical and mental equal of the Gentile." Bushnell presupposed that successful Jewish athletes had "dropped all evidence of clannish prejudices." Ironically, while Jewishness may have limited previous athletic activity, Judaic practices could extend an athletic career. "The Jew can credit much of his athletic success to his diet and abstemious manner of life." For Bushnell, as well as Bernarr McFadden, the editor of *Physical Culture*, the article served as a prime example of physical culture's benefits to a previously abnormal person.[85]

---

[83] Frank, "It Was Obvious – But Here is the First Man to See It."

[84] Edward Bushnell, "The Jew as an Athlete," *Physical Culture* 14, no. 4 (October 1905). The article appeared in the *American Hebrew* on November 25, 1905. Local Jewish newspapers often contained bulletins of institutions with information on physical education departments and athletic teams. See "Official Bulletin YMHA," *Boston Advocate*, January 5, 1906; "Phoenix Club," *The Jewish American* (Detroit), July 12, 1907; "Columbian Settlement: Annual Report," *Jewish Criterion* (Pittsburgh), January 24, 1908.

[85] Bushnell, "The Jew as an Athlete." During the 1900s, Bernarr McFadden's *Physical Culture* published a wide range of articles on the physical activities of different groups in order to prove the benefit of McFadden's concept of physical culture. See "The Art of Japanese Jujuists," *Physical Culture* 5, no. 6 (September 1901); "Kaffir Athletes," *Physical Culture* 7, no. 3 (June 1902); "The Aborigines of Australia," *Physical Culture* 10, no. 4 (October 1903); "Strong French Canadians," *Physical Culture* 12, no. 1 (July 1904); "Jesus as a Physical Culturist," *Physical Culture* 21, no. 6 (June 1909). McFadden promoted feminine beauty, but his greatest efforts focused on developing masculine strength in previously weak members of society. See Jan Todd, "Bernarr McFadden: Reformer of Feminine Form," *Journal of Sport History* 14, no. 1 (Spring

Bushnell's article provided a detailed and theoretical examination of Jewish athleticism. He included one of the first lists of Jewish athletes in a variety of sports, although not basketball, in a national magazine. Bushnell commented that boxing had become the "one sport for which the Jew shows predilection," and believed that this dispelled charges that the "Jew will not fight."[86] He also addressed the absence of Jewish baseball players, caused "partly to a physically peculiarity of his race." According to Bushnell, "one of the methods employed by a manager to select his players is an examination of the eyes, for it is a little known and singular fact, that the best batsman are men with light-colored eyes." Bushnell explained that dark-eyed men could compete if they brought other skills or qualifications, but Jews, the majority of whom had dark eyes, faced continued racial prejudice. "The time may come when the Jew will be able to break down the prejudice in question, but as it now stands, the average manager declines to experiment with him as a team unit."[87] Bushnell placed the burden of breaking down racial barriers squarely on Jewish athletes. In 1908, the *American Hebrew*, one of the most influential Anglo-Jewish newspapers during the early years of the twentieth century, differed slightly on this theme.

1987): 61-75. David Roediger explained that McFadden's ideal was blond, pure, and Anglo-Saxon. See Roediger, *Working toward Whiteness*, 187.

[86] Bushnell, "The Jew as an Athlete." Jewish boxers often fought under Irish names. Previously, English Jews in the late eighteenth century had risen to fame. On commentary of Jewish boxers, see Hendrick, "The Skulls of Our Immigrants,"; "Boxers of Many Races," *National Police Gazette*, August 22, 1903. Jewish boxers remained a prominent presence in the ring for decades. See Ken Blady, *The Jewish Boxers Hall of Fame* (New York: Shapolsky Publishers, 1988); Allen Bodnar, *When Boxing was a Jewish Sport* (Westport, CT.: Praeger, 1997). The magazine did not exclude basketball out of ignorance since it published a regular 'Athletic World' section offered commentary and analysis on basketball. This analysis focused primarily on internal development of the sport such as rule changes and generally ignored participants and competitive outcomes. See the 'Athletic World' section, *Physical Culture* from February 1905-February 1907.

[87] Bushnell, "The Jew as an Athlete." This physical characteristic had little connection to the stereotypical 'ghetto eye' as indicative of Jewish degeneration. For stereotypical depictions of Jewish physicality and the 'ghetto eye,' see Ripley, *The Races of Europe*; Hendrick "The Skulls of Our Immigrants." Hendrick explained that "In the popular mind there is a clearly defined Jewish type – black-haired, black-eyed, thick-lipped, swarthy-complexioned, hook-nosed, short-statured, somewhat narrow-chested, and bent." Also see Cesare Lombroso, "The Hereditary of Acquired Characteristics," *Forum* (October 1897): 200-208.

In December 1908, the *American Hebrew* explained that Jewish youth had previously been barred from athletic participation due to discrimination. Progressive organizations, however, had changed the landscape and provided opportunities for athletic participation. The *Hebrew* specifically praised the PSAL because it had "encouraged and made possible for hundreds of Jewish boys to attain athletic leadership by fair and sportsmanlike competition. Formerly, the same boys were prevented from accomplishing this by petty prejudice and unfair management." This opportunity served a valuable purpose. A Jew would benefit when "he becomes a real factor in the every-day activities of his environment, then and then only can a Jew hope to receive from his Gentile rivals the respect and credit due him."[88]

Like Bushnell, the *Hebrew* ultimately evaluated Jewish activity in relation to Gentile respect and acceptance. Prejudicial attitudes would be contested with American activities and Jewish athleticism would produce normality. Sport's goodness and power as a means to provide moral and physical benefit for its participants could transform Jewish athletes who remained marked as different, whether through a legacy of non-athleticism, dietary practices, or eye-color. Yet, a modern Jewishness that included athletic participation required Jews to discard, according to Bushnell, their "clannish prejudices." According to this principle, Jewish tradition and culture remained barriers to normalization. This dichotomy blamed Jews for any continued prejudice and allowed Jews to become physically normal only if they participated in sport. The *American Hebrew*, as well as many American Jews, willingly connected athletic participation to social acceptance after a controversy illustrated that Jewish athleticism involved more than improving the immigrant body.

In December 1907, Harvard University president Charles Eliot addressed Harvard's Menorah Society, which had been formed the previous year as a way for Harvard's Jewish students to study "Jewish culture." Eliot spoke before approximately 200 people, including Jewish students from Brown, Dartmouth,

---

[88] "The Jewish Athlete," *American Hebrew*, December 11, 1908.

Tufts, Boston University, MIT, and Radcliff. According to the *New York Times*, Eliot stated: "If you take any representative gathering of, say a thousand Jews, you will find that they are distinctly inferior in stature and physical development to a similar gathering of representatives of any other race." President Eliot did not claim that Jews could not physically regenerate, but he placed the responsibility on Jews to conform to the American physical ideal. He believed that the freedom offered by America provided an opportunity for modern Jews to recapture the "glorious times in the history of the Jews when there was a martial spirit among you." Eliot indicated that Jewish physical inferiority occurred because of centuries of suffering, but also claimed: "Here at Harvard, you young men, members of the Jewish race, neglect the out-of-door life, and do not get out into the fresh air and develop physically as you should, although you are taking every advantage of the intellectual opportunities offered you."[89]

Eliot's comments, which imposed a unified Jewish cultural and racial identity that included both physical deficiency and lack of physical activity, received an immediate, and public, response from American Jews. Jewish newspapers in Denver, St. Louis, Detroit, Pittsburgh, and elsewhere published editorials, letters, and rabbinical sermons on the subject of Jewish normality. Most commentary focused on Eliot's condemnation of Jewish physicality. Some Jews posited 'vitality' as an alternative definition of physicality in order to illustrate that traditional Judaism promoted health. Rabbi Joseph Silverman of New York's prestigious Temple Emanu-El denied that Jews, including eastern European Jews, had ever degenerated, and claimed "stature and development are matters of leisure." Rabbi Samuel Margolies of Cleveland's Anshe Emeth agreed

---

[89] Eliot's statements quoted in "Urges Jews to be Strong," *New York Times*, December 21, 1907, 1. Also see "Dr. Eliot on Jewish Physique," *American Hebrew*, December 27, 1907. Jewish papers were printed on Fridays, so the response in the Jewish press occurred the following week. For quote on the Menorah Society's goal, see Seth Korelitz, "The Menorah Idea: From Religion to Culture, from Race to Ethnicity," *American Jewish History* 85, no. 1 (1997): 79; Jenna Weissman Joselit, "Against Ghettoism: A History of the Intercollegiate Menorah Association, 1906-1930," *American Jewish Archives* 30 (1978): 133-154. Eliot's speech was the second lecture in a series given by Menorah. Eliot was no proponent of Jewish assimilation and argued that Jews should not intermarry. See "Dr. Eliot Urges Jews to Uphold Traditions," *New York Times*, December 13, 1924.

and stated that, "the best authorities on this subject…call attention to the pronounced vitality of the Jews and to their physical strength."[90]

During the controversy, the *American Hebrew* acquiesced to the intellectual-physical dichotomy that rendered Jews a non-athletic 'other' in American society. The *Hebrew* endorsed sport as the primary means to overcome the negative characteristics associated with the Jewish body. Ghettoization had partially caused the degeneration of the Jewish body, but "there is a certain amount of truth in Prof. Eliot's statements" since Jews' intellectual activity caused inadequate physical training. This did not change the fact that Jewish boxers, runners, and weight-lifter E.L. Levy proved that, "Jews are capable of developing their muscular system equally as well as other folk and that there is no inherent difficulty in acquiring athletic qualifications if these be desired." The *Hebrew* implied that too few Jews had this desire and appealed to "Jewish students at Harvard and elsewhere" to take Eliot's advice and "devote even a greater amount of time to their outdoor sports than the ordinary student whose frame has been built up by generations of life in the country."[91]

Eliot's comments also received attention at the 92nd Street YMHA, where a *Bulletin* editorial agreed that, "our Jewish young men are not sufficiently

---

[90] "Rabbi Excerpts to Eliot Speech," *New York Times*, December 22, 1907, 14. Editorial, *Jewish Outlook* (Denver), January 3, 1908. Also see "Rabbi Chas. Fleischer's Reply to President Eliot," *Jewish Voice* (St. Louis), January 10, 1908; "President Eliot at the Menorah Society," *Jewish Advocate* (Boston), December 27, 1907; Editorial, *Jewish Criterion* (Pittsburgh), December 27, 1907. During the decade, and in response to a hostile environment, American Jews formed various defense organizations. Among the most important was the American Jewish Committee (AJC), founded in 1906 following the Kishinev pogroms. On the early development of the AJC, see Gerald Sorin, *A Time for Building: The Third Migration, 1880-1920* (Baltimore: Johns Hopkins University, 1992), 204-207. In 1908, the New York police commissioner claimed that Jews constituted half the city's criminals, which broadened rhetorical denouncements of the cunning Jewish mind. T.A. Bingham, "Foreign Criminals in New York" *North American Review* 188 (September 1908). Arthur Goren explained that New York Jews established the Kehillah in 1908 in response to Bingham's charges regarding Jewish criminality. See Goren, *New York Jews and the Quest for Community: The Kehillah Experiment, 1908-1922* (New York: Columbia University Press, 1970). The perception of Jewish economic and intellectual strength led to broad conspiracy theories and Jewish bankers were a central figure in anti-Semitic texts. According to E.A. Ross, Jewish criminals were those of "cunning" not violence. See Ross, *The Old World in the New*, 155-157; Hendrick, "The Jewish Invasion of America," 125-128.

[91] Editorial: Jewish Physique, *American Hebrew*, December 27, 1907.

developed physically," and claimed that the relatively few Jewish athletes served as "the best proof of this." The solution would be for "the Jewish philanthropist to remove the stigma by giving larger support than heretofore to institutions like the YMHA," which was "engaged in the all-around development of young men."[92] Officials extended the YMHA's commitment to competitive sport in the 1908 annual report. "We hope some day to see some of our own boys take a prominent part in athletic competition and thus disprove that our people do not give proper attention to our physical development." Finally, in October 1908, a *Bulletin* editorial stated: "Let us therefore from now on determine to win honors in the athletic world…the Association will do its share toward encouraging athletics in the building."[93]

Institutional officials blamed the lack of athletes on the absence of communal support for institutions interested in "all-around development." The YMHA hoped to illustrate that it offered programs unavailable elsewhere in organized Jewish communal life, and thus deserved more attention, finances, and support. Yet, only months before Eliot's speech, the Atlas Athletic Club had decided to "sever its connection…as a subordinate society of your Association," and established for itself an independent clubhouse in the Bronx. Atlas president Henry Lang, who served on the AAU's Metropolitan Basketball Committee during the mid-1900s, explained to the YMHA Board of Directors that, "the fostering of athletics, with the hope that some day might see Jewish athletes gain recognition and merit (as Jews have done in other fields of life) has been the goal we have been striving to attain." Lang lamented "the inability of the Association to specialize in the direction of and cater to athletics; at the same time, we have held together in the Association, hoping that some day the hand of fortune might

---

[92] "Are the Jews Really Inferior," *Y Bulletin*, February 1908.

[93] Young Men's Hebrew Association, *Thirty-Fourth Annual Report, 1908* (New York: 1909). The *Report* was re-published in the *Y Bulletin*, March 1908. "Athletics in the YMHA," *YMHA Bulletin*, October 1908.

shower on you to enable you to augment Jewish athletic prowess."[94] Despite Lang's complaint regarding the YMHA's "inability" to provide financial support for athletic specialization, "unwillingness" may have been a more fitting word. Atlas's hope for a YMHA athletic culture had produced no appeal to 'philanthropists.' Eliot's comments, on the other hand, raised an immediate cry for help and appear to have been the necessary catalyst to produce a cultural change at the YMHA.

One must be careful in drawing too broad a conclusion regarding the 92nd Street YMHA's response to Eliot's comments. YMHA officials remained silent regarding Atlas's departure, which allowed them to blame the broader community for Jewish physical deficiencies. They could therefore justifiably demand more support in *their* (not Atlas') fight to "remove the stigma."[95] Yet, the YMHA had supported, ideologically if not financially, Atlas's desire to produce Jewish athletes. At the formal opening of Atlas's new clubhouse in the Bronx, YMHA Superintendent William Mitchell foreshadowed what would become the YMHA's project only months later, but at the time, seemed to be the exclusive property of Atlas: "it is necessary that you stick to your resolution to do purely athletic work." Mitchell explained that even if Atlas did not develop champions, "your work will

---

[94] Henry Lang to the Board of Directors of the 92nd Street YMHA, March 20, 1907, Young Men's Hebrew Association records, 92nd Street Y Archives, New York; According to information found in the Atlas minute book, the club was repeatedly denied use of the YMHA gymnasium for basketball practice. In response, Atlas began practicing at other area gymnasiums and furthered their separation from the YMHA. Club members also consistently asked the Association to purchase or rent a running track, but were ignored or denied. According to the Atlas Athletic Club minute book, the club began looking for a new 'home' in January 1905. The *Bulletin* announced Atlas' departure and focused on the lack of "outdoor training quarters" since the "Association did not cover this phase of athletics." See "Jewish Athletic Club," *Y Bulletin*, May 1907. Lang's name was listed as a member of the AAU Committee, "Basket Ball Leaders Purifying the Game," *New York Times*, December 15, 1906.

[95] Additional funding in the late 1900s permitted the hiring of an "athletic coach," though one official complained that, "too much stress was being placed on athletic work." See Minutes of Class Committee, March 19, 1910, Young Men's Hebrew Association records, 92nd Street Y Archives, New York. Young adult males had an additional outlet in the late 1900s. In 1906, the City Athletic Club was formed to "promote athletics and sociability." Though the vast majority of its members and leaders were Jewish, it was not considered an exclusively Jewish club. On the City AC, see Riess, "Sports and the American Jew," 10; "The City Athletic Club," *American Hebrew*, November 20, 1908.

not have been in vain. I am a great believer in young men, in young Jewish men, and in physical sport, as a builder of manhood and character."[96]

Mitchell unified his concept of manhood with 'character,' which indicated the influence of the American Physical Education Association (APEA) on the YMHA gymnasium program. Although physical educators had various levels of commitment toward sport, including some opposition to it, the APEA promoted a manhood of self-control that produced a symmetrical body and the harmonious development of the whole person. Educators generally did not equate health with muscles or physical size, which provided the YMHA with an attractive model with which to build its physical education department. Yet, the YMHA still had to conform to an external ideal and APEA manhood remained informed by the racial superiority, if not the physical size and strength, of the Anglo-Saxon male. The APEA model also could not provide an adequate defense to counter charges of Jewish weakness. When Charles Eliot spoke of Jewish physical inferiority, the YMHA decided that 'all-around' development would no longer be enough to produce masculine Jews. Rather than forcing the Jewish man to live up to the physical ideal of muscular size and strength, the YMHA opened a dialogue with dominant conceptions of athleticism and became determined to 'win honors in the athletic world.'[97] The YMHA had sought to avoid any engagement with the

---

[96] For Mitchell's speech, see "Jewish Athletic Club, *Y Bulletin*, May 1907. Lang remained a life-long YMHA member, which is likely why the Atlas records are located at the 92nd Street Y Archives. In the letter to the Board of Directors, Lang referred to the lack of a Jewish athletic tradition, but did not discuss the Jewish body. He thus legitimized one aspect of the stereotype (non-athleticism), but would have likely argued against the other (physical weakness).

[97] On the APEA and physical educators, see Park, "Healthy, Moral, and Strong," 148-154. See Mrozek, *Sport and American Mentality*, 36-41. On the football player as athletic ideal, see Oriard, *Reading Football*, 189-273 passim. On Jewish discomfort with aspects of physical or athletic aggressiveness, see Eisen, "Jewish History and the Ideology of Modern Sport," 512-514, 520-521. Some physical educators like Luther Gulick worked closely with Progressive reformers while others had little interest or contact with reform efforts. Debates over competitive sport generally revolved around the need for good management as a bulwark against it succumbing to unhealthy competitive or commercial pressures. The APEA studied muscular activity, symmetry; anthropometry, and other 'sciences.' As a member of the APEA, YMHA physical education director George Schoening would have been keenly aware of the studies, debates, lectures, and symposiums occurring throughout the country. Schoening first appeared in the membership role of the APEA in 1903, the year after becoming the YMHA physical education director.

stereotype of the non-athletic, weak Jew. Yet, its response to Eliot's comments indicated the strength of the stereotype at a time when the question of Jewish physical regeneration had important implications regarding Jews' place in American society.

In 1907, only months before Eliot addressed the Menorah Society, the United States Congress formed the Dillingham Commission to examine immigration. Opponents of immigration argued that the 'new' immigrants of southern and eastern Europe including Jews, Italians, and Slavs were racially inferior to the 'old' immigrants from northern Europe such as the English, Scottish, and Scandinavians. Jewish anthropologist Franz Boas attacked racial science and argued that physical changes occurred due to environmental rather than racial factors. Boas challenged the basic premises of racial nativism and argued that changes in head form and body type illustrated the assimilatory tendencies of the children of immigrants. Boas depicted the 'new' immigrant body as degenerative and abnormal compared to an idealized 'American' physical type.[98]

The Dillingham Commission's report nominally supported the notion that Jews would assimilate to the American physical norm. The commission's report, published in 1911, stated: "Physically the Hebrew is a mixed race," although "to a less degree than most." Their adaptability meant that "they are found to approach the type the people among whom they have long resided." The commission endorsed Boas' argument that "the form of the head seems to have become quite the reverse of the Semitic type." The report also stated that, "the 'Jewish nose' and to a less degree other facial characteristics, are found well-nigh everywhere

---

[98] On Boas's struggle with dominant racial scientists in the early twentieth century, see Gossett, *Race*, 422-425, 429. "Say Aliens Soon Get American Physique," *New York Times*, December 17, 1909; "Jewish Heads" *American Hebrew*, December 24, 1909. Robert Wiebe marked 1907 as the beginning of a serious drive for immigration restriction. See Wiebe, *The Search for Order*, 288. On the Dillingham Commission, see Arad, *America, its Jews, and the Rise of Nazism*, 41-44, 63; Goldstein, *The Price of Whiteness*, 105-114.

throughout the race."[99] Jews' physical characteristics confirmed their racial identity. Boas denied race as a biological category, which meant he could not, or would not, use race to define Jewishness within mainstream society. Neither would a Ukrainian-born anthropologist, Maurice Fishberg, who like Boas, took skull measurements and affirmed that environmental factors influenced physical characteristics. His work culminated in the 1911 study, *The Jews*, in which he denied the existence of a Jewish "physical type." Any similarities among Jews, such as posture or facial expressions, had been caused by "centuries of persecution and social isolation."[100]

Some Jewish leaders hoped Fishberg's study would help discredit negative notions of the "race Jew." Yet, race pride often intruded upon these efforts. According to historian Eric Goldstein, Fishberg's denial of racial difference led to the "logical conclusion" that Jews would assimilate into white society. Goldstein explained that many American Jews "respected Fishberg's efforts to protect Jews from criticism and attack, but could not countenance what they saw as a denial of Jews' most basic and enduring ties to one another."[101] Jews wanted inclusion in 'white' society, but they also wanted to retain racial identifiers that allowed for the survival of the Jewish people. Some American Jews believed that Jewishness itself, defined not as cultural practice but as racial identity, could contribute to athletic success even within a Jewish body.

In 1908, the *American Hebrew* published its first series of articles on Jewish athleticism. The first article, "Activity of the Jews in Athletics," celebrated the fact that teams from either the Clark House or University Settlement, "solely made up of Jewish boys, has held the basketball championship

---

[99] *Dictionary of Races or Peoples*, Reports of the Immigration Commission, 61st Congress, 3rd Session, Senate Document No. 662 (Washington: Government Printing Office, 1911), 73-74.

[100] Goldstein, *The Price of Whiteness*, 110-114. Quote from page 113.

[101] Quote from Goldstein, *The Price of Whiteness*, 112; Eric L. Goldstein, "Contesting the Categories: Jews and Government Racial Classification in the United States," *Jewish History* 19, no. 1 (January 2005): 93-94. Abram Lipsky, "Are the Jews A Pure Race?" *American Hebrew*, July 12, 1912.

of the settlement league…ever since the league came into existence." The newspaper focused on basketball played on the lower East Side in an environment predominated by Jews, which led to the conclusion that, "it is a well established fact that in basketball, the Jew has no superior." More significantly, the newspaper attempted to examine the root of Jewish success. This urban, frenetic and hurried sport, according to the *Hebrew*, "requires a good deal of quick thinking, lightning like rapidity of movement and endurance; it does not call for brutality and brute strength and that is why the Jews excel in it."[102]

The *Hebrew*'s assertion of Jewish basketball superiority fit into the dominant writing about the sport's required characteristics. Early accounts of the sport noted that "basket-ball requires the most rapid kind of play," which necessitated a certain kind of player. The focus on passing placed a premium on quickness and speed. A 1912 treatise explained that "agility and alertness are two of the fundamental and principle characteristics." In 1903, *Spalding's* editor pronounced: "Basket ball is a game of skill and not of brute force. I have seen a team weighing on an average fifteen pounds less than the other win a game by skill in passing the ball."[103] Even inventor James Naismith commented: "The first principle on which the game was based was that it should demand of, and develop in, the player of the highest type of physical and athletic development. This type in the mind of the writer was the tall, agile, graceful, and expert athlete, rather than the massive muscular man on the one hand, or the cadaverous greyhound type on the other."[104] The stereotyped Jewish immigrant body did not fit Naismith's ideal, but it was not negated as either the 'cadaverous greyhound' or the 'massive muscular' type.

---

[102] "Activity of the Jews in Athletics," *American Hebrew*, September 18, 1908.

[103] Paret, "Basket Ball," 227; "Basket Ball and Its Success," *New York Times*, November 12, 1893. The press explained that playing positions were virtually interchangeable with the exception of center, which required an additional characteristic: height. Guerdon N. Messer, *How to Play Basket Ball: A Thesis on the Technique of the Game* (New York: American Sports Publishing Co., 1912); "Order v. Chaos," *Spalding's Official Basket Ball Guide 1902-03* (New York: American Sports Publishing Company, 1903).

[104] Naismith, "Basket Ball," 340.

The *Hebrew* took the dominant writing about basketball and applied it to the imagined category of the 'Jew.' The *Hebrew* proposed, possibly for the first time, that the Jewish body could serve as an advantage in athletic competition. The *Hebrew* inverted the lack of physical size from a determinant of Jewish non-athleticism and weakness into an advantage in basketball. Jewish vitality could be transformed into endurance and intellectual ability translated into mental acuteness in a rapid game that required instinctual quickness. Yet, ascriptions of Jewish intelligence perpetuated the underpinnings of the stereotype. The implication that Jews did not have "brute strength" meant Jewish masculine identity had not escaped perceptions of Jewish physical inferiority. Jews succeeded because of quickness and thinking, not because of physical strength.

The *Hebrew*'s 'basketball Jew' possessed the immigrant body and an essential Jewishness. Speed and the ability for fast play served as important characteristics, but the Jew also had the necessary mental makeup needed to succeed. Thus, the Jew succeeded as, and because of being, a Jew. The racial pride involved in celebrating this distinctiveness indicated that although Bushnell and others presented Jewish athleticism as a way to overcome 'clannish' tendencies, Jews did not have to change their racial or cultural identity to become American. In fact, the underlying assumption of the *Hebrew's* argument was that if Jews lost either their small body or their Jewish intellect, they would also lose their status as superior basketball players. American Jews had found an activity that proved their willingness to participate in mainstream society without losing their positive racial identity.

The *American Hebrew* attached Jewish excellence to a style of play that it presumed predominated in basketball. The *Hebrew* could do this because discontinuity between amateur and professional basketball prevented the game from gaining a national reputation in the early twentieth century, which allowed observers to define their own notions of superiority. The abstract notions involved in Naismith's invention had been challenged by participants who attached different values to the sport, constructed different ways to play, and determined what physical attributes proved useful. Professionals often used brute strength to move their way toward the basket, thus turning the game into a slow, rugged, and sometimes dull affair.[105] Groups or individuals who wanted to participate in basketball could do so even if they offended a particular ruling body. If players or teams found themselves unwanted in one location, they could easily find another. By 1914, some commentators estimated that five sets of rules existed within basketball.[106] The sport remained recognizable to all those involved, but the confusion meant that various groups could play the game with little contact or knowledge of one another.

In the 1910s, young Jews who began their careers in the settlements and public schools would help bridge the gaps. The PSAL and the Inter-Settlement League provided a pathway to a mainstream culture otherwise unavailable to the children of immigrants. In the mid-1900s, immigrant Jews in New York and Philadelphia made their entrance into the public space of the basketball guides in photographs of championship public school and settlement house teams.[107] These

---

[105] Peterson, *Cages to Jump Shots*, 80-83.

[106] Horger, "Play By The Rules," 73. The AAU associated itself closely with *Spalding* while *Physical Culture* promoted the Protective Association, which opposed the perceived hypocrisy of the AAU's registration rules and rigid standards of amateurism. The editor of Spalding guides served as the AAU's secretary and president in the 1890s and 1900s. On the Protective Basket Ball Association, see Thomas H. Smith, *Official Basket Ball Guide and the Protective Association Rules for 1906-07* (New York: Fox's Athletic Library, 1907). Naismith, "Basket Ball," 342-343. Naismith described four sets of rules: AAU, college, professional, and women's; others described a fifth set of rules played in Canada.

[107] In the mid-1900s, Jewish names appeared with more frequency in both *Spalding* and *Reach*. Though it is risky to make broad conclusions based on names, it can be safely assumed that Cohens, Goldsteins, and Shapiros were Jews. *Reach* was published in Philadelphia and covered that city's school teams, and *Spalding*, which primarily followed the amateur, school, and settlement competitions of New York. Examples of Jewish names in the guides can be seen in the *Spalding's Official Basket Ball Guide 1906-07* (New York: American Sports Publishing Company, 1906) which contained articles on the "Metropolitan Junior Championships" held at the 92nd Street YMHA, "Basket Ball in the Public Schools of New York City," and "Inter-Settlement Basket Ball"; Also see "School Basket Ball in Philadelphia," *Reach Official Basketball Guide, 1907-08* (Philadelphia: A.J. Reach & Co., 1908), which followed the exploits of Philadelphia schoolboys in an article; For the increase of Jewish names in the guides, see *Spalding's* listed the top scorers in "Basket Ball in New York City Playgrounds and Recreation Centers," *Spalding's Official Basket Ball Guide 1912-13* (New York: American Sports Publishing Company, 1912), which indicated that the top 20 scorers in the complication were Jewish. Settlements also produced opportunity for immigrants to engage in other cultural forms. On modern dance, see Julia L. Foulkes, *Modern Bodies: Dance and American Modernism from Martha Graham to Alvin*

specialized leagues produced skilled Jewish players who participated in a competitive environment that encouraged consumer, and thus potentially commercial, activity. Among the teenage players that Harry Baum taught at the University Settlement, Barney Sedran, Marty Friedman, Louis Sugarman, Ira Streusand, and Harry Brill became professional players. They consciously broke away from Progressive reformers who believed that sport would transmit moral values and prepare participants for work in an industrial society, not become work itself. In the process, these Jewish players served as the vanguard of a Jewish basketball culture that would eventually receive national attention and would serve a Jewish project of producing social acceptance through the development of strong, athletic, Jewish men.

Jewish basketball exemplified the growth of Jewish athletic participation in the late nineteenth and early twentieth century. The general acceptance of sport in American society increased opportunities for young Jews in a variety of locations and sports, but Jews found greater collective success in basketball than in other team sports. At settlement houses, public schools, Jewish institutions, and playgrounds, Jews played basketball in locations that espoused an amateur ethos informed by Progressive moralism.[108] The *Hebrew's* racially informed basketball Jew emerged out of this location and reflected the concerns of American Jews regarding their place in American society. During the 1890s and 1900s, acceptance of the stereotype of the weak Jew strengthened, as did both the immigration restriction movement and the importance of sport in society. The three converged in the late 1900s and intensified the need among mamong many American Jews to prove their normality in physical and racial terms. Sport

---

Ailey (Chapel Hill: University of North Carolina Press, 2002). Quote on "the game" from Postal, Silver, and Silver, *Encyclopedia of Jews in Sports*, 77.

[108] An example of Jewish participation in various environments is Barney Sedran, who played basketball at the University Settlement. He was mentioned in the *New York Times* on a number of occasions in the 1900s when the paper ran articles on the athletic events of the lower East Side. See "Boy Athletes Race for Special Prizes," *New York Times*, July 2, 1905; "Little Boys elect Mayor of Fish Park," *New York Times*, August 16, 1905; "Championship Basket Ball," *New York Times*, April 10, 1907. Some individuals played professionally while at settlement houses or in public school. See Postal, Silver, and Silver, *Encyclopedia of Jews in Sports*, 83, 95.

became the primary tool to achieve this goal, and the birth of the basketball Jew served as a derivative of the Jewish desire to construct an identity that included both modern and traditional elements.

Chapter Two

The Emergence of Jewish Basketball

Progressive reformers had believed basketball would transform the children of immigrants into productive citizens, but found that basketball could not easily be controlled. For Jewish players from the University Settlement and Clark House who dedicated time and effort to succeed, the sport offered the possibility of individual advancement. As these Jews stepped into the tense world of college and professional basketball, Jewish institutions accepted a model of Jewish athleticism in which male athletes became symbols of Jewish normality, masculinity, and modernity. This model contained the assumption that physical change would be the byproduct of a more important cultural change. Yet, the burden of the stereotype of the weak Jew, the demand of representing the broader community, and communal pressure to conform to middle class norms complicated the incorporation of this 'champion' model at Jewish institutions. Success would help destroy perceptions of Jewish weakness, but only if it did not change the Jewish identity of participants.

Not all Jews supported an expanded conception of Jewish athleticism. During the Eliot controversy, some Jewish commentators denied that sport would prove a satisfactory activity for physical improvement. Boston rabbi M.M. Eichler believed that general physical education, but not sport, could positively transform Jewish manhood because "in the matter of physical culture, our colleges are in need of reform." Eichler feared competitive sport would harm the Jewish body because non-Jewish college athletes were simply "physical giants, fit to enter a circus." An editorial in Boston's *Jewish Advocate* claimed Jewish boys *did* enjoy "open-air sports," but this caused a lack of stamina because sports "tend to develop one set of muscles at the expense of the whole body."[1] Even the *American Hebrew*, which hoped that "Jews of intellect" would participate in sport, did not endorse unrestrained athleticism. "There is little danger that they will push this side of their activities to such an exaggerated extent as is found in the case of the ordinary university students."[2]

Faith in Jewish students' ability to balance athletic and intellectual pursuits indicated that some American Jews believed that sport could only produce positive change if participants avoided the behavior of "ordinary," or non-Jewish, students. Eichler repeated criticisms from academics that sport harmed the education system by overwhelming the intellectual side in American colleges. For instance, Charles Eliot battled Harvard's athletic culture for much of his reign and believed competitive sport had become the bane of college life.[3] According to one historian, Yale's social and athletic culture meant "there was little place for an intellectual attitude or a concern for study." The non-Jewish

---

[1] "Agrees with President Eliot," *Jewish Advocate* (Boston), January 3, 1908; Editorial, *Jewish Advocate*, December 27, 1907. The editorial also blamed poor dietary habits of Jewish students for their weak stamina, though most commentators of the era concluded that Jews' diet – keeping *Kashrut* (Kosher) – contributed to the remarkable Jewish vitality despite their physical deficiencies. Editor Jacob de Haas was a noted Zionist whose editorial was entitled 'Muscular Judaism.' This was one of the few instances when the concept appeared in the Jewish press in the early twentieth century.

[2] "Jewish Physique," *American Hebrew*, December 27, 1907. During the controversy, a Jewish commentator argued that discrimination at Harvard and other elite schools meant the Jewish student "finds himself gradually forced out and knowing the condition he leaves the [sports] field to others. See "President Eliot Before the Menorah Society," *Jewish Advocate* (Boston), January 3, 1908.

[3] For Eliot's opposition to highly structured and competitive sports, see Horger, "Play By The Rules," 163-176, 208-209; Oriard, *Reading Football*, 182, 207. On the growing separation between the physical and mental in American colleges and universities in the late nineteenth and early twentieth century, see Gorn and Goldstein, *American Sports*, 165-168; George Meylan, "Athletics," *American Physical Education Review* 10, no. 2 (June 1905): 157-163; Clark W. Hetherington, "Analysis of Problems in College Athletics," *American Physical Education Review* 12, no. 2 (June 1907): 154-181; C.W. Savage, "The Professional Versus the Educational in College Athletics," *American Physical Education Review* 20, no. 4 (April 1915). On the development of 'all-around' education and development, see Burton J. Bledstein, *The Culture of Professionalism: The Middle Class and the Development of Higher Education in America* (New York: Norton, 1976).

elite could discount the academic side. Jewish student needed to take advantage of the opportunities offered at American colleges to advance in society.[4] In the late 1900s and 1910s, however, college basketball began to provide Jewish students with the opportunity to challenge elite Americans on the court, if not in the larger society.

In the early years of the twentieth century, basketball thrived at small colleges. For instance, one historian found that Oberlin College, located in Ohio, did not have the resources to build a 'big-time' football program, so it offered basketball as a way to provide athletic opportunities to students, attract loyalty and funds from alumni and fans, and build institutional prestige.[5] For similar reasons, New York City colleges such as New York University (NYU), and the City College of New York (CCNY) established basketball programs in the mid-1900s. Along with Columbia University, which focused on basketball after de-emphasizing football, these schools expanded the athletic opportunities of Jewish students. Jews from the lower East Side competed for these schools as Samuel Melitzer starred at Columbia and Joe Girsdansky played for NYU. CCNY's vast Jewish student population and high number of Jewish players, however, led the school to symbolize Jewish athletic achievement in college basketball.[6]

During the 1900s, Jewish players helped turn CCNY into an early basketball power. The tuition-free CCNY primarily served a Jewish population and Jewish players from the University Settlement such as Barney Sedran, Ira

---

[4] Dan A. Oren, *Joining the Club: A History of Jews and Yale* (New Haven: Yale University Press, 1985), 19-20.

[5] Horger, "Play By The Rules," 210-215. 'Big-time' programs existed as an abstraction between the absolutes of professional and amateur sport. 'Student-athletes' received no pay, but universities often earned large amounts of revenue from competitions. On the history of college basketball, see Neil D. Isaacs, *All The Moves: A History of College Basketball* (New York: Harper and Row, 1984); Peter C. Bjarkman, *Hoopla: A Century of College Basketball* (Indianapolis: Masters Press, 1996). On college sport, see Smith, *Sports and Freedom*.

[6] On early college basketball, see Isaacs, *All The Moves*, 39-45. Columbia abolished football in the early 1900s and expanded the basketball program to compete with professional, non-college, and amateur teams. New York provided the infrastructure and acceptance for Columbia basketball to thrive in the 1900s and 1910s as it dominated the Ivy League.

Streusand, and Harry Brill led CCNY to a record of 9-2 in 1908. During the 1909 season, Jews made up the entire team and served as manager, assistant manager, and coach. The team finished 8-3 and its competitive success drew the notice of the New York press and *Spalding* guides.[7] More importantly, a 'Jewish' team in college sports drew the attention of Jewish newspapers. In December 1908, at the beginning of the basketball season, the *American Hebrew* claimed CCNY's victories over Princeton and Yale, "stamps them as the premier college five."[8] Yet, even as CCNY became a prominent program due to its Jewish players, the school experienced problems associated with the basketball program.

In November 1907, the student newspaper *The Campus* had exclaimed that basketball could "advertise" the school "to the public outside of New York City." The paper equated the fame of Harvard, Yale, and Princeton, known as the "Big Three," to their prestige in the athletic world, and stated, "there can certainly be no harm in athletics flourishing in any college." Commentators had been denouncing the commercial and competitive pressures of 'big time' college sport since the 1890s, and *The Campus* ignored the recent 'crisis' of college football caused by brutal and violent play. Instead, the newspaper claimed, "athletics have not been detrimental to the growth of any institution or impaired their high standard."[9]

The Campus wanted basketball to be a positive force at the college. The editor criticized students in December 1907 for "hissing" at opponents, which "violated the first laws of hospitality." The paper condemned similar behavior

---

[7] For information on the CCNY team, see Basketball, *CCNY Microcosm*, 1909. The *New York Times* provided regular coverage of CCNY games during the late 1900s, although with only brief commentary on the game. On CCNY in *Spalding*, see the guides in 1906, 1908, and 1909.

[8] "The Jewish Athlete," *American Hebrew*, December 18, 1908.

[9] Editorial, *The Campus*, November 25, 1907. In 1907, CCNY moved from 23rd Street to 137th Street (its present location). The new campus included expanded facilities, including a gymnasium. That same year, the college hired Leonard Palmer as a "tutor in the department of Physical Instruction and Training at a salary of $600 per annum." In October, Palmer's salary was increased to $800. See Proceedings of the Board of Trustees of the College of the City of New York, February 25, 1907 and October 21, 1907. On the football crisis of 1905, see Smith, *Sports and Freedom*, 191-208; Oriard, *Reading Football*, 164-165, 170-171.

during a 33-23 loss to Columbia, but had little to say about CCNY's overwhelming victory over Adelphi the following week by a score of 95-11. Later that season, an editorial again asked fans to "be manly and display some courtesy toward visitors."[10] Controlling crowds upwards of 1,500 proved difficult. So did attempts to limit basketball's impact on other campus activities. In March 1908, *The Campus* stated that athletics "are not everything. Last Friday evening, with the game as a counterattraction, not a single one of the literary societies could muster a quorum and conditions very much the same as this have been the rules since the opening of the basketball season."[11]

As much as the basketball team's success drew students away from other campus activities, a lack of success hurt the basketball program. In 1910, CCNY remained a predominantly Jewish team, although without Sedran, Streusand or Brill. The basketball team lost early and often, including to Navy, whose "coach told our [coach] Mr. Palmer that his team learned how to play the game from us." Such praise meant little to the students who, during the season, became "indifferent and failed to support the team." The lack of attendance proved financially costly because the school's Athletic Association had provided "our basket-ball men with the best outfits that money could purchase." As a result, the team barely made a profit since "it was never dreamt that our student body could be so devoid of any semblance of college pride as to be interested in a team only so long as it is always the victor."[12]

CCNY's basketball fortunes returned in 1911 and students looked to avenge the previous season's loss to Yale. As the date of the rematch drew close,

---

[10] Condemnation of fan behavior as well as Adelphi score in Editorial, *The Campus*, December 11, 1907. Columbia score found in *The Campus*, December 4, 1907. The second condemnation found in *The Campus*, January 8, 1908.

[11] Editorial, *The Campus*, March 18, 1908. The same issue contained an article entitled "Basketball Statement," which illustrated the team had produced net revenue of $440.14 for the season. On the financial considerations involving basketball at CCNY in the 1900s and 1910s, see reports in the *CCNY Microcosm: Official Annual of the College*.

[12] "Basketball," *The Campus*, February 9, 1910; "Athletics: The Last Straw," *The Campus*, February 23, 1910.

The Campus appealed for the students to organize more cheers in order to "help the players." It became important to beat Yale in order to "maintain the reputation which we have built up by the hardest kind of work."[13] CCNY's 20-15 victory merited a three-page article in *The Campus*, which exclaimed: "the high standards of our curriculum could not have done, in years, what the glorious triumph of the varsity basketball team over Yale accomplished in one short evening."[14]

In the 1900s and 1910s, CCNY's commitment to basketball surpassed that of elite colleges, yet led to unwholesome fan behavior. The "discourteous attitude" of some fans toward both the Yale players and the referees marred the victory in 1911. Some decisions "were generally met by noises that may be quite proper in the cheaper sort of playhouses, but which are wholly unsportsmanlike among college men."[15] As a college that served an immigrant, and largely Jewish, population, CCNY needed its spectators to conform to the ideal, if not the reality, of amateur sport. The 'big three' of Yale, Harvard, and Princeton had been guilty of the worst offenses in college football during the 1890s and 1900s. Their elite status protected them even as they faced critical condemnations.[16] CCNY did not have such freedom, especially as basketball served as one of CCNY's most public activities during the Progressive era.

---

[13] "Athletics: Soon," *The Campus*, December 7, 1910.

[14] "Our Recent Victory," *The Campus*, December 21, 1910.

[15] Ibid. Much like the handbook for settlement athletes, *The Campus* attempted to differentiate cheap entertainment with the more sophisticated activity of college basketball. This may seem a dubious distinction today, but at the time, the separation of commercialized leisure activities remained important, especially for a college striving for prominence.

[16] The crisis in 1905 led President Theodore Roosevelt to call a meeting of the 'Big Three' at the White House in October. The absence of real reform led a number of colleges to meet in December 1905 and form the Intercollegiate Athletic Association, which eventually became the National College Athletic Association (NCAA) in 1910. Yale did not join the NCAA as Walter Camp strenuously attempted to maintain his position of authority in college football. Smith, *Sports and Freedom*, 91-108; Oriard, *Reading Football*, 25-26, 30-34; John R. Thelin, *Games College Play: Scandal and Reform in Intercollegiate Athletics* (Baltimore: Johns Hopkins University Press, 1994), 15-17. CCNY joined the Intercollegiate Athletic Association in 1909. See Proceedings of the Board of Trustees of the College of the City of New York, May 20, 1909.

CCNY's victory over Yale occurred at a time when basketball remained a 'minor' sport in the college athletic world. At the 'Big Three' and other elite colleges, the 'major' varsity sports of football, baseball, track, and crew generally refused to share their resources and funds. Entrepreneurial students thus controlled basketball, which led to increased commercial behavior. Administrators at elite schools often found the sport disreputable due to roughness and professionalism. College teams also resisted efforts of the Amateur Athletic Union (AAU) to control the sport, frequently ignored AAU rules and formed a separate rules committee. The split meant that even as some schools built strong basketball programs that could provide both publicity and financial success, college basketball remained a marginal sport in the 1910s.[17] This marginality also occurred because many Americans viewed college basketball as feminine due to its popularity among college women. Women's basketball, however, existed almost as a separate sport due to an ideology of moderation that contrasted sharply with the dominant competitive and commercial culture of American male athleticism.

In the late nineteenth century, some middle class American women began to demand access to physical education. During the 1890s, the 'New Woman' entered American public life. Men who felt threatened by the 'New Woman' used medical arguments to claim that women were 'prisoners' of their reproductive systems and should not participate in any physical activity. Female physical educators challenged this biological argument by asserting that in order to produce strong offspring and improve the race, women needed exercise. These educators admitted the physical inferiority of women, but argued that 'culture' rather than 'nature' had imprisoned women in weak, Victorian bodies. The belief that culture could influence gender caused many educators to fear that women

---

[17] Horger, "Play By The Rules," 74-75, 170-174, 189-196. In particular, Harvard's Charles Eliot and Princeton's Woodrow Wilson were concerned with basketball's unsavory reputation as elements of the professional game crept in. Eliot strongly opposed competitive athletics in all forms, and when Harvard basketball's "degenerated" into roughness, the school abolished it Harvard did not have a basketball program from 1910-1921. Yale basketball found itself blacklisted by the AAU for playing non-registered teams.

would become 'masculine' if they participated in competitive sport. The danger of transgressing accepted gender prescriptions made competitive sport a controversial activity and led female educators to construct an ideology of 'moderation' that did not directly challenge accepted gender distinctions.[18] They attempted to balance the demands of physical activity with the problem of the unrestricted emotions released by sport.

Women began playing basketball soon after Naismith invented the game. Senda Berenson, the assimilated daughter of Jewish immigrants and women's basketball preeminent leader, explained: "Games are invaluable for women in that they bring out as nothing else just those elements that women find necessary today in their enlarged field of activities." The presence of 'masculine' elements such as roughness and competitiveness, however, led educators to reevaluate the sport's form and function. Fearing a loss of autonomy if they did not make basketball acceptable for women, female educators codified a 'feminized' version with distinct rules governing space, touch, and movement.[19] Berenson, who had close ties with Luther Gulick, agreed that basketball "may be made an influence for good so may it be made a strong influence for evil. The gravest objection to the game is the rough element." Berenson ultimately decided that "modifications

---

[18] On the 'New Woman,' see Peiss, *Cheap Amusements*; Ellen Wiley Todd, "Art, the 'New Woman' and Consumer Culture," in *Gender and American History Since 1890*, ed. Barbara Melosh, (New York, Routledge, 1993), 128-152; Nancy S. Dye, "Introduction," in *Gender, Class, Race, and reform in the Progressive Era*, eds., Noralee Frankel and Nancy S. Dye (Lexington, KY: University Press of Kentucky, 1991), 1-9; Jean V. Matthews, *The Rise of the New Woman: The Woman's Movement in America, 1875-1930* (Chicago: Ivan R. Dee, 2003). On late nineteenth century doctors and medicine in relation to women's body image and health, see Peter N. Stearns, *Fat History: Bodies and Beauty in the Modern West* (New York: New York University Press, 1997); Carroll Smith-Rosenberg and Charles Rosenberg, "The Female Animal: Medical and Biological Views of Women and their role in 19th Century America," in *From 'Fair Sex' to Feminism: Sport and the Socialization of Women in Industrial and Post-Industrial Eras*, eds., J.A. Mangan and Roberta Park (London: F. Cass, 1987), 14-20; Paul Atkinson, "The Feminist Physique: Physical Education and the Medicalization of Women's Education," in Mangan and Park, *From 'Fair Sex' to Feminism*, 40-44, 53-54. Susan K. Cahn, *Coming on Strong: Gender and Sexuality in 20th Century Women's Sport* (New York: Free Press, 1994), 7-22; ; Park, "Physiology and Anatomy are Destiny!?," 56-57; Roberta Park, "Sport, Gender, and Society in a Transatlantic Victorian Perspective," in Mangan and Park, *From 'Fair Sex' to Feminism*, 75-77.

[19] Horger, "Play by the Rules," 250-270; Cahn, *Coming on Strong*, 83-87; Allen Guttmann, *Women's Sports: A History* (New York: Columbia University Press, 1991), 114-120.

in the rules" and the "division of the playing field" would help "do away with undue physical exertion."[20]

Berenson's rules standardized women's basketball and restricted the space in which players could move. Berenson divided the court into three sections with two players from each team located in each section. Players could not leave their section, although they could move around within the section. This cut down on the possibility of roughness and ensured that women did not exhaust themselves. Berenson did not believe the rule changes diminished basketball's educational value of teaching teamwork, restrained competitiveness, and moral behavior. Much like the cages in professional basketball, which indicated primitive masculinity, the rules governing women's basketball constructed the sport as a performance of gender. The 'New Woman' may have challenged Victorian womanhood, but she did not alter the belief in gender difference.[21]

In the 1890s and 1900s, Berenson's line basketball became a popular sport at private northeastern schools such as Smith and Vassar and public universities in the west. Whereas male physical educators had virtually no influence on college athletics due to the presence of professional coaches, the institutional control of female educators allowed them to stress cooperation and participation over individual success and winning.[22] Female educators argued that women's sport

---

[20] Berenson quote from "Line Basketball for Women" in *Major Problems in American Sports History*, ed. Steven A. Riess (Boston: Houghton Mifflin, 1995), 253-54. On Berenson, see Carole A. Oglesby, ed., *Encyclopedia of Women and Sport in America* (Phoenix: Onyx Press, 1998), 133-134. Berenson was an instructor at Smith College, and the daughter of Jewish immigrants. Her father insisted the family assimilate into society and Berenson married a non-Jewish English professor, Herbert Abbott.

[21] On Berenson and women's basketball, see Horger, "Play By The Rules," 251-262. On 'performing' gender, see Judith Butler, *Gender Trouble: Feminism and the Subversion of Identity* (New York: Routledge, 1990), 24-25.

[22] On defined 'gender distinctions' in sport, see Donald J. Mrozek, "The 'Amazon' and the American 'Lady': Sexual Fears of Women as Athletes" in Mangan and Park, *From 'Fair Sex' to Feminism*, 284-89. According to the Patricia Vertinsky, the shift toward a more athletic 'new' woman was not as pronounced and drastic as Mrozek argues. Vertinsky agreed, however, that the 'athletic girl' did become fashionable at the turn of the century. See Patricia Vertinsky, "Body Shapes: The Role of the Medical Establishment in Informing Female Exercise and Physical Education in Nineteenth-Century North America" in Mangan and Park, *From 'Fair Sex' to Feminism*, 270-275. Male physical educators supported assertions that women needed their own

could provide "ethical value," but warned that "men's athletics to-day should not serve as a model for women's athletics" since the "predominating note in women's sports should always be the joy and exhilaration and fun of playing, not the grim determination to win at any cost."[23] A similar philosophy emerged among Progressive reformers who provided female immigrants with limited athletic opportunities in comparison to male immigrants.

Progressive reformers looked at female recreation as a response to industrialization's impact on the female body. Physical education would improve health, provide recreation, and rejuvenate tired bodies. Educators focused on moral and physical health rather than character, democracy, or citizenship. Luther Gulick's theory of repetitive activity did not extend to women and he argued that, "athletics do not test womanliness as they test manliness." He agreed that "a city girl must be provided with outdoor exercise," but these activities needed to be "for recreation and pleasure…not for serious, public competition."[24] Gendered notions of athleticism frequently separated the activities of boys and girls. In 1910, the *New York Times* commented that for "Jewish girls…the athletic appeal

---

version of basketball, including Dudley Sargent, "What Athletic Games, If Any, Are Injurious for Women in the Form in Which They Are Played By Men," *American Physical Education Review* 11 (September 1906): 175-179.

[23] Frances A. Kellor, "Ethical Value of Sports for Women," *American Physical Education Review* 11 (September 1906): 160-162. Alice Katharine Fallows, "Athletics for College Girls," *Century Illustrated Magazine* 66 (May 1903): 58-65; W. Bengough, "The New Woman, Athletically Considered," *Godey's Magazine* 132 (January 1896): 23-29; C. Gilbert Percival, "Athletics at Wellesley College," *Health* 54 (July 1904): 223-224. For other articles on the need for women to 'learn' traits to cope with their expanding opportunities, see Alice Bertha Foster, "Basket Ball for Girls," *American Physical Education Review* 2 (September 1897): 152-154; Harriet I. Ballantine, "The Value of Athletics to College Girls," *American Physical Education Review* 6 (June 1901): 151-153. For articles on class games, see Women and Home, *Los Angeles Times*, November 25, 1894; "Women at Basket Ball," *Chicago Tribune*, March 7, 1896; The annual game at Smith College received attention around the country as freshmen and sophomores dressed in specific colors, sang songs, and cheered for their classmates. Media representations in the 1890s often depicted participants in women's basketball as the 'athletic girl,' who existed within the character of the complicated 'New Woman,' and may have contributed to notions of the 'New Woman' as a middle class college woman.

[24] Luther Gulick, "Athletics from a Biological Viewpoint," *American Physical Education Review* 11 (September 1906): 159-160.

is small. They and the Italian girls prefer to weave baskets. Here and there a star arises on the basket ball field, but they are rare."[25]

Female settlement sport did not wholly conform to prescribed gender norms. In 1906, the Henry Street *Settlement Journal* commented that a loss to Educational Alliance occurred because, "our girls were at a disadvantage in that their coach, Miss [Frances] Kellor, was absent and besides they could not overcome the rough tactics of the opposing side." The journal's defense of the loss, as well as Henry Street's willingness to arrange a "return game" despite the Alliance's roughness, indicated that some settlement girls wanted the intense experience of competitive sport. Yet, virtually no competitive leagues existed during the 1900s and 1910s. Shut out of public competition, girls had far fewer athletic opportunities than boys in a Progressive environment.[26]

Jewish and non-Jewish officials willingly made space for boys, but racial and gendered notions of sport influenced a broader initial unwillingness to grant women athletic privileges. Women's and girls' gymnasium classes met less frequently, for less time, and received less institutional support than men's classes and activities. For instance, the Educational Alliance's 1900 annual report indicated that gymnasium classes for 'young men' occurred every weeknight whereas 'young women' and 'girls' had classes only twice a week. A similar situation existed at the University Settlement and Henry Street Settlement. Many Jewish women attempted to break free of social restrictions by participating in a variety of physical and athletic activities.[27] Basketball's 'masculine' elements,

---

[25] "Personally Directed Sorts Are Popular with Children," *New York Times*, July 24, 1910. On women's fashion and athletics, see Lois Banner, *American Beauty* (New York: Knopf, 1983), 142-152.

[26] Gym Notes, *The Settlement Journal*, May 1906. In New York, the PSAL did not initially include female sports in city competitions and inter-settlement leagues rarely provided competitive outlets for girls. For PSAL's slow inclusion of female competition, see Riess, *City Games*, 163. Outside competition remained generally limited to older or 'senior' girls within 'women's' basketball, see St. Paul Neighborhood House, *Twenty-Second Annual Report* (St. Paul: 1919-20).

[27] Educational Alliance, *First Annual Report, 1900* (New York: 1901). Borish, "'An Interest in Physical Well-Being Among the Female Membership,'" 61-93; Borish, "'Athletic Activities of Various Kinds'" 241-250; Paula E. Hyman, "Gender and the Shaping of Modern Jewish Identities," *Jewish Social Studies* 8, nos., 2-3 (Winter-Spring 2002); Hasia R. Diner and Beryl

however, meant that Jewish women had to proceed carefully into an athletic world that continued to denigrate male Jewish athleticism.

In the late nineteenth century, American Jewish men identified Jewish women as "saviors" of the race. Women's domestic qualities proved to be essential to preserving a Jewish culture and identity.[28] Proper female behavior served an important part of successful integration and Jewish men attempted to limit the public role of Jewish women. In response, Jewish women devised political strategies to widen their role in the community and claimed their domestic qualities gave them the moral authority to provide public service to the Jewish community. They established independent organizations, such as the National Council of Jewish Women (NCJW), and extended their public influence by fusing their cultural roles in Judaism with modern society's notion of femininity.[29]

Lieff Benderly, *Her Works Praise Her: A History of Jewish Women in America from Colonial Times to the Present* (New York: Basic Books, 2002), 185-192 and 225-241. Economic and political activity proved one method of Jewish women's public activity, but they often faced more direct resistance from communal leaders in other endeavors. In their examinations of Jewish female athleticism, historians George Eisen and Linda Borish explained that traditional Jewish culture placed different values on women's participation in society. See Borish, "An Interest in Physical Well-Being Among the Female membership," 62-64; George Eisen, "Sports, Recreation, and Gender: Jewish Immigrant Women in Turn-of-the-Century American (1880-1920)," *Journal of Sport History* 17, no. 1 (1991): 103-120. An example female physical education's popularity can be seen at the University Settlement, where the 1896 Annual Report listed the attendance in the "'girls' gymnasium" at 697 over 22 meetings for an average of 31, while the "boys gymnasium" had a total attendance of 686 over 40 meetings for an average of 17. See University Settlement, *Report for the Year 1896* (New York: 1897).

[28] Eric L. Goldstein, "Between Race and Religion: Jewish Women and Self-Definition in late 19th Century America," in *Women and American Judaism: Historical Perspectives*, ed. Jonathan D. Sarna and Pamela Nadell (Hanover, NH: University Press of New England, 2001), 182-196.

[29] See Paula Hyman, "Gender and the Shaping of Modern Jewish Identities." Prior to the 1890s, Jewish women were generally segregated into various 'Ladies Auxiliaries' such as the Sisterhood of Personal Service at the prominent Reform synagogue Temple Emanu-El. On Sisterhoods and the National Council of Jewish Women, see Diner and Benderly, *Her Works*, 233; Paula Hyman, "Gender and the Immigrant Jewish Experience in the United States," in *Jewish Women in Historical Perspective*, ed. Judith R. Baskin (Detroit: Wayne State University Press, 1998); Eric L. Goldstein, "Different Blood Flows in Our Veins: Race and Jewish Self-Definition in late 19th Century America," *American Jewish History* 85, no. 1 (March 1997): 29-55. Goldstein explains that many Jewish women initially used religion to justify their participation in the non-Jewish world but when they found religion inadequate in explaining their Jewish identity, they tended to turn to racial language. Goldstein, "Between Race and Religion," in Sarna and Nadell, *Women and American Judaism*, 188-89.

The arrival of eastern European Jewish immigrants complicated the identity of middle class Jewish women. Immigrant families aspired to a middle class ideal, but female wage earning did not carry much stigma among immigrants and "economic activity was recognized as appropriate and normal for Jewish women."[30] Though laboring immigrant women did not abandon their aspiration for marriage and middle class status, many Jewish men projected their fears of social rejection onto the stereotype of the "Ghetto Girl." This stereotype, according to historian Riv-Ellen Prell, contained various elements, including a lack of refinement, abhorrent behavior that often led to prostitution, and excessive Americanization that caused immigrant girls to abandon their Jewishness. By participating in 'male' behavior, the "Ghetto Girl" discarded her role as a racial 'savior' that had been constructed to allow Jewish men to join the broader society. In the late 1900s, Jewish leaders responded to widespread beliefs regarding the supposed predominance of Jewish women in prostitution and institutions made a more concerted effort to develop wholesome activities to counteract harmful behavior.[31] The institutional response would indicate that American Jews differed

---

[30] Quote from Aviva Cantor, *JewishWomen/Jewish Men: The Legacy of Patriarchy in Jewish Life* (San Francisco: HarperSanFrancisco, 1995), 171. Cantor explained that despite their presence in working class urban neighborhoods, many Jewish working parents, both men and women, regarded themselves as a 'temporary' proletariat. Also see Melissa R. Klapper, *Jewish Girls Coming of Age in America, 1860-1920* (New York: New York University Press, 2005), 201-207; Quote from Hyman, "Gender and the Immigrant Jewish Experience," 314. For information on immigrant women, see Donna R. Gabaccia, *From the Other Side: Women, Gender, and Immigrant Life in the U.S., 1820-1990* (Bloomington: Indiana University Press, 1994); Elizabeth Ewen, *Immigrant Women in the Land of Dollars: Life and Culture on the Lower East Side, 1890-1925* (New York: Monthly Review Press, 1985); Susan A. Glenn, *Daughters of the Shtetl: Life and Labor in the Immigrant Generation* (Ithaca: Cornell University Press, 1990), 210-214, 238-39; Heinze, *Adapting to Abundance*; Paula E. Hyman, "The Jewish Body Politic: Gendered Politics in the Early Twentieth Century," *Nashim* 2 (1999): 45-48. Immigrant women constructed a "Jewish New Womanhood" that justified a public presence through domestic roles as they Americanized their families through consumption. They developed political strategies that allowed for communal activism, and to maintain their 'Jewishness' through the purchase of kosher food. Politically, Jewish immigrant women participated in a number of boycotts of kosher butchers in opposition to exorbitant prices and were generally supported by male communal leaders.

[31] Riv-Ellen Prell, *Fighting to Become Americans: Jews, Gender, and the Anxiety of Assimilation* (Boston: Beacon Press, 1999), 21-57. Hyman, *Gender and Assimilation in Modern Jewish History*, 25-41; Hyman, "The Jewish Body Politic," 38-44. Male leaders focused on the anti-Semitic ramifications whereas female leaders wanted to 'rescue' the victims and address the social conditions that led to "white slavery." For the history of prostitution, see Vern L. Bullough and

among themselves regarding their belief in how female physical education and competitive sport could encourage the Americanization process and construct Jewish female identity.

In the 1900s, New York's Young Women's Hebrew Association (YWHA) became one of the most prominent Jewish institutions to exclusively serve women. Founded in 1902, the YWHA had female board members and officials who organized talks on social hygiene, offered classes on millinery, cooking, and stenography, and developed a Sewing School. The Association also offered public gymnastic exhibitions open only to female spectators.[32] In December 1909, the YWHA superintendent reported that the lack of "clean amusements" for Jewish immigrant women had become a serious problem. Officials added gymnasium apparatus and equipment for basketball in February 1910 and the superintendent reported that, "the girls are enthusiastic over the basket-ball practice which they now have." Within three months, the YWHA cancelled its elocution class in order to devote an additional evening to gymnasium work. The following year, it devoted one evening a week to basketball and other "athletic games."[33] YWHA basketball's monopoly over the gymnasium mirrored that of

---

Bonnie Bullough, *Women and Prostitution: A Social History* (Buffalo, NY: Prometheus Books, 1987).

[32] For information on a children's gymnasium exhibition, see the YWHA Superintendent Report, March 1908, Young Women's Hebrew Association records, 92nd Street Y Archives, New York. Soon after the exhibition, the YWHA increased its number of gymnasium classes. Due to the increased interest, a class for girls' aged 14-16 was added, and the superintendent reported that the physical culture classes combined for over 80 registered members. See the YWHA Superintendent Report, January 1909, Young Women's Hebrew Association records, 92nd Street Y Archives, New York.

[33] By the end of 1909, the YWHA offered only one gymnasium class with an average daily attendance of six members. See the YWHA Superintendent Report, November 1909, Young Women's Hebrew Association records, 92nd Street Y Archives, New York. Quote on 'clean amusements' from YWHA Superintendent Report, December 1909, Young Women's Hebrew Association records, 92nd Street Y Archives, New York. According to the January 1910 YWHA superintendent report, the declining interest in physical culture had occurred because "the girls did not feel it was worth while to pay for a gymnasium with as little equipment as ours." The first mention of basketball appeared in the YWHA Superintendent Report, February 28, 1910, Young Women's Hebrew Association records, 92nd Street Y Archives, New York. In 1914, the YWHA moved into a new building that included a world-class swimming pool. The YWHA hosted national tournaments and events that frequently supported the suffrage movement. The prominence of swimming at the YWHA was partly due to a Jewish woman, Charlotte Epstein,

men's basketball at Jewish settlements, but basketball remained a tense sport to provide female athletic opportunities.

Basketball did not serve a single path toward female Americanization. As late as 1914, physical educators debated the best form of basketball for women. They found that "the vigorous girl athlete" had no interest in basketball played by "Women's rules."[34] Educators generally opposed women playing "Men's rules," but they found it difficult to root out the sport. For the exclusively female YWHA, public attention needed to be positive and the institution thus used basketball for recreation rather than public competition. In contrast, the Council of Young Men's Hebrew and Kindred Association (CYMKHA), a national organization that oversaw the activities of YMHA's and YWHA's, promoted basketball because "so few sports are open to girls, it may be well to form basketball teams among them."[35] Aware of the controversies involved in basketball, most Jewish institutions played the more moderate and less 'vigorous' form of women's basketball. One of the few that did not, the Chicago Hebrew Institute (CHI) provided its female members with a public and competitive space in which to play women's basketball with "Men's rules."

---

who helped found the female-controlled club, the Women's Swimming Association (WSA). The WSA, which used the YWHA pool for practices, broke free from the National Women's Life Saving League in 1917. See Borish, "Athletic Activities of Various Kinds," 258-262; Borish, "An Interest in Physical Well-Being Among the Female Membership," 71-77. According to historian Susan Cahn, swimming was widely seen as an acceptable female activity. The sport contained many benefits in the public imagination, including a version of beauty, which in the 1910s was idealized in the Anglo-Saxon woman. The middle class accepted swimming in opposition to basketball and track and field because both sports supposedly contained 'masculine' elements. See Cahn, *Coming on Strong*, 44-46, and 128-30. Just as Anglo-Saxon masculinity impacted the identity of the modern American Jewish male, feminine beauty had a similar effect on Jewish women. On the influence of body image to Jewish girls and women, see Klapper, *Jewish Girls Coming of Age in America*, 202-204. As historian Julia Foulkes illustrated, Jewish female dancers faced rejection if they did not 'look' American or have the "WASP face." Foulkes, *Modern Bodies*, 138-139. On the negative associations of the Jewish nose, see Sander L. Gilman, *The Jew's Body* (New York: Routledge, 1991), 169-193. Also see Marianne Sanua, *Going Greek: Jewish College Fraternities in the United States, 1895-1945* (Detroit: Wayne State University, 2003), 154-156.

[34] Harry E. Stewart, "A Critical Study of the Rules and Present Day Conditions of Basket Ball for Women," *American Physical Education Review* 19, no. 2 (March 1914): 242-246.

[35] Coleman Silbert, *Clubs for Jewish Work* (Publications of the Council of the YMH and Kindred Associations, 1915).

Formed in 1903, the CHI opened a new gymnasium with equal facilities for both men and women in 1913.[36] The institution's *Observer* declared female physical education would provide "the mental and moral growth of their daughters and the latter's descendents depend upon a sound and well-controlled constitution." CHI officials declared a need for wholesome recreation because "dance halls contribute much towards the disintegration of the morals of the young."[37] The CHI also directed women's gymnasium classes toward physical and social well-being. An English class for Foreigners required compulsory attendance in a gymnasium class where, "the clumsy immigrant girl…[is] changed to a graceful and spritely girl."[38]

Within this environment, officials defined sport as a masculine activity. The male CHI athletic director declared: "Some of the boys come to wrestle, others to box, and still others to play basketball; the girls come to dance and become graceful." The female physical director concurred. "His aim is proficiency in athletics. The woman cares not so much to become an athlete as to develop good posture and grace of movement. Grace is much admired by women as a quality which most women strive to acquire." 'Grace' remained undefined except as in opposition to 'clumsy.' It may have been implicitly connected to an ideal state of beauty, motherhood, and Jewish women as racial 'saviors.'[39] Some

---

[36] Gems, "Sport and the Forging of a Jewish-American Culture," 15-26; Kaufman, *Shul with a Pool*, 118-121. Officials appealed to philanthropist Julius Rosenwald for expansive gymnasium facilities to be included in the Institute's rebuilding. The CHI raised $100,000 for this purpose. CHI President Jacob M. Loeb then made a further appeal for additional funds in order to build separate gymnasium facilities for women. Rosenwald declined to aid the construction of a women's gymnasium. Linda Borish examined the relationship between Loeb and Rosenwald in building the CHI gymnasium. See Linda J. Borish, "Settlement Houses to Olympic Stadiums: Jewish American Women, Sports, and Social Change, 1880s-1930s," *Journal of Sport History* 23, no. 2 (1987): 8-11.

[37] Quote from Editorial, *CHI Observer*, May 1913. On reformers' attempts to keep women out of dance halls, see Peiss, *Cheap Amusements*, 88-112, 164-184.

[38] Report of the Superintendent, *CHI Observer*, May 1914.

[39] Harry Berkman, "Growth of Our Athletic Department, *CHI Observer*, April 1914; Gertrude Pochter, "What Physical Training Does for Women," *CHI Observer*, April 1916. Dance was most associated with 'grace,' a feminine quality important for American wives. See Klapper, *Jewish Girls Coming of Age in America*, 201. Also see Foulkes, *Modern Bodies*, 105.

female members, however, hoped the opening of the gymnasium would provide athletic opportunities, not just 'grace.'

In January 1915, CHI member Rose Rodkin praised the new gymnasium for providing women the "equal right" to compete in athletics. She also indicated the importance that the media would play in Jewish athleticism. Public recognition would come since "we now have space in the Observer to write up our activities, just like our men folks do."[40] Rodkin helped form a competitive basketball team in January 1916, and the *Observer* reported on the team's first game, a 25-15 victory over Hull House. "It was the first time that the Institute's 'softer sex' has attempted to match its skill against another institution." The *Observer* described the outcome of the game, and added: "Our ladies – perhaps we better say girls; it sounds less dignified – displayed much better team work than Hull House."[41]

By the late 1910s, women's basketball became a popular competitive activity at the CHI. As the *Observer* diligently reported on the team's success, the female education director recognized basketball as "one of the best exercises for 'all around' development of the mind as well as for the body." In February 1918, the publication praised the team for going undefeated after ten games and outscoring their opponents, 115-10, including a 43-2 victory over Palantine High School.[42] In 1920, the *Observer* reported that the basketball team had a record of 14-1 with attendance of over 500 at some games. The following year, the CHI finished undefeated, outscored its opponents 447-116, and won the Central AAU championship.[43] The disparate scores revealed the intensity that accompanied

---

[40] Athletics, *CHI Observer*, January 1915.

[41] Ladies Basketball, *CHI Observer*, January 1916.

[42] Quote from Gertrude Pochter, "The Girls' Gym," *CHI Observer*, March 1917. Gems, "Sport and the Forging of a Jewish-American Culture." Ladies Basketball, *CHI Observer*, February 1918. The following month, the CHI hosted a 'ladies basketball tournament,' described as the "first of its kind in the history of Chicago." See Rose Rodkin, "Ladies' Basketball Team," *CHI Observer*, March 1918.

[43] Gymnasium, *CHI Observer*, June 1920. The *Observer* reported game-by-game results of the women's team and noted that a fundraising game made about $130 for the team and broader

CHI women's basketball. This sort of activity occurred throughout American society and led female educators to question the wisdom of competitive female sport.

Following World War I, a new generation of female educators sought to restrict the commercial and competitive pressures seen in men's sport from intruding on women's sport. These educators vigorously attacked competitive sport and contested the AAU's use of "men's rules" in basketball.[44] According to historian Ellen Gerber, the second generation of female physical educators feared the AAU would "exploit" women's sexuality for promotional and financial gains. The AAU seemed to confirm these fears by organizing beauty pageants in tandem with AAU events, including basketball games or tournaments. The AAU's support of both public displays of female sexuality and athletic competitiveness occurred at a time that, as historian Donald Mrozek explained, public female excellence lay on the edge of middle class respectability.[45]

In the 1920s, female educators formed the Women's Division of the National Amateur Athletic Federation (NAAF), which according to Gerber, reflected a "conservative social viewpoint regarding appropriate female behavior." The NAAF promoted a "participation for all" philosophy that stressed involvement over winning and virtually eliminated competitive team sports from

---

women's gymnasium department. On the AAU championship, see Borish, "Settlement Houses to Olympic Stadiums," 12-13.

[44] Cahn, *Coming on Strong*, 72-74, 94-96; Ellen Gerber, "The Controlled Development of Collegiate Sport for Women, 1923-1936" *Journal of Sport History* 2, no. 1 (1975): 1-28. For a denouncement of women playing by men's rules, see Stewart, "A Critical Study of the Rules and Present Day Conditions of Basket Ball for Women," 242-246. Stewart, a doctor, was the physical director at a girls' school in Connecticut warned that 'men's rules' were potentially dangerous and appealed for a compromise between the rules.

[45] Gerber, "The Controlled Development of Collegiate Sport for Women," 6-8; Mrozek, "The 'Amazon' and the American 'Lady'," 291-293; Cahn, *Coming on Strong*, 78-79. An example is 'Babe' Didrikson, great female athlete who society did not fully accept until she let her hair grow and got married. Her success in track, baseball, basketball, golf, and countless other sports identified her as a tomboy, not a normative athlete.

American educational institutions, especially colleges, by the late 1920s.[46] Local newspapers sometimes included game scores with brief descriptions or 'women in sports' columns, but their minimal and cursory inclusion normalized male athleticism within the sports page.[47] With no media attention and educators who opposed competitive sport, Jewish women found themselves without the essential elements necessary to develop a competitive basketball culture beyond a single institution.

Within this environment, Jewish women did not represent public notions of Jewish athleticism. The CHI, renamed the Jewish People's Institute in the 1920s, continued to produce excellent women's teams during the interwar period. Yet, neither the Jewish nor the mainstream press provided much coverage of women's basketball. Even in the late 1910s, as the CHI's female basketball team won awards and attracted fans, the institution's *Observer* attached far more symbolic importance to male athleticism than it did to female athleticism. In 1917, the periodical explained that the athletic success of "Jewish young men" had begun to eliminate "the prejudice that has long existed" against the Jewish people. They did this by winning championships and through their "gentlemanly conduct and sportsmanship."[48] The CHI presented Jewish athleticism, as related to the project of "eliminating" discrimination, as a masculine activity. At the same time, New York institutions provided a similar power to the successful male athlete who would both reduce prejudice and modernize Jewish culture. New York's large Jewish population also allowed for an institutional network that transformed the project of Jewish athleticism.

---

[46] Gerber, "The Controlled Development of Collegiate Sport for Women," 9-14. Quote on 14. Also see Guttmann, *Women's Sport*, 138-141. Where competitive basketball was played, "women's rules" remained firmly entrenched.

[47] For an example of women's sport in the mainstream media, see The Sportswoman, Washington *Post*, December 23, 1925. The column was a regular feature in the *Post*. Michael Messner has commented on the continued ghettoization of women's sport and pointed to *Sport's Illustrated for Women* at a contemporary example. See Messner, *Taking the Field*, 93-94.

[48] "The Jews and Athletics in Chicago," *CHI Observer*, May 1917.

In April 1907, an editorial in the 92nd Street YMHA's *Bulletin* had elucidated what would become the dominant paradigm about Jewish athleticism during the first half of the twentieth century. "The Jew as an Athlete" presented a familiar narrative: "Jews as a nation have never been actively identified with the manly sports, either in ancient or modern times." The Jews could be partially blamed for this absence. "Had the manly sports been more indulged…the Jews might have been treated with greater respect by their enemies." In the United States, "more attention is being paid by the Jews to the harmonious development of the human form and as a result, we are gradually developing a number of promising Jewish athletes." The editorial praised the public school system for helping produce successful athletes, especially in the "game of basket-ball, [where] Jewish young men are acknowledged leaders." Sport needed to become more important to Jewish 'peoplehood,' but with one important caveat. "There is something in athletics which appeals to all manly men and if the Jews will pay more attention to it and through it develop a number of champions, it will do more to raise the status of the race in the eyes of the world than any other single achievement."[49]

The editorial demanded change in the relationship between American Jewish culture and sport and constructed a new model of Jewish athleticism. The *Bulletin* published the editorial the month before the Atlas Athletic Club left the YMHA and eight months before Eliot spoke before the Menorah Club. It provided a model with which YMHA officials could respond to the Eliot controversy. The absence of "manly sports" within Jewish culture had served as a barrier to Jewish integration. Thus, individual Jews could benefit if Jewish culture moved closer to sport. This model included a new concept of Jewish athleticism. Mainstream society would accept Jews and provide a space for modern, and normal, manhood only if Jewish "champions" proved their worth in the athletic world. The champion model encouraged the development of a communal athletic culture that served both an internal project of Jewish

---

[49] "The Jew as an Athlete," *YMHA Bulletin*, April 1907.

socialization and an external project of proving Jewish athleticism, and thus normality, to mainstream society.

In 1912, New York area YMHA's formed the YMHA Athletic League.[50] The league provided young Jews with competitive athletic opportunities, and the *Bulletin* explicitly connected the league's public presence to an internal Jewish project. Jews should socialize with, and play against, other Jews. An article, "Jews in Athletics," stated that the absence of a Jewish athletic club culture had forced Jews to join athletic clubs or even YMCA's and their names became "linked with some Christian Association." As a result, the athlete "was not recognized as a Jew. This league will have the tendency to bring these Jewish young men together."[51] YMHA officials also believed competitive sports were "splendid preparation for the duties and obligations of citizenship." The league's initial mention in the *Bulletin* stated it had formed "to develop and encourage clean sport between the boys of the different Associations."[52]

Commitment is needed for competitive structures to succeed. Organized rules, governance, and scheduling meant the league supported elite specialization in sport over mass participation. The league's competitiveness encouraged member institutions to develop the hierarchical structures that would support an athletic club culture. At the 92nd Street YMHA, internal competitions and

---

[50] The Athletic League was first proposed in April 1912. See Minutes of the Board of Directors, April 3, 1912, Young Men's Hebrew Association records, 92nd Street Y Archives, New York. The YMHA Athletic League was mentioned in Gym Notes, *Y Bulletin*, October 1912. The section declared, "Our YMHA is looked to as the Mecca of all similar institutions and it was up to us to lead this undertaking and only with our guidance and active support could the league be assured of success."

[51] Mike Taub, "Jews in Athletics," *Y Bulletin*, January 1913. The league encouraged a number of Jews to transfer to the YMHA from prominent athletic clubs. The year after the formation of the league, the *American Hebrew* covered a controversy over a Jewish youth's desire to join the 23rd Street YMCA in New York City. The youth objected to the YMCA's policy to restrict the number of Jews to 5% of its membership. The *Hebrew* denounced the youth's desire to join the YMCA rather than the restrictive policy and stated: "a Jewish youth man should become a member of the YMHA if he desires club privileges." See "Jews and the YMCA," *American Hebrew*, December 5, 1913.

[52] Young Men's Hebrew Association, *Fortieth Annual Report, 1913* (New York: 1914); re-printed in the *Y Bulletin*, March 1913. The report's budget contained an "Athletics" column, probably in reference to the league. Also see "Athletic League," *Y Bulletin*, October 1912.

tournaments between house and club teams expanded the pool from which representative teams could draw talent. Intra-association teams swelled from thirty in 1910 to more than fifty in 1915 and "representative" teams such as the Mohegans received attention in mainstream newspapers as they played against athletic clubs, public schools, YMCA's, settlements, and even the occasional college team.[53] All of this activity served the Association's participation in the YMHA League, which limited participation to "only five regular players and a few substitutes [who] can represent us *directly* on the field." Members, however, could "represent us *indirectly* by their presence," at games as attendance became a "duty" and "organized rooting" encouraged the team to victory. At the end of the first season, the 92nd Street YMHA captured the league title in front of "an average attendance of 150 visitors."[54]

Soon after the formation of the league, YMHA basketball became a financial endeavor. In 1914, the 92nd Street YMHA's *Bulletin* explained: "Athletics should be self-supporting. We have the opportunity to make it so by attending the basketball games…every cent taken in at these games goes to encourage track and field sports and baseball, as well as basketball itself." During the 1910s, the physical department needed to fund itself in order to grow and survive, and basketball's success allowed the YMHA to develop boxing,

---

[53] On the number of inter-association teams in 1910 as well as information on the Mohegans, see "Gymnastic Notes," *Y Bulletin*, December 1909. On the number of teams in 1915, see "Athletic News," *Y Bulletin*, December 1915. The YMHA used the term 'representative' to describe any team that competed against outside teams. Most of the 'representative' teams in the early 1900s were club teams that also competed in inter-association tournaments. The most successful team was the Mohegans, led by Lazarus Joseph, a player and coach at YMHA. Joseph played at NYU prior to joining the 92nd Street YMHA and was the grandson of Rabbi Jacob Joseph. The Mohegans and other "representative" teams occasionally traveled to New Jersey to compete. In 1912, the Mohegans had a record of 25-1.

[54] Editorial, *Y Bulletin*, November 1912. Though competitive sport was intended to provide a wholesome environment and not deride the opposition, "organized rooting" was seen as providing an advantage to the home team. On the championship season, see "YMHA Athletics," *Y Bulletin*, March 1913. The team defeated YWHA teams from Yonkers, Brooklyn, Brownsville, Perth Amboy (NJ), Mt. Vernon, Bayonne (NJ), and even Philadelphia in a post-season contest.

handball, and swimming programs.[55] Athletic departments at other institutions also increased their commitment to competitive sport out of economic necessity.

The YMHA League provided a centralized location for Jewish athletes, their fans, and the media to find a Jewish presence in sport. The success of the 92nd Street YMHA basketball team led to expanded coverage in the *Bulletin*. An "Athletic News" column reported on star players and representative teams as they competed against a vast array of amateur and college teams, succeeded in AAU tournaments, and won league championships. The *Bulletin* also published articles such as "Clear the Floor for Basketball", "Basketball and its Possibilities", and "Play Fair," that educated, informed, and entertained readers.[56] Beginning in August 1912 and covering a number of months, the *American Hebrew* ran sporadic articles on the activities of the YMHA League, including swimming, cross-country, and basketball.[57] The mainstream media also noticed the growth of Jewish basketball at the YMHA, thus confirming the notion that Jewish athletes would gain public recognition as Jews.

In the 1910s, *Spalding* published two articles on YMHA basketball. The 1913-14 guide explained that New York's large Jewish population supported a competitive league that "popularized the game more than ever" at YMHA's.[58] Three years later, *Spalding* published an article entitled "Basket Ball in YMHA's"

---

[55] Basketball, *Y Bulletin*, December 1914. The statement regarding self-sufficiency indicates the desire that athletics not take funding away from other programming, and thus ensure the relative autonomy of the athletic department.

[56] "Clear the Floor for Basketball," *Y Bulletin*, December 1912; "Basketball and its Possibilities," *Y Bulletin*, October 1913; "Play Fair," *Y Bulletin*, March 1915; The 'Athletic News' column began in December 1913.

[57] See "YMHA Athletic Games," *American Hebrew*, August 16, 1912; "The YMHA Athletic League," *American Hebrew*, November 8, 1912.

[58] "YMHA Athletic League, 1912-13," *Spalding's Official Basket Ball Guide 1913-14* (New York: American Sports Publishing Company, 1913). The YMHA League was not the first mention of a specific Jewish league, but it was the most extensive. In the 1910-1911 *Spalding Guide*, under the section "Basket Ball in Detroit," there was a brief mention of a four-team league in the local YMHA. No further mention of this specific league occurred. Spalding provided only a single article on the league compared to annual publication of various YMCA leagues. Also see "Local YMHA in the Lead," *New York Times*, December 16, 1912 for a report on early results during the first year of the YMHA Basketball League.

which included Associations in a variety of locations, including Portland (Oregon), Kansas City, Louisville, Richmond (Virginia), New Orleans, Syracuse, and of course, New York. The author, Harry Henshel of the 92nd Street YMHA, explained that YMHA basketball existed in "various stages of development" comparable to the "difficult struggles which our Christian [YMCA's] friends suffered for many years." Due to a lack of financial support, a number of Associations struggled to complete "successful" seasons.[59] Many YMHA's had not "developed to the point where they have big enough gymnasiums to encourage basket ball of high caliber." Both *Spalding* articles singled out the 92nd Street YMHA for having a "splendidly equipped building, including a fine gymnasium and basket ball court."[60]

Henshel based his *Spalding* article on a questionnaire issued by the Council of Young Men's Hebrew and Kindred Association (CYMHKA). Formed in 1913, the organization intended to merge settlements and YMHA's into a national Jewish Center movement. Officials believed the Jewish community center (JCC) would overcome the fragmentation of Jewish communal life based on religious, 'ethnic,' and class differences by providing social, cultural, and religious programs that unified "all members of the community."[61] An official CYMHKA publication stated: "Athletics are absolutely necessary and a gymnasium is an essential feature of the YMHA." The Council primarily promoted outdoor sports over basketball, which as an indoor game, was "perhaps the least to be recommended." The Council's attitude toward basketball

---

[59] Harry Henshel, "Basket Ball in YMHA's," *Spalding's Official Basket Ball Guide 1916-17* (New York: American Sports Publishing Company, 1916). Despite these struggles, YMHA's had decided to go down the path that YMCA's had determined *not* to go. YMCA's continued to play basketball, but refused to become full-fledged athletic clubs.

[60] Ibid.

[61] Kaufman, *Shul with a Pool*, 63.

notwithstanding, Henshel stated that basketball had become "the feature indoor sport in YMHA's throughout the country."[62]

During the 1910s, an increasing number of Jewish individuals, settlement houses, and YMHA's appeared in the *Spalding* and *Reach* basketball guides, which provided the closest example of national basketball news for fans, coaches, and players of the game.[63] These annual guides represented insiders' opinions on the development of the game, albeit from competing perspectives regarding professionalism. With introductory sections intended to promote the guides' respective philosophies, as well as to inform and educate the reader, both guides examined a wide range of leagues, organizations, and institutions. The guides did not overtly comment on either an immigrant or Jewish presence, and though names identified participants as Jewish, the guides did not qualify this identity as they occasionally did with African-Americans or Native-Americans.[64] Jewish players may have presented basketball's promoters with an opportunity to illustrate the sport's invigorating qualities, but since the sport continued to

---

[62] Quote from Harry Glucksman, *The Boys' Club in the YMHA* (Publications of the Council of YMH and Kindred Associations, 1915); Coleman Silbert, *Clubs for Jewish Work* (Publications of the Council of the YMH and Kindred Associations, 1915). On the Council, see Rabinowitz, *The Young Men's Hebrew Association*, 85-87. Among the financial and ideological leaders of the Council were Louis Marshall, Judah Magnes, Julian Mack, and the 92nd Street YMHA's president, Felix Warburg. Henshel, "Basket Ball in YMHA's."

[63] The mainstream sport media of the 1900s and 1910s reported on the exploits of college, professional, and amateur basketball, but they remained strictly local and rarely commented on events in other sections of the country. In terms of a national press, *Outing* promoted an amateur ideal that involved a strong class bias while the *National Police Gazette* deplored the hypocrisy of the elite who promoted violent sports like football yet denounced boxing. See Oriard, *Reading Football*, 216-228.

[64] Participation of Jewish individuals and institutions in mainstream competitions may have been seen as the inevitable product of basketball's expansion since immigrants were intended to be part of the larger basketball culture. Thus, it may have been that basketball's proponents identified Jews within a more generalized immigrant identity as representatives of the game's growth and power. The breadth of coverage by both guides meant that Jewish names appeared in a variety of other locales, including the PSAL of Troy, New York. The Jewish Educational Alliance played in the Public Athletic League of Baltimore and the Chicago Hebrew Institute appeared in the Central AAU Championship. *Spalding* also included comment on the YMHA in "Basketball in New Orleans" *Spalding Guide* (1918-19) and the Maccabean House in the Public Athletic League of Baltimore in 1909-10. The guides did qualify the participation of African-Americans and Native-Americans, though these occurred only sporadically.

struggle with acceptance within American society, highlighting Jewish prominence would not have furthered the guides' goal. Even among professionals, the guides commented on their excellence and made no explicit reference to their Jewishness.[65]

In 1913, the *Reach Basketball Guide* commented on the success of a group of Jewish players from the lower East Side without identifying them as Jews. The Newburgh (NY) team received "a hard jolt when three of its best players jumped their contracts at the beginning of the season." To replace these players, the manager "was able to get the entire Clark House team together to represent Newburgh and they played grand ball." The guide made a seemingly minor mistake in its discussion of Newburgh's new players. Most of them had played at the University Settlement, not Clark House. Though this illustrated bad reporting by the guide, it also indicated the significant step these players had to make into the world of professional basketball.[66] They advanced into professional basketball at a time when it existed as a marginal and unstable sport. In the process, they both helped construct a path from the street to college and professional basketball and transformed the professional game.

The Jewish players on Newburgh's team had started formally to play professional basketball in the early 1910s. Though many young Jews from the

---

[65] "The Introduction of Basket Ball into the Levant," *Spalding's Official Basket Ball Guide 1903-04* (New York: American Sports Publishing Company, 1903); "Basket Ball in Cuba," and "Basket Ball in Southern California," *Spalding's Official Basket Ball Guide 1906-07* (New York: American Sports Publishing Company, 1906); "Basket Ball in Maine," *Spalding's Official Basket Ball Guide 1911-12* (New York: American Sports Publishing Company, 1911); "Basket Ball in Wisconsin," *Reach Official Basketball Guide 1906-07* (Philadelphia, A.J. Reach & Co.: 1907); "Basket Ball in the West," *Reach Official Basketball Guide 1911-12* (Philadelphia, A.J. Reach & Co.: 1912). The inclusion of small leagues and organizations in these publications required participants to provide the relevant information. Unlike the relatively few collegiate or professional leagues, the sheer number of smaller organizations meant the guides needed some sort of filter. It remains unclear how the guides determined what to include, but the priority appears to have been covering the breadth of basketball's expansion. This is important to recognize in using the guides as texts as well as sources and complicates their use as a 'reflection' of social acceptance.

[66] Hudson River Basket Ball League, *Reach Official Basketball Guide 1912-13* (Philadelphia: A.J. Reach & Co., 1913). A couple of the Jewish players in professional basketball did come from the Clark House, but most of the players – and the most recognized – had played at the University Settlement.

lower East Side played in professional games while in high school or college, they often did so under assumed names to keep their amateur status. Among the most prominent and skilled players, former settlement and CCNY basketball players Barney Sedran and Harry Brill joined their friend Marty Friedman, who had not played in college, on an independent professional team in New York City called the Roosevelt Big Five. The Jewish players also played in the newly formed Hudson River League, which had teams located in upstate New York towns such as Newburgh, Utica, and Kingston.[67]

In the 1910s, professional basketball existed as a chaotic sport. The Hudson League existed alongside many other professional leagues that predominated in northeastern towns. Teams often folded in the middle of a season. Leagues struggled financially and occasionally disbanded after only a couple of seasons. Players jumped from team to team for better pay and without fear of reprisal. Sedran, Friedman, and the other Jewish players quickly adapted to the professional culture. They too moved from team to team and league to league as players enjoyed a player-centered market system that allowed them to partially control their own labor.[68]

Jewish players adjusted to the tactics of the professional game. In the 1900s and 1910s, professionals often played games in cages that made the game faster and rougher. The ball remained in constant play with no out-of-bounds. Players wore knee-pads and expected harsh treatment from opponents, fans, and sometimes even the referee. The roughness and threat of violence influenced the style of play. Barney Sedran remembered that two-handed set shots predominated. "It was suicide to shoot for the basket with your feet off the

---

[67] Biographies of Marty Friedman and Barney Sedran in Postal, Silver, and Silver, *Encyclopedia of Jews in Sports*, 82-84, 92-94. Also see folders of Barney Sedran, Marty Friedman, and Nat Holman in the Edward and Gena Hickox Library at the Basketball Hall of Fame, Springfield, MA. A Picture of the Roosevelt Big Five in *Spalding's Official Basket Ball Guide 1912-13* (New York: American Sports Publishing Company, 1912). *Reach* first mentioned the players, including Barney Sedran, Marty Friedman, William Cone (nee Cohen), Lou Sugarman, Ira Streusand, and others, in Hudson River League, *Reach Official Basketball Guide 1910-11* (Philadelphia: A.J. Reach & Co., 1911).

[68] On early professional basketball, see Peterson, *Cages to Jump Shots*, 46-68.

ground because you'd be lucky to come down alive." While playing for a team in Carbondale, Pennsylvania, the 5'4" Sedran was being punched by an opponent. His backcourt partner, Marty Friedman, the two became known as the 'Heavenly Twins,' remembered that he told "Barney to run at full speed past me and as the bully boy came alongside me I stepped in front of him and down he went." The move produced a near riot.[69]

Neither Friedman nor Sedran ever claimed the attack occurred because of anti-Semitism. The early Jewish players experienced varying level of anti-Semitism during their careers. Friedman claimed: "I ran into little anti-Semitism among the players," although it occasionally emerged "in the Midwest among the fans." Ira Streusand's experience differed: "I ran into anti-Semitism everywhere, from my first collegiate game until I retired from basketball."[70] Anti-Semitism did not restrict access to professional basketball for Friedman, Streusand, or other Jewish players, but the rough culture of the sport made it difficult to isolate incidents of anti-Semitism from the everyday occurrences of violence.

Not all involved in professional basketball accepted the roughness and violence. William Scheffer, the editor of the *Reach Basketball Guide*, sought to control the chaotic state of the sport by inventing an industry along the lines of *Spalding*. Scheffer wanted a national governing organization to control professionalism and legitimate the sport, much like baseball had done in the late nineteenth century. Significantly, Scheffer decried unnecessary roughness that "needs a strong hand to keep down." He promoted a game of speed since basketball "was never intended to be a rough game, but a scientific educator."[71]

---

[69] Postal, Silver, and Silver, *Encyclopedia of Jews in Sports*, 83, 92-93.

[70] Ibid., 83, 96.

[71] Introduction, *Reach Official Basketball Guide 1909-10* (Philadelphia, A.J. Reach & Co.: 1910). Scheffer was supported the president of the Eastern League and wanted the sport to function under a stable capitalistic system to allow for growth and respectability. No standards existed for the size of the court or ball and he believed the absence of unification, control, or authority led to roughness. Quote from Stephen Fox, *Professional Baseball, Football, and Basketball in National Memory* (Lincoln: University of Nebraska Press, 1998), 275.

Scheffer particularly welcomed passing styles that reduced the violence as a step in the right direction. Sedran, Friedman, and other Jewish players brought such a passing style that they had initially learned under Harry Baum to the professional basketball. In 1915, Sedran, Friedman, William Cohn (nee Cohen), and Jack Fox played for Utica in the New York State League. *Reach* explained that the Utica "team, with one exception, [consisted] of youngsters that came fast, and it was the same old story of youth replacing older players with speed." Utica won the league championship and the guide commented that their teamwork and passing honored the sport's origins, since "basket ball was invented as a passing game."[72] Scheffer saw Utica's players as a group of young players who used a preferred passing game that could legitimate professional basketball.

The introduction of passing did not preclude Jewish players from having to adjust to the dominant form of play. Equipment frequently determined the rules, form, and style of play of professional basketball leagues.[73] Among the stories later turned into legend, Sedran scored 17 baskets in one game on an open basket (no backboard) while playing with Utica. The following year, the New York State League folded and Sedran, along with Utica's other Jewish players, entered the Eastern League. *Reach* explained that they were initially "handicapped at the start by the change in style of play." They had become "accustomed to shooting at an open basket, while the Eastern rules call for backboards."[74] Sedran's accomplishment with Utica, though quite remarkable, occurred in a space in which he felt comfortable. Regardless of their passing style, had Sedran and the other Jewish players not been able to adjust to playing

---

[72] Introduction, *Reach Official Basketball Guide 1914-15* (Philadelphia: A.J. Reach & Co., 1915). The guide discussed the Utica team that captured the New York State League title, and ended the five-year reign of the Troy Trojans, one of the greatest teams of early basketball. Five of Utica's top six players were Jewish.

[73] Stephen H. Hardy, "Entrepeneurs, Organizations, and the Sport Marketplace: Subjects in Search of Historians," *Journal of Sport History* 13, no. 1 (Spring 1986): 19-21; Hardy, "'Adopted by All the Leading Clubs.'"

[74] Introduction, *Reach Official Basketball Guide 1916-17* (Philadelphia, A.J. Reach & Co.: 1917).

with backboards, their welcome in the Eastern League would have been short-lived and their professional careers stalled.

By 1917, Sedran had won a number of championships in the various leagues of the northeast. He also achieved financial success. By his own account, Sedran made $12,000 in one year while playing "sometimes two or three times a day."[75] Yet, he achieved this competitive and financial success as an individual, not part of a community project. The professional success of Sedran, Friedman, and other Jews did not change the fact that communal Jewish athleticism needed to facilitate Jewish acceptance and integration without negatively impacting Jewish identity. This proved difficult as Jewish leaders found that individual Jews often had their own ideas about sport.

In the 1910s, both the YMHA League and its member institutions banned Saturday play, which indicated that officials believed Jewish athletic culture could function adequately on a six-day athletic week. Some young Jews found the official separation of Jewish athleticism from mainstream sport unsatisfactory. In a July 1915 letter to physical director George Schoening, 92nd Street YMHA President Felix Warburg explained that a few members had ingeniously "formed themselves into the so-called Manhattan Club, making it appear by using the cut of our building, that the same was their club-house." They did this in order to "play in competition on Saturdays, which the Board had ruled should not be permitted."[76]

Writing on behalf of the Board of Directors, Warburg communicated their concerns regarding "the attitude of our young men toward athletics." Besides the Sabbath incident, which officials never fully confronted in either private meetings or public declarations, he spelled out two other matters that needed to be addressed, gambling and professionalism. Competition could be a healthy activity for "our young men, handicapped as a good many of them are by

---

[75] Postal, Silver, and Silver, *Encyclopedia of Jews in Sports*, 90-91.

[76] Felix Warburg to George Schoening, July 26, 1915, Young Men's Hebrew Association records, 92nd Street Y Archives, New York.

generations of ancestors who have been forced to live in unhealthy surrounding and crowded districts." The YMHA needed to refocus its efforts toward fair play and sportsmanship since "the desire to excel and to win prizes has led us to give an undue importance to those young men who may turn out to be the winners." Placing blame squarely on themselves, YMHA directors and officials "feel that we may have been guilty of driving them forward in these ambitions, rather than warning them to improve their standing all around and thus causing them to specialize to a dangerous degree to the detriment to other boys, whom they have crowded out." Warburg appealed to Schoening to teach and develop "the ethics of sport…rather than the muscles alone."[77]

The *Bulletin's* 1907 call for champions had not foreseen that problems would arise. It assumed competitive sport would be easily incorporated into American Jewish culture. Aggressive behavior, whether associated with professionalism, gambling, or disregard of Jewish tradition, illustrated that YMHA members had learned 'American' values, but potentially at the expense of 'Jewish' values. Individualism and the pursuit of financial success were not the values Association officials sought to teach its "young men." The YMHA's desire to develop strong and modern American Jewish men meant that Saturday competition would not be tolerated. Neither would disreputable behavior that transgressed middle class norms.

When confronted with the consequences of competitive sport, YMHA officials became determined to reign in their champions. The hierarchical structure of the YMHA League encouraged specialization and competition, which meant officials confronted the ultimate paradigm of American sport, elite or mass participation. Yet, Warburg's reference to Jews' ghetto existence indicated that an additional burden influenced his perspective. The perceived absence of sport in Jewish culture meant that despite concerns regarding the YMHA's developing

---

[77] Ibid. Warburg's concerns regarding gambling had been caused by betting at various events, but specifically at baseball games. The league cancelled the baseball season.

athletic culture, neither Warburg nor other YMHA officials ever contemplated abolishing competitive sport.[78]

In 1917, the YMHA formed an official Athletic Committee to replace an informal committee that possessed no authority to control members' actions since it focused solely on financial matters.[79] Both directors and members governed the new Committee. Indeed, the first official committee to include members, it sought to protect the YMHA's growing reputation in mainstream sport. New YMHA President Irving Lehman placed the responsibility for developing "clean" sports in the hands of the members. At the committee's opening meeting, Lehman stated: "This is an experiment. If this experiment fails it hurts the kind of work in which you are especially interested…pick out the kind of men [Committee members] who are going to stand for straight, clean athletics."[80] Before the Athletic Committee could produce results, America's entry into World War I diminished competitive sport at the YMHA and caused the suspension of all YMHA League activities.

World War I provided an opportunity for YMHA officials to promote the institution as a location that served both the Jewish community and the American nation. Regular columns such as "Our Honor Roll" and "In the Service of the USA" praised YMHA members for their efforts to defeat the "enemy." The YMHA helped "weave those moral principles which will best serve the young

---

[78] The incident appears to have resulted solely in a *Bulletin* article that praised YMHA athletes for not competing on the Sabbath. The article was written by a member of the Board of Directors, the Reverend Dr. Samuel Schulman. See "The Opportunities for the Jewish Character," *Y Bulletin*, May 1916. Athletes guilty of gambling and professionalism were briefly suspended.

[79] An example of praise awarded on the basketball team is found in the 1917 YMHA *Annual Report*, which proudly reported the 32-1 record of the team. The following year, the *Bulletin* editor and physical director picked an All-YMHA team from 'in-house' teams. The existence of this all-star team is the best indication of a shifting ideology toward basketball as honored players were chosen solely for 'playing ability,' and 'points scored,' with no mention of sportsmanship, moral value, or other Progressive ideals. On the formation of the initial committee in 1913, see "Committee on Athletics," *Y Bulletin*, April 1913.

[80] For Lehman's speech, see "Athletic Committee Re-Organized," *Y Bulletin*, April 1917. Felix Warburg resigned as YMHA president in April 1916. The Athletic Committee was the first committee at the Association to contain members.

American Jew." It also produced strong men: "We do not forget our duty to our country...the YMHA boy is keeping himself in good physical condition."[81] The YMHA connected the physical and moral condition of its members, their American Jewish identity, and their loyalty to the United States.

As the war approached, CCNY basketball symbolized the democratic environment of America's tolerant athletic world. The school had continued basketball success in the 1910s, but remained largely out of the media spotlight. In December 1916, the *New York Times* declared that CCNY had "upset" their mighty opponents from Yale University. Such a report relied more on assumptions regarding Yale's athletic supremacy than the reality of college basketball. For the *American Hebrew*, which commented on the outcome weeks after the game occurred, the victory served an important symbolic function. The CCNY victory occurred only months before America entered World War I, and the outcome served as "a striking example of real American democracy." Victory "rested with the immigrant boys, the red-blooded aristocrats of America's future."[82] Jewish immigrants, and thus all Jews, represented America's future.

Not all Americans would have agreed with the *Hebrew*. Despite Franz Boas' efforts, the Dillingham Commission's report in 1911 had legitimized the use of racial scientific theories that ranked immigrant races below an idealized Anglo-Saxonism. During the 1910s, the eugenics movement provided further power to the belief of 'new' immigrants' racial inferiority.[83] Unlike late nineteenth century Social Darwinists, eugenicists opposed laissez-faire policies regarding racial propagation. E.A. Ross, Madison Grant, Charles Davenport, and

---

[81] "Is the YMHA Making its Members Fit?," *Y Bulletin*, November 1918; 1917 YMHA *Annual Report*, published in the *YMHA Bulletin*, March 1917.

[82] "Yale Five Upset by City College," *New York Times*, December 24, 1916; *American Hebrew*, January 15, 1917. On Yale's team was Charles Taft, son of the former president.

[83] See Higham, "The Rise of Social Discrimination," 124-132; Daniels, *Coming to America*, 177-178. The commission endorsed a literacy test intended to limit the number of eastern and southern European immigrants. Presidents Taft and Wilson both vetoed literacy test bills, though one eventually passed over Wilson's veto in 1917. This test had little impact on Jewish immigration, since Jews had high literacy rates, but it nonetheless illustrated the growing strength of the immigration restriction movement.

others believed biological, not environmental, factors influenced inherited characteristics and immutable racial identity threatened American society.[84] Grant, who would have tremendous influence following World War I, warned in 1916: "the Polish Jew, whose dwarf stature, peculiar mentality, and ruthless concentration on self-interest are being engrafted upon the stock of the nation." Grant connected physical and mental characteristics to an immutable Jewishness and condemned the "melting pot" as "mongrelization" that would destroy America since, "the cross between any of the three European races and a Jew is a Jew."[85] Few Americans knew of Grant's treatise in the 1910s, but even before America entered World War I, the perception that millions of 'unassimilated' immigrants remained loyal to the 'old world' had intensified.

World War I destroyed the Progressive movement. Never completely united, Progressives split into factions that viewed the war as either constructive or destructive. Some reformers believed the war would provide further opportunity to direct social order. Others feared the war would disrupt reform efforts. Settlement workers confronted charges that Americanization had not occurred.[86] Americanization evolved into the conception of 'One Hundred Percent Americanism,' which enforced conformity to American ideals. Expressions of loyalty and patriotism became synonymous and "hyphenated Americanism" became seen by Americans such as Theodore Roosevelt as an aberration and indicated that immigrants had dual loyalties. For Jews, the threat

---

[84] On the eugenics movement, see Wendy Kline, *Building a Better Race: Gender, Sexuality, and Eugenics from the Turn of the Century to the Baby Boom* (Berkeley: University of California Press, 2001), 19-29; Bederman, *Manliness and Civilization*, 108-120. At a time of social reform, eugenicists took advantage of, and promoted, the fear of 'race suicide' as they encouraged Anglo-Saxon women to have more children and hoped to reduce the number of immigrant children

[85] Grant, *Passing of the Great Race* 16-18.

[86] Carson, *Settlement Folk*, 151-159; Archdeacon, *Becoming American*, 166-168; Daniels, *Coming to America*, 277-278. On reformers during the 1910s and World War I, see Alan Dawley, *Changing the World: American Progressives in War and Revolution* (Princeton: Princeton University Press, 2003).

of violence, especially Leo Frank's lynching in Georgia in 1915, warned them that many Americans continued to view them as outsiders.[87]

World War I transformed American Jewish life. Jews initially had varied responses to the war. Leaders such as Jacob Schiff encouraged Jewish support of the war effort whereas many immigrants despised America's ally, Russia. The Russian Revolution and hope for the establishment of a Jewish homeland in Palestine changed the attitude of many Jews toward the American war effort. Zionism, which until the war had remained a relatively small movement due to strong opposition from some American Jews who feared charges of dual loyalty, became a more important part of American Jewish life as some Jews also challenged the idea of the 'melting pot.'[88]

In 1914, Louis Brandeis joined the movement and his leadership leant legitimacy and prestige to American Zionism. A prominent Progressive and first Jewish Supreme Court Justice, Brandeis promoted a version of Zionism that fit into academic Horace Kallen's notion of cultural pluralism. As opposed to the coercive assimilating tendency of the American 'melting pot,' cultural pluralism allowed immigrants to maintain their cultural differences as they joined mainstream society.[89] Brandeis believed that Zionism reflected Progressive ideals

---

[87] Higham, *Strangers in the Land*, 247-249; Daniels, *Guarding the Golden Door*, 33-34.

[88] Christopher M. Sterba, *Good Americans: Italian and Jewish Immigrants during the First World War* (New York: Oxford University Press, 2003), 163-172.

[89] For information on cultural Jewishness, see Korelitz, "The Menorah Idea," 84-95; Goldstein, *The Price of Whiteness*, 177-182. Also see Sidney Ratner, "Horace M. Kallen and Cultural Pluralism," *Modern Judaism* 4, no. 2 (May 1984): 185-200. For Kallen's reaction to the nativist literature and his use of cultural pluralism in the 1910s, see Horace M. Kallen, "Democracy versus the Melting Pot, A Study of American Nationality," *The Nation* 100 (February 18 and 25, 1915): 190-194, 217-220. There has been much debate regarding Kallen's cultural pluralism. See William Toll, "Horace Kallen: Pluralism and American Jewish Identity," *American Jewish History* 85, no. 1 (1997): 57-74. Toll reacts in particular to critiques by David Hollinger, Werner Sollars and Orlando Patterson who define Kallen's viewpoint of cultural pluralism only through his original essay, which limits choice within ethnic identity. See David A. Hollinger, *Postethnic America: Beyond Multiculturalism* (New York: Basic Books, 1995), 92-94; Werner Sollors, *Beyond Ethnicity: Consent and Descent in American Culture* (New York: Oxford University Press, 1986), 183; Orlando Patterson, *Ethnic Chauvinism: The Reactionary Impulse* (New York: Stein and Day, 1977), 167-169. William Toll explained that those one must read all of Kallen's work to understand the complexity of his thought.

and served an integrated American Jewish identity. He famously wrote: "to be a good Americans we must be better Jews, and to be better Jews, we must become Zionists."[90] The Brandeis branch of American Zionism promoted Palestine as a homeland for the European Jew who faced widespread anti-Semitism. American Jews could thus support the development of Palestine without disturbing their loyalty to the United States.

The American Jewish community emerged onto the world stage during World War I. In 1914, American Jews of all religious denominations, nationalities and classes united to form the Joint Distribution Committee, which raised millions of dollars to aid in relief for European Jewry. That same year, the war effectively stopped immigration and the "Jewish center movement came to realize that in the future it would no longer administer to immigrants but to their children." In April 1917, only days after the United States entered the war, American Jews organized the Jewish Welfare Board (JWB) to provide social and religious services to Jewish soldiers in camps.[91] The JWB served as a central Jewish organization as Americans rallied around the flag during the Great War. The war provided Jews an opportunity to 'become' Americans. It also helped transform American sport.

Leading up to America's entry into the war, the "preparedness" campaign shocked Americans as they learned of the physically unfitness of a majority of American men set to join the armed forces. Physical educators took advantage of the crisis to encourage physical education in high schools. The APEA sought federal legislation to encourage proper education since "German brutality and unsportsmanlike conduct are directly attributable to a poorly balanced scheme of military and physical training, resulting as it does in overemphasis of formal mass

---

[90] For Brandeis's initial involvement in the Zionist movement, see Melvin I. Urofsky, *American Zionism from Herzl to the Holocaust* (Garden City, N.Y.: Anchor Press, 1975), 111-118; Mark A. Raider, *The Emergence of American Zionism* (New York: New York University Press, 1998), 25-27. Quote from Urofsky, 120.

[91] Sorin, *A Time for Building*, 201; Goren, *New York Jews and the Quest for Community*, 214-230. Quote from Kaufman, *Shul with a Pool*, 127. The JWB also enlisted Jewish soldiers and raised money for the war effort.

activity to the neglect of athletic games and sports and thus causing a deadening of individual initiative and courage."[92]

During the war, the armed forces made competitive sport central to the war effort. The YMCA initially worked with reformers such as Luther Gulick to use sport as "invisible armor" against the sexual activity of soldiers. The JWB played a role in the War Department Commission of Training Camp Activities, which coordinated the efforts of various organizations and hoped competitive sport would serve moral ends. By the end of the war, however, sport served to distract and entertain soldiers, not provide a moral education. Training camps and the American Expeditionary Forces (AEF) helped "create not only an army of soldiers," but also "an army of athletes." As historian Steven Pope explained, the war furthered the link between sport and the military in order to "cultivate national vitality, citizenship, and the martial spirit."[93] Ultimately, the army's commitment to sport encouraged the emergence of America's national sporting culture.

Professional basketball leagues suspended their operations during the war and Jewish professional players made their mark in the armed services. In 1919, Marty Friedman and Jake Furstman, another former player from the University Settlement who played professional basketball, were named first team All-AEF. *Stars and Stripes* described Friedman as "one the slipperiest men in basketball" who had played "with several world's championship teams."[94] Lt. Friedman led the Tours Inter-mediate Section, S.O.S. to the AEF championship as "the greatest

---

[92] Frank L. Kleeberger, "American Athletics vs. German Militarism," *American Physical Education Review* 24, no. 2 (February 1919): 83. On the preparedness campaign as well as debates over the effectiveness of military drills versus sport, see Timothy P. O'Hanlon, "School Sports as Social Training: The Case of Athletics and the Crisis of World War I," in *Sport in America: From Wicked Amusement to National Obsession*, ed. David K. Wiggins (Champaign, IL: Human Kinetics, 1995), 189-206.

[93] Steven W. Pope, "An Army of Athletes: Playing Fields, Battlefields, and the American Military Sporting Experience, 1890-1920," *Journal of Military History* 59, no. 3 (July 1995): 436. Pope quoted a sportswriter in *Outing* as commenting on the "army of athletes."

[94] "Some of America's Best Basketball Players Are on All Star A.E.F. Team," *Stars and Stripes*, April 25, 1919.

all-round basketball player in the game today.' Private Furstman, "better known in the basketball world as 'Jakie' Fuller, an alias under which he played the game in the Eastern, Hudson Valley, and New York State League" also received praise from *Stars and Stripes*. The newspaper stated that, "those who saw 'Jakie' perform in the Paris series believe few, if any guards, in the game are better men."[95] The celebrations of Friedman and Fuller in the army's newspaper reflected the removal of Progressive meanings from basketball. By the end of the war, the chaotic conditions of the pre-war era had largely disappeared as the sport's popularity grew in high schools, colleges, AAU, industrial leagues, and various other organizations. This popularity would help spread the sport's commercialization and a broader acceptance of professional basketball.

At the end of World War I, Jewish basketball had become poised to emerge as an important part of the broader American basketball culture. Friedman, Sedran, and other Jews had helped establish a pathway from urban areas to the professional game at a time when the two existed in different spheres. Among the first of a new breed of professionals who had grown up playing basketball, they began their careers as boys, but had become mature men by the end of the Progressive era. They took advantage of the game's form that allowed participants to play every day, in any location. Yet, they were neither typical nor symbolic representatives of Jewish immigrants of the era. They succeeded due to the prevalence of college and professional basketball in New York. The idea of an athletic career remained distant for the vast majority of urban youth.[96] These

---

[95] Tours Team Is Winner in A.E.F. Basketball Race," *Stars and Stripes*, April 18, 1925. Pope, "An Army of Athletes," 436. Both General Pershing and James Naismith attended the final basketball game of the tournament On the changing use of sport during World War I, see Allan Brandt, *No Magic Bullet: A Social History of Venereal Disease in the United States since 1880* (New York: Oxford University Press, 1987), 59-61; Donald J. Mrozek, "Sport in American Life: From National Health to Personal Fulfillment, 1890-1940," in *Fitness in American Culture: Images of Health, Sport, and the Body, 1830-1940*, ed. Kathryn Grover (Amherst, MA: University of Massachusetts Press, 1989), 22-23. The basketball tournament and Inter-Allied Games increased the popularity of basketball in Europe. Friedman organized the American team, which defeated France in the final by a score of 93-8.

[96] According to Steven Riess, fewer than ten percent of urban children used playgrounds. See Riess, *City Games*, 167. Most of the experienced professionals prior to the late 1910s had previous athletic experience at YMCA's or athletic clubs. Unlike football or baseball, basketball was

players, however, entered a marginalized, yet open, profession, expanded the promise of sport to include commercial possibilities, and helped established a Jewish basketball culture that would surpass that of other immigrant groups.

In the 1910s, YMHA's and JCC's helped expand public recognition of Jewish male athleticism. Philadelphia and New York Jewish communities produced organized, hierarchical structures that encouraged competitiveness, facilitated the propagation of skills, and developed champions. The champion model demanded that athletes, not the institutions that produced them, be publicly recognized as Jews in mainstream sport. After the war, the Jewish press began to use a variation of the champion model as the basis for celebrations of sport's positive influence on American Jews. As Jewish basketball emerged into mainstream society, the desire for positive expressions of racial Jewishness led to further connections between racial identity and athletic achievement. The emerging discourse had minimal impact on the play of Sedran, Friedman, or other early Jewish professionals, but their activities laid the groundwork for future conceptions of Jewish athleticism and would influence how future players, coaches, and the press saw Jewish basketball.

---

intended as an indoor sport, though outdoor courts and baskets quickly proliferated across the country. In addition, basketball is often played in various forms, including half-court, and can be easily played with only two players.

Chapter Three

From Caged to Court Jews: Jewish Basketball
and the 'Basketball Jew' in the 1920s

In the 1920s, Jewish basketball expanded further into mainstream society. The decline of Progressive sport in tandem with immigration restriction ended basketball's connection to Americanization. American Jewish men participated in an emerging consumer culture that intensified the commercialization of American sport and legitimized professional basketball. As Jews succeeded in college and professional basketball, they received public recognition. Writers and commentators in both the Jewish and mainstream press expressed the belief that Jewish excellence in basketball occurred due to specific racial characteristics. During a time of anxiety and fear that they would continue to face social exclusion, American Jews increasingly valued the Jewish presence in basketball.[1] Public participation in American sport, however, also unleashed criticisms over the Jewish impact on modern American culture.

During the 1920s, Henry Ford saw something sinister in Jewish athleticism. Ford's *Dearborn Independent* exclaimed: "Jews are not sportsmen. This is not set down in complaint against them, but merely as analysis. It may be a defect in their character, or it may not." The *Independent* did not deny Jewish participation in sport. Rather, if the Jew "takes up golf it is because his station in society calls for it, not that he really likes it; if he goes in for collegiate athletics, as some of the younger Jews are doing, it is because so much attention has been called to their neglect of sports that the younger generation thinks it necessary to

---

[1] For information on American Jews immediately after World War I, see Henry L. Feingold, *A Time for Searching: Entering the Mainstream, 1920-1945* (Baltimore: Johns Hopkins University Press, 1992), 1-15.

remove that occasion of remark." Part of a Jewish conspiracy intent on controlling the world, the Jewish "exploiter and corrupter" had become the "bane of American sports." Unlike the "sportsman" who played for "fun and skill," the Jew participated only for money and power.[2]

The *Dearborn Independent's* use of sport to depict Jewish racial inferiority and moral degradation reflected the broader anti-Jewish feeling among groups and individuals who feared a 'foreign' invasion during the 1920s. The United States emerged from World War I a strong, but uneasy world power. The belief in a worldwide Bolshevik conspiracy led to the Red Scare in 1919 and 1920. The Ku Klux Klan re-emerged in the 1920s, demanded conformity to '100% Americanism' based on Nordic purity, and expanded its hatred beyond African-Americans to include Catholics and Jews, who represented "alien" threats to American society. Jews became seen as racially inferior urban dwellers, assertive, greedy and deceptive businessmen, radical intellectuals; a general threat to American society.[3] The *Independent's* rhetoric intensified the feeling that Jews had not assimilated, would not assimilate, and in fact, could not assimilate. Ford blamed Jews for destroying traditional American values through commercial activities that encouraged the growing dominance of a consumer-based economy. Yet, Jews did not participate in this consumer culture any more than other

---

[2] *The International Jew: The World's Foremost Problem*, vol. 3 (Dearborn, MI: The Dearborn Publishing Co., 1921), 38-39. The chapter was titled, "Jewish Gamblers Corrupt American Baseball." Ford blamed the 'Jew' for baseball's 1919 Black Sox Scandal (when the heavily favored Chicago White Sox lost the World Series on purpose) and virtually every gambling scandal in American sports since the turn of the century. Also see Higham, *Strangers in the Land*, 281-285; Levine, *Ellis Island to Ebbet's Field*, 4.

[3] Historian Warren Susman made clear that the 1920s were not solely a consequence of the horrors of war, see Warren Susman, *Culture as History: The Transformation of American Society in the Twentieth Century* (New York: Pantheon Books, 1984), 105-107. On American society after World War I, see, Michael E. Parrish, *Anxious Decades: America in Prosperity and Depression, 1920-1941* (New York: W.W. Norton, 1992); William E. Leuchtenburg, *The Perils of Prosperity, 1914-1932* (Chicago: University of Chicago Press, 1958). On the 'Jewish Problem,' see Goldstein, *The Price of Whiteness*, 119-122. On 100% Americanism, see Higham, *Strangers in the Land*, 204-205, 247-250; Knobel, *America for Americans*, 263-266. On the language of Americanism, see Gary Gerstle, *Working-class Americanism: The Politics of Labor in a Textile City, 1914-1960* (New York: Cambridge University Press, 1989).

Americans who wanted amusement, entertainment, and leisure after decades of reform.

Meanwhile, Americans in the 1920s, Americans celebrated a sporting culture that rejected Progressive moralism. Baseball, college football, golf, tennis, and other sports became public spectacles. Athletes such as Babe Ruth, Red Grange, Bill Tilden, and Bobby Jones became national heroes. Some commentators expressed concern about the impact of competitive, commercialized sport on traditional American values. Most Americans simply accepted sport as leisure, relaxation, and part of the emerging consumer culture. As one sport historian explained, the commercialized and competitive sport culture of the 1920s helped Americans compensate for the powerlessness they felt in a bureaucratic and complex society.[4] The decade's sport culture legitimized the celebration of athletic champions as symbols of Jewish normalization and proof that Jews could "rank with the stars of the sport and on par with his Gentile friends."[5]

During the decade, the Jewish press constructed a discourse of Jewish athleticism. This discourse included a variety of elements, but overall, it conformed to a larger project of balancing perceived notions of difference with Jews' ability to attain physical normalization and gain acceptance from the rest of

---

[4] On the emerging spectacle of American sport, see Mark Dyreson, "The Emergence of Consumer Culture and the Transformation of Physical Culture: American Sports in the 1920s," *Journal of Sport History* 15, no. 4 (Winter 1989): 261-281. During the 1920s, the press included lengthy description of games, featured articles on players, coaches, teams, and commentary on the internal developments of specific sports Columnists gained national followings, cartoons of the top stars expanded their appeal, and letters debating and comparing the minutia of sports increasingly appeared. On the expanded sports media, see Oriard, *King Football*, 24-32, 52-59. For an analytical examination of Babe Ruth, see Susman, *Culture as History*, 141-148. The new culture ended the influence of professional educators on the play activities of American youth, though the APEA continued to promote sport's function in the "future of civilization." See Percy Hughes, "Emotionality in Athletics" *American Physical Education Review* 27:6 (June 1923): 274; Weaver Pangburn "American Learns to Play," *McClure's* (July 1925); Robert Kilburn Root, "Sport versus Athletics," *Forum* 72 (November 1924): 657-664. Physical educators began to voluntarily remove themselves from children's sport. See Jack Berryman, "From the Cradle to the Playing Field: America's Emphasis on Highly Organized Competitive Sports for Preadolescent Boys," *Journal of Sport History* 2. no. 3 (Fall 1975): 112-131.

[5] Sidney Cohen, "The Jew as Athlete," *American Hebrew*, September 10, 1920.

society. The press occasionally published articles on individuals as examples of the modern Jew in American society. The more common annual compilations and weekly columns rarely contained information beyond the name and association of athletes and merged mass participation with individual achievement.[6] Public denunciations of the male 'Jew' led the Jewish press to find heroes with the most power and influence. Women illustrated the willingness of Jews to participate in social endeavors, but they served as supporting, not primary, evidence of Jewish athleticism.[7] Among male athletes, sports such as handball did not have sufficient popularity in mainstream society to allow the press to idealize the world's greatest handball player, although such an individual could also be used to prove Jewish athleticism. Jewish basketball, on the other hand, served a unique function. It reinforced the connection between athletic ability and racial identity. Non-Jewish commentators also noted this connection, but attached negative meanings to Jewish success in basketball. In contrast, the Jewish press's use of the basketball Jew reflected a belief that Jewishness provided an advantage in the mainstream sport culture.

---

[6] For examples of annuals in the Jewish press, see "A Banner Year in Sports," *The Buffalo Jewish Review*, September 27, 1935; "Jewish Athletes of the Year," *American Jewish World*, September 3, 1926; "The Year in Sports," *Philadelphia Jewish Times*, September 30, 1927. Not as rigidly structured as the annuals or columns, articles sometimes provided information on whether an individual self-identified as a Jew, but more often included factual information on their careers that may or may not have had anything to do with their Jewishness. Stories of overcoming prejudice and discrimination were the most common. See "Harvard's Prize Hero," *American Jewish World*, November 18, 1927. YMHA's, Jewish teams or athletic clubs were sometimes mentioned in annuals or broad articles, but this was an uncommon occurrence. Some commentary on Jewish athlete's social impact was generally an underlying, though ubiquitous, presence.

[7] Female athletes were not completely excluded from annual compilations or columns, but fewer articles were written on Jewish women. Individual athletes in swimming, track, golf, tennis and few in team sports were included in media representations. See "Thrice Western Women's Golf Champion," *American Hebrew*, November 6, 1925 on golfer Elaine Rosenthal. "A Rising Tennis Star," *American Hebrew*, August 3, 1928 on Clara Greenspan. According to the article, Greenspan "has one great ambition…to meet [baseball player] Andy Cohen!" For a rare exception on women in team sports, see "Jewish Sport Notes," *Philadelphia Jewish Times*, January 22, 1926, which included a story of the women's team from the Jewish People's Institute (formerly the Chicago Hebrew Institute) and praised the team for playing under 'boy's' rules. Also see George Joel, "The Year in Sports," *Philadelphia Jewish Times*, September 30, 1927. Joel commented that "Jewish women basketball were scarce," though players at NYU and Chicago led "the slim field in America."

The *American Hebrew* certainly did not represent all American Jews, but its increased interest in sport after World War I symbolized sport's growing importance in American society. In 1920, the *American Hebrew* produced its first annual 'Who's Who' issue that celebrated achievement in a variety of endeavors, including sports. Between April 1920 and April 1921, the newspaper also published four lengthy articles on the subject of Jews in sport. The *Hebrew's* initial articles helped set the form and function of the Jewish press' interwar depictions of Jewish athleticism which proved that "the Jew of America has found a new vocation."[8]

The Jewish press blamed historical intolerance, not inherent Jewish difference, for the lack of athleticism in Jewish culture. Lists of names, articles, and columns illustrated that young Jews did participate in American culture. Lists, however, could not refute charges of inherent Jewish difference. The Jewish press thus incorporated the notion of Biblical athleticism into the narrative. The *American Hebrew* claimed in 1920 that although "athletics was not a national feature of the Jew's life, he always possessed a strain of athletic ability in his blood." To prove such an assertion, the *Hebrew* pointed to "Naphtali, the ninth son of Jacob, who, according to legend, could have made any Varsity track team," the famed Biblical hero Samson, "the lion tamers of the Spanish Royal Court" and others. The *Hebrew* also drew attention to Israel Abrahams' *Jewish Life in the Middle Ages*, which "has a whole Chapter or two on 'Games.'"[9]

---

[8] Quote from Cohen, "The Jew as Athlete.". The first "Who's Who" annual appeared in the *American Hebrew* on December 3, 1920. "Who's Who" often occurred during High Holidays, but other lists were present at the end of the Julian calendar and sometimes in the spring. An example of the breadth of these annual lists, the 1921 "Who's Who" included Literature, Drama, Sciences, Music, National Welfare, and Politics. See *American Hebrew*, December 2, 1921. The *Hebrew* often served as the Jewish paper of record in American society. Specifically, see "Say Fraternities are Un-American," *New York Times*, May 22, 1910; "Will the Jews Ever Lose Their Racial Identity?," *Current Literature* 50 (March 1911): 292-294; "Jobs and Jews," *Time*, May 21, 1934.

[9] "American Jews as Sportsmen," *American Hebrew*, April 2, 1920; Cohen, "The Jew as Athlete." Also see Gurock, *Judaism's Encounter with American Sports*, 8-27; Postal, Silver, and Silver, *Encyclopedia of Jews in Sports*, 1-18. Alternatively, George Eisen has argued that such a narrative has misled historians. See Eisen, "Jewish History and the Ideology of Modern Sport," 486-488.

The Jewish press did not examine whether it could legitimately define biblical or medieval archery, running, or fighting as modern sport.[10] English Olympian Harold Abrahams confronted the irony when he declared "references to games in the Old Testament are merely metaphorical and must not be taken literally." According to Abrahams, one did not need to link to Biblical texts to see "the Jew (I use the word through the article in its racial, not in the narrower religious sense) is in every way as fine a physical entity as any other man." Historical examples of Jewish physical prowess and masculinity illustrated that Jews had lacked opportunity since Biblical times since "oppression, exiles, and later pogroms and imprisonment in 'pales' occupied the attention of the Jew, and the opportunity of free play was stifled."[11]

The portrayal of Biblical figures as athletic heroes did not completely destroy the belief that Jewish culture traditionally opposed violent physicality and aggressive masculinity. Israel Abrahams stated that Biblical "figures introduced as devoted hunters—Nimrod and Esau—are by no means presented in a favorable light." Even Samson, who one would think could easily be placed into the athletic arena, had been primarily viewed as a 'mighty' man who contained not brute strength, but rather "spiritual strength."[12] This complicated the incorporation of supposed Biblical athleticism into Jewish culture, although commentators continued to promote such a notion even as they claimed that no Jewish athletic culture had existed in the pre-modern, and intolerant, era.

---

[10] For both non-Jewish commentators in the Progressive era and the Jewish press during the interwar period, the fact that sports were a modern invention was irrelevant. For theoretical explanations of modern sport, see Allen Guttmann, *From Ritual to Record: The Nature of Modern Sports* (New York: Columbia University Press, 1978; Adelman, *A Sporting Time*.

[11] Harold M. Abrahams, "The Jew and Athletics," in H. Newman, *The Real Jew: Some Aspects of the Jewish Contribution to Civilization* (London: A&C Black Ltd., 1925), 240. Quote from Sidney Cohen, "The Jew as Athlete"; Haskell Cohen, "The Jew in Sports – A Historical Retrospective of His Participation in Athletics since Bible Days," *American Hebrew*, September 20, 1935.

[12] Israel Abrahams, *Jewish Life in the Middle Ages* (Philadelphia: Jewish Publ. Soc. of America, 1903), 375; Frank Vizetelly and Cyrus Adler in "Athletes, Athletics, and Field-Sports," *Jewish Encyclopedia* (New York: 1906).

The belief in a 'tolerant' non-Jewish athletic culture minimized sport's potential conflict with Jewishness. Supporters of Jewish athleticism virtually drowned out the voices of those who opposed athleticism on the grounds of its negative impact on Jewish culture or identity. The Jewish press rarely questioned whether Jewish manhood should include the aggressive masculinity associated with competitive sport. Neither did the Jewish press examine sport's impact on the Jewish psyche or a racial Jewishness that existed separately from Judaism.[13] Few Jews publicly confronted whether athleticism and Jewishness could be compatible. One of those who did, Maurice Samuel, examined this relationship within the context of racial Zionism's desire to construct a modern identity separate from both non-Jewish modern society and traditional Judaism.

Following World War I, eastern European newcomers transformed the American Zionist movement as they drove out Brandeisian, or "Americanized Zionists." Many of the eastern Europeans promoted an identity that historian Eric Goldstein described as a "strongly racialized view of Jewishness." This identity incorporated a vigorous nationalism that denied Jewish whiteness and cultural or 'ethnic' identity.[14] During the 1920s, neither cultural pluralists nor racial Zionists had a widespread following since American Jews wanted to construct an integrated identity between American whiteness and distinctive racial Jewishness. Nonetheless, Samuel boldly examined the explicity racial distinctions between Jews and non-Jews in his 1924 treatise, *You Gentiles!*.

Samuel expressed the belief that Jewish tradition opposed sport and thus obstructed normality as defined by non-Jews, but he felt no need to apologize for the situation. Sport and war, "the sublimest of the sports and therefore the most deeply worshipped," symbolized the "savagery" of western civilization. Speaking to non-Jews, Samuel declared "Your spirit *is* sport." In the non-Jewish world, the

---

[13] See Gurock, *Judaism's Encounter with American Sports*, 1-7. Commentators often identified athletes based on names or other undefined criteria, and though debates often raged over Jewish heritage or ancestry, rarely did commentators attempt to define or discuss the degree of an individual's Jewish identity.

[14] Goldstein, *The Price of Whiteness*, 170, 180-182.

"moral instinct is trained on the football and baseball field." He denigrated sport because the arbitrary rules brought "into life from the athletic field have no relation to the ultimate moral value of your acts and serve only to give you the moral satisfaction of having obeyed some rule or other while doing exactly what you want to do." Jews were not natural sportsmen and Jewish participation in sport represented a form of self-deception. "There is no touch of sport mortality in our way of life. …Our life morality cannot be symbolized in a miniature reproduction. We have no play-presentation of life." Jews who searched for self-respect through athletic or military activities would only find despair and a continued inferiority complex.[15]

Samuel did not deny that Jews willingly participate in modern society, so examples of Jewish athleticism could only illustrate ability, not whether participants confronted psychological tensions due to inherent Jewish difference. The Jewish press generally did not consider the possibility that sport and Jewish identity could be oppositional or whether sport represented negative forces in western society.[16] Neither did the press recognize the inherent contradiction of attempting to become 'normal' through a constructed cultural form that had helped brand them as inferior. Ignoring the underlying implication of Samuel's charges, the press continued to use athletic success as evidence of Jews' ability to overcome external charges of inferiority and abnormality. In direct response to Samuel, the *American Hebrew* argued that Zionist athletic clubs in Europe served as "a virile refutation of this ridiculous sophistry," and commented that,

---

[15] Maurice Samuel, *You Gentiles!* (New York: Harcourt, Brace, and Co., 1924), 38-61. Some commentators praised Samuel for his "courageous" race pride, but *You Gentiles!* generally received negative reviews. For the connection between military and sport in the late nineteenth century, see Mrozek, *Sports and American Mentality*, 46-64; Donald J. Mrozek, "The Cult and Ritual of Toughness in Cold War America," in *Sport in America: From Wicked Amusement to National Obsession*, ed. David K. Wiggins (Champaign: Human Kinetics, 1995), 257-262.

[16] Few historians have examined whether Jewish culture and sport are oppositional. For a theoretical examination, see Hoberman, "Why Jews Play Sports."

"Palestine will in good time have its stadium, where the speed and sinew of Jewish youth will prove on a pal with contenders of whatever origin."[17]

The *Hebrew's* mention of Zionist athleticism reflected the "muscular Judaism" movement. Max Nordau coined the term in 1898 at the Second Zionist Conference when he demanded that Jewish physical regeneration become a central goal of the Zionist movement. Nordau believed that physical development served a *moral* purpose for the modern Jew and "muscular Judaism" connected sport to nationalistic political principles that symbolically included physical components. Zionists asserted that since the Diaspora had produced the degenerated Jewish body, only a Zionist state could normalize the Jew.[18] Zionist sport became important in Central Europe where clubs such as Hakoah and Maccabi attracted tens of thousands of young 'muscular Jews' who embraced athletic competition as a means to build strong bodies and a strong nation.

The relative weakness of American Zionism hindered the formation of nationalistic athletic clubs. Instead, American Jews celebrated Jewishness within American society through "highlighting the ways Jewish racial distinctiveness contributed to the upbuilding of American rather than to its instability."[19] This became increasingly important in the early 1920s after the immigration restriction bill set quotas on the number of immigrants allowed in the United States each year. The restriction movement included the belief that Jews encompassed all the negative characteristics of modern America, which necessitated certain actions to limit their impact on society.

---

[17] For reviews of Samuel's book as well as direct reactions, see "Soccer versus Sophistry," *American Hebrew*, May 14, 1926; "In the Library" *The Jewish Youth*, November 1925; "Our Sport Column," *American Jewish World*, March 6, 1925; and "Jewish Sport Notes," *Philadelphia Jewish Times*, November 6, 1925.

[18] Max Nordau, as translated by Dr. George Jeshuran, "Of What Value is Gymnastics to us Jews?," *Maccabaean*, November 1913; George L. Mosse, *Confronting the Nation: Jewish and Western Nationalism* (Hanover: Brandeis University Press, 1993),168-170.

[19] Quote from Goldstein, *The Price of Whiteness*, 172. On Diaspora sport, see Haim Kaufman, "Jewish Sports in the Diaspora, Yishuv, and Israel: Between Nationalism and Politics," *Israel Studies* 10, no. 2 (2005): 154-158.

In the early 1920s, Harvard president A. Lawrence Lowell, a proponent of immigration restriction, expressed the opinion that his university had a Jewish problem. He proposed a solution that would limit Jewish enrollment to 15%, which he believed had become necessary because "the anti-Semitic feeling among the students is increasing, and it grows in proportion to the increase in the number of Jews. If their number should become 40% of the student body, the race feeling would become intense."[20] Lowell discussed the rude and crude manners of Harvard's Jewish students and believed the quota would help them assimilate. He declared that Jewish students did not "fit in" to Harvard's social environment due to their interest in academic achievement rather than athletic participation.[21]

As other elite colleges followed Harvard's lead in establishing Jewish quotas, American Jews celebrated college sports as reflective of Jewish modernity and integration. American Jews believed college provided a gateway toward greater social opportunity and acceptance. University of Michigan quarterback Benny Friedman became a Jewish race hero for his athletic and academic success and Harold Rigelman, a leader of the Jewish fraternity Zeta Beta Tau (ZBT), proposed the idea of 'Pro-Semitism.' Jews would "continuously and persistently, by their sportsmanship on the athletic field," illustrate their "race appreciation" and positive contribution to society.[22]

The idea that athletic success could encourage acceptance and facilitate integration gained credence due to a controversy over Jewish basketball at Yale, which occurred at the same time that Harvard's Lowell began publicly arguing for

---

[20] "Lowell Tells Jews Limit at College Might Help Them," *New York Times*, June 17, 1922, 3.

[21] On the quota controversy, see Feingold, *A Time for Searching*, 16-22; Marcia Graham Synnot, *The Half-Opened Door: Discrimination and Admissions at Harvard, Yale, and Princeton, 1900-1970* (Westport, CT.: Greenwood Press, 1979). Harvard's Jewish population increased from approximately 7% in 1900 to 21% in 1922. See Jerome Karabel, *The Chosen: The Hidden History of Admission and Exclusion at Harvard, Yale, and Princeton* (New York: Houghton Mifflin, 2005), 86-109. The result of the quota was the introduction of non-academic requirements, including 'character.' Harvard, Yale, and Princeton pushed for the use of standardized tests.

[22] Marianne R. Sanua, *"Here's to Our Fraternity": One Hundred Years if Zeta Beta Tau, 1898-1998* (Hanover, NH: Zeta Beta Tau Foundation, 1998), 70-72; Quote from Sanua, *Going Greek*, 144-145.

quotas. After the Yale basketball team finished last in the Ivy League during the 1922 season, Yale alumni demanded an end to discriminatory practices against Jewish basketball players in order to field a winning team. The school's final defeat of the season occurred against the Atlas Athletic Club of New Haven, a Jewish club, as a fundraiser for the Jewish War Relief Campaign.[23] Games between colleges and community teams occurred frequently in the early 1920s and some independent clubs proved superior to colleges who placed little emphasis on basketball.[24] Yale's marginal commitment to basketball proved disastrous when Sam Pite, a former Atlas player who had starred for both the New Haven and Hartford YMHA's quit the Yale team during the 1922 season because he believed he had been "frozen out" by the anti-Semitic coach. Rumors of this situation had existed for years, but Yale alumni did not oppose such behavior until the basketball team finished in last place in the Ivy League.[25]

Pite played the central role in both Yale's decline in 1922 and its triumph in 1923. Prior to the 1922-1923 season, Yale hired a new coach, Joe Fogarty, who told newspapers: "It makes no difference to me whether a player is black or white, Jew or Gentile, so long as he can play basketball." Fogarty's tolerance directly contrasted his predecessor's intolerance, but elite Jewish players like Pite did not depend on the whims of coaches. "Basketball followers" considered Pite one of the "best players in the state," while others "went farther" and called him

---

[23] "Yale Alumni Assail Heads of Athletics," *New York Times*, June 17, 1922. On the Atlas-Yale game, see House Notes, *Community News*, March 1922. Also see Oren, *Joining the Club*, 78. Oren explained that the game attracted three thousand fans, the largest basketball crowd in New Haven up to that point. On other athletic clubs, such as the Brooklyn Dux, see Levine, *Ellis Island to Ebbet's Field*, 30-34. On the Brownsville Boys Club, see Gerald Sorin, *The Nurturing Neighborhood: The Brownsville Boys Club and Jewish Community in Urban America, 1940-1990* (New York: New York University Press, 1990).

[24] The *Connecticut Hebrew Record* relished the prominent role of three former YMHA stars in Yale's title in 1922. See "Yale: Joseph and his Brethren," *Connecticut Hebrew Record*, April 6, 1923. The New Haven YM-YWHA simply published the *American Hebrew's* article with no additional commentary, see *Community News* 4, no. 8 (August 1922); "Round the Town," *Community News* 4, no. 11 (November 1922).

[25] Quote on 'frozen out' from "Sam Pite Decides to Play for Yale," *Hartford Courant*, November 10, 1922; On Jewish basketball at Yale prior to the controversy, see Oren, *Joining the Club*, 79-80.

"the best of the lot." Pite initially stated he would not return to the Yale team despite the coaching change. He eventually did, and along with other Jewish players, led Yale to the conference championship in 1923.[26]

The Yale situation indicated that college alumni, if not the broader society, had started to recognize Jews as excellent basketball players even as Jews continued to face exclusion. Yale alumni's desire for Jewish basketball players served competitive and commercial ends. It did not indicate a decline of anti-Semitic feeling at elite colleges. Widespread competitive failures led Yale alumni to demand the entire athletic program be rebuilt and basketball remained a minor sport for years within the restructured program.[27] The presence of Jewish players on Yale's varsity did nothing to end quotas at Harvard, Yale, Princeton, or other elite colleges. Yale never stopped Jewish admission and Pite remained a student throughout the controversy. If admitted Jewish students could play basketball, college authorities would have welcomed their inclusion.

The singling out of Jewish players led the *American Hebrew* to use the incident as representative of American tolerance. One week after Yale alumni publicly demanded an end to the discrimination against Jewish players, the *American Hebrew* examined Jewish basketball on both a macro and micro level. The newspaper declared that the incident indicated an end to the "hysterical anti-everything spirit" that had hindered Jews from taking their rightful place as productive citizens in society. The attack on Yale athletics would seem trivial "from a purely Jewish standpoint" had Jews not been "mentioned as objects of discrimination." According to the *Hebrew*, public recognition of Jewish basketball meant that "no college worthy of the name can go on record as

---

[26] "Nutmeg Boys May Star," *Hartford Courant*, December 19, 1922. Fogarty played with Jewish professionals in the 1910s; Oren, *Joining the Club*, 78-80.

[27] On the Yale basketball team, see "NCAA," *Spalding's Official Basket Ball Guide 1923-24* (New York: American Sports Publishing Company, 1924); *Yale Alumni Weekly*, January 5, 1923. The *Spalding* guide simply stated that the championship team, "made places on the reconstructed Blue team" for three players, though it did not identify them as Jews. The *Yale Alumni Weekly* focused more on the decline of Yale athletic prestige than the inclusion of Jews on the basketball team and stated that the 1922-23 season would not be a repeat of previous failure, because of "a new coach and system."

favoring their elimination from a sport in which they [Jews] so notably excel." The *Hebrew* traced a historical narrative of Jewish basketball from the lower East Side to the professional game. It focused primarily on Jewish basketball within the New York environment and concluded that basketball had become a "sport in which Jewish athletes are known to excel." The newspaper also idealized a professional player, which illustrated the changing position of professional sports in American society. "Today in the United States, there is no more speedy or more accurate player than Nat Holman of the Celtics."[28]

During the 1920s, many sports commentators considered Nat Holman the best player in professional basketball. Born on the lower East Side to Jewish immigrant parents, Holman played in settlements and public schools before moving to a variety of Northeastern leagues in the late 1910s. Unlike the majority of professional players of the era, Holman attended college and began his professional career while still at the Savage School of Physical Education. After his first full season of professional basketball in 1918, *Reach* recognized his ability, and stated that he "is a natural-born basket ball player, has a wonderful physique, a good head, and there is every reason to believe that with a little experience, he will exceed in skill and cleverness the best man that ever stepped on the court."[29]

In 1920-21, Holman played with Barney Sedran and Marty Friedman for the New York Whirlwinds. That season, the Whirlwinds scheduled a three-game series against the Original Celtics to determine basketball's 'world champion.' The first two games drew thousands of fans in New York City. They did not play the third game. The reason remains unclear, although the *Reach* basketball guide indicated that gamblers attempted to fix the game. Although the teams did not

---

[28] Elias Lieberman, "Yale Athletics and Jewish Athletes," *American Hebrew*, June 30, 1922.

[29] For information on the Holman's career, see Murry Nelson, *The Originals: The New York Celtics Invent Modern Basketball* (Bowling Green, OH.: Bowling Green University Popular Press, 1999), 1, 5-6, 34-36. Quote from "Norwalk, CT," *Reach Official Basketball Guide 1917-18* (Philadelphia, A.J. Reach & Co.: 1917). Upon his retirement, Holman had become widely considered the greatest player in the history of the young game. In 1950, the Associated Press named Holman the third best basketball player of the first half of the twentieth century.

complete the series, it illustrated the popularity of professional basketball and helped launch the sport into a new era.[30]

The Celtics' owners took advantage of the growing importance of spectators in America's post-war athletic culture. The Celtics offered exclusive contracts to players, and turned the former settlement house team into an all-star team. For instance, two weeks after the 1921 series, Holman signed with the Celtics. These contracts allowed the team to take long barnstorming tours to the Midwest and South, which increased the team's popularity and profitability.[31] The Celtics frequently played over 100 games in a single year, and rarely lost more than ten games in one season. One basketball historian emphatically stated: "The Celtics were so superior to most of the teams they played that they were able to perfect their new theories under actual game conditions without much fear of losing."[32]

During the early 1920s, the Celtics perfected a switching man-to-man defense, a give-and-go offense, and the pivot play, in which a player stood with his back to the basket and either passed to teammates cutting to the basket or pivoted and went to the basket himself. Holman later explained that the Celtics "built its offense around it [the pivot play] with such startling success that it captivated the East and Middle West, where the Celtics flourished, and found its way into the offensive systems of a great many teams."[33] The Celtic players also used their free throw shooting acumen to their advantage. "Whenever the Celtics were involved in a tight game, Holman would handle the ball and invariably draw

---

[30] Peterson, *From Cages to Jump Shots*, 70-72; Postal, Silver, and Silver, *Encyclopedia of Jews in Sports*, 86-88. The series attracted close to 10,000 fans, but was not mentioned in the *New York Times*.

[31] On the reaction of intellectuals to spectatorship in the 1920s, see Dyreson, "The Emergence of Consumer Culture and the Transformation of Physical Culture," 262-279. On the importance of contracts, see Peterson, *Cages to Jump Shots*, 69-79.

[32] Zander Hollander, ed., *The Modern Encyclopedia of Basketball* (Garden City, NY: Doubleday and Co., 1979), 274.

[33] Nat Holman, *Winning Basketball* (New York: Charles Scribner's Sons, 1932), x.

a foul, frequently as a result of imaginary contact that sent Holman careening and drew a sympathetic whistle from the official."[34]

Holman helped change professional basketball into an entertaining spectacle. According to a Jewish commentator in the late 1920s, Holman's "first concern is to put on a show for the patron's money." The commercial pressure meant that "sometimes he deliberately tries to get himself disliked and there are many towns in the country that pack an armory for the express purpose of booing and razzing Holman."[35] Holman's tactics reflected the reality of post-war American sport. Yet, one did not need to look only at Holman or organized professional basketball to find American Jews participating in the commercialized and competitive basketball culture of the 1920s.

Competitive sport grew quickly at Jewish community centers (JCC) and YMHA's after World War I. Returning veterans helped institutional membership grow to unprecedented numbers, and centers expanded their facilities and athletic programs to accommodate demand. At the 92nd Street YMHA, basketball games helped finance 'Welcome Home' celebrations for returning veterans. Basketball also became the major source of revenue for the athletic department.[36] A representative team called the Harmony Big Five played in front of capacity audiences and helped the physical department recover from a $28 deficit in 1919 to reach a budget surplus of just under $5,000 the following year. In support of basketball's growth, the *Bulletin* expanded its coverage of games and ran articles such as "Qualifications of Basketball Men," which instructed players on correct

---

[34] A. Hollander and A. Sachare, *The Official NBA Basketball Encyclopedia* (New York: Villard Books, 1989), 19.

[35] Bob Shelley, "Basketball Jews," *The Jewish Daily Forward*, November 3, 1929.

[36] "Athletic Notes," *Y Bulletin*, February 28, 1919. This was the first issue of the *Bulletin* as a weekly publication. While the 'Welcome Home' celebrations were nominally intended to honor the veterans, the *Bulletin* article indicated that the financial rewards of the basketball games proved equally, if not more, important to the Association. The income gave the athletic department autonomy from the YMHA Finance Committee, which the board encouraged so Association funds could go to other departments and programming.

technique, positioning, and style of play, but contained no moral or 'character-building' valuations.[37]

Professionalism accompanied the commercial and competitive success of the Harmony team. In October 1922, the YMHA Athletic Committee held a special meeting to discuss professionalism and decided that "members who engage in a sport professionally shall not be permitted to engage in the same sport in our gymnasium."[38] The following year, the YMHA denied Harmony the use of the gymnasium for practice and games because "it would be undesirable to have this team, which has been continuing to play professional ball, use our gymnasium for their training." The physical education department issued a memorandum against professionalism, but the YMHA did not expel Harmony players and they eventually returned as the representative team, albeit in an amateur state.[39]

In the mid-1920s, 92nd YMHA officials established a structure in which management would control basketball, including player activity. Rather than allowing players to form a team that 'represented' the institution, a coach would select a varsity team composed of the best players. The new model restricted the sort of activity in which Harmony had engaged in but did not decrease the commercial importance of basketball. In 1926, members formed the Athletic

---

[37] Budget numbers found in a miscellaneous folder, Athletic Committee records, Young Men's Hebrew Association records, 92nd Street Y Archives, New York. The YMHA did not have competitive sport during World War I, which led to the deficit. A.A. Eustis, "Qualification of Basketball Men: The Forward," *Y Bulletin*, December 29, 1922 and January 5, 1923. The article was also published in the *Athletic Journal* 3, no. 4 (December 1922). On the back cover of the *Athletic Journal*, a listing of other articles by Eustis indicated that the "The Forward" was one of many such articles. No others ran in the *Bulletin*.

[38] Minutes of the Athletic Committee, October 5, 1922, Young Men's Hebrew Association records, 92nd Street Y Archives, New York. Some of the Harmony players, including Rube Gordon and Harry Davis, became full-time professionals in the late 1920s and 1930s. Another Harmony player, Willie Marron also played professionally before becoming a member of the American Communist Party.

[39] Quotation on Harmony found in Minutes of the Athletic Committee, October 3, 1923, Young Men's Hebrew Association records, 92nd Street Y Archives, New York. Harmony was mentioned in the *Bulletin* articles as the YMHA 'representative' team in 1925. See "Harmony's Victory in Harmony with Expectations," *Y Bulletin*, October 16, 1925. The team defeated CCNY.

Council, which served as a representative body of gymnasium members, controlled its own activities and had a level of autonomy unseen elsewhere in the institution.[40] The following year, basketball coach 'Spike' Spunberg criticized the YMHA membership for their lack of support at games and appealed to the Council rather than the board-controlled Athletic Committee. In response, the Council placed a representative on the Bulletin Committee to "guarantee the proper representation." Two years later, the Council took over total control of the business management of varsity basketball and abolished free admission to any game.[41]

Similar to the 92nd Street YMHA, the structure of the Metropolitan League, formerly known as the YMHA League, evolved during the 1920s. The original YMHA Athletic League had member institutions in Westchester (Mt. Vernon and Yonkers), Brooklyn, and New Jersey (Bayonne and Perth Amboy). Re-named the Metropolitan League to represent non-YMHA members such as the Educational Alliance, the league's expansion in the 1920s reflected the changing demographic patterns of New York Jews. Economic prosperity allowed Jews to leave the lower East Side, and by 1925, only 15% of New York Jews remained in

---

[40] Harry Henshel, Athletic Committee chairman, to prospective representatives. See miscellaneous file, Physical Education department files, October 6, 1926, Young Men's Hebrew Association records, 92nd Street Y Archives, New York. The first mention of the Council in the *Bulletin* was in "Athletic Council," *Y Bulletin*, November 26, 1926. The Council's original goal was to overcome overcrowding by bringing "members of the gymnasium in closer contact with each other." The Council was divided into representatives from 'major' and 'minor' sports. Basketball was declared a 'major' sport along with baseball, track, and others. 'Minor' sports included tennis, gymnastics, and handball. The Council also formed an Executive Committee, which included the physical director, athletic coaches, the Athletic Committee chairman and elected gymnasium members.

[41] The varsity coach, 'Spike' Spunberg, was a former member of Harmony and one of those charged with professionalism. He began coaching the YMHA basketball team in 1926. Appeal by Spunberg found in the Minutes of the Athletic Council, October 1927, Young Men's Hebrew Association records, 92nd Street Y Archives, New York. In 1928, the Board of Directors decided to rebuild the YMHA. During a two-year construction period, the Association moved into the building of the New York YWHA. Smaller facilities meant the physical department confronted a drastic loss in membership and the basketball team was forced to use the gymnasiums of independent organizations. The decision of the Athletic Council to take over the business management of the basketball team was found in Minutes of the Athletic Council, December 3, 1929, Young Men's Hebrew Association records, 92nd Street Y Archives, New York.

the immigrant neighborhood.[42] The migration to the Bronx and Brooklyn made communal contact among Jews more difficult. Jewish centers attempted to fill the void caused by the dispersal. By the mid-1920s, sport served as the "principal means of establishing cordial relations between the members of the YMHA's in the Metropolitan district." In 1925, the Metropolitan League existed as "solely an athletic group," although officials hoped to "enlarge the scope of activity…to include debates, oratorical and music contests, etc." That same year, the league issued a report that asked the Jewish Welfare Board (JWB), a national organization that oversaw YMHA's and JCC's, to help stimulate "athletic competition on a larger scale."[43]

In the mid-1920s, the league formed an Athletic Committee to control member behavior, standardize rules and regulations, and encourage league competition by awarding cups and trophies. Minutes of the league's various committees reveal an inordinate amount of time spent ruling on the validity of team protests, the suspension and reinstatement of players, the standardization of rules, referees decisions, and decisions regarding awards, trophies, and other minutia.[44] The Metropolitan League also confronted gambling, which it banned at all events:

> No man who has been found guilty of placing or attempting to place a bet or acted as an agent for others in betting on athletic contests in the Metropolitan League shall be eligible to represent a constituent organization in any League activity one year from the date of the occurrence of the act. The Board of Directors of the

---

[42] Beth S. Wenger, *New York Jews and the Great Depression: Uncertain Promise* (New Haven: Yale University Press, 1996), 83.

[43] "1925 – Its History, Aims, and Plans," folder, 1922-26, Metropolitan League Records, Young Men's Hebrew Association, 92nd Street Y Archives, New York. Samuel Leff to Jack Nadel, April 29, 1925, Correspondence Files, Metropolitan League, Young Men's Hebrew Association, 92nd Street Y Archives, New York. Metropolitan League, "Metropolitan League of YMHAs to Extend Activities," press release, May 11, 1925.

[44] For minutes of the Athletic Committee, Presidents Committee, Administrative Council, and Physical Directors Society, see Metropolitan League records, 92nd Street Y Archives, New York at the 92nd Street YMHA archives.

organization of which he is a member is to be notified and requested to take similar action.[45]

The wording of the ban indicated the familiarity of such activity within YMHA sport and the mention of 'agents' meant players themselves may have gambled. Jewish institutions outside of New York also confronted gambling. A reader's letter in the *Baltimore Jewish Times* commented that "open gambling is being conducted by Jewish young men." During YMHA games in the Baltimore Basketball League, "they flash their money in the open and call aloud for bettors." The *Times'* columnist stated the gamblers "leave a bad taste in the mouth of the respectable Jewish young men."[46] Officials became concerned that incidents of gambling reflected poorly on the larger community. They also remained concerned about professionalism at Jewish centers and sought to restrain the capitalistic behavior of their basketball champions.

During the early and mid-1920s, Metropolitan League officials had frequent discussions regarding the professional status of individual players. The league's Athletic Committee declared: "No man who has ever competed as a professional shall be eligible to play in this League." The committee generally gave Centers the benefit of the doubt regarding their ignorance of a players' professional standing. The sheer volume of incidents indicated, however, that institutional control and supervision was often lacking. As a result, the Athletic Committee also "went on record disapproving any YMHA giving out free athletic membership as an inducement to enroll athletes."[47]

---

[45] Report on Minimum Standards of Health Education Recommended by the Metropolitan League, undated, Metropolitan League records, Young Men's Hebrew Association, 92nd Street Y Archives, New York.

[46] "Thru Sportdom," *Baltimore Jewish Times*, December 17, 1926.

[47] Report on Minimum Standards of Health Education Recommended by the Metropolitan League, no date, Metropolitan League records, 92nd Street Y Archives, New York. A similar document titled "Athletic Committee Rules" was found in a miscellaneous folder titled '1922-26,' Athletic Committee records, Young Men's Hebrew Association, 92nd Street Y Archives, New York. Minutes of the Athletic Committee, September 22, 1924, Metropolitan League records, 92nd Street Y Archives, New York. Minutes of the Athletic Committee are located in the Metropolitan League records, 92nd Street Y Archives, New York. Though not complete, the minutes provide a good

The Metropolitan League limited the ability of New York institutions to circumvent the code of amateur sport, but other YMHA's felt less external pressure to establish rigid standards regarding professional behavior. In the early 1920s, the Hartford YMHA participated primarily in citywide competitions and won three consecutive city championships. In December 1923, a game against the Original Celtics caused some YMHA officials to question the commercialism and rumored professionalism of the basketball team. With pressure to decrease their commercial activity, the 'representative' team declared its intention to break off from the institution and call themselves 'City Champs' as an independent team. Not surprisingly, YMHA officials opposed this development and insisted that the title belonged to the Association, not the players. The rift appeared irreconcilable until a local businessman offered the YMHA $5,000 if the team again captured the city championship. Upon this news, the players returned to the YMHA, supposedly on a 'pure' amateur standing.[48]

The reconciliation did not alleviate the concerns of some YMHA officials regarding the team's activities. Rumors grew that the manager would pay the players. The YMHA Advisory Board left the team's fate in the hands of the president, who told the *Hartford Courant* that the YMHA paid the team's expenses on out-of-town trips, but "that is all." When the *Courant* reported that statement, YMHA board members explained that strictly paying expenses was a "new" arrangement and that players had previously "split the money [profits] amongst themselves." This new arrangement, however, did not stop the team's professionalism. The *Courant* also reported that the team had "three players who live in other cities," all of whom the manager "paid by means of padded expense

---

amount of detail regarding the internal workings of the league. For examples of rulings on the professional status of players, see January 9, 1923. In these minutes, the Committee ruled on establishing a reinstatement policy for professionals.

[48] See the *Hartford Courant*, December 25, 1923; January 10, 1924; January 13, 1924. In 1921, Hartford joined a YMHA state league. Five YMHA's (Springfield, Hartford, New Haven, New London, Bridgeport) met to organize a state league, "along three lines: athletic, educational, and camp and miscellaneous." A basketball league was not initially formed because "most organizations...made up their schedules." See "House Notes: YMHA League is Organized," *Community News*, December 1921.

allowances." The controversy resulted in the resignation of the Hartford YMHA's executive secretary because of "numerous clashes" with the institution's president over the status of the basketball team.[49]

The Hartford team's recruitment and compensation of star players indicated a complexity not often associated with YMHA sport. Among the players on Hartford's team was Sam Pite, the central player in the 1922 Yale controversy. Considering his New Haven origins, Pite's presence indicated that a dissatisfaction with members' talent led YMHA management to search outside the institution's local area to find players. The *Courant* also reported that the YMHA team had a neighborhood following of over one thousand fans, including non-members. To remedy this situation, and end the competitive and commercial pressures that had caused the problems during the 1924 season, YMHA officials declared at the end of the season that they would no longer allow "non-membership players" on the team.[50]

New York's Metropolitan League also contained player movement that indicated the league did not exist as a local endeavor. A report on the 92nd Street YMHA basketball team in 1931 revealed that only one of nine varsity players lived near the Association on the upper East Side. In contrast, five players lived in Brooklyn at a time when fewer than ten percent of the Association's membership came from the borough.[51]

---

[49] "Only Remote Possibility that YMHA will have City Series Team Next Year," *Hartford Courant*, March 13, 1924.

[50] The *Connecticut Hebrew Record* simply commented on the initial fracture between the YMHA and the players over the commercialization of basketball. "Hartford Sports," *Connecticut Hebrew Record*, January 10, 1924.

[51] Nat Beckelman to Nat Holman, April 6, 1931, Correspondence files "Young Men's Hebrew Association," Executive Director records, Young Men's Hebrew Association, 92nd Street Y Archives, New York. According to the letter, the roster included one player from Manhattan, three players from the Bronx, and five players from Brooklyn. In a separate letter, an Association official indicated to Charles Bernheimer of the JWB that 39.46% of the total membership was from Manhattan, 46.73% was from the Bronx, and only 9.28% was from Brooklyn. The sender of the letter is unknown, though most likely was YMHA executive director, Jack Nadel, September 5, 1931, miscellaneous folder, Jewish Welfare Board records, Young Men's Hebrew Association, 92nd Street Y Archives, New York. For information on player movement, which generally did not occur during a season, see the *Y Bulletin* in the 1920s and 1930s. According to historian Beth

Autonomous teams, players, and institutions often conducted capitalistic activity more commonly associated with colleges and universities. The athletic marketplace included an aggressiveness, competitiveness, and commercialization that changed the goals of institutional sport. Some players moved back and forth between institutions while others remained at an institution for years, established close relationships with coaches, and controlled positions on the varsity team.[52] These conditions transformed the institutional 'spirit' in which members, as both players and spectators, shared a common experience. The introduction of outsiders, as well as the entrenchment of some players, transformed Center sport into a smaller version of commercialized college and professional sport.[53]

In the 1920s, promotion of the champion model established an environment that commodified the Jewish athlete. The competitive and commercial pressures led Jewish centers to search for better players who would bring publicity and success. The champion model made athletic ability the primary variable of an individual's worth within a competitive athletic culture. At the 92nd Street YMHA, annual preseason commentary examined individual players as athletic "material" to be shaped into the final product, a successful team.[54]

Wenger, the Jewish population in the YMHA's Yorkville neighborhood was only 4%. It is therefore not surprising that the YMHA sought players from other boroughs, though it is odd that one player traveled from Coney Island to play for the YMHA.

[52] In 1937, Lester Trokie was rumored to return to the 92nd Street YMHA varsity basketball team because he was "not exactly happy at Union Temple." See Spike Spunberg, "Basketball Bounces," *Y Bulletin*, April 16, 1937.

[53] Such activity repeated that of universities at the end of the nineteenth century as informal student activities became structured, formalized, and hierarchical, controlled by faculty, coaches, and administrations rather than the students themselves. Colleges increasingly looked outside their institutions for athletes and actively recruited individuals strictly for the athletic ability. See Smith, *Sport and Freedom*, 184-187.

[54] For information on the commodification of college athletes in relation to individual athletes, see A.G. Ingham, B.J. Blissmer, and K. Wells-Davidson, "The Expendable Prolympic Self: Going Beyond the Boundaries of Sociology and Psychology of Sport," *Sociology of Sport Journal* 16 (1999): 236-285.

A similar situation existed in college basketball, which increasingly served an important role as American Jews celebrated their participation in mainstream society. College basketball grew rapidly after World War I. The number of college basketball teams increased from 195 nation-wide in 1915 to approximately 440 only seven years later. Conferences became the predominant competitive structure and some schools constructed large arenas that could accommodate over 10,000 spectators.[55] In the West, Midwest, and South, large universities in major conferences played in campus arenas and often served as the predominant focus of community sport. Officials took control away from students and hired professional coaches, who formed the National Association of Basketball Coaches (NABC) in 1927. The NABC allowed coaches to promote their sport through conventions, the media, clinics, and public appearances as "community ambassadors." Much like their counterparts in college football, basketball coaches often overwhelmed school officials in their promotion of competitive and commercial concerns. Nat Holman, whom CCNY had hired as its varsity basketball coach in 1919, expressed the basic principle for many college coaches when he stated: "first and foremost, my principle desire is to WIN games."[56]

---

[55] Horger, "Play by the Rules," 136-138, 194-198. In the 1910s, the AAU, YMCA, and the National Collegiate Athletic Association (NCAA) had formed the Basket Ball Rules Committee to govern amateur basketball. The committee provided college basketball with stability. On the development of the NCAA, see Smith, *Sports and Freedom*, 191-208. Albert Applin explained that by 1924, there were three types of leagues: interstate conferences like the Ivy League and Big Ten, state conferences composed of smaller schools, and small state conferences consisting of both large and small schools. The Metropolitan league would have fallen into the third category. See Applin, "From Muscular Christianity to the Marketplace," 161-168. Among the large arenas were that of the Ivy League's University of Pennsylvania and the Big Ten's Indiana and Ohio State

[56] On the NABC, see Applin, "From Muscular Christianity to the Marketplace," 165-166. On the professionalization of coaching in football, see Smith, *Sports and Freedom*, 147-164, 171. Schools in the Midwest and West also hired professional coaches, though they were generally former college or amateur players since professional basketball remained underdeveloped in those regions. The national press was often quite critical of college coaches. See Correspondence, *The Nation*, November 27, 1929. The quote was from a copy of Everett S. Dean, *Progressive Basketball* (Stanford University, 1942). Nat Holman file, Edward and Gena Hickox Library at the Basketball Hall of Fame, Springfield, MA.

During the 1920s, Holman built a successful program as he split his time between coaching and playing for the Original Celtics. As CCNY coach, he brought a professional demeanor to his position. He dressed in tailored suits and simulated an acquired English accent, demanded excellence from his players, and perhaps most importantly, introduced stylistic elements from the Celtics to college basketball. His teams played a switching man-to-man defense and the offense involved constant movement without the ball and quick cuts to the basket. CCNY experienced instant success under Holman and won the unofficial 'eastern' championship in 1922 and 1923. Despite this success, CCNY and other New York schools played in the media shadow of the Ivy League, which remained the predominant presence of 'eastern' basketball in the early 1920s.[57]

In the 1920s, the Jewish presence grew slowly in a New York college basketball culture that compared poorly with other regions. New York City schools had neither the space nor resources to compete in large arenas so they generally played in armories in front of two or three thousand fans or in small campus gymnasiums that held even fewer people.[58] New York schools did, however, have access to a seemingly limitless supply of talented, local, and, quite often, Jewish players. Basketball powers Fordham and St. John's infrequently included Jews as Irish players predominated at these local Catholic schools. In contrast, CCNY and NYU became the favored schools of New York Jews. The

---

[57] "CCNY Has New Offense," *New York Times*, December 26, 1919; On the Celtics' style, see Nelson, *The Originals*, 41-56; Peterson, *Cages to Jump Shots*, 77-78; For information on the "city" style, see Isaacs, *All the Moves*, 67-68; Bjarkman, *Hoopla*, 29-30. On the differences between eastern and western basketball, see George Richardson, "Improving the Game," *Spalding's Official Basket Ball Guide, 1924-25* (New York: American Sports Publishing Co., 1924); See F.W. Luehring, "Comparison Between Eastern and Western Basketball," *Athletic Journal* 2 (February 1922). New York newspapers reported on CCNY, but basketball guides used the Ivy League to represent. This slowly changed as Ivy League deemphasized their athletic programs, but the Ivy League remained the dominant presence in 'eastern' basketball even after in the early 1930s.

[58] CCNY and NYU played their annual contest in front of 10,000 fans in 1920, but this event would not be matched until the early 1930s. Unlike the Celtics-Whirlwinds series mentioned in Chapter 4, the college contest was covered by the local press, including the *New York Times*, see "NYU vanquishes CCNY, 39 to 21," *New York Times*, March 7, 1920. NYU, with two Jewish players, would win the AAU championship later that year. The largest crowds of the decade were about five to six thousand.

1926 season finale between the two schools included seven Jewish starters; all five for CCNY and two for NYU. Jews also increasingly appeared on Ivy League teams, and in 1924, made up six of the league's top eighteen scorers.[59]

The Jewish press took notice of the growing presence of Jews in college basketball. Even newspapers that generally focused on local athletes gazed outward at the pervasiveness of Jewish basketball. In 1924, Minneapolis' *American Jewish World* (AJW) published an article that had little to do with Minneapolis Jews, but which the newspaper's editor believed would serve as a "splendid refutation of the charge that Jews fail to take part in college athletics." The section entitled "Leads in Basketball" stated: "practically every team contending for championship honors has from one to four Jewish court players." The article commented on Yale's elimination of "race prejudice," and stated that in the Ivy League, "two of the captains and more than half of the outstanding stars are Jewish." The article also lauded the achievement of the predominantly Jewish CCNY team and stated that Holman, who "holds the distinction of being the greatest player and coach of basketball in the United States, has made a habit of turning out winners."[60] The celebration of Jewish basketball reflected the participation of Jews as well as other racial and ethnic groups in American sport. This presence led to 'studies' on the connection between race and athleticism.

In 1922, the *American Physical Education Review* published a series of articles entitled "Racial Traits in Athletics." The author, non-Jewish physical educator Elmer Mitchell, wrote: "Nowhere, does it seem to me, can we find people closer and truer to their fundamental character than in their free and spontaneous play." The *Eugenical News* printed a summary of the series, which reinforced the dominant racial paradigm in American society. Mitchell analyzed fifteen racial groups, although he arranged Latins, The South American, and The

---

[59] On NYU-CCNY game, see *New York Times*, February 28, 1926. On final scoring tally of the Ivy League, see "Ivy League Standings," *New York Times*, March 10, 1924.

[60] Sidney S. Kluger, "Jews in College Sports: An Account of Jewish Athletes as Jewish Stars," *American Jewish World*, April 18, 1924.

Oriental into broader classifications than the Irish, Greek, or Jew. Mitchell explained that the 'American' athlete, "a composite of many races: conspicuously the English, Irish, German, and Scandinavian," had become the "greatest in the world." Southern and eastern Europeans, however, "are less ready assimilable" than northern Europeans and they illustrated this on the athletic field.[61]

Mitchell believed that Jewish athleticism demonstrated Jews' racial inferiority. "We see the same distaste of the Jew for outdoor life, his industry in the intellectual side of his pursuit, his subtlety in applying social or individual weakness to his own benefit, and his lack of moral sensitiveness." He explained that contradictory to public opinion, Jews possessed both physical and moral courage, although certain "distinctive qualities cling to the Jew when he participates in athletics." Sport did not change the Jewish temperament: "The average Jew is an unpopular team-mate; he is assertive, individualistic, and quarrelsome." Mitchell concluded that any observer would concur "by watching a group of Hebrew children on the playground." Even more disturbing, Jews' ability to "face adverse circumstances" often manifested itself in "the villain role," which he believed they seemed to enjoy.[62]

Mitchell's imaged Jew remained physically inferior in the small immigrant body. The Jew had vitality, caused by "clannishness," sacred family ties, and adaptability to "the bustle and change of modern commercial life." This vitality was "a wonderful thing," especially since sport did not produce the physical change many had expected. "The typical Jew is not robust in appearance," explained Mitchell. He used football to prove his point. Only in "exceptional cases" do Jews star in this team sport, "where size plays so important a part." Yet, a small body could help Jews succeed in other sports. "Along with

---

[61] Elmer D. Mitchell, "Racial Traits in Athletics," *American Physical Education Review* 27, no. 3 (March 1922), 93; The summary was in the *Eugenical News* 7 (1922). Mitchell cited studies from Charles Davenport, Madison Grant, and other prominent eugenicists. In the late 1910s, the APER included a permanent eugenics section under its monthly bibliography.

[62] Elmer D. Mitchell, "Racial Traits in Athletics," *American Physical Education Review* 27, no. 5 (May 1922): 197.

boxing and dancing, gymnastics and basket ball are popular, all of them types of athletic exercise demanding dexterous footwork and dodging ability and carried on indoors. Basket ball is easily their favorite sport."

The unchanged Jewish body reflected, in Mitchell's view, Jews' unchanged intellectual ability that served as an advantage in the athletic world. Jews retained their mental advantage as "quick thinkers, alert to grasp the strategy of the game, both of their own team and of their opponents." Yet, the intelligent Jew corrupted pure sport since his "individualistic tendency" produced "a spirit fostering the professional game, rather than the game which is played solely for the joy of participating."[63] Mitchell did not view Jewish athleticism in similar terms as Henry Ford's *Dearborn Independent*, but he attached negative characteristics to Jewish intelligence. Mitchell believed that when Jews willingly participated in American sport, it resulted in professional or tricky behavior that reflected Jews' racial inferiority. Throughout the 1920s, columnists in the Jewish press, though informed by the same assumptions used by Mitchell, used the belief in innate Jewish intelligence to construct a positive form of racial marking within the athletic world. In doing so, they constructed a discourse that led to the reemergence of the basketball Jew.

During the interwar period, syndicated sports columnists such as George Joel, Harry Conzel, and others wrote articles, columns, and annuals that appeared in a variety of Jewish newspapers. Joel, for instance, wrote for the Jewish Telegraphic Agency (JTA), which had his columns, articles and annuals published in the *Philadelphia Jewish Times* and the *Detroit Jewish Chronicle*.[64] These columnists merged the broad outlook of the distant and lionizing annuals with experiential content of local columns as they provided information on the accomplishments of well-known Jewish athletes and identified Jewish athletes to the readership. They infrequently included non-elite athletes as evidence of

---

[63] Ibid. For analysis of Mitchell's articles, see Oriard, *King Football*, 255-257, 283-284.

[64] Oriard, *King Football*, 34. According to Oriard, Joel published the first Jewish All-America football team in 1925.

Jewish athleticism, but these athletes rarely informed compilations beyond claims that "Americanized, practically every Jewish youngster participates in some sport or another."[65]

Jewish newspapers rarely contained sport pages, so readers in various cities often received their information on Jewish athletes from syndicated columnists. Letters from readers countered claims of an athlete's Jewish identity or the greatness of a team or individual, but few challenged the idea that "sport should be encouraged. It is a good school for life; it prepares us to will and to do."[66] Yet, some commentators noted that because of the annuals and columns, "the Jewish reader makes the inference that his strong brethren have conquered all the American sports and are equally successful at them all. ...Can we, however, honestly claim that the Jewish athlete takes to all sports with the same degree of success?"[67]

Most columnists asserted that Jews succeeded in basketball more than any other sport. Outside of Nat Holman, the columnists generally emphasized the collective importance of Jewish basketball rather than individual players.[68] Throughout the 1920s, columnists argued, "from a Jewish angle," that basketball had become the "the king of sports." George Joel stated in his 1927 syndicated annual that, "it is hard to find a college team without at least one Jewish player on the squad."[69] The previous year, Harry Conzel boldly claimed, "it would be

---

[65] "Sports are in the Air," *American Hebrew*, June 4, 1937.

[66] Harry Conzel, "Our Sport Column," *American Jewish World*, January 30, 1925.

[67] "Jewish Sports Notes," *Philadelphia Jewish Times*, December 18, 1925.

[68] Baseball allowed for more extensive examinations regarding the Jewish place in the sport and in-depth analysis regarding individual ability. Hank Greenberg's MVP award in 1935 was essential in representing his athleticism as a Jew. Likewise, Barney Ross' success as a boxer was never separated from his championships.

[69] "Thru Sportdom," *The Jewish Times*, December 3, 1926. Local papers across the country concentrated on the activities of clubs, institutions, and organizations that would never have garnered the attention of the *Hebrew*; George Joel, "The Year in Sports," *Philadelphia Jewish Times*, September 30, 1927. Joel had been a member of ZBT and wrote for the fraternity's publications.

useless to list Jewish basketball players. Collegiate and professional basketball teams all over the country contain almost a majority of Jews." As late as 1930, columnists continued to assert that in basketball, it remained "impossible to attempt to name the Jewish players. This is a sport that Jews dominate."[70]

The perception of Jewish 'dominance' led columnists to ask "why Jewish athletes show such marked superiority in basketball above all other sports." This question "has puzzled the leading exponents of the game, although some advance the theory that their ability lies in their brainy playing and their uncanny accuracy in locating the basket."[71] In 1926, Conzel decided that since "it is a generally accepted fact that Jewish athletes dominate the sport of basketball," he would make "a study of this puzzle." He concluded that, "basketball is the least dangerous sport. Basketball requires more speed and rapid thinking than brute strength. …Basketball does not necessitate too rigorous training. So there you are. It is not an indictment against Jewish athletes; it is probably a tribute to their intelligence."[72]

In the middle of the 1920s, Jewish basketball remained rooted in the racial scientific assumptions that had constructed the stereotype of the weak Jew. Conzel confidently expressed his theory as he, like Elmer Mitchell and other commentators, fully accepted Jewish intelligence as a racial marker. Jews succeeded in basketball because of the Jewish mind, if not the immigrant body. As basketball moved further away from the Progressive moralism expressed by Elmer Mitchell, the APEA, and officials at Jewish centers, the American sport culture intensified the connection between Jews' racial identity and their basketball abilities. It also led to expanded opportunities for Jewish professionals to achieve fame, fortune, and success.

---

[70] Harry Conzel, "Jewish Athletes of the Year," *American Jewish World*, September 3, 1926. The annual stated that Conzel was the "foremost American authority on Jews in sports." "The Year in Sport," *American Jewish World*, September 19, 1930.

[71] Sidney S. Kluger, "An Account of Jewish Athletes as Jewish Stars," *American Jewish World*, April 18, 1924.

[72] "Jewish Sports Notes," *Philadelphia Jewish Times*, January 29, 1926.

In the mid-1920s, Nat Holman received recognition as the coach of CCNY, a star for the Original Celtics, and as a prominent Jewish athlete. The multi-ethnic identity of the Celtics contributed to the team's popularity, and reflected the interwar sport culture that brought people of various backgrounds together. Irish and German players joined Holman and Davey Banks, the team's Jewish representatives.[73] The Celtics' barnstorming trips served as a unique attraction in places where few locals had seen quality basketball or had opportunities to identify with specific players. Fan loyalties and identifications frequently crossed geographic boundaries and young American Jews who participated in the American sport culture had a strong desire to cheer for Jewish athletes. Conscious of his status as a Jewish player on the Celtics, Holman explained that during barnstorming trips, "I was very much aware of the Jewish following that supported me in a number of cities on the circuit. While I always played at my very best, I tried even harder when I knew the Jewish community was rooting for me."[74]

Commentators had nominally noted basketball's ethnic presence during the Progressive era, but the importance of group identification intensified as spectators gained more power in the 1920s consumer culture. *Reach* noted that a Jewish team called the Danbury Separatists "enjoyed a prosperous season" in 1923 as "one of best attractions" in northeastern basketball. The basketball guide believed that "the coming season is sure to find them supplanting that great old Roosevelt team that harbored players like Sedran and Friedman years ago in the

---

[73] On the Celtics, see Nelson, *The Originals*. Neighborhoods, ethnic, racial, and religious groups, unions, department stores, and virtually every other type of organization developed athletic teams in order to participate in the broader athletic culture. Communal and ethnic identification during a fractious and anxious decade likely contributed to the situation. Lizabeth Cohen explained that historians assumed consumption encouraged assimilation into mainstream society, but have provided little evidence. She explained that there is evidence that during the Depression, mass culture united previously fractured ethnic and racial groups. See Lizabeth Cohen, "Encountering Mass Culture at the Grassroots," in Glickman, *Consumer Society in American History*, 147-162.

[74] Quote in Nelson, *The Originals*, 15-16.

hearts of Hebrew basketball lovers."[75] Danbury's name did not identify it as a Jewish team, but knowledgeable basketball fans would have been aware of the team's makeup.

Basketball's growth in urban areas and among immigrant groups attracted both Jewish and non-Jewish entrepreneurs who sought to expand the sport's scope. Basketball promoters and commentators had discussed forming a 'national' basketball league in the 1910s and a national commission failed to control the various professional leagues of the northeast in the early 1920s. In the middle of the decade, however, promoters formed the American Basketball League (ABL) as a 'national' league and attempted to reconstruct professional basketball into a mass, commercialized sport.[76]

The ABL attempted to turn basketball into a respectable sport. The league banned profanity, used amateur rules, abandoned the 'cage,' and played its games in large urban arenas. Moral condemnations of professional basketball declined as outright violence occurred less frequently.[77] The ABL became the first league to serve as the pinnacle of a linear, though unstable, basketball hierarchy as a younger generation of former college players entered professional basketball.

---

[75] "Interborough Professional Basketball League of New York," *Reach Official Basketball Guide 1923-24* (Philadelphia, A.J. Reach & Co.: 1924).

[76] For information on the national commission and discussion of the need for a national league, which would standardize rules of professional basketball, see Introduction, *Reach Official Basketball Guide 1921-22* (Philadelphia, A.J. Reach & Co.: 1922); Applin, "From Muscular Christianity to the Marketplace," 194-196; Peterson, *Cages to Jump Shots*, 55.

[77] As a 'national' league, the ABL had teams in New York, Brooklyn, Cleveland, Washington D.C., Rochester (N.Y.), Fort Wayne, Boston, Chicago, Detroit, and Buffalo. On the ban against profanity, see "'Oh, Pshaw,' Limit in Epithets for Pro Fives; $10 a violation," *New York Times*, December 31, 1927. For sporadic incidents of violence during basketball games, see "Celtics Win from Rosenblum Five, "*New York Times*, April 15, 1924; "Fist Fights as Jewels Defeat Celtics," *Brooklyn Daily Eagle*, November 26, 1932. Jewish players were involved in both fights as Marty Friedman and Nat Holman squared off in 1924 during a game played for U.S. Olympic fund under the auspices of the Mayor's Committee on Municipal Athletic Activity. The 1932 fight occurred during another fundraiser, this time for a retired player.

Media attention remained fairly sparse, however, until the Celtics joined the league during its second season in 1926-27.[78]

ABL owners wanted to leave behind the chaos and instability of Progressive-era professional basketball where players had more control over their production. The Celtics had illustrated the importance of continuity in building team success. Other teams adopted the contractual model that both intensified the commodification of players and provided a massive salary surge. ABL owners attempted to challenge all aspects of local basketball cultures, including scheduling, ticket prices, and most importantly, fan loyalties. In some cities, fans decried an ABL team's "unpopular attendance charge" and the possibility that the league would "unfavorably affect the popularity of local basketball games."[79]

The ABL used major league baseball as a model as owners sought to structure fan loyalty solely around the team. Ethnic spectatorship had led New York baseball managers in the 1920s to hire Jewish players who would attract a specific audience. Basketball teams had the opposite problem as ethnic identification competed with the local team identification that ABL owners desired.[80] The Celtics had succeeded as a multi-ethnic team and its broad popularity meant it felt little pressure to change its internal structure. For other independent teams, however, the ABL exerted a tremendous amount of influence to discard, at least to some extent, pre-ABL identities.

---

[78] "Youngsters Crowding Cage Pros," *Los Angeles Times*, December 25, 1927. The article describes the generational transfer within the professional game as "college-trained youngsters" began to replace "old-timers."

[79] The ABL owners suspended a Brooklyn player during the first season for playing with a non-ABL team during the season. See "Brooklyn Basketball Star Suspended," *Washington Post*, November 20, 1925. Quote from "Thru Sportdom," *Baltimore Jewish Times*, September 19, 1926. On salaries, see Peterson, *Cages to Jump Shots*, 84-94. Holman received an annual salary of $10,000 from the Celtics during the mid-1920s.

[80] For other Jewish professionals of the mid- to late 1920s, see "Jewish Sport Notes," *Philadelphia Jewish Times*, January 15, 1926. The column contained an "All-Jewish All-American" professional basketball team. Levine explained he used name identification. See Levine, *Ellis Island to Ebbet's Field*, 61. Levine explained he used a similar method as Paula Fass in her book, *Outside In: Minorities and the Transformation of American Education* (New York: Oxford University Press, 1989).

Teams in Rochester and Philadelphia altered their identifiably Jewish rosters in the ABL. Rochester's entry in the ABL, the Centrals, had formed at the Rochester YMHA in the 1900s and the team remained exclusively Jewish into the 1920s. In the ABL, however, the Centrals included "players of other nationality on its roster, [though] it retains its Jewish identity."[81] In Philadelphia, promoter Eddie Gottlieb owned the Philadelphia Sphas (South Philadelphia Hebrew Association), a team that had emerged out of Philadelphia's Jewish basketball culture in the late 1910s. By the mid-1920s, many commentators considered the Sphas one of the top teams in professional basketball. Yet, Gottlieb disbanded the Sphas and formed a new team called the Warriors, which included both Jews and non-Jews, as Philadelphia's ABL team.[82] In order to successfully compete in the ABL, Rochester and Philadelphia had to represent the entire city and overcome their traditional identification as 'Jewish' teams.

Other teams included Jews for other reasons. In contrast to existing teams, a new team in Washington attracted Jewish fans by including recognizable players. The *Baltimore Jewish Times* celebrated the inclusion of three local Jewish players on Washington's ABL entry, including "'Lefty' Stern [who] has

---

[81] Quote from Original Celtics Game Program, 1927-28, Nat Holman file, Edward and Gena Hickox Library at the Basketball Hall of Fame, Springfield, MA. The Rochester Centrals were mentioned in the *Encyclopedia of Jews in Sports*, but strictly as a team that emerged from the Rochester YMHA, with no comment regarding its connection to the ABL. See Postal, Silver, and Silver, *Encyclopedia of Jews in Sports*, 91.

[82] For information on the Sphas, see Postal, Silver, and Silver, *Encyclopedia of Jews in Sports*, 84, 91; Also see "Philadelphia Sphas" in *Encyclopedia of Ethnicity and Sports in the United States*, eds. George B. Kirsch, Othello Harris, and Claire E. Nolte (Westport, CT: Greenwood, 2000), 360-361. A group of young Jews formed the Combine Club as adolescents. The members then competed for the South Philadelphia Hebrew Association, which eventually broke its affiliation with the team. The kept the name and began to play in the Philadelphia League in the early 1920s. The Sphas were first mentioned in *Reach* as a member of a local professional league and "the leading traveling club" of the city. They were nicknamed the "Wandering Jews" by some locals. During the 1925-26 season, the Sphas defeated both the Original Celtics and an African-American team, the Harlem Renaissance in a special series. The team included non-Jewish players during its participation in the Eastern League in the late 1920s. The Warriors played two seasons in the ABL and then moved to the Eastern League. See Abe Radel, "South Philadelphia Hebrew Association," *Reach Official Basketball Guide 1924-25* (Philadelphia, A.J. Reach & Co.: 1925). On the Hakoahs and Warriors, see the files of Nat Holman and Eddie Gottlieb in the Basketball Hall of Fame.

abandoned college in favor of signing with the team."[83] The inclusion of three local Jews indicated that unlike Rochester, the newly-formed Washington team had to build a fan base from the ground up. Cleveland owner, department store magnate Max Rosenblum who humbly named his team the Rosenblums as a cheap form of advertising, brought in Marty Friedman to serve as player-coach during the ABL's first two years. Friedman's presence in Cleveland indicated the true character of the league. Before he arrived in Cleveland, Friedman had played his entire 15-year professional career for northeastern teams. Friedman's skill and knowledge as an 'old-timer,' not his identity as a Jew, best served the Rosenblums as he led them to the first ABL championship.[84]

The ABL provided a central location in which to examine the Jewish presence in basketball. By the middle of the decade, many of 'old-time' players of the pre-war era had started to retire, and though a new infusion of Jewish talent began to trickle into the professional game, only Holman and teammate Davey Banks served as preeminent Jewish talents. In the first two years of the ABL, Holman and Banks of the Celtics were joined by Washington coach Lou Sugarman, also from the lower East Side, as prominent Jewish representatives of the league. In addition, Eddie Gottlieb owned and Jules Aaronson managed the Philadelphia Warriors. According to historian Peter Levine, Jews made up 19 of 101 players on ABL rosters during the 1927-28 season.[85] At a time when American Jews consisted of less than four percent of the American population, such a disproportionate number of Jews in the major professional basketball league would have legitimized the claims of Conzel, Joel, and other commentators that Jews 'dominated' basketball. The notion of Jewish dominance

---

[83] "Thru Sportdom: Basketball Again," *Baltimore Jewish Times*, September 19, 1926.

[84] Friedman led Cleveland to the ABL's first title, called the "world series" in 1925-26, the year before the Celtics joined. On Friedman's role with the Rosenblums, see Peterson, *Cages to Jump Shots*, 85-86. According to Albert Applin, Rosenblum was the true force behind the league. Other owners included sport promoters like George Halas and George Marshall (both NFL owners) or business groups. See Applin, "From Muscular Christianity to the Marketplace," 200-204.

[85] Levine, *Ellis Island to Ebeet's Field*, 61.

and innate ability also received notice in one of the era's most thorough articles on Jewish basketball.

On November 3, 1929, the English-section of the Yiddish daily, the *Jewish Daily Forward*, published "Basketball Jews." The *Forward* and other Yiddish papers served a distinct role in American Jewish life. They provided the daily news that English readers of the *American Hebrew* and other weekly Jewish newspapers would get from the mainstream media. The *Forward* contained a full weekend sports page in Yiddish that provided information on broad athletic events as well as Jewish athletes, although in general, the Yiddish press provided little information on sports. For instance, the same weekend as the publication of "Basketball Jews" in the English section, the newspaper's Yiddish sports page contained no information on basketball.[86] Nonetheless, "Basketball Jews" reflected the growing presence of Jews in a changing sport.

The *Forward* article did not view Jewish participation as illustrative of Jewish acceptance, but rather as a normal experience within basketball. The author stated that basketball had become "a major activity among the young Jewry of New York and the vicinity. In the YMHA's of innumerable small cities in the New York region, regular Saturday night games are staged, where dancing before and after the games are a feature of the evening." These "community houses" produced "excellent basketball players, whose names later appear in the rosters of high school, college, and professional teams." The article also provided the name of 17 Jewish professional players and singled out Nat Holman, who remained "the greatest basketball player in the country. ...[He] has been taken for granted for so long that one runs the risk of becoming a bore to repeat his

---

[86] Oriard, *King Football*, 34. According to historian Eddy Portnoy, many immigrants received their sports news from the *New York Daily Mirror*, whose Jewish readership was large enough that the paper occasionally printed messages in Yiddish on the sports page. Portnoy also explained that the Yiddish press contained virtually no coverage of sport during the interwar period. The author's brief examination of the *Forward* confirmed this. Eddy Portnoy, e-mail message to author, October 12, 2006.

praises." The *Forward* claimed Holman "is as full of deception as the traditional fox," and praised the professionalism that made him "a great showman."[87]

"Basketball Jews" advanced the notion that basketball "may almost be said to be a Jewish sport." Basketball became popular among Jews because "there are no football fields or baseball diamonds to speak of in lower Manhattan." Popularity, however, did not explain success and Jewish athleticism remained embedded to racial identity. The Jewish professional presence was so great because basketball "is not essentially a sport where a huge body is a requisite. Brains, nimble thinking and speedy coordination between mind and muscle are more important and effective than mere physical brawn and power." The ideal player needed intelligence as much, if not more, than strength. "The average athlete is a chap whose brains are located in his biceps and whose head is stronger outside than inside. Not so, however, with the average basketball player. …Of course, a strong and husky physique is an asset in basketball as in other sports, but in general basketball players are not so dumb."[88]

Like previous commentators, the author of "Basketball Jews" presented basketball as a sport that required certain characteristics. He distinguished Jewish basketball players from the 'average athlete.' The Jew succeeded because of Jewish intelligence and an unchanged Jewish body. The Jewish athlete did not, and should not, need to conform to the physical ideal to succeed. Indeed, the body of the basketball Jew could not change if Jews wanted to maintain their advantage in the sport.

"Basketball Jews" served as the final commentary on Jewish basketball in the 1920s and within the ABL. The Celtics broke up in 1928, which led to a declining interest in the league. After the Celtics disbanded, Nat Holman and Davey Banks played with the New York Hakoahs (*Hakoah* is Hebrew for 'strength'), but the ABL disbanded in 1931 due to financial troubles intensified by the Depression. The league's 'national' model had failed to subdue the provincial

---

[87] Bob Shelley, "Basketball Jews," *The Jewish Daily Forward*, November 3, 1929.

[88] Ibid.

and local nature of traditional basketball. In 1933, promoters established a reformatted and 'regional' ABL in the northeast.[89]

Within the regional ABL, the Philadelphia Sphas returned to their all-Jewish origins and became one of the best teams in professional basketball. They won seven ABL championships in a thirteen year period, barnstormed in the off-season, and frequently played non-league opponents during the season. The team wore Hebrew letters on their uniforms and the mainstream press sometimes mentioned the team's Jewishness. More often, sportswriter stated that the Sphas, "don't need much introduction to basket ball fans."[90] Yet, the Sphas' success and entrepreneurial spirit received very little mention in annuals or nationally syndicated columns in the Jewish press due to the regional ABL's 'minor' status among professional sport leagues.[91]

During the interwar period, other professional basketball leagues existed in the northeast, but the ABL's semi-professional and often local nature maintained the permeable boundaries between Jewish participation and spectatorship that had encouraged the development of Jewish basketball. Young players lived in the same neighborhoods as professional players, most of whom had other jobs even during the season. Former professional stars such as Barney Sedran coached in the ABL and an entire generation of Jewish players made a relatively seamless transition from the streets to the professional game. In the mid-1930s, Jews made up almost fifty percent of the league, but their meager

---

[89] On the ABL's rise and fall, see Peterson, *Cages to Jump Shots*, 84-94; Applin, "From Muscular Christianity to the Marketplace," 199-205. According to Albert Applin, there were actually two 'ABL's', the first disbanding in 1928 due to financial difficulties directly related to the Celtics. Their dominance of the competition removed spectator interest in other cities. The 'first' ABL folded in November 1928 and the 'second' reformed immediately with some of the old ABL teams as well as teams from the Metropolitan Basketball League.

[90] "Philadelphia SPHA Cagers Tackle Heurich Brewers Today," *Washington Post*, February 17, 1935. On the Sphas' success in the ABL, see Peterson, *Cages to Jump Shots*, 120-123.

[91] The author examined annuals in the *American Hebrew* from 1920-1945, as well as syndicated annuals published in the *American Jewish World*, 1920-1939. As a 'minor' sport in the 1930s and early 1940s, professional basketball remained on the back pages of sports pages across the country. Like some other 'minor' sports of the era (such as soccer), professional basketball had not attained a level of popularity from which it could withstand a massive economic downturn.

'salaries,' often only $30-40 per game, illustrated that players happily entered professional basketball to continue playing a game they loved, not to achieve financial stability. Jewish writers did not celebrate any single player as they had Nat Holman during the 1920s, and unlike Holman, Jewish professionals competed in relative anonymity in a marginal sport.[92] Jewish players would have an even greater impact on mainstream basketball in the 1930s, but only after college basketball surpassed the professional game in its popularity as a national sport.

Professional basketball's minor status during the 1930s should not minimize the importance of the *Forward's* representation of Jewish basketball or its connection to commentaries during the decade. "Basketball Jews" contained the essential elements of Jewish basketball in the 1920s. The competitive culture of Jewish basketball encouraged its blending with college and professional basketball, which grew due to America's emerging consumer culture. From New Haven's Atlas Club to Yale to the ABL, Jews thrived in a basketball culture that provided examples of success and opportunity during a time of anxiety and exclusion. By the end of the 1920s, the cultural meanings associated with Jewish basketball had, in some ways, become more important than the game on the court. Yale alumni in 1922 did not explicitly attach racial characteristics to their demand for Jewish players, but the Jewish press had wholeheartedly accepted the connection between racial identity and Jewish basketball success. The racial pride associated with this success became expressed through the basketball Jew. This image inverted the stereotype of the weak Jew and served as an example of the athletic participation of modern Jews in American society.

---

[92] Levine, *Ellis Island to Ebbets Field*, 65-67. Levine estimated that in 1938, 45 of 91 players in the ABL were Jewish. Among the New York dailies, the *New York Times* virtually ignored the regional ABL whereas papers such as the *Brooklyn Daily* Eagle, *Brooklyn Standard Union*, and *New York Herald Tribune*, among others paid some attention to it. Often, the mainstream media discussed the financial difficulties of the professional game. Unlike contemporary times, however, the best college players did not automatically turn professional since the financial incentives often could not compare to other vocations.

Chapter Four
"Mental Agility" not "Physical Strength": Jewish Basketball and the Rise of Depression-era College Basketball

On March 21, 1931, soon after the end of the college basketball season, headlines in New York newspapers screeched with news of a scandal: "NYU Fires Basket Team!"; "NYU Bars Court Stars from Athletics for Professionalism; St. John's Suspends Five." Both St. John's and NYU investigated "charges that the men received money with several teams," including those at Jewish Centers around the New York area. The schools quickly suspended the guilty parties, including the entire starting five at St. John's. Rumors soon surfaced regarding similar activities of players at Fordham, Yale, Columbia, CCNY, Syracuse, Georgetown, Providence, Villanova, and Manhattan. *New York Daily News* columnist Paul Gallico quoted St. John's forward 'Rip' Gerson as saying: "I don't believe a man is a professional unless he gets at least $20 per game." The *News* condemned the "recalcitrant players," who were "old enough to know the definition of a real amateur." Gallico declared: "the practice of playing with or against professionals has become so commonplace…[the players] figured they were merely following a precedent of long standing or an old established college custom."[1]

---

[1] "NYU Fires Basket Team," *New York Daily News*, March 21, 1931; "NYU Bars Court Stars from Athletics for Professionalism; St. John's Suspends Five," *New York Herald Tribune*, March 21, 1931; Also see "NYU, St. John's Bar 10 From Sports as Professionals," *New York Evening Post*, March 20, 1931; "St. John's Suspends Five Players Pending Hearing," *New York Times*, March 21, 1931; Paul Gallico, "Blowing the Whistle," *New York Daily News*, March 24, 1931; Paul Gallico, "Who's Sensational Now?," *New York Daily News*, March 27, 1931. Rumors of this situation had existed for years and future Philadelphia Spha star Joel 'Shikey' Gotthoffer did not play in college because of his 'professional' status. He eventually attended NYU and paid his own way. He remembered: "What struck me as strange was that some of the NYU ballplayers were playing for money on the side at the same time." See Peterson, *Cages to Jump Shots*, 10. Two St.

The 1931 scandal transformed New York college basketball. Critics had denounced college sport for decades and only two years before the basketball scandal, an independent study called the Carnegie Report had condemned the "commercialization of college sports, the employment of highly paid professional coaches, and all the other well-known athletic abuses of our institutions of higher learning."[2] The basketball scandal differed from the activities mentioned in the Carnegie Report since it involved players, not college programs. The 'Big Six' of New York City basketball, CCNY, NYU, St. John's, Manhattan College, Columbia, and Fordham, still responded quickly and barred their players from participating in any 'outside' game which charged admission.[3] The schools' action helped stabilize New York college basketball in the midst of the Depression when small colleges and large universities alike began allocating resources toward basketball programs. Beginning in December 1934, Madison Square Garden hosted annual series of double-headers, two games in one night, in

---

John's players were accused of playing for the Elizabeth (New Jersey) YMHA in the Elizabeth City League. City College's Moe Spahn was rumored to have played for a professional team against the Newark YMHA. In addition, Yale exonerated its captain Ed Horowitz, who played with the Atlas Athletic Club of New Haven and the New Haven Collegians at the Bridgeport (Connecticut) JCC after his college career had ended. The St. John's players denied professionalism with any YMHA and All-America Mac Kinsbrunner explained that he was a member of four YMHA's. For information on Yale's Horowitz, see "Yale Stars Deny Professionalism," *New York Evening Post*, March 21, 1931; "Horowitz Plays Outside Yale, But Not as Pro," *New York Herald Tribune*, March 21, 1931.

[2] On the Carnegie Commission report, see Oriard, *King Football*, 7-8, 105-107. Also see Thelin, *Games Colleges Play*, 13-37. The report blamed coaches, alumni, presidents and faculties for ignoring the amateur ideal of college athletics and allowing football to become a professionalized and commercialized entity. The Report had little say about basketball since the sport's commercial and competitive pressures were minimal compared to football. And though the commission's finding received press attention, the call for voluntary restraint fell on deaf ears. Editorial, *Nation*, January 15, 1930.

[3] On the new rule, see "Local Colleges Rule Out 'Pros'," *New York Evening Post*, March 24, 1931. The scandal remains virtually unknown today. Not surprisingly, the scandal went unmentioned in the Jewish press as the Wonder Five maintained their reputation as successful Jewish players at a Catholic college. St. John's turned professional as a team the following season, but not before being dismissed from the university. The colleges did not restrict players from participating in games that did not charge admission. College officials reasoned that the new rules would preempt claims that a player did not receive pay for their services.

which New York schools competed against the best of college basketball.[4] The Garden games led the national media to provide college basketball with the sort of attention previously confined, at least among college sports, to football.

Jewish basketball helped produce the "rise" of college basketball. During the 1930s, Jewish players turned CCNY, NYU, St. John's, and Long Island University (LIU) into nationally-known programs. A significant Jewish presence existed at the Garden as players with names such as Goldman, Klein, Rubenstein, Pincus, and Rosen headlined the double-headers. The mainstream press rarely commented directly on the Jewish presence in New York basketball, although *Newsweek* declared in December 1935 that basketball was "a sport at which Jews excel."[5] *Newsweek* did not attach any explicit meaning to this statement, but it served as a powerful piece of information and a potential source of pride for American Jews.

As Jews helped transform basketball, the Jewish press contained a mix of anxiety and confidence that reflected the continued, though less central, project of promoting Jewish athleticism as symbolic of Jewish normality. In the early 1930s, some Jewish commentators argued that the Depression provided more opportunity for Jewish athletes because fewer non-Jews attended college. In 1931, an annual compilation commented that no longer did the press have "to overplay the few isolated athletes that come to one's attention."[6] Yet, quotas in elite colleges remained a reality and the 1931 book entitled *Christians Only* argued that Jews continued to face prejudice in college athletics. The authors

---

[4] For the Depression's impact on college basketball, see Ted Vincent, *The Rise and Fall of American Sport: Mudville's Revenge* (Lincoln, NE.: University of Nebraska Press, 1994), 255-258; Rader, *American Sports*, 269-270. According to Albert Applin, college basketball grew during the Depression due to public works programs, an expanded number of spectators caused by the 'enforced' leisure of unemployment, and charitable causes for the sport to be promoted and used, thus furthering its reach and popularity. See Applin, "From Muscular Christianity to the Marketplace," 161-169.

[5] "Basketball: Peach Basket Soccer Goes on the Big Time," *Newsweek*, December 14, 1935.

[6] "Topnotchers in Intercollegiate Sports," *American Hebrew*, December 18, 1931. For New York Jews' economic situation during the Depression, see Wenger, *New York Jews and the Great Depression*.

quoted an unnamed state university that had reported "no prejudice" against Jews, but which qualified its statement: "between a Gentile and Jew of the same ability, the Gentile will get the position."[7]

In the mid-1930s, rhetorical attacks by Father Coughlin, charges of the 'Jew Deal,' and the possibility of Nazi-inspired American fascism intensified Jewish fears of social exclusion.[8] The 1936 Berlin Olympics, which the Nazis attempted to use to promote their theories of Aryan racial supremacy, led to a boycott movement that reflected American Jews' fear of exclusion and the possibility of acceptance. It also led to the reemergence of the basketball Jew, which remained remarkably similar to the 1920s' version despite changing ideas of race. A black-white racial paradigm became increasingly dominant in American society in the 1930s, but it did not diminish the connection between racial identity and Jewish athleticism. As Jewish players influenced American basketball, they remained distinct from both black and white players. Jewish racial identity continued to inform the basketball Jew even as Jewish basketball gained its greatest public recognition.

In the late 1920s and early 1930s, New York became increasingly important to Jewish basketball. In particular, Jews began to play at St. John's, a Catholic school, in addition to their continued presence at NYU and CCNY. In 1928, a column in Minneapolis's *American Jewish World* provided a fairly detailed account of Jewish basketball and commented on a loss by CCNY's "all-Jewish team" to St. John's, "a Catholic college, [that] had three Jews on its team." The column did not include the score (33-24), but stated that the three St. John's players had "accounted for fifteen of the [team's] points." The *AJW* also

---

[7] "Jewish Sports Notes," *American Jewish World*, May 13, 1932. The column included a section titled; "The Depression and Jewish Athletes." For examples of annuals, see "The Year in Sport A Review of Jewish Athletic Achievement," *American Jewish World*, September 22, 1933; "Sports are in the Air," *American Hebrew*, June 4, 1937. Heywood Broun and George Britt, *Christians Only: A Study in Prejudice* (New York: The Vanguard Press, 1931), 97.

[8] On Jewish powerlessness and intense anti-Semitism during the interwar period, see Arad, *America, Its Jews, and the rise of Nazism*, 62-69, 130-156. Also see Dinnerstein, *Anti-Semitism in America*, 78-127; David Biale, *Power and Powerlessness in Jewish History* (New York: Schocken Books, 1986).

contextualized the game by explaining it was "the first big basketball game of the season between two first class teams" largely unknown outside of New York.[9]

This St. John's team, which would become the focus of the 1931 scandal, represented the growth of Jewish basketball within New York City's basketball culture. The *AJW* actually undercounted the number of Jews on the St. John's team. Nicknamed the 'Wonder Five,' the team consisted of four Jewish starters, the fifth being Polish, from the New York area. The victory over CCNY occurred at the start of a remarkable three year run in which the team compiled a 67-4 record against both powerful programs like CCNY and 'minor' teams like the Albany Law School. Prior to the 1931 scandal, New York sportswriters hailed them as the greatest college team *ever*. Despite such praise, however, the Wonder Five's prominence remained a local affair, even as the mainstream press began to play a pivotal role in promoting New York college basketball.[10]

In the late 1920s, the New York press increased its coverage of the sport. Sportswriters and coaches named annual All-Metropolitan teams that unofficially rewarded the best players in the city. Often the only contact between teams and fans, sportswriters constructed a historical narrative of city basketball in which participants challenged legends and continued traditions. Writers included pre-season forecasts, statistical analysis, and individual scoring totals alongside box scores, critical columns, and detailed descriptions of games. Columnists debated strategies, coaching acumen, and players' abilities. Box scores and description of

---

[9] "Jewish Sports Notes," *American Jewish World*, December 28, 1928. The Jewish press often discussed championships, but disregarded mid-season games except in regards to local interest. For an exception, Los Angeles's *B'nai B'rith Messenger* commented on St. John's victory over CCNY in 1931. Nonetheless, the need to inform readers illustrated the continued anonymity of the Wonder Five outside of New York. See See Levine, *Ellis Island to Ebbet's Field*, 77. After the scandal, the team turned professional together as the New York Jewels in the regional ABL.

[10] For information on the 'Wonder Five,' see Isaacs, *All the Moves*, 73-75. On the victory over CCNY in 1928, see "City College Bows to St. John's, 33-24," *New York Times*, December 16, 1928. Also see "St. John's Routs Albany Law School," *New York Times*, January 19, 1929. "St. John's Wins 30-16," *New York Evening Post*, March 5, 1931; *Brooklyn Standard Union*, March 5, 1931. The sportswriter exclaimed the Wonder Five was: "the greatest team this reporter has ever seen." The four Jewish players were guards Mac Kinsbrunner and Mac Posnack, and forwards Allie Schuckman and Jack 'Rip' Gerson. The fifth starter was center Matty Bergovich.

games provided information to readers about schools that played before relatively small crowds. For instance, only 1,300 people attended the 1928 St. John's-CCNY game.[11]

The Depression provided the foundation for the remarkable growth of New York college basketball. The economic downturn had a negative impact on most sports by 1931. Baseball attendance declined, professional leagues such as the ABL and the American Soccer League (ASL) shut down, and college football teams often had difficulty filling the large stadiums built during the architectural boom of the 1920s.[12] In contrast, the Wonder Five headlined a triple-header fundraiser for the city's unemployment relief fund. In January 1931, 15,000 spectators filled Madison Square Garden for a 'Carnival' that raised over $20,000. Similar events occurred the following two years, which illustrated that basketball fans wanted first-hand exposure to local teams like the 'Wonder Five.'[13]

During the 1931 Carnival, St. John's played a slow and deliberate style of basketball. The *New York Times* reported that St. John's 17-9 victory over CCNY was "extraordinary" since St. John's "froze the ball practically the entire second half." Likewise, the *New York Post* explained that St. John's had "too comfortable a lead to excite the gallery" and they held CCNY to only "a pair of field baskets."[14] The following season, the Basketball Rules Committee instituted the mid-court line and the ten-second rule to restrict stalling and encourage a

---

[11] "St. John's Wins Two Posts on Holman's All-Met Five," *New York Evening Post*, March 18, 1930; "NYU Five Face Georgetown Team in Tourney Final," *New York Evening Post*, January 3, 1929.

[12] Rader, *American Sports*, 169.

[13] On the Wonder Five and the triple-header, see Bjarkman, *Hoopla*, 30-32, 33-34; Isaacs, *All the Moves*, 74-75. The team was certainly talented as Holman had named all five starters to his 1930 All-Met team and Mac Kinsbrunner and Mac Posnack were named All-America during their careers.

[14] According to the *New York Times*, the triple-header raised $22,854.40. See "15,000 See St. John's, Columbia, and Manhattan Quintets Triumph," *New York Times*, January 20, 1931; "Basketball Sets Attendance Mark at Garden Games," *New York Evening Post*, January 20, 1931. Without radio, print remained the most powerful media form in the 1930s. There were also fundraisers in 1932 and 1933.

faster pace and higher scores. Officials believed the rule changes would speed up the game, attract fans, and turn college basketball into commercial entertainment. To survive and thrive during the Depression, college basketball had to ensure that tactics would not slow down the growth of the sport.[15]

Following the 1931 season, CCNY replaced the Wonder Five as the darling of the New York media. Holman had retired from professional basketball the previous year, although he occasionally played games in the New York area. During the 1931 scandal, the *Daily News* had accused Holman of using CCNY players in a game against professionals. This charge, leveled against a coach and not players, received extra attention due to Holman's prestige and popularity. CCNY students overwhelmingly supported the coach, who university officials quickly vindicated.[16] CCNY then won the 'mythical' eastern championship in 1932 and 1933 and in January 1934, the *New York Post's* Stanley Frank ranked CCNY No. 1 among eastern teams.[17]

Bolstered by CCNY's success, New York sportswriters increased their boosterism in 1934 and presented New York as "the college basketball center of the East." Other schools contributed to notions of New York superiority. St. John's remained an excellent program after the 1931 scandal and NYU defeated Yale, Temple, and St. John's over a five day span in February 1934. Stanley Frank declared that NYU's 47-30 "whaling" of St. John's was "the most impressive display of power shown this year."[18] The strength of CCNY, NYU,

---

[15] Teams could no longer use the entire court to stall and defensive teams had less area to defend as they attempted to get the ball back. See Bjarkman, *Hoopla*, 35.

[16] "Lavender Five in Pro Focus," *New York Daily News*, March 22, 1931; Jack Farrell, "Manhattan's OK – but Take Slant at This!," *New York Daily News*, March 24, 1931; "Holman Denies News' Charge," *The Campus*, March 23, 1931; "Metropolitan League Colleges to Bar All Professional Players Next Year; Holman Suspension Rumor Untrue, *The Campus*, March 25, 1931.

[17] On Frank's rankings, see Stanley Frank, "Court Chatter: Rating the East," *New York Evening Post*, January 15, 1934. The media celebrated City College's 38-game home win streak (and seventeenth win overall) after defeating Providence. See Stanley Frank, "Court Chatter: Mid-season All-Met," *New York Evening Post*, January 12, 1934.

[18] Stanley Frank, "Court Chatter," *New York Evening Post*, February 19, 1934.

and other city schools during the 1934 season led sportswriters to discuss the possible formation of a Metropolitan League, made up of the 'Big Six.' If Columbia could not leave the Ivy League, sportswriters begrudgingly decided that it would be replaced by Long Island University (LIU), which had only started its basketball program in the late 1920s.[19]

Considered "small-time" in the early 1930s, LIU found itself denigrated by other New York schools. Unlike the city's top programs, this latecomer to New York basketball allowed freshmen to play and had not been included in the first charity triple-header at the Garden. The program slowly increased its prestige after Claire Bee became the head coach and recruited top high school players from New York. Bee's acumen at recruiting had brought some of the best Jewish players to LIU, which became the fourth 'Jewish' basketball school in New York, joining NYU, CCNY, and St. John's. Yet, its invitation to play in the 1933 charity 'carnival' did not mean that sportswriters or fans considered LIU to be in the class of NYU or CCNY. In 1934, the school announced it would no longer allow freshmen to play on the varsity, but sportswriters belittled LIU's 20-game winning streak against "second-class competition." Ironically, a 33-28 *loss* to St. John's provided the school legitimacy as "a new basketball power."[20]

The 1934 LIU-St. John's game illustrated the intense passion that basketball could produce. Thirteen hundred spectators "formed the most rabidly partisan gathering of the campaign," and watched a "tense, thrilling battle that was worthy of its setting." During the game, "the players kept remarkable control of themselves until just 35 seconds before the final gun" when St. John's Rip Kaplinsky slammed into LIU's Bill Schwartz. "Fists started to fly and in an instant one end of the court was a mass of fighting players." Eventually, "the constabulary arrived in time to stop a few zealous spectators from throwing sucker punches in the players' private fight."[21]

---

[19] Claire Hare, "How About It?" *New York Evening Post*, January 20, 1934.

[20] "LIU Joins Court Leaders," *New York Evening Post*, February 15, 1934.

[21] "St. John's Topples LIU Five, 33-28," *New York Times*, February 15, 1934.

Violence contributed to professional basketball's marginalization, and officials hoped to avoid such a fate for college basketball. During the late 1920s, the Basketball Rules Committee developed a Code of Sportsmanship that encouraged players and coaches to "accept decisions of officials without question" to "discourage booing and hissing among their own supporters and aid greatly in teaching the public the proper attitude toward the game."[22] Some coaches believed spectators needed to be controlled. In 1934, Kansas coach Forest 'Phog' Allen stated that the ten-second rule and mid-court line had sped up basketball, but "the game still has its drawbacks." Specifically, Allen denounced "blatant rowdyism, expressed in the form of booing, hissing, and the well known 'Bronx Cheer.'" He explained:

> I think that booing and rowdyism in basketball crowds are getting so bad that unless definite steps are made to curtail them, they will kill the game. To me it seems all wrong that we permit the public, because it pays money, to deride, cajole, and abuse the officials. Serve notice at the games that booing will not be tolerated, that it is considered unsportsmanlike, that offenders will be escorted to the box office by ushers, and after the money is refunded will be asked to leave the building… spectators are close to and practically upon the players. Every opinion uttered is almost a personal remark.[23]

Allen's call for reform fell on deaf ears. Soon after his appeal, college basketball entered the "big-time" as mass spectacle, which contributed to the degeneration of player and spectator behavior in the eyes of coaches like Allen. Others, however, celebrated the new culture that provided commercial and competitive benefits to participating schools and brought national attention to the sport, schools, players, and coaches. This new culture would be centered in New York, where Jews, as both players and fans, would play an important role in college basketball's emergence into the national spotlight.

---

[22] "Sportsmanship First and Always," *Spalding's Official Basket Ball Guide, 1928-29* (New York: American Sports Publishing Co., 1929).

[23] Forrest C. Allen, "Booing a Real Menace in Basketball," *Spalding's Official Basket Ball Guide, 1933-34* (New York: American Sports Publishing Co., 1934).

By 1934, Jewish players had become commonplace at New York colleges. Jews occasionally played at Fordham, Manhattan, and Columbia, but had more of a presence at CCNY, NYU, St. John's and LIU. During the 1934 season, CCNY fielded an almost exclusively Jewish team while St. John's had two Jewish starters and both NYU and LIU had four. These four schools proved important in college basketball's new model and each took advantage of the growth of Jewish basketball as it related to the experience of New York Jews during the Depression.

Historian Beth Wenger illustrated that New York Jews survived the Depression in a better position than other immigrant groups. A decade of anxiety and economic insecurity intensified threats from American fascists who supported Nazi Germany, but Jews avoided employment in the heavy industries or large corporations, due in part to the belief that corporate anti-Semitism would restrict upward mobility. Many Jews found employment in the garment industry and white collar positions, or owned small businesses. Their relatively stable economic situation allowed Jews to attend college basketball games and cheer on players from the Jewish neighborhoods of New York.[24]

New York Jews did not constitute a unified community in the 1930s. Eighty percent of New York Jews lived in Brooklyn and the Bronx, and class divisions remained strong even as differences in nationalities became less important. Immigrant associations built around identification with a region or town in eastern Europe had virtually no appeal for native-born Jews who became more important in American Jewish life due to immigration restriction. Their world revolved around the neighborhood, whether a middle class neighborhood like Flatbush or the working class neighborhoods of East New York and Brownsville. By the 1930s, 75% of New York Jews lived in "neighborhoods with

---

[24] Wenger, *New York Jews and the Great Depression*, 1-3, 15-24, 83. Also see Feingold, *A Time for Searching*, 126-128. The author conducted interviews with former players, all of whom indicated that friends and family watched their games. Norm Drucker, phone interview with author, September 5, 2005; Irwin Rothenberg, phone interview with author, September 3, 2005; Dutch Garfinkel, interview by author, Brooklyn, New York, April 18, 2005.

predominantly Jewish populations."[25] From the streets of Brownsville to the Williamsburg YMHA and the Brooklyn Jewish Center in Eastern Parkway, playing basketball became a daily experience for many young Jews in New York.

The Brooklyn Jewish Center (BJC) represented the changing demographic pattern of New York Jews. The BJC was constructed in 1920 as a 'synagogue-center' in the middle class neighborhood of Eastern Parkway. Historian David Kaufman defined the 'synagogue-center' as "any institution whose program merges the religious, the educational, and the social within one unified 'center.'"[26] The 'synagogue-center' intended to merge secular American life with Judaism, and in the early 1920s, the BJC served as the "new community center of Brooklyn Jewry." The building itself, an impressive structure that served as a "functional institution," reflected the architectural boom of post-World War I America. The BJC placed its gymnasium in the basement, along with a bowling alley, swimming pool, billiard room, locker rooms, and the boiler room. The institution's president hoped young members would leave the "lower regions" of the gymnasium and look "upward where Godliness and Holiness dwell." He conceded, however, that "we would rather have them in the Center's basement than in Goyishe [non-Jewish] clubs and organizations." Other 'synagogue-centers' formed soon after the BJC and became an important part of Brooklyn Jewish life.[27]

The BJC helped expand competitive basketball among New York Jews. In the 1920s, New York 'synagogue-centers' had formed the Inter-Center Basketball League. During the 1930s, the BJC competed against top local amateur teams, including the 92nd Street YMHA, Union Temple, another

---

[25] On immigrant associations, see Daniel Soyer, *Jewish Immigrant Associations and American Identity in New York, 1880-1939* (Cambridge: Harvard University Press, 1997). Quote from Wenger, *New York Jews and the Depression*, 81-96.

[26] Kaufman, *Shul with a Pool*, 4.

[27] Annual Message delivered by Mr. Isidore Fine, president, January 19, 1933, Ratner Center, JTS, Brooklyn Jewish Center Records, box 3/folder 8. On Brooklyn 'synagogue-centers, see Kaufman, *Shul with a Pool*, 249-257. The floor plans of the BJC on 255.

'synagogue-center,' and Ohrbach's Department store, which like other department stores, sponsored a team as a promotional device. In 1936, the BJC won the Kings County AAU championship. Sam Schoenfeld, who also served as the head basketball coach at Brooklyn's Jefferson High School, directed BJC basketball and produced a number of college players at both locations, which contributed to the growth of Jewish basketball. [28]

Along with the BJC, a street culture in Brownsville contributed to Jewish basketball. Located just east of middle class Eastern Parkway and eighty percent Jewish during the Depression, Brownsville contained a vibrant Jewish culture and became known among some residents as the "Jerusalem of America." It served as the home to Danny Kaye, Alfred Kazin and other young Jews who would later become public figures. Poverty, however, existed alongside its Jewishness. Outside the Hebrew Educational Society (HES), there existed few neighborhood facilities and resources. Wenger explained that streets in working class neighborhoods often served as second homes. This certainly occurred in Brownsville, where basketball players learned the game on streets, playgrounds, and schoolyards. [29]

The *Spalding* basketball guide published articles in 1929, 1931, and 1934 that captured the relationship among Jewish neighborhood, college, and professional basketball. Contributor Barney Ain focused on the heavily Jewish areas of Brownsville and East New York and explained in the first article that basketball "is now the principle athletic sport in every section of Brooklyn...Night after night, hundred of teams, and thousands of players fought

---

[28] For information on the formation of the basketball league, see "Basketball League," *Brooklyn Jewish Center Bulletin*, October 22, 1926. The teams in the league were the BJC, Union Temple (also located on Eastern Parkway), Ahaveth Sholem of Flatbush, the New York Jewish Center, and the Far Rockaway Jewish Center. The following year, it was called the Jewish Temple Basketball League. It returned to being named the Inter-Center League in 1928. On AAU title, see "Basketball Season Ends," *Brooklyn Jewish Center Review*, March 1936. Schoenfeld was first mentioned as the BJC coach in 1929-30 while he was a star player at Columbia University. One of the BJC players in the mid-1930s was Irwin Witty, who played for NYU at the same time.

[29] Wenger, *New York Jews and the Great Depression*, 85-96. Quote on 'Jerusalem,' from Soyer, "Brownstones and Brownsville," 184.

for supremacy on every available playing court." The second article expanded on the impact of Brooklyn basketball as clubs and teams produced "more and better championship quintets than any other section of the city." Finally, in 1934, Ain claimed Brooklyn "is recognized as the 'Basketball Hotbed of the East.'" Jewish players in colleges, high schools, middle schools, amateur clubs, 'synagogue-centers,' and other independent organizations dominated his articles.[30]

Street basketball's close relationship with the other forms of Jewish basketball helped construct a fluid New York basketball culture. Even as the New York mainstream press provided more attention to college basketball during the 1934 season, they retained a relatively balanced coverage of New York basketball. Colleges, and sometimes the ABL, received the most attention, but the press also provided information on more obscure teams, leagues, and organizations. On any given day, the New York daily newspapers may have provided bold headlines of CCNY or NYU games as well as results from the ABL, YMHA or YMCA games, municipal leagues, or AAU games and tournaments. Soon after Ain's third article, however, promoters began to exploit this relationship and turned college basketball into a modern, national spectacle.

The CCNY-NYU game in March 1934 served as the spark that led to college basketball's emergence into the national spotlight. The extensive media attention during the season peaked for this final game. The pre-game coverage generally focused on the strengths and weakness of the teams, players, and coaches. Sportswriters excitedly discussed the matchup, and used increasingly more elaborate imagery and symbolism in anticipation of a mythic contest. Both teams entered the contest undefeated and the *New York Times* stated that the

---

[30] Barney Ain, "Brownsville and East NY Sections of Brooklyn," *Spalding's Official Basket Ball Guide 1928-1929* (New York: American Sports Publishing Company, 1928); Barney Ain, "Brownsville and East New York Sections of Brooklyn," *Spalding's Official Basket Ball Guide 1930-1931* (New York: American Sports Publishing Company, 1931); Barney Ain, "Basketball in Brooklyn," *Spalding's Official Basket Ball Guide 1933-1934* (New York: American Sports Publishing Company, 1933).

twentieth annual meeting between the two schools had "never before ... aroused such widespread interest."[31]

One central discussion involved speculation whether Holman would play his All-American center, Moe Goldman. In the days leading up the CCNY-NYU game, Goldman had publicly indicated his intention to join the Philadelphia Sphas immediately following the NYU game.[32] A conflict emerged between Holman and Goldman, although it did not involve the player's decision to turn professional. Rather, Goldman's "desultory attitude" became the problem as he placed his own aspirations before the team. Holman hoped a CCNY victory would lead to a "post-season" game against Notre Dame, considered the best team in the Midwest. Goldman's decision to turn professional would make him ineligible for a contest many believed would crown a 'national' champion.[33] Writers firmly backed Holman and blamed Goldman for a lack of focus. In the end, Goldman played, which led the *New York Post* to state: "In the normal course of events, Holman undoubtedly would keep Goldman on the bench, but this is no normal situation."[34]

The 1934 CCNY-NYU game involved competitive pressures previously unseen in New York college basketball. Prior to the season, Holman had won eighty percent of his games at CCNY and had almost complete authority and influence over the basketball program. The revenue and publicity connected to a possible CCNY-Notre Dame game, however, prevented him from banishing his star player. NYU ended discussions of a 'national' championship by beating

---

[31] "Unbeaten City College and NYU Fives Clash Tonight in 20th Annual Game," *New York Times*, March 3, 1934.

[32] On Goldman's post-CCNY career, see Levine, *Ellis Island to Ebbets Field*, 66-68.

[33] "Coach May Bench Captain Goldman for NYU Game," *New York Times*, March 1, 1934. Goldman was named Converse second team All-America. He first skipped practice and then Holman barred him from practice.

[34] "Lavender Choice as Smarter Five; Goldman to Play," *New York Evening Post*, March 3, 1934.

CCNY 24-18. Goldman played, but NYU's Irwin 'King Kong' Klein and Joe Lefft held him to only three points.[35]

Fan interest in the CCNY-NYU game aroused the curiosity of promoters. The game had been played before 5,000 fans at the 102nd Armory, but reports indicated that three times as many people wanted tickets. Promoters made a failed attempt to move the game to Madison Square Garden, although they successfully organized a series of double-headers at the Garden the following season.[36] Lead promoter Ned Irish explained that he left his job as a sportswriter at the *New York World Telegram* to run the double-headers because: "Basket ball in the Metropolitan area should have the greatest ready-made market of any sport. It is played in colleges, high schools, elementary schools, at playgrounds." Speaking to the same fluidity of New York basketball that Barney Ain had described in *Spalding*, Irish stated that "games in college gymnasiums and armories have been well-attended – but principally by younger enthusiasts who were willing to brave the discomforts of first-come first-served ushering, makeshift seats with somebody's legs hanging over your shoulders and abominable ventilation." These conditions could only attract the most dedicated – and partisan – fans, whereas "adult fans were not attracted." Irish intended to transform the audience experience and hoped to exploit basketball's popularity by giving "the fans a good place in which to watch games."[37]

---

[35] "NYU Five Stages Lat Spurt to Halt City College," *New York Times*, March 4, 1934; "NYU Quintet May Play Irish," *New York Evening Post*, March 4, 1934. Both NYU and CCNY played Jewish clubs after their game. In late March 1934, NYU played against the New Haven YMHA and helped raise $160 for the Hebrew Institute, the Home of Jewish Children, the Jewish Home for the Aged, and the YM-YWHA camp. See "Final Basketball Game – Benefit Performance," *Community News*, March 30, 1934. CCNY played against the Brooklyn Dux. See Levine, *Ellis Island to Ebbet's Field*, 33-34. Beginning in 1934-35, Holman established a policy of preseason news releases that were provided to all New York area newspapers. Other city schools followed his lead. See Applin, "From Muscular Christianity to the Marketplace," 170.

[36] Isaacs, *All the Moves*, 76, 78-79.

[37] "Basket Ball Cashes Big Time in New York, Seen as Threat to Football in Crowds, Dollars," *Washington Post*, January 7, 1935.

Not everyone celebrated the new model of New York college basketball. Prior to a double-header in December 1935, NYU students publicly complained of being relegated to "gallery" seats. A student publication declared that, "one can easily deduce that the non-commercialism of NYU athletics is just so much talk and nothing more." Two student publications boycotted basketball and refused to include news on the team until officials remedied the situation. Upon being informed of the controversy, Irish denied any responsibility. A media report stated that Irish believed the "matter rested solely between the students and the university officials." He also provided assurances to all fans "that there was no foundation for the claims of poor visibility from the balcony."[38]

The failed boycott did not prevent the isolation and marginalization of students purposely implemented by Irish. Promoters of the March 1934 CCNY-NYU game limited student tickets to 500 from each school, but students remained well represented at a contest with an audience of 5,000. Irish's desire to exploit an existing mass culture and cater to an older audience led to a scathing critique in the *Nation*. In March 1935, columnist 'Left Wing' stated: "a college basketball team has no more place in a professional sports arena… than a Jew in Hitler's bathtub." 'Left Wing' connected the Garden double-headers to the 'evils' of college athletics, which "today is in the control of thoroughly venal men" who only cared about the commercial benefits of sport. They hypocritically called college sports amateur while "making it professional in everything but name, with paid athletes, games played before enormous throngs, and a professional atmosphere surrounding the whole thing."[39]

Few commentators or sportswriters joined 'Left Wing' in condemning the new model. The double-headers assured college basketball's place in the pantheon of American sport. They received national media attention and praise

---

[38] "NYU Papers Urge Basketball Boycott," *New York Times*, December 20, 1935. The cited quote is from the *Washington Square College Bulletin*. NYU had recently de-emphasized football due to commercialism.

[39] "The Build-Up of Basketball," *The Nation*, March 27, 1935.

from national sportswriters as articles marveled at the sudden rise of college basketball into the "big-time." Magazines and newspapers produced familiar storylines as teams, players, and coaches became recognizable figures. New York schools welcomed the financial opportunities provided by the Garden. One media report stated that CCNY's Holman "looks with high favor upon the development" of basketball's "prosperous future."[40] Yet, whereas the charity double and triple headers of the early 1930s had been local or regional events, the regular double-headers brought teams from across the nation to play New York schools. This posed a problem.

Before Garden basketball could succeed in constructing a new model in college basketball, it had to overcome the sport's fragmentation. In 1934, *Time* explained that college basketball "is played almost entirely within regional leagues." This restricted the sport's nationalization because "the argument of each league that it has the best team in the land is more forceful than most such controversies, since the strongest teams play on courts of different sizes under rules differently interpreted."[41] Stanley Frank pointed out that the root of the problem was "a vague negative set of rules, lending itself easily to all sorts of conflicting interpretation, is the stumbling block which makes college basketball a purely sectional sport." Any 'championship' contest would "prove exactly nothing" since "the home team most probably would win because the visiting squad would be bewildered and crucified by the wholly unfamiliar rule enforced by home officials." Frank quoted officials who that the rule book caused many problems since it merely "tells what a player cannot do and leaves everything else to the imagination."[42]

---

[40] "Playing the Game," *Literary* Digest, January 12, 1935.

[41] "Sport: Basketball," *Time*, February 19, 1934. The centrality of conferences in college sport led New York schools to discuss forming a Metropolitan League as a way to provide publicity and revenue. The advent of regular Garden basketball made such a league irrelevant, but even if it had been formed, it would have contributed to the confusion of college basketball.

[42] Stanley Frank, "Court Chatter," *New York Evening Post*, January 10, 1934.

The first Garden double-header in December 1934 demonstrated Frank's supposition. In the highly anticipated second game, St. John's played Westminster College in the opener, NYU's predominantly Jewish team and Notre Dame provided "hardly a dull moment all evening" before a crowd of 16,000 "that knew its basketball thoroughly." *Literary Digest* declared that "the packed galleries" in the arena had acted "as they do at a professional hockey game." This influenced the outcome since "the conduct of the partisan crowd kept nervous Notre Dame players from sinking a lot of free shots at the basket." To offset the partisanship, the Garden brought in a Midwestern referee to officiate alongside a New York referee. The *New York Times* explained that "the Midwestern interpretation of guarding cost NYU…a heavy penalty in fouls." *Literary Digest* concurred that the "interpretation of the guarding rule inflicted a heavy penalty on the NYU team." NYU, which fielded largely the same team that had gone undefeated in 1934, defeated Notre Dame 25-18 despite the rulings of the Midwestern official.[43]

Rule interpretation remained the most pressing problem of Garden basketball during the 1934-35 season. In the second double-header, NYU played Kentucky, considered the best team in the South. In the final minute of play, New York ref Jack Murray called a foul on Kentucky's star player, 6'5" center Leroy Edwards. NYU's Sid Gross converted the free throw, which proved to be the deciding basket in a 23-22 NYU victory. The questionable foul, "set off the most raucous and liveliest argument the sport has yet provoked." Kentucky coach Adolph Rupp claimed his team had been "robbed" by Eastern officials since they had not punished NYU's rough players for fouling Edwards throughout the entire game. *Literary Digest* stated that Rupp and Notre Dame's coach both "contend that they would have made a far better showing against NYU had their games been handled by home officials. No team can lay claim to a 'National Championship' as long as officials are unable to agree on their definitions of fouls

---

[43] "Playing the Game," *Literary Digest*, January 12, 1935; "NYU Five Downs Notre Dame, 25-18, as 16,000 Look On," *New York Times*, December 30, 1934.

in a game." The mainstream media begrudgingly agreed that "NYU has the strongest claim of the [national] title."[44]

NYU's competitive success proved vital for the Garden, whose promoters remained primarily interested in commercial success. The promoters structured Garden basketball as spectator-centered rather than player-centered. Promoters used glass backboards so that no fans would have their views blocked, but these proved to be a "handicap to the visitors" accustomed to solid wood backboards.[45] The court brought additional complaints. The charity events previously held at the Garden had a canvas floor that "frequently sagged, tripped players, interfered with their dribbling and disrupted passing." In contrast, regular double-headers used a "floor board that will afford all the security of a college gymnasium."[46] Some visiting teams complained that the Garden court did not meet regulation requirements for length since it: "is the maximum width, 50 feet, and is 84 feet long, which is halfway between the minimum and maximum for length." Defenders of the Garden court explained "there is no 'regulation' size for the basketball floor," and declared: "probably the complainants would have found everything satisfactory at the Garden if they hadn't happened to run into N.Y.U. under that roof."[47]

NYU became the first school to achieve national recognition from New York's "Metropolitan" district. In January 1936, during the second season of Garden double-headers, *Newsweek* remarked that basketball had relegated boxing

---

[44] "Eastern Candidates for Basketball's Crown," *Literary Digest*, February 9, 1935. For coaches' "contention," see "Melvin Goldsmith, "College Basketball in the Far West," *Literary Digest*, January 26, 1935. The NYU-Kentucky game led to the three-second lane in order to restrict roughness under the basket.

[45] "College Quintets to Play in Garden," *New York Times*, December 5, 1934.

[46] "NYU Meets Notre Dame Five in Feature of College Double Bill at Garden Tonight," *New York Times*, December 29, 1934.

[47] John Kieran, "A Few Drops in the Bucket," *New York Times*, January 25, 1936.

to a "minor place" at the Garden and "surpassed football's attendance figures."[48] The article featured NYU, which continued its success after finishing undefeated in 1934 and 18-1 in 1935. By mid-January 1936, NYU had an 18-game winning streak and some in the New York press compared it to the greatest teams in history, although Nat Holman declared that the "Wonder Five would have taken them." NYU won two more games over North Carolina and St. John's at the Garden before traveling to Washington, D.C., where the "team of one Swede, one Irishman, and eight Jews" lost to Georgetown, 36-34.[49]

The centrality of New York schools at the Garden meant that even after NYU's loss, 'Metropolitan' basketball remained the predominant form of 'eastern' basketball. By March, at the end of the 1936 season, LIU had compiled a 30-game winning streak and *Time* declared that on the "strength of its amazing record," the school had become "New York City's basketball favorite."[50] In 1936, LIU had four Jewish players among the top 16 scorers in the Metropolitan district and Julie Bender became the school's first All-American player. Two years later, the Garden featured the school on six of its twelve double-headers. LIU's rapid rise from obscurity to national prominence exemplified how Depression-era schools used basketball for prestige, publicity, and commercial interest. The school also continued the dominance of predominantly Jewish teams at the top of eastern college basketball that had started with the 'Wonder Five'

---

[48] "Basketball: NYU Quins Make it More Popular than Football," *Newsweek*, January 18, 1936. NYU was retroactively awarded the Helms National Championship by the Helms Foundation, which began awarding championships and other awards to college teams in 1936.

[49] "Holman Thinks NYU Beatable," *New York Evening Post*, January 23, 1936. Quote on loss from "Naismith Week," *Time*, February 24, 1936.

[50] "Sport" *Time*, March 2, 1936. The 'Metropolitan' district became a recognizable entity only after the beginning of Garden basketball, although *Time Magazine* described the district in February 1934. See "Basketball: Midseason," *Time*, February 19, 1934. The previous year, *Time* restricted its attention to the 'East.' See "Basketball," *Time*, March 13, 1933. Also see *Spalding's Official Basket Ball Guide, 1933-34* (New York: American Sports Publishing Co., 1934). The issue did not include a listing of a 'Metropolitan' league, but rather focused on "Basketball in Eastern Colleges." For information and a broader history of New York City basketball, see Isaacs, *All the Moves*, 67-92.

and continuing with CCNY and NYU.[51] This succession caused New York to become the undisputed center of Jewish basketball and the prime representative of Jewish champions during an era of anxiety and increasing anti-Semitism.

In December 1935, the *American Hebrew* began its first regular weekly sports feature called the "Sports column." The first column stated: "A new basketball season looms. Last year, teams such as NYU, Temple, and LIU – for the most-part all-Jewish teams – were at the forefront."[52] The *Hebrew's* column the following month stated that, "Jewish supremacy on the basketball courts this season doesn't end with NYU." At LIU, "you will find such stars as Bender, Merson, Kramer, Schwartz, and Hillhouse. I can't attest to the Jewishness of all five of these men, but I believe I am safe in at least four of them." NYU's loss to Georgetown brought more attention to LIU, "a largely Jewish aggregation." The column correctly identified four Jewish starters and explained that "there is a possibility that Art Hillhouse (our scouts haven't checked yet) may be also. A number of their subs are likewise of the faith."[53]

The *Hebrew's* columns provided readers with mid-season commentary, but sometimes included errors or omissions. The columnist failed to discover the identity of LIU's Art Hillhouse. The normative presence of Jews in New York college basketball led to the *Hebrew* to incorrectly assume that Hillhouse was Jewish. The newspaper also did not report a controversy covered by *Time* in the "aftermath" of NYU's loss to Georgetown. A "sizzling editorial" in a NYU student newspaper demanded that the school sever athletic relations with Georgetown because "the 'health and safety of the [NYU] players' was

---

[51] Isaacs, *All the Moves*, 81-86; Charley Rosen, *Scandals of '51: How the Gamblers Almost Killed College Basketball* (New York: Holt, Rinehart, and Winston, 1978); Claire Hare, "How About It?," *New York Evening Post*, February 8, 1934; Bjarkman, *Hoopla*, 37-38. Between 1935-1939, Bee compiled a remarkable record of 149-11 at LIU. Within a three-year period, the school moved from playing obscure and small schools such as Seth Low College and Oglethorpe to nationally recognized teams such as Duquesne.

[52] "Sports Column," *American Hebrew*, December 20, 1935.

[53] "Sports Column," *American Hebrew*, January 17, 1936; "Sports Column," *American Hebrew*, February 14, 1936.

endangered by 'Georgetown's insane...Jew-hating following.'"[54] That the newspaper failed to report the incident is surprising since the "Sports column" began in the midst of a boycott movement of the 1936 Olympics, scheduled to be held in Nazi Germany.

Leading up the Olympics, the first to include basketball on the official program, the American Olympic Committee (AOC) organized a series of qualifying tournaments to determine the Olympic team. After the completion of the national tournament held at Madison Square Garden, *Time* explained that many fans had believed in the superiority of college basketball teams until "two organizations as thoroughly non-academic as Universal Pictures Corp. of Hollywood and Globe Oil and Refining Co. of McPherson, Kansas met in the final." A professional team in all but name, McPherson's players were "employed by a central Kansas oil concern in a town of 5,000." The company paid for "their basketball ramblings," and much "like Universal Pictures five, and thousands of similar groups in the United States, they are a company promotion scheme."[55] New Yorkers had expected LIU, NYU, CCNY or even Brooklyn College to win the Olympic berth, but none of the predominantly Jewish teams competed in the tournament. CCNY's Nat Holman "found his players unwilling to participate in any competition with an Olympic tinge."[56]

Holman's players made their decision after an Olympic boycott movement had failed. Following the Nazi rise to power, many Americans, both Jews and non-Jews, demanded the Olympic Games be removed from Germany. Boycott supporters believed that Aryan racial theories, German anti-Semitism, and the Nazis' refusal to allow German Jews to compete in tryouts mocked the Olympic

---

[54] "Naismith Week," *Time*, February 23, 1936. One of Georgetown's top players was Jewish, Harry Bassin. Neither NYU nor Georgetown validated the charge.

[55] "Sport: Basketball," *Time*, April 13, 1936. Quote from Arthur Daley, "Awesome Kansas Giants Reverse Basketball Lay-up Shot Process," *New York Times*, March 10, 1936.

[56] "Sport: Long Island's Streak," *Time*, March 2, 1936; "City College Opposed," *New York Times*, March 4, 1936.

spirit of brotherhood.[57] The issue received only marginal attention in America in 1933 and 1934, but reached a fevered peak leading up to the national AAU Convention in December 1935. Catholics, college officials, and many other Americans joined with Jews in supporting the boycott. The AAU, however, decided to send a team to Germany, much to the disappointment of American Jews.[58]

Some boycott opponents had denigrated Jewish athleticism as part of their argument. Prior to the AAU Convention, *New York Daily News* sports editor Paul Gallico stated in *Life* that, "the make-up of the German team would seem to be their own business. The truth of the matter is that the agitation on this side of the water is nothing but political attention-calling. There are very few Jewish athletes here or in Germany of Olympic calibre."[59] Gallico's comments did not elicit a public reaction among American Jews. By the time of his article's publication, the Jewish press had already become embroiled in a controversy over Jewish athleticism.

In the fall of 1935, General Charles Sherrill, a member of the International Olympic Committee (IOC), had traveled to Berlin and 'convinced' the Germans to include a minimum of Jewish athletes in Olympic training. Upon his return to the United States in October 1935, Sherrill stated that a boycott would generate a

---

[57] "Jewish Leaders Claim Boycott," *Los Angeles Times*, October 23, 1935; Editorial, *The Nation*, November 29, 1933; Harry Conzel, "The Year in Sport – A Review of Jewish Athletic Achievement," *American Jewish World*, September 22, 1933. Conzel mentioned that Germany "had outlawed all Jews from athletic activity." In addition to Jewish opposition, the boycott movement was supported by American Catholics.

[58] For a detailed examination of the failed boycott movement and the events leading up to the 1936 Olympic Games, see Richard D. Mandell, *The Nazi Olympics* (New York: MacMillan, 1971). The boycott movement eventually failed in large part because of the efforts of Avery Brundage, head of the American Olympic Committee, who was a Nazi sympathizer and member of the America First Committee. Brundage later became the president of the International Olympic Committee. On German attitudes toward German Jewish athletes, see Arnd Kruger, "'Once the Olympics are through, we'll beat up the Jew': German Jewish Sport, 1898-1938 and the Anti-Semitic Discourse," *Journal of Sport History* 26, no. 2 (1999): 353-375; Gertrud Pfister and Toni Niewerth, "Jewish Women in Gymnastics and Sport in Germany, 1898-1938," *Journal of Sport History* 26, no. 2 (Summer 1999): 287-325.

[59] Paul Gallico, "Sports Parade," *Life*, December 1935.

series of "pogroms" by American athletes and their supporters: "I would not surprised if it reached such proportions as it did in Spain in 1492 [when the Jews were expelled]." Describing himself as a "friend of the Jews," Sherrill depicted the boycott movement as a strictly Jewish concern and stated that, "the whole trouble in Germany started when the Jews…overplayed their cards." Jewish newspapers, syndicates, and institutional publications responded with sarcasm and anger at Sherrill's comments. In particular, the Jewish press condemned his claim that, "it was not easy to get a good Jewish athlete" and "there was never a prominent Jewish athlete in history."[60]

Sherrill's and Gallico's comments reminded Jews that the stereotype of the weak Jew remained a force in American life. Not since the Eliot controversy had Jewish athleticism been front page news in the Jewish press. The mockery directed toward Sherrill contained an underlying anxiety that Jews remained seen as non-productive outsiders. The Jewish press could not hide the fear that anti-Semitic depictions of Jewish difference would lead to exclusion or even violence. The controversy also led to the most extensive examination of Jewish athleticism during the interwar period. In direct response to Sherrill, sportswriter Stanley Frank published *The Jew in Sports* in the spring of 1936, "to repudiate a preposterous concept of the Jew."[61]

Frank viewed sport as a positive element in American Jewish life. He represented the native-born generation for whom sport had become a normal part of American Jewish life. A varsity athlete while at CCNY, Frank served as editor of *The Campus* before becoming a sportswriter for the *New York Post*. He

---

[60] "A General Warns Jews to Lay Low or Else," *The American Hebrew*, October 25, 1935. For a study of race within the 1936 Olympics, see D.A. Kass, "The Issue of Racism at the 1936 Olympics," *Journal of Sport History* 3, no. 3 (1976): 223-235. For information on Sherrill's service on the IOC, see John Lucas, "An Analysis of an 'Over-Crowded Worried Life': General Charles Hitchcock Sherrill's Tenure on the International Olympic Committee, 1922-1936," *Olympika: The International Journal of Olympic Studies* 11 (2002): 143-168. Some commentators ridiculed Sherrill's assertion of pogroms and others focused on the discriminatory policies of the Nazis against German athletes. Most believed that Sherrill had been tricked by Hitler and the Nazis and viewed the Third Reich through distorted glasses.

[61] Stanley Frank, *The Jew in Sport* (New York: The Miles Publishing Co., 1936), 18.

believed that Jewish athleticism did not just dispel anti-Semitic stereotypes, but also symbolized the end of Judaism's hostile relationship with modernity. In his book, he argued that "the Jew" had constructed a "hypothetical ghetto…after his migration to tolerant countries." This Jew had avoided athletic participation because he "remembered the teachings of his rabbis" who opposed the "strange intensity for sport." In America, however, Jews had emerged from this ghetto to fully embrace sport as they joined "modern civilization." Frank expressed faith in America, where "the invigorated Jew has been given half a chance to expand and to breed a strain constantly growing stronger and swifter. That is all the Jew wants – or needs."[62]

Frank provided athletes with a tremendous amount of power as he explicitly denied the concept of racial Jewishness. In his preface, he explained that, "the Jew is a member of no distinct race or nationality." Religion served as the "only denominator which unifies the Jew in a group." Any "physiological characteristics of the Jew" had not emerged due to "any organic peculiarities of a racial origin, but to social, historic, and economic causes." He condemned racial scientific theories and extolled academics who commented on the extraordinary "adaptability" of Jews. Science, however, could only provide statistical proof of Jewish normalization. The Jewish athlete had "blasted the legend of Jewish physical weakness, which remained unchallenged, particularly by the Jew, for too many centuries." In order "to command popular attention, it is necessary to speak the popular language of champions and records. And the only Jew who can do a thorough job of it is the athlete."[63]

Frank balanced his celebrations of Jewish athletic success with explanations of Jewish contributions to sport. Because golf "demands painstaking attention to minute details, absolute concentration on every premeditated move," the "dour, phlegmatic Scotch" succeeded. In contrast, "the nervous, impatient Jew does not find golf the best suited to his temperament and talents." In football,

---

[62] Stanley Frank, *The Jew in Sports* (New York: The Miles Publishing Co., 1936), 28, 43.

[63] Ibid., 23-25, 27.

discrimination no longer prevented Jewish success since fans and coaches only cared "whether the Jew has courage and the mental and physical staying power which football sternly demands of the men who play it. The Jew has these essential qualities; he had them when the pyramids of ancient Egypt were still young." Boxing provided ample evidence of Jewish physicality since "if the legend concerning the physical weakness of the Jew were true, he would have raised the white feathers in boxing long ago. Instead, he raises clasped hands high above his head – the traditional salute of the winner."[64]

To normalize Jewish athleticism, Frank confronted the question of Jewish difference. In baseball, the Jewish presence "still is surprisingly small." Commentators had long struggled to understand the situation, especially since "most Jewish boys, at one time or another, play baseball and Jewish adults make up a large proportion of the crowds attending major league games." Frank argued that, "neither his temperament nor the environment from which he springs are well suited for the game." Jewish intelligence caused problems since "baseball, quite bluntly, does not call for intellectual giants." In addition, "the long period of apprenticeship necessary is most discouraging to the impulsive, impatient Jew." A Jewish physical characteristic also hindered success: "Jews develop flat feet early in their careers and seem to slow up prematurely." Despite providing ample evidence to justify the lack of Jewish baseball stars, Frank concluded that "the Jew in baseball is a normal citizen, no better than the average and no worse."[65]

In contrast to the defensiveness of the baseball chapter, the basketball chapter included an unparalleled confidence. Frank began his chapter by claiming: "no other game in sports, not even the rugby of the British, golf of the Scots…is dominated so completely as basketball is by the Jews." Frank defended this assertion by constructing a historical narrative that began in "the crucible of basketball," New York's lower East Side, "where more great, lasting luminaries

---

[64] Ibid., 97-99, 114-117, 168-170.

[65] Ibid., 75-91.

of America's most popular indoor game have been born and developed than in all other communities combined." From there, Frank examined New York's outer boroughs, the "wealthier sections of the city," where Jews played basketball in "YMHA's, the community centers, the school-yards." One could find similar environments in other cities: "everywhere that the Jew constitutes more than merely a fragmentary proportion of the population." This culture developed because "basketball is essentially a game to be played in large cities. The Jew by tradition gravitates naturally to large cities," and because "Jewish boys come into contact with basketball very early in life," they "meet with extraordinary success."[66]

Frank quantified and qualified Jewish dominance. He explained that Jewish players "are constantly popping up in the headlines on the Pacific Coast, in the Middle West, in the deep South." These players only provided support for his argument that 'eastern' basketball proved Jewish superiority. "Five of the last dozen leading scorers" in the Ivy League "have been Jews." More importantly, from 1929-1935, St. John's, CCNY, and NYU had "only a grand total of five Gentiles." Frank's used the three schools over that specific time period because they had succeeded one another as 'eastern' champions leading up to the Garden double-headers. Frank also stated the debate over regional rivalry between the east and the west (or "Middle West") was "silly, futile, and cannot hope to convince either faction." Nonetheless, Frank decided that after "looking at the controversy dispassionately, it would seem that the East has the stronger points for rebuttal" due to supremacy in the professional game. Frank concluded that, "the success of CCNY's basketball-playing alumni in the pro game also serves to emphasize the talent of the Jew."[67]

---

[66] Ibid., 52-53.

[67] Ibid., 50-51; 65-69. Frank named individual players from Oregon, Temple, Dartmouth, Northwestern, Wisconsin, Providence, Pittsburgh, Tulane, and Rice among others. Frank only paid cursory attention to LIU since his book came out just as LIU began to receive media attention outside of the New York area.

Frank examined the achievements of St. John's 'Wonder Five' and NYU's "Violent Violet Jews," but focused primarily on Nat Holman's CCNY teams. Under Holman's tutelage, CCNY played a rational and rigid style with constant movement, limited improvisation, and authority that rested exclusively with Holman. Called the 'Holman Wheel,' historian Neil Isaacs described the style of basketball as a "four-man weave around a post." Since Holman's team often found themselves "outmanned and outsized," they "by necessity specialized in the long set shot and the clever little man, in a game of short pass, quick score, and dribble away to run out the clock."[68]

CCNY's playing style matched the characteristics of basketball described by Frank. Urban life and cultural encouragement may have served to attract Jews to the sport, but they succeeded because "the elements of the game are admirably suited to those qualities commonly attributed to him." In particular, "instincts largely figure" and "things happen so quickly and situations change with such bewildering rapidity…that a player has little time to think." Frank did not mean to imply that intellect played no role in basketball, but that the ideal player needed instinctual intelligence. Frank also used public perceptions of "the Jew" in his construction of Jewish basketball and stated:

> The popular conception of the Jew fits in perfectly with the hair-trigger reaction which basketball demands. The Jew is reputed to be fast on the pick-up, quick-witted. He is also supposed to be shifty on his feet. Speed is the dominant keynote of all sports, but sheer straight-away speed is worthless on a 90-foot basketball court if not blended with the ability to navigate quickly and easily in close quarters. The Jew in basketball possesses the required shiftiness.[69]

Frank's basketball Jew remained unchanged from earlier media and textual descriptions. Jewish intelligence and the shifty body provided Jews an advantage in a sport that did not contain the same level of physical roughness as football,

---

[68] Isaacs, *All the Moves*, 87. Frank, *The Jew in Sports*, 66.

[69] Frank, *The Jew in Sports*, 50-55.

boxing, or even baseball. Frank provided evidence that the short, quick, smart player not only fit the characteristics of basketball, but produced the ideal.

The achievements of Nat Holman and Barney Sedran heavily influenced the construction of Frank's basketball Jew. Frank idealized Nat Holman, who "had perfect coordination, speed, stamina, a keen sense of situation, and superb poise which sometimes was mistaken for arrogance." Frank praised Holman's showmanship and explained that, "Holman never left a fan cold; he inspired tremendous admiration or deep-seated hatred." Holman also remained connected to the Jewish ghetto. "It was no accident of birth that the most vivid personality in basketball was moulded in the crucible that is the East Side."[70] Frank further connected Jewish basketball to the immigrant ghetto through Barney Sedran. This "little giant," who stood 5'4", informed Jewish basketball more than even Holman, since: "The meek inherited the basketball earth when Barney Sedran played. He put the weak on par with the strong. And he, above all others, for twenty-five years has given inspiration to undersized, underprivileged Jewish boys, who can never hope to be tall and strong – but can always hope for a full measure of success in sports as long as they have ambition and perseverance."[71]

Frank's "little giant" and "crucible" of basketball suggested that the dimensions of the ghetto had produced Jewish basketball. Tight spaces required quick movement, quick passing, quick reactions, and quick thinking. Frank's Jew 'dominated' basketball because of his urban background, mental ability, and shifty feet. Jewish players could not help but succeed since "the characteristics inherent in the Jew and the nature of basketball have served as natural irresistible magnets." In basketball, "the volatile Jew finds that imagination and subtlety, qualities inherent in him, pay the heaviest dividends."[72]

---

[70] Ibid., 55-60. Frank had long idealized Holman. In 1933, he authored a series of stories titled "Basket Ball That Wins," with Holman in *Sport Story Magazine*.

[71] Ibid., 63.

[72] Ibid., 50, 54.

Jewish excellence in basketball occurred *despite* the absence of the physical and athletic traits idealized by Anglo-Americans. Frank's description of Jewish basketball proved remarkably similar to that of Nat Holman, who told the 92nd Street *Bulletin* in 1937 that, "it is in basketball that the Jew finds mental agility and perception overpowering sheer physical strength."[73] Athletic masculinity in American society remained defined by physical size and strength and the focus on 'mental agility' over 'physical strength' implied that Jewish players had the former, but not the latter. In his text, Frank ignored examples that could have contradicted his notion of Jewish basketball. After NYU's "Violent Violet Jews" had defeated Kentucky in January 1935 on Sid Gross's last minute free throw, Adolph Rupp complained of NYU's roughness.[74] NYU's physical domination would not have described Jewish basketball players any better than mental agility or shiftiness. At the time of Frank's representation, tall or large men did not serve as the ideal player in basketball, although participants valued height due to the vertical nature of the game. The form and function of basketball rewarded the short, "shifty" player and Frank based his textual representation on the perception that Jewish distinctiveness produced Jewish success.

Frank's belief in Jewish distinctiveness did not prevent him from attempting to dress his basketball Jew in an ethnic, not racial, identity. The notion of ethnicity, which some Jews began using in the 1920s, became an acceptable replacement for race to describe immigrant groups. Unlike race, cultural practices would not distance immigrants from 'whiteness' within a strengthening black-white paradigm. During the 1930s, anthropologist Franz Boas – who Frank cited in his text – argued with some success that 'race' could not serve as a valid

---

[73] "Jews in Sports," *YMHA Bulletin*, December 10, 1937. In 1935, the *American Hebrew* quoted a London rabbi as stating that Jewish athletic success in Europe occurred primarily in "sports as boxing, swimming, gymnastics…and biologically considered, one would expect superiority in a type of exercise calling for speed rather than endurance, for rapidity of nerve transmission rather than for the fibre which makes up the marathon runner." See Cohen, "The Jew in Sports – A Historical Retrospect of his Participation in Athletics Since Bible Days," *American Hebrew*, September 20, 1935.

[74] *New York Daily News*, January 6, 1935; *New York Herald Tribune*, January 6, 1935; *New York Times*, January 6, 1935.

category. Yet, ethnic identity assumed a level of normalization that would have denied Jewish difference, and could possibly lead to assimilation. Historian Eric Goldstein argued that even after World War II, the use of ethnicity among American Jews "did not represent a thoroughgoing reconceptualization of Jewish identity. Instead, it was largely a linguistic strategy designed to recast their continued attachment to a racial self-understanding in terms more acceptable to the non-Jewish world."[75] Frank's ideal basketball player remained the racialized Jew. Religion could not explain the athletic success of Jews. Neither could ethnic Jewishness. Only race informed athleticism.

Frank combined a positive expression of the Jewish body as a cultural product of the ghetto with the notion of Jewish intelligence, a racial characteristic, to construct the ideal basketball player. The "temperament" of the basketball Jew – impulsive, nervous, and impatient – proved a perfect match for an urban sport. Jewish basketball represented the trappings of modernity and urbanization: rapid movement, instinctual intelligence, and frenetic activity. Jewish athleticism, manhood, and basketball success served as "irresistible magnets."

Frank's text indicated that Jewish success in track and field events had diminished. The perceived reason for this decline reflected the strengthening of the black-white racial paradigm, and differences between the perception of Jewish and African-American athleticism. Frank explained that Jews had success in the sprints and broad jump, "events requiring sudden explosion of energy." By the time of publication in 1936, however, "these are events which the Negro, granted a measure of athletic equality in this country, has controlled despotically in recent years." This success led "scientists and theorists" to explain that "the Negro is outstanding because he is so many generations closer to the jungle." Frank did not overtly refute this racial science: "The cause is open to conjecture but the effect is conclusive. The Negro rules the sprints and jumps." Frank did not believe that the black athlete would permanently replace Jews. "The athletic

---

[75] On Boas, see Gossett, *Race*, 418-423; Korelitz, "The Menorah Idea," 85-87; Goldstein, *The Price of Whiteness*, 206.

liberation of another underprivileged group has resulted in a brief slump of Jewish track and field athletes, but the situation, unfortunate in its untimeliness, will be remedied by the law of compensation after a period of readjustment."[76] Frank's belief in the power of Jewish athleticism did not diminish his acceptance of an emerging racial discourse in which the black athlete would become a dominant force.

African-Americans faced a different fight in the American sport culture than did American Jews. After black boxer Jack Johnson lost the world heavyweight championship in 1915, white society maintained a fairly strict policy of segregation to ensure that other black athletes could not destroy the myth of white superiority.[77] White Americans also constructed a stereotype of African-American physical weakness to support the notion of black intellectual, mental, and spiritual inferiority. In his 1922 series "Racial Traits in Athletics," Elmer Mitchell explained that a "Negro" who played on integrated teams in the north would generally be "quiet and unassertive." If "allowed authority," however, he showed "the tendency to be theatrical or to play for the grandstand." Like he did with the 'Jew,' Mitchell used prejudicial racial science to construct his depiction of the 'Negro,' who had a "shuffling gait" and specific physical characteristics, including "unusually long arms, narrow hips, high placed calves, and flat feet." The black body did not alone define the Negro since, "temperamentally he is inclined to be lazy." Finally, Mitchell characterized the black athlete through "his imitativeness, his love of frankness, and especially his love of praise."[78]

Black success in the 1930s challenged the American athletic discourse. White Americans believed that athletic supremacy, especially at the Olympics,

---

[76] Frank, 148-149.

[77] For information on Johnson, see Bederman, *Manliness and Civilization*, 2-5, 40-44; Also see Geoffrey C. Ward, *Unforgivable Blackness: The Rise and Fall of Jack Johnson* (New York: A.A. Knopf, 2004). On segregation in sports, see David K. Wiggins and Patrick B. Miller, eds., *The Unlevel Playing Field: A Documentary History of the African-American Experience in Sport* (Urbana: University of Illinois Press, 2003).

[78] Elmer D. Mitchell, "Racial Traits in Athletics," *American Physical Education Review* 27, no. 4 (April 1922), 151.

illustrated racial vitality and national strength. The success of Jesse Owens and other African-American track and field stars at the 1936 Berlin Olympics destroyed Aryan theories of athletic supremacy. Two years later, world heavyweight boxing champion Joe Louis knocked out German Max Schmeling. White Americans celebrated the success of both Owens and Louis, but black athletic success, as well as the success of other 'colored' races throughout the world, hinted at the decline of white supremacy. White America thus transformed the racial discourse of American sport to maintain the racial hierarchy.[79] Science informed this paradigm and white Americans connected biological, not social or cultural, factors to black success. Although it would seem as though black 'laziness' and 'shiftiness' would prove more difficult to integrate into notions of natural athleticism than Jewish 'intelligence,' white Americans felt a more intense need to protect the racial hierarchy from black supremacy than Jewish normality.

In the 1930s, white Americans began to assert that black athletes succeeded due to "natural" ability. Natural athleticism meant whites could accept black athleticism without changing stereotypes of lazy, shiftless, and unintelligent African-Americans. They succeeded because of physical strength, but not hard work or intelligence, and thus remained the opposite of the 'civilized' white. The belief in the primitive African-American produced a different stereotype than the

---

[79] For information on the "natural" black athlete's lack of intelligence, see John M. Hoberman, *Darwin's Athletes: How Sport Has Damaged Black America and Preserved the Myth of Race* (New York: Houghton Mifflin Co., 1997), 19-20, 23-24, 43-44. In 1935, the APEA discussed the "natural" physical gifts of African-American runners, which allowed for their success. See "A Comparison of the Patellar Tendon Reflect Time of Whites and Negroes," *The Research Quarterly of the APEA* 6, no. 2 (May 1935). Following the Games, scientists measured the body of Jesse Owens in order to determine whether his leg muscles determined his athletic success. Marc Dyreson, "American Ideas about Race and Olympic Races from the 1890s to the 1950s: Shattering Myths of Reinforcing Scientific Racism?," *Journal of Sport History* 28, no. 2 (2001): 173-215; David K. Wiggins, "'Great Speed but Little Stamina': The Historical Debate Over Black Athletic Superiority," *Journal of Sport History* 16, no. 2 (1989): 158-185; Jon Entine, *Taboo: Why Black Athletes Dominate Sports and Why We Are Afraid to Talk About It* (New York: Public Affairs, 2000). At the 1936 Games, two Jewish sprinters, Marty Glickman and Sam Stoller, were removed from the 4x100 relay race at the last minute and replaced by two African-American runners (including Owens). Historians generally agree that anti-Semitism caused the change. See Marty Glickman with Stan Isaacs, *The Fastest Kid on the Block: The Marty Glickman Story* (Syracuse: Syracuse University Press, 1999); For information on the Olympic controversy as well as the Louis-Schmeling fights, see Levine, *Ellis Island to Ebbet's Field*, 184-188, 219-229. American Jews especially celebrated Louis's victory over Schmeling. See David Margolick, *Beyond Glory: Joe Louis vs. Max Schmeling, and a World on the Brink* (New York: Knopf, 2005).

overcivilized, over-intellectual Jew, whose athleticism had not escaped notions of physical weakness and 'mental agility.' Their respective stereotypes remained rooted in their perceived inferiority to white Americans, but their position as 'underprivileged' groups in American society influenced their ability to challenge the stereotypes. Jews may have frequently faced exclusion, but they *could* participate in the relatively tolerant mainstream sport culture. African-Americans, on the other hand, faced discrimination and exclusion in sport similar to their experience in society.

In professional basketball, two teams represented black basketball to mainstream society. One, the Harlem Renaissance, also known as the Rens, had formed in the early 1920s and like many other teams of the era, played in a ballroom where dances occurred before and after games. Success against the Original Celtics, Philadelphia Sphas, and other top barnstorming teams in the mid-1920s proved that the Rens played as well (or better) than their Jewish or Irish counterparts.[80] The other team, the Harlem Globetrotters, owned by Jewish immigrant Abe Saperstein, also participated within the boundaries of the traditional basketball culture that encouraged the distinct racial identity of the Celtics, Sphas, Olson's Terrible Swedes, the Buffalo Germans, Jim Thorpe and His World-Famous Indians, among others. In the late 1930s, the Chicago-based Globetrotters began to "clown" because Saperstein recognized its entertainment value. Despite their undeniable talent, the Globetrotters' clownish antics defined them. Historian David Wiggins explained that the Globetrotters "perpetuated the black Sambo stereotype." The clowning and "style of play reflected all the prejudices that the dominant culture had built up about blacks in this country. The Globetrotters had innate physical skills, exhibited 'natural rhythm,' but were in need of 'mature white handling.'" Their disparate playing styles aside, both the Rens and Globetrotters inspired pride and dignity within their communities. Yet,

---

[80] On the Rens, see Connie Kirchberg, *Hoop Lore: The History of the National Basketball Association* (Jefferson, NC: MacFarland & Company, 2007), 35-37; Peterson, *Cages to Jump Shots*, 95-101.

they remained excluded from organized leagues during the interwar period and had to continue barnstorming into hostile environments.[81]

During the interwar period, no other minority group was as racially qualified by the mainstream press as African-Americans. The mainstream press lauded the play of Columbia University's George Gregory and LIU's Dolly King, the two best black college players in New York during the 1930s, but also qualified them as 'colored' and 'Negro.' Press reports of a 1932 charity game between CCNY and Howard University, an African-American school, qualified racial identity on a black-white paradigm. The depiction of Howard as the "colored intercollegiate champions" meant that CCNY's Jewish players became 'white.' The mainstream press also used racial language to explain that City College was "too smart" in their "intelligently" played victory over Howard.[82] This certainly fit into the dominant black-white racial paradigm of American society, but also conformed to the generalized notion of the 'smart' basketball Jew.

In the 1930s, American Jews viewed the defense of black civil rights and advancement of full integration as an indirect attack on anti-Semitism. Historian Eric Goldstein explained that during the interwar period, American Jews often expressed their difference from white society in racial terms even as they sought the benefits of white identity. In 1935, African-Americans rioted in Harlem and attacked over 200 Jewish-owned businesses. The next three years saw black leaders, newspapers, and street orators claim that Jews exploited urban black populations. The anti-Semitic rhetoric shocked American Jews who saw themselves as the oppressed brethren of African-Americans, but Jews' non-

---

[81] Wiggins, "Great Speed But Little Stamina," 165. Like the Rens, the Globetrotters were founded in connection to a dance hall. Owner Abe Saperstein named the team the Harlem Globetrotters because: "Harlem was to the fellows what Jerusalem is to us." On Saperstein and the Globetrotters, see Ben Green, *Spinning the Globe: The Rise, Fall, and Return to Greatness of the Harlem Globetrotters* (New York: HarperCollins Publishing, 2005).

[82] Quote 'too smart,' from *New York Times*, March 6, 1932. Quote 'intelligently' from *New York Herald Tribune*, March 6, 1932.

blackness defined their relationship with American blacks.[83] In 1934, a basketball game illustrated both Jewish distance from blackness and basketball's unique position within the athletic world.

In April, the Communist Party's Labor Sports Union (LSU) sponsored a basketball game as a fundraiser for the Scottsboro Boys, nine African-American teenagers, including a 12-year-old, who had been accused of raping two white women in Alabama three years earlier. The defendants agreed to be defended by the International Labor Defense (ILD), associated with the Communist Party, and who retained New York lawyer Samuel Leibowitz, himself not a Communist, as defense counsel. Prosecutors tried the Scottsboro defendants four times and the case reflected the racial inequalities in the South.[84] According to historian Matthew Jacobson, the promotion of racial integration served as the highest profile "practical work" of the Party, while the defense of the Scottsboro Boys became the most recognized feature of this activity. The Party also attempted to use sport as a way to illustrate to Americans that "Communism is nothing strange and foreign."[85]

The LSU promoted the Scottsboro game as symbolic of Communist inclusion in contrast to capitalist exclusion and segregation. The *Daily Worker* reported that the game, in which the Harlem Rens defeated a collection of

---

[83] Hasia R. Diner, *In the Almost Promised Land: American Jews and Blacks, 1915-1935* (Westport, CT: Greenwood Press, 1977), 79-81. Goldstein, *The Price of Whiteness*, 159-160, 164; Jaher, "Antisemitism in American Athletics."

[84] On the Scottsboro case, see Dan T. Carter, *Scottsboro: A Tragedy of the American South*, Rev. ed. (Baton Rouge: Louisiana State University Press, 1979). On American Jews and the Scottsboro Boys, see Diner, *In the Promised Land*, 42-43, 99, 114.

[85] Jacobson, *Whiteness of a Different Color*, 249-256. *Daily Worker*, August 31, 1935. During the Popular Front in the mid-1930s, Communists developed a fairly relaxed attitude toward mainstream sport. In 1935, the *Daily Worker's* Mike Gold, author of *Jews Without Money*, declared the need for regular sports news in the paper. Soon after Gold's column, the *Worker* established a Sunday edition with an expansive sports page that reported on mainstream sports. Nonetheless, this inclusion served political ends and the *Worker's* sports editor Lester Rodney became one of the few non-black journalists to attack segregation in sports. See Irwin Silber, *Press Box Red: The Story of Lester Rodney, the Communist Who Helped Break the Color Line in American Sports* (Philadelphia: Temple University Press, 2003). On Communist and leftist sport, see Robert F. Wheeler, "Organized Sport and Organized Labour: The Workers Sports Movement," *Journal of Contemporary History* 13 (1978): 202-205.

professional 'All-Stars' by the score of 36-27, served as a true location of integration where "Negro and white stars" united under Communism. The sporting culture overwhelmed the passions of "regular" fans, who forgot "their prejudices and one-sided rooting fervor for a couple of hours" to appreciate the true nature of sport. In this vein, the *Worker* proclaimed that for the Rens, the game served as "one of the few times they have played a white team where they were entirely satisfied, where they were treated as social equals."[86]

The *Worker's* claim of the Rens' satisfaction contrasted with the treatment the team usually confronted in hotels, arenas, and by some fans, but despite claims to the contrary, the Rens' participation remained a sign of difference rather than inclusion. Jacobson asserted that the Communist Party's emphasis on the social significance of the 'Negro Question' helped establish the unquestioned 'white' identity of the majority of the Party's ethnic members.[87] This focus on racial difference allowed the Party to represent blacks in the wider society, and by qualifying the Rens as the "undisputed world's Negro champions," the *Worker* subtly reinforced Communist 'whiteness.' The *Worker* also ignored the Jewishness of all the 'All-Stars,' as well as the referee and umpire, and assigned them 'white' identities.[88] Instead of celebrating the participation of two minority groups who faced discrimination, the Communist Party used the Scottsboro game to focus on black exclusion rather than Jewish inclusion.

---

[86] For the initial notice of the game, see "Basketball Mania," *Daily Worker*, March 16, 1934. For the report on the game, see "Sports," *Daily Worker*, March 31, 1934. On the Rens' satisfaction, see "A Revealing Rebound," *Daily Worker*, April 2, 1934. Also see "Sports: Charity Tilt on Thursday," *New York Amsterdam News*, March 24, 1934. The *News* did not report on the outcome.

[87] Jacobson, *Whiteness of a Different Color*, 249-256.

[88] The *Worker* merely mentioned that the 'white' players were "practicing especially for this game at the YMHA on Lexington Avenue." See "Sports: A Basket for the Nine Scottsboro Boys," *Daily Worker*, March 26, 1934; In contrast, the 92nd Street *YMHA Bulletin* proudly commented on the Jewish identity of the 'All-Star' players who practiced for the game at the YMHA. See "Former Y Court Stars to Play in Benefit Game," *Y Bulletin*, March 23, 1934. The *Bulletin* declared that "four former 'Y' varsity basketball stars...performing in a game to be played for the benefit of the Scottsboro Defense Fund";.

The Scottsboro game did not serve as an example of an integrated game between racially mixed teams, but rather a game played on an integrated court. The *Worker* downplayed the professional status of the Rens as well as their participation in a sport that provided more acceptance of blacks than baseball or football. Unlike baseball, no Negro League existed and black basketball teams frequently competed against whites. The audience at the 1932 charity game between CCNY and Howard had also served as a "model of sportsmanship and appreciativeness."[89] The CCNY-Howard contest or even the Rens' regular competition indicated that the Scottsboro game was not truly a unique experience for players and spectators. The Scottsboro game only differed from CCNY-Howard and countless other games in the symbolism attached by the *Daily Worker*.

During the interwar period, basketball's environment differed from other team sports. Historian Michael Oriard explained that coaches, the press, and others judged black college football players by their ability to play the 'right,' or white, way. Basketball, however, did not contain a dominant style, approach or 'right' way. Regional differences defined styles which meant that the discourse surrounding the "natural" black athlete did not whiten Jewish basketball. The basketball Jew stood racially and athletically apart from other groups and meant that Jews' distance from whiteness, although not the same as from blackness, remained considerable. Even as the racially-informed Jew stood alone in the basketball world, however, basketball began to change. How this would influence conceptions of the basketball Jew became evident at Madison Square Garden soon after Frank published *The Jew in Sports*.

After a successful opening season, college basketball continued to grow at the Garden. The complaints from some coaches during the first season did not diminish the Garden's appeal and many teams returned during the second season of double-headers. In December 1935, Kentucky again lost to NYU, 41-28, although "Kentucky had no excuse tonight. The officiating…was not

---

[89] *New York Herald Tribune*, March 6, 1932.

questioned."[90] The Garden also attracted Pacific Coast schools during the 1936 season. After the University of California lost to NYU 41-26 in the opener, the team's coach praised the referees and said: "I prefer the way the game is played in the East. Nobody got hurt and the action was faster."[91] The coach's comments demonstrated the important role the Garden double-headers played in college basketball. Without discussing any problems associated with officiating or rule interpretation, he concentrated on the 'way' basketball was played in New York.

Standardized officiating allowed commentators directly to discuss the decades-old question of regional supremacy. As they had since the early 1930s, the New York press portrayed the city's basketball as superior to the rest of the country. Others, however, viewed the sport from a difference perspective. In 1935, *Literary Digest* had commented that college basketball had been "long dominated by the Midwest."[92] The importance of conferences in the Midwest and West Coast likely contributed to this impression, but historical success meant little during inter-regional games. Commentators nonetheless distinguished the various forms of basketball through spatial considerations that often contained implicit racial differences.

Differentiated styles conformed to generalized regional differences within the United States. In reality, styles varied within regions, cities, and even schools as some coaches changed strategies based on personnel.[93] Most commentators ignored such intricacies, however, and viewed basketball through the lens of regionalism. *Time* magazine's mid-season report in February 1934 represented the basic summary: "bred on small gymnasium courts, Eastern teams play a

---

[90] "New York U. Crushes Kentucky Cats 41-28," *Kentuckian*, January 9, 1936.

[91] "Maidman is Best to Bears' Coach," *New York Evening Post*, December 19, 1935.

[92] "Eastern Candidates for Basketball's Crown," *Literary Digest*, February 9, 1935.

[93] St. John's illustrated the power of a college program as the team adapted to new personnel and played a different style than they had as the 'Wonder Five.' With "fast and shifty," but "undersized" players, the St. John's coach transformed the team into one that used a "fast-breaking offense" of "short passes and hard cutting." See "St. John's Quintet Due to Poor Year," *New York Evening Post*, November 24, 1933.

cunning, fast game; usually with spontaneous maneuvers. The larger Western courts develop long passers, elaborate strategies."[94] *Time* ignored a 'Southern' style, but after the first NYU-Kentucky game in January 1935, the *New York Times* had explained that Kentucky "demonstrated something quite new to metropolitan court circles." They used "a slow, deliberate style of offense" that "was so sharp a contrast that the spectators, used to the swift-moving panorama of metropolitan basketball, were inclined to be impatient with the other type."[95]

The Garden double-headers both served as a laboratory to determine regional supremacy and slowly decreased stylistic and regional differences. Teams observed, studied, and embraced the strategies, styles, and methods of their opponents even as the debate over dominance stopped being theoretical. The Garden's commercial and popular success led promoters in Buffalo, Chicago, Philadelphia, and other cities to imitate the double-headers. This structure encouraged annual tours by western schools during winter breaks. One particular visit revolutionized the sport.[96]

In December 1936, Stanford traveled east during the holiday break. After defeating Temple, 45-38 in front of 9,000 fans in Philadelphia, Stanford arrived at the Garden to play LIU in one of the most anticipated games in college basketball history. The predominantly-Jewish LIU team remained basically the same as the year before when the school rose to national prominence, and the New York media stated that the contest "will for the first time…[provide] the definite answer to the question of East-West supremacy." As the "smartest, smoothest team in the East," LIU would defend eastern honor. The game's competitive pressure led LIU to follow "the example set by major colleges in football" by preparing at a "training camp" at Grossinger's Resort in the Catskills. According to the *New York Times*, "this is believed to be the first training camp trip any basketball team

---

[94] "Basketball: Midseason," *Time*, February 19, 1934.

[95] "NYU Defeats Kentucky Five, 23-22," *New York Times*, January 6, 1935.

[96] Isaacs, *All the Moves*, 79-80.

ever has made during the Christmas holidays."[97] New Yorkers believed that LIU's zone would stop Stanford's All-American Hank Luisetti but before a crowd of 17,623, Stanford ended LIU's 43-game winning streak by a score of 45-31. The result shocked 'eastern' basketball and resulted in the further standardization of basketball.[98]

In contrast to the east's two-handed set shot, Luisetti and the rest of the Stanford team shot one-handed. Some eastern commentators and coaches had doubted the effectiveness of the shot until Luisetti shredded the vaunted LIU defense for 15 points. CCNY's Nat Holman, an adamant defender of the set shot, had called Luisetti's shot a "prayer" before the game.[99] Within the decade, some CCNY players would use the one-handed shot even as others remained committed to the set shot. The changing shooting style illustrated the impact of the Garden on New York, and Jewish, basketball. Some players willingly incorporated improved methods of play into the traditional culture. Others took a bigger step and began to leave the local area to play college basketball.

In the 1930s, William Silberstein traveled from Brooklyn to Indiana University and Bernie Opper left the Bronx to attend Kentucky. Opper in particular found success as he received honors as All-Southeast Conference and All-America during his career. Opper reportedly contacted Kentucky coach Adolph Rupp after seeing the 1935 NYU-Kentucky game as a high school student.[100] Prior to the Garden games, personal contact with the larger basketball world was limited to the print media. Sport radio remained relatively minor and

---

[97] "East-West Court Feud Ideal Test of Stanford," *New York Evening Post*, December 30, 1936; "On Basketball Courts," *New York Times*, December 24, 1936.

[98] Isaacs, *All the Moves*, 111-115. The result helped Stanford capture the Helms National championship that season.

[99] "LIU Victory String Now 43 as Result of 3 More Triumphs," *New York Times*, December 28, 1936; "East-West Court Feud Ideal Test for Stanford," *New York Evening Post*, December 30, 1936.

[100] On Sliberstein, see John Laskowski with Stan Sutton, *John Laskowsk's Tales from the Hoosier Locker Room: A Collection of the Greatest Stories Ever Told* (Sports Publishing Company, 2003), 77-81. Silberstein later established the first endowed athletic scholarship at Indiana.

television had yet to become a standard feature in American homes. Garden promoter Ned Irish's desire to attract an older audience notwithstanding, the Garden could exist as a space where players' and spectators' identities blended. Opper's first-hand exposure to teams from across the country was a common experience among Jewish youth in the New York area and his experience indicated the unique opportunity provided New York youth.[101]

Though Opper and Silberstein represented the expanding breadth of Jewish basketball, the basketball Jew remained connected to New York. Following the 1936-37 season, the New York press declared that "eastern basketball lost prestige" due to Stanford's victory over LIU. Reports of the game also contained an implicit racial tone. One member of the New York press argued that LIU's loss meant that "New York's fundamental concept of basketball will have to be radically changed if the Metropolitan District is to remain among the progressive centers of court culture in the country." In particular, "coaches must cease looking for the smart, shifty player and focus attention on big, nimble athletes who can drive and put the ball through the hoop." It remained unclear where this type of player could be found, but "nothing can be done about it as long as home-bred talent tries to play an intellectual game while invaders are forcing the breaks, instead of waiting for them, with terrific speed and hell-for-leather tactics."[102]

The none-too-subtle coding of the 'Metropolitan' player as the 'Jew' indicated that New York's Jewish basketball had not informed the larger athletic ideal. Commentary on size, stylistic improvements, and the weakened

---

[101] For brief information on Opper, see Tom Wallace, *Kentucky Basketball Encyclopedia* (Sports Publishing LLC, 2002), 105. After his Kentucky career, Opper returned to the northeast to play professionally with the Philadelphia Sphas and other ABL teams. Opper also played in the National Basketball League (NBL), a Midwestern based professional league. The Garden used radio to promote the double-headers and former football and track star Marty Glickman became the voice of college basketball during the 1940s. He helped pioneer the sport on radio. Also see Isaacs, *All the Moves*, 80.

[102] "Pop Knick's 'Big Nine' of Court Sets Mark – Wrong One, though," *New York Evening Post*, January 4, 1937; "Stanford, Notre Dame Won Fame as New York Quintets Faltered," *New York Times*, December 26, 1937; "Speed Wrecks L.I.U.'s Guile and Accuracy Seals Verdict," *New York Evening Post*, December 31, 1936.

"intellectual game" indicated that some doubted whether the 'Jew' could adapt to a changing game. Coaches needed to find a new type of player who was not just 'smart' or 'shifty.' The older culture of regional distinctiveness had idealized the basketball Jew in the east. Nationalization, however, brought the rest of America to Madison Square Garden and revealed the limits of the racially informed ideal. The sportswriter believed that the entire structure of New York and Jewish basketball would have to change in order to keep up with big, nimble and *white* athletes.

The *Times* article did not attach an explicit racial identity to the 'Metropolitan' player, but others viewed Jewish basketball through the lens of race. Sportswriter Paul Gallico explained in 1938 that basketball "appeals to the Hebrew with his Oriental background" as well as "the temperament of the Jews" because it "places a premium on an alert, scheming mind, flashy trickiness, artful dodging, and general smart aleckness."[103] Gallico's representation of 'the Hebrew' basketball player, while clearly anti-Semitic, consisted of characteristics remarkably similar to those used by the Jewish press within the discourse of Jewish athleticism.

Gallico's comments must be viewed in relation to Stanley Frank's. Notions of Jewish "trickiness" and "scheming" perpetuated the stereotype of the immoral and dishonest Jew. Yet, they could also conform to the idea of the intellectual Jewish athlete. A player's 'artful dodging' sounded quite similar to the ability of Frank's 'shifty' Jewish player. The difference was that Frank believed Jews had integrated into society as normal Americans. Gallico's use of the word 'Hebrew' reinforced the notion of a racial Jewishness that differentiated American Jews from the normative white ideal. The imagined Jew could not challenge the "big, nimble athlete" who would become more common in basketball soon after Gallico's comments. At the time, however, Gallico and Frank's basketball Jew remained a distinctive character in the basketball world.

---

[103] Paul Gallico, *Farewell to Sport* (New York: Knopf, 1938), 324.

Although they differed in their opinion regarding Jewish integration, they agreed that Jews succeeded because of their innate Jewishness.

In the 1930s, Jewish basketball emerged as a force within the national spectacle of college basketball and played an important role in the remarkable rise of the sport. This success occurred as the native-born generation began to pave new paths toward acceptance and Americans began to accept the concept of ethnicity. Stanley Frank viewed Jewish athletic success as a reflection of Jewish normality that would inevitably lead to acceptance and illustrative of an integrated, and modern, American Jewish culture. The Olympic controversy reminded American Jews, however, that they had not yet achieved complete acceptance or integration.

Even as Frank defended and Gallico attacked Jewish athleticism and its connection to Jewish racial identity, the Jewish project that had produced so many prominent Jewish players began to change. As American Jews felt increasingly more comfortable in American society, their need for Jewish champions would diminish. Some Jewish leaders became concerned about how competitive sport would impact modern Jewish identity. They believed sport should provide Jews a means toward broader social acceptance for the group not financial success for individuals. In the 1930s, Jewish institutions and organizations either backed away or avoided the promotion of a competitive basketball culture. As a result, the champion model, which had played an important role in the project that connected Jewish athleticism to integration and acceptance, would disappear from organized Jewish life.

Chapter Five

"We Are Average Americans": Jewish Political Identity, and Jewish Basketball

In December 1936, the *American Hebrew* celebrated Jewish participation in American sport. "Among its most devoted followers are millions of Jews. No better indication of the Americanization of the Jew is to be noted than this joining in with the trend."[1] The *Hebrew's* article spoke to the fact that many Jews did not have the athletic ability to play at CCNY, in the ABL, or even at the 92nd Street YMHA, but still enjoyed playing and watching sports. The article also reflected the ongoing impact of immigration restriction, which transformed the American Jewish community. Groups recognized basketball's popularity among native-born Jews and used the sport to attract Jewish youth to their cause.[2] They did not, however, attempt to produce elite Jewish athletes. As a result, the champion model soon ceased to exist and Jewish athleticism became reformulated within organized American Jewish life.

During the 1930s, basketball increasingly served a new project for American Jews. One that had less to do with proving athleticism and more with building unity, communal strength, and an integrated American Jewish identity. In particular, the socialist Workmen's Circle focused on labor sport and cared little about Jewish athleticism while the Zionist youth group Young Judaea focused on internal, Zionist activities. Both used spectatorship to express unity

---

[1] *American Hebrew*, December 11, 1936.

[2] Ezra Mendelsohn, *On Modern Jewish Politics* (New York: Oxford University Press, 1993), 75-90. For information on Socialist and Zionist sport, see Eisen, "Jewish History and the Ideology of Modern Sport," 515-520. On Jewish Communists, see Paul Buhle, "Jews and American Communism: The Cultural Question," *Radical History Review* 23 (1980): 9-31; Bat-Ami Zucker, "American Jewish Communists and Jewish Culture in the 1930s," *Modern Judaism* 14, no. 2 (May 1994): 175-185; Jacobson, *Whiteness of Another Color*, 253.

and identity in their attempt to attract the "mass" of young American Jews, but neither cared to produce Jewish athletes. This restrictive form of supervised sport provided little attraction for elite athletes who found few communal outlets for their competitive desires.

At the center of this new concept of communal Jewish athleticism, the Jewish Welfare Board (JWB) sought to construct a national movement to control previously independent YMHA's and JCC's. JWB educators and officials accepted the notion that traditional Jewish culture opposed physical activity. They did not, however, promote solutions that conceptually diminished Jewishness or produced disreputable behavior such as gambling. Neither did they view Jewish athleticism through the lens of racial ability or achievement. Historian David Kaufman stated that officials founded the Center movement on the belief that "Jewish religious life was obsolete" and needed "to be replaced by the cultural and ethnic Jewishness of the secular center."[3] JWB officials blamed religious leaders for neglecting physical activity and producing the weak Jewish body. The JWB would correct this abnormality. In doing so, the Jewish center confronted the champion model and effectively ended the culture of Jewish basketball in which players learned competitive skills at Jewish centers before playing in college or professional basketball.

Physical education served an important role in the JWB's attempt to become the central authority of Jewish life. During the interwar period, Jewish leaders debated the role of the Jewish center in communal life and sport's place within the Center. Professionalism and commercialism had become a normal part of American sport, but a Center's identity could not become too closely associated with competitive sport. Physical education needed to "bridge the gulf that might exist between the European father and his American-born children." The executive director of Savannah, Georgia's Jewish Educational Alliance warned "there is the danger that to the community at large the Center may stand

---

[3] Kaufman, *Pool with a Shul*, 279.

for nothing besides athletics. Such a situation should be foreseen and provisions made to guard against it."[4]

JWB officials attempted to contend with the champion model in three ways. First, they denigrated institutional sport as containing the harmful 'evils' associated with college athletics. Second, they constructed a Jewish physical education program that could be incorporated into the modern, Jewish culture advocated by the JWB. Finally, they changed the concept of Jewish athleticism by appealing to the value of recreation for *all* institutional members, not just top athletes.

In October 1922, in the first issue of the *Jewish Center*, JWB officials began their attack on the champion model. Competition became dangerous "when the object becomes winning at any cost. Rather than lose, unfair practices may be resorted to by players or winked at by managers. Ineligible contestants may then be introduced. ...[T]he outcome is a decline in sportsmanship, which is the flower of civilized play." Four years later, Newark executive director Aaron Robison denounced the elitist athletic structure that encouraged "aggressive self-assertion," which he believed "Jewish life now suffers too much from."[5]

In June 1926, the Jewish Welfare Board's (JWB) *Jewish Center* focused on physical education in YMHA's and Jewish Community Centers (JCC). Abraham Rosenthal, the executive director of the Bronx YMHA, wrote an article based on a questionnaire the JWB sent to institutions across the country. The questionnaire asked about gymnasium facilities, affiliations with summer camps, and athletic programs. The majority of respondents declared their facilities 'good' and three-fourths had "full-year, all-season [athletic] programs." Three centers "limit themselves to the competitive sport in which Jewish stars predominate – basketball." According to Rosenthal, basketball:

---

[4] William Pinsker, "Physical Education in the Jewish Community Center (discussion)," *Jewish Center* 4, no. 3 (June 1926): 47.

[5] E.J. Londow, "Inter-Association Activities," *Jewish Center* 1, no. 1 (October 1922). Aaron G. Robison, "Physical Education in the Jewish Community Center (discussion)," *Jewish Center* 4, no. 3 (June 1926): 49.

is responsible for every evil in a Jewish Center attributed to football and baseball in intercollegiate competition. Despite every effort to submerge the star player, to prevent betting and interference with the more important work of the gymnasium, a representative team in outside competition, in proportion to the number of games it wins, [gains] a cumulative, hectic interest on the part of a large number of our young people as worshipful spectators.[6]

Rosenthal's attack on Center basketball occurred because the champion model had become defined by competitive, and often commercial, behavior. During the interwar period, athletes at Jewish institutions progressed from the junior level through intermediate onto the senior, or varsity, team. The Philadelphia YMHA's physical director summarized his Center's 'program.' "Each player on the [varsity] team coaches a team in the Inter-Fraternity League, which is made up of clubs. …The captains of these teams, in turn, coach the teams in the Junior League, and the same arrangement is maintained so that even 8 and 9-year-old boys are playing the same game in our gym under the guidance of the older and experienced boys."[7] Such a program existed within a broader culture in which the best Jewish players would play for centers and high school teams and then progress to college basketball. From college, many would either proceed to the ABL or return to a Jewish center to continue their career. Often, players would move back and forth between professional and institutional basketball, thus continuing the culture of basketball champions within Jewish communities. The champion model had been constructed to facilitate integration through communal involvement in the 'manly' sports. It had accomplished its goal too well.

---

[6] Abraham W. Rosenthal, "Physical Education in the Jewish Community Center: In Relation to the Entire Program of the Jewish Center," *Jewish Center* 4, no. 3 (June 1926): 42. Rosenthal began the article by explaining that physical education "has reawakened a physical courage and a practical, cheerful idealism dormant for centuries…beautified and glorified the neglected physique of an entire race."

[7] "Basketball Team Excels," *Philadelphia Jewish Times*, December 20, 1927.

Centers profited financially from the players' labor, but players exhibited quite a bit of agency in their migratory practices. Champions like Sam Pite often controlled their market value and demanded compensation for their efforts. Teams such as the Philadelphia Sphas, which began at a Jewish center, removed themselves from institutional control in order to manage their own labor. In many ways, the victims of such an athletic culture were the anonymous members who may have tried out for varsity teams and found their abilities lacking. The JWB hoped to attract those individuals who did not have the skill, talent, or desire to become champions and mold them into integrated American Jewish men.

In 1930, Samuel Leff, field secretary of the JWB, produced the most direct attack on competitive sport published in the *Jewish Center*. He explained that the champion athlete had become harmful. "The silent, unspectacular large membership is the heart and soul of the gymnasium group, not the specialized teams. If we analyze impartially the sports situation in most Jewish Centers as well as elsewhere in America, we find that we are suffering from useless hero worship of spectacular athletes…at the expense of a physically, undeveloped mass of people." Leff praised the 1929 Carnegie Report, which condemned the excesses of competitive college sport and included "constructive reforms [that] offer shining examples for Jewish Centers to follow." Leff also believed that, "Jewish values" had been "neglected" in the gymnasium or even "destructively mistaught." Competitive sport had led to "the intense and often savage fight for athletic victory." Leff explained that, "physical education in a Center must be judged by the universality of its use and not by the false, but unfortunately intrenched standard of championship teams composed of a small number of specially trained athletes."[8]

Leff singled out basketball as a sport containing "17 character values" that could be expressed in positive or negative ways, including "cooperation or the lack of it, self-control or the opposite, loyalty or disloyalty, etc." He admitted

---

[8] Samuel Leff, "Health and Physical Education in Jewish Community Centers," *Jewish Center* 8, no. 3 (September 1930): 13-21, passim. JWB workers often examined the role of sport in Jewish Centers through 'scientific' surveys.

members enjoyed playing and watching the sport, but "the disadvantages far outweigh the benefits." Basketball monopolized the gymnasium as a "fatiguing game" suited only for the young, and demanded too much time from physical directors who then neglected the larger membership. YMCA officials had made similar comments, but YMCA's "never have depended on this sport to fill their gymnasiums with larger numbers of members than YMHA's ever had." Leff condemned the "exaggerated emphasis on basket ball in many of our Jewish Centers," and suggested that "if the overemphasis on this sport cannot be curbed, I would favor its gradual elimination from all our Jewish Centers."[9]

JWB physical education connected the modern Jew to the historic legacy of Jewish health, hygiene, and vitality. In 1923, Abraham Rosenthal had explained that the Jewish Center needed to provide facilities for Jewish youth since public playgrounds and other institutions "lack the appreciation and understanding of the physical and mental background of the Jewish youth." Physical education could be incorporated into the Jewish center program because "the ideals and problems of the modern physical educator are in accord with the practice of the best Jewish teachings."[10] In 1930, Leff concurred, noting "the importance of health, both personal and public, has historically been recognized by Jews. Medical science owes a debt of gratitude to Moses, who first enunciated fundamental laws and practices of health that have aided in the survival of the Jews to this day."[11]

JWB physical education emerged from the same milieu that had encouraged the construction of the 'champion' model. Leff prevailed upon Jewish Centers to help Jews "overcome a measure of their ancestral tradition of over emphasis on mental development," and believed physical education could

---

[9] Ibid, 12.

[10] Abraham W. Rosenthal, "Objectives in Physical Education for the Jewish Center," *Jewish Center* 1, no. 3 (May 1923): 36.

[11] Leff, "Health and Physical Education in Jewish Community Centers." This survey was based on results from 59 Centers rather than the 43 from 1926.

serve as a preventive measure since "physical defects are prevalent among members." JWB officials blamed Jewish physical weakness on the fact that "the emphasis on our survival has been place primarily on religious and cultural factors, on the Jewish education of our youth." Leff stated that, "Jewish physical survival is an indispensable condition for the preservation and development of Jewish group life…[as] the humble, but vital foundation on which the more inspiring superstructure of Jewish life is created." JWB physical education would improve the Jewish body and Leff argued the ideal Jew would use the gymnasium "as an important medium for mental, moral, and spiritual development necessary in the well-balanced all-around, trained Jewish personality."[12]

Officials expressed the belief that Jewish physicality and manhood had been restricted by the rabbinic and cultural authorities who had traditionally controlled Jewish life. JWB officials believed that "recreational activity in the Center is an educational process," and defended their use of recreation and physical education in comparison to the "more limited scope of formal Jewish activities." It had become necessary to include "social and athletic activities to impart interests that one may continue through life and not consider merely those that require youthful vigor and agility." Physical education at the Jewish Center would attract *all* Jews to the Center as an activity that encompassed the lifespan of American Jews and helped "develop the Jewish consciousness."[13]

The JWB hoped to integrate sport into their attempts to mold Jewish youth along character building principles. The 92nd Street YMHA physical education department issued a memorandum in 1925 that stated the institution sought "to develop the highest type of virile manhood," while giving "members a better understanding of the Jewish faith" because "neuro-muscle habits play a very important part in the development of character." The memorandum also indicated

---

[12] Ibid.

[13] Louis Kraft, "Proceedings of the 11th Annual Conference of National Association of Jewish Community Center Secretaries: Address of the President," *Jewish Center* 7, no. 2 (June 1929); Leff, "Health and Physical Education in Jewish Community Centers"; Robison, "Physical Education in the Jewish Community Center," 49.

that athletic tournaments remained central to the organized department because supervised sport served as "a means of development of character through self-control, temperate living, and fair play."[14] The 92nd Street YMHA's memorandum promoted the supervised and controlled athletic tournaments that conformed to the JWB model. Yet, the JWB had difficulty controlling competitive sport at Jewish centers because many, including the 92nd Street YMHA, structured their entire physical education departments around the champion model. In the 1930s, officials who hoped to prevail over the competitive athletic culture found an unlikely ally in Nat Holman.

In spring 1930, the 92nd Street YMHA moved into a new, modern building and hired Holman as the physical education director. He retired from professional basketball to take the position, although he continued to coach at CCNY. Holman's eight-year tenure reflected the Center movement's struggle for athletic balance. Despite his own career as a professional player and college coach, Holman unrelentingly promoted mass participation over varsity athletics in his new position, stating, "the super-athlete is not our goal but one wherein those interested in our activities will develop a fair amount of skill so that he can obtain a reasonable amount of enjoyment from actual participation."[15]

A little more than one year into his appointment, Holman attacked competitive basketball. In September 1931, Holman suggested abolishing the

---

[14] "Policy of the Department of Physical Education of the YMHA," 1925, Young Men's Hebrew Association records, 92nd Street Y Archives, New York. The memorandum was written by physical director was George Cornell, a long-time member of the APEA whose influences included Luther Gulick and G. Stanley Hall. Cornell was hired to replace long-time director George Schoening. He had previously served at YMCA's in New York. The memorandum only subtly hinted at Hall's recapitulation theory, but more overtly repeated Gulick's theoretical use of muscular repetition to influence moral 'reflexes.' On Cornell, see "Dr. Cornell Appointed Physical Director," *Y Bulletin*, February 20, 1925.

[15] Holman retired from professional basketball to accept the position at the YMHA. Holman's view toward mass participation was mentioned in various *Bulletin* issues. See "Participation is Keynote of Next Year's Sports Program," *Y Bulletin*, June 26, 1931; "Holman Asks Clubs to Use Mass Games," *Y Bulletin*, September 18, 1931. Quote from Monthly Report of the Physical Director, October 1934, Young Men's Hebrew Association records, 92nd Street Y Archives, New York. Some YMHA officials hoped Holman's opposition to 'super-athletes' would correspond to their desire to abolish all varsity athletics. Holman refused to take such an extreme measure.

Metropolitan League because "the effects of institutional basketball are not to be found by studying the game, but by studying the spirit of the institution." He stated that:

> Winning basketball teams are sometimes necessary evils among certain institutions to attract new members to the building; possibly the incoming revenue from these games covers the expenses incurred by other sports. The question centers around control. Visiting or home teams who bring their enthusiasts along to bet on games in a most unscrupulous manner, to question every decision of the officials, to desire to win at any price by the players and coaches; to deliberately employ unfair tactics in order to get a star player our of the game, to boo at the time an opponent is shooting a foul – make for a very unwholesome influence in our Jewish centers.

Holman discussed pervasive problems associated with Center basketball. Betting, booing, arguing, and excessive competitiveness had no place in organized Jewish communal life. Rather, sport should "uphold all the ideals and principles of clean sportsmanship, honesty, and fair play." Expanding on these points at considerable length, Holman concluded by reiterating his objective, "we have got to consider the interest of the mass rather than any specialized few."[16]

The article sparked a wave of discussion. In mid-October, the YMHA Physical Education Committee studied the "defects" of the league's basketball competition, including "bitter feeling among the Associations, disorder, gambling, and other vices." Holman's proposal faced strong opposition from Committee members, who voted that the Association should remain in the league to ensure "better spirit and closer supervision."[17] One week later, the Metropolitan League's Physical Director's Society discussed how "the element of championship had stimulated excessive rivalry." They concluded that an "over-emphasis upon basketball," had led to "unsportsmanlike situations." The

---

[16] "Holman Suggests Abolition of Met. League Basketball," *Y Bulletin*, September 25, 1931.

[17] Minutes of the Athletic Committee, October 13, 1931, Young Men's Hebrew Association records, 92nd Street Y Archives, New York.

directors commented on the difficulty of controlling the "attitudes of the spectators" due to the established rivalries. The directors decided that if Centers played each other less often, the tensions involved in bitter contests would decline. League competition would be organized into three divisions "in such a manner that each association will rotate in relation to its competitors from one year to another."[18]

Samuel Leff, who had condemned Center basketball in the *Jewish Center* the previous year, proved to be one of the most adamant opponents of Holman's proposal. Leff believed that Holman misunderstood the situation. He agreed that "evils" plagued the league, but "these faults are not inherent in the league." Rather, they "are foreign growths that have attached themselves to league games. These growths can be removed by stricter regulations." Leff believed his long-time association with the league allowed for a more accurate assessment of the situation. He explained: "merely because some of the organizations or to be more exact, some of the players representing some YMHA's display very bitter and unsportsmanlike feelings and conduct toward one another, there is no reason to abolish the league." He added that "similarly, there is no justification for ending the leagues because of any betting that may go on by members or other spectators at the games." The league controlled institutional actions and its abolition would mean that, "no standing of eligibility would exist and high school players, college players, professionals and even 'ringers' would be brought in to win important games. There would also be a great temptation to professionalize the sport by paying good players."[19]

Holman's proposal led to increased supervision in the Metropolitan League. In 1932, Holman required all varsity athletes at the 92nd Street YMHA to sign a form that included "a pledge of loyalty and sportsmanslike conduct."

---

[18] Minutes of the Physical Directors Society, October 19, 1931, Metropolitan League records, Young Men's Hebrew Association, 92nd Street Y Archives, New York.

[19] Edward Kramer, "Leff Expresses Disagreement with Nat Holman's Views," *Y Bulletin*, October 2, 1931.

Officials attempted to institute a four-year eligibility rule for varsity basketball players and the Athletic Council passed a resolution that: "No member competing for a high school, college or another institution may represent the YMHA in open competition at the same time."[20] The resolution repeated previous statements, which illustrated the ineffectiveness of such rules. Increased supervision did little to remove 'evils' from the national culture of Center basketball. Then, at the 1933 YMHA National Championship, officials accused the Boston YMHA team, the tournament winner, of using a professional player. The controversy caused the Metropolitan League to re-examine New York center basketball.[21]

Metropolitan League officials bickered amongst themselves about the future of Center basketball. Samuel Leff suggested abolishing tournaments during this controversy and argued: "competitive tournaments have interfered with sound development of physical education in Jewish Centers." He pointed to the Bensonhurst Jewish Community House, which "abolished all varsity teams," and found "membership interest and participation in intra-association athletics is at its highest point in the history of the organization." Powerful league officials opposed Leff. Charles Ornstein, a future member of the U.S. Olympic Committee, believed abolishment would "stifle competitive sports within the YMHA." E.J. Londow agreed, and explained that "the difficulty lies in the fact that the activity had been put in the hands of professionals [coaches], whose main

---

[20] "Require Pledge of Y Athletes," *Y Bulletin*, October 14, 1932. For Holman's initial mention of the pledge form, see Monthly Report of the Physical Director, May 1932, Young Men's Hebrew Association records, 92nd Street Y Archives, New York. The four-year eligibility rule was first mentioned in "Y to Enter in Basketball and Other Tourneys of Metropolitan League," *Y Bulletin*, November 7, 1930. In 1933, the *Bulletin* reported that "the ruling almost went through when something happened." See Waxing Confidential, *Y Bulletin*, February 24, 1933; "Athletic Council Opens Season," *Y Bulletin*, October 13, 1933. The Council addressed the question of whether or not to allow members under the age of 16 onto varsity teams. Another discussion involved the "management and handling of spectators at the basketball games...precautions will be taken this season to prevent crashing. Bulletin writers were brought up for special mention. It was decided that their girl friends' ticket will have to be paid for."

[21] "Quintet Battles in Boston for National YMHA Title," *Y Bulletin*, April 7, 1933. The 92nd Street YMHA basketball team had to pay their own way because of the Metropolitan League's lack of funds (due to other institutions' failing to pay their dues). The 92nd Street YMHA, which lost to Boston in the championship game, claimed it could appeal the verdict due to the controversy, chose not to.

interest lay in a winning record of their teams." Abraham Rosenthal went so far as to suggest the league should appoint a basketball commissioner to standardize the "dissimilarity of membership standards," which had been caused by the "employment of professional talent for Jewish center basketball teams, due to the need for money to carry out the organizations' physical education program."[22]

In October 1933, Metropolitan League officials declared a "one-year moratorium" on all athletic tournaments. The league's Athletic, Health, and Physical Education Committee appointed Judge Aron Steuer to head a sub-committee that would investigate "whether tournament competition is the basic cause of the unpleasantness or if the fault lies in curable defects in the administration of these tournaments."[23] Leff supported the decision. His reversal on the abolishment of tournaments would seem curious if not for the fact that he often acted as an arbiter of athletic activities and expected his opinion to steer the direction of Center athletics. Correspondence between Leff and 92nd Street YMHA officials, especially executive director Jack Nadel, was cordial and friendly, but often contained an underlying tension. This tension surfaced during a controversy over basketball in 1933.

At roughly the same time as the formation of the Steuer Committee, the 92nd Street YMHA's Athletic Council went on record that the YMHA would not play professionals. It cancelled its regular season opener against the Harlem Rens. The Council soon reversed its position, however, because the opening game "was not a contest but an exhibition." The Council decided that since the game would be "held for revenue only, in order to outfit the team properly," it found no problem with scheduling "against a team that would be the most certain to bring us the needed revenue." A poorly attended first game "would surely

---

[22] "Met League Abolishes All Athletic Tournaments," *Y Bulletin*, October 20, 1933. Former 'Wonder Five' member 'Rip' Gerson coached the Williamsburg YMHA and CCNY's Lou Spindell coached the Wilkes-Barre (Pennsylvania) YMHA while professionals in the ABL. For mention of Spahn, see "Cagers to Face Wilkes-Barre Y," *Y Bulletin*, February 28, 1936. For Gerson, see "Varsity Five Earns First Victory, 29-27," *Y Bulletin*, October 30, 1931.

[23] "Met League Abolishes All Athletic Tournaments," *Y Bulletin*, October 20, 1933.

lower the attendance for the remainder of the season." The Council then scheduled the Original Celtics in order to "insure a large crowd for the opening contest." The Council's president told the *Bulletin*, however, that in the future, "the 'no-professional' policy will be adhered to."[24]

The Celtics game blatantly violated amateur rules. The YMHA received a letter from the AAU demanding an explanation, and Leff, who had reported the YMHA to the AAU, confronted the Athletic Council. Leff asked the YMHA to clarify "the present policy of your YMHA" in relation to "such games with professionals." Jack Nadel retorted: "we engage in competition with amateur teams only."[25] The following year, Leff returned to the subject upon learning that the YMHA had again scheduled games against professional teams, including the Harlem Rens. He demanded the YMHA stop playing against these teams since "there is danger that your team will be regarded as violating amateur rules, and the reputation of your organization in all amateur sports will likewise suffer." Leff appealed to the YMHA's importance within the Center movement. If the YMHA established a strict policy of amateurism to guarantee the "gradual elimination of any danger of professionalism," it would "set a high standard for the other YMHA's and Jewish Centers throughout the country"[26]

---

[24] Minutes of the Athletic Council, September 14, 1933 and October 10, 1933, Young Men's Hebrew Association records, 92nd Street Y Archives, New York. In the late 1920s and early 1930s, ticket prices for games against professionals were higher than to other games. See Minutes of the Athletic Council, October 9, 1930, Young Men's Hebrew Association records, 92nd Street Y Archives, New York; "Athletic Council Opens Season," *Y Bulletin*, October 13, 1933. This was actually a different Celtics team, though it remained nominally connected to the Original Celtics of the 1920s. The team was called the Kate Smith Celtics in the mid-1930s after singer Kate Smith leant her name and money to promote the team. See Peterson, *Cages to Jump Shots*, 91, 102-103.

[25] Correspondence between Athletic Council president Ellis Banov and the AAU registration chairman, October 28-31, 1933, Young Men's Hebrew Association records, 92nd Street Y Archives, New York. Correspondence between Samuel Leff to Jack Nadel, November 6, 1933, December 27, 1933, December 29, 1933, January 4, 1934, Correspondence Files, "National Jewish Welfare Board," Executive Director records, Young Men's Hebrew Association, 92nd Street Y Archives, New York.

[26] Samuel Leff to Nat Holman, October 8, 1934, Correspondence files "Metropolitan League of Jewish Community Associations," Executive Director records, Young Men's Hebrew Association, 92nd Street Y Archives, New York.

The 92nd Street YMHA's willingness to play the Celtics and Rens indicated that the basketball program had become a commercial enterprise. The Steuer Committee blamed all the 'evils' of the Metropolitan League, such as gambling and competitiveness, on this sort of commercial behavior. The committee believed proper supervision would solve the problems and recommended that all Centers needed to organize athletic councils "to finance and supervise athletic activities."[27] Experience indicated, however, that athletic councils would focus on the financial, rather than supervisory side. At the 92nd Street YMHA, the Athletic Council relied on the basketball program to fund the entire athletic department. Between July 1931 and January 1933, income from basketball games constituted 98 percent of the total revenue of the Athletic Council. In 1935, receipts from basketball games reached over $4,000 and the "net receipts" generated more than $1,500. Two years later, the basketball team averaged 530 spectators per game and generated almost $2,000 in revenue, an impressive sum during the Depression.[28]

The continued commercialism of Jewish center sport did not stop the Steuer Committee from recommending in May 1935 that the Metropolitan League resume basketball tournaments after a two-year absence. The following year, the Metropolitan League incorporated as the New York Metropolitan Section-JWB, Inc.[29] Neither development immediately changed the priorities of Centers in the Metropolitan League, which contained approximately 35 member institutions

---

[27] "Met League Abolishes All Athletic Tournaments," *Y Bulletin*, October 20, 1933.

[28] Financial figures from miscellaneous Athletic Council files, Young Men's Hebrew Association records, 92nd Street Y Archives, New York. Much of the money raised went to charities and funds, including the Maccabi Association in Palestine, the Hebrew Orphan Asylum, the Jewish Federation, and the YMHA's special fund, Keren Ami (Fund for My People). What is important to note, however, is that these charities and funds were by-products of the revenue from basketball games and did not constitute the end goal for basketball. Most of the basketball revenue was used by the Athletic Council to benefit the athletic program rather than social programs or the broader institution.

[29] "Metropolitan League Plans to Restore Competitive Tournaments," *Y Bulletin*, May 3, 1935. M. Maldin Fertig to Jack Nadel, January 31, 1936, Correspondence files "National Jewish Welfare Board," Executive Director records, Young Men's Hebrew Association, 92nd Street Y Archives, New York.

spread throughout New York City, New Jersey, Long Island, and Westchester County. Competitive basketball at the 92nd Street YMHA flourished as former college players from LIU, St. John's, Brooklyn College, and even Minnesota starred for the team. The Athletic Council continued to encourage a 'champion' culture. In 1936, the Council formed a Varsity Club to reward the best athletes. The following year, it began to grant an annual Outstanding Athlete Award.[30] Through the end of the decade, the YMHA played the top amateur teams in New York City, regular competition in the Metropolitan League, and replaced professional opponents with College All-Star teams until the AAU forbade them to do so.[31]

The YMHA's continued use of the champion model in spite of the Steuer Committee's recommendations reflected the fragmented nature of American Jewish life in the 1930s. Even within a relatively unified organization such as the JWB, tensions remained strong. Despite external perceptions of unity, American Jews played out their internal divisions in a variety of public locations, including sport. In the mid-1930s, tensions involving the Olympic boycott movement illustrated the lack of uniformity and absence of a central authority among American Jewry.

In March 1934, a *Bulletin* columnist called 'Job' had claimed that the AAU could not legitimately oppose German discrimination since the Nazis could "cite our own prejudice against the Negro."[32] The column raised an immediate

---

[30] During a November 1937 Board of Directors meeting, the YMHA president urged the institution to "emphasize special activities among Jewish athletes who are individually outstanding." Minutes of the Board of Directors, November 16, 1937, Young Men's Hebrew Association records, 92nd Street Y Archives, New York.

[31] For information on players and games, see the *Y Bulletin*. On the AAU decision to eliminate All-Star games from the Y schedule, see Minutes of the Athletic Council, October 10, 1940, Young Men's Hebrew Association records, 92nd Street Y Archives, New York.

[32] "Job," *Y Bulletin*, March 16, 1934. In December 1933, *Time* reported that at the national AAU Convention, Gustavus Kirby had demanded that Germany allow Jewish athletes to compete in Olympic tryouts for the 1936 Games. Kirby offered a resolution that the American Olympic Committee (AOC) boycott the Games if discrimination against Jewish athletes did not cease. "Boycott into Protest," *Time* (December 4, 1933). General Sherrill opposed the resolution and demanded "it be amended so as to be a protest." 'Job' denigrated Kirby and seemed to have little

response from Louis Kraft, Director of the JWB's Jewish Center Activities, who wrote to Nadel and claimed 'Job' revealed "an outstanding ignorance concerning the history of sport under the direction of the AAU with reference to the so called question of race discrimination." Kraft understood that the columnist "is more concerned about being cleveristic than he is about accuracy of facts; but he has done a good deal of damage." He hoped the YMHA would make "an official disavowal and apology," especially since "the YMHA is a constituent society of the JWB and the JWB is the only Jewish national organization that is represented on the AAU and the American Olympic association." As a result of this power, "we have a right to expect the loyal support of all constituent societies in the stand taken by the parent body on this momentous issue."[33] Kraft's appeal, demand really, that the 92nd Street YMHA silence dissenters illustrated the JWB's desire to become the authority of American Jewish communal life.

The tension involved in the 'Job' incident intensified after the Olympic boycott failed. Individual Jewish athletes received tremendous pressure to boycott the Olympics from communal leaders who expressed the belief that no self-respecting Jew could compete in Germany. The *American Hebrew* praised Tulane University sprinter Herman Neugass for refusing to compete in the Olympic trials and waited for "the opportunity to announce the names of other athletes, Jews and Gentiles, who feel likewise."[34] Others viewed the Games as an opportunity to prove Jewish athleticism. Sam Balter, the sole Jewish player on the U.S. basketball team, explained that, "the most effective way to enforce our side of the argument is to show Herr Hitler that a Jew has as much right to be an

---

faith that the United States could rely on the leaders of "the great business of amateur athletics" to truly commit to a boycott.

[33] Louis Kraft to Jack Nadel, March 20, 1934, Correspondence files "National Jewish Welfare Board," Executive Director records, Young Men's Hebrew Association, 92nd Street Y Archives, New York.

[34] "Sports Column," *American Hebrew*, December 27, 1935.

athlete as an Aryan or anyone else."[35] In June 1936, the *Hebrew* denounced Jewish Olympians and exclaimed, "the disheartening side of the picture is that three Jews have accepted posts on the 1936 Olympic team." The *Hebrew* hoped no others would join since "three are enough black sheep."[36] Eventually six American Jewish athletes traveled to Germany.

After the boycott failed, participation in any event connected to the Olympics became controversial. In January 1936, one month after the AAU Convention, the *Jewish Examiner* stated, "it must be a benighted notion that the German Olympics is something every decent Jew is trying to avoid, for the sports pages reveal that we Jews in New York are training athletes to send over to the black Reich." The *Examiner* incredulously asked: "and which, of all institutions, is supporting the work? The [92nd Street] YMHA." The newspaper condemned both the YMHA, which had been prominently involved in the boycott movement, for hosting the Metropolitan AAU championship and Nat Holman, who as CCNY coach, "has his own team entered in the tourney." Holman had supported the boycott and declared: "the Olympic oath of fair play and sportsmanship should be upheld."[37] Holman's support for the boycott as a Jewish educator, however, conflicted with his role as a basketball 'ambassador.'

---

[35] Jewish Cager Says He Will Play in Olympics, *American Jewish World*, April 10, 1936. Balter's individual choice to compete in Berlin may have been more difficult that the collective decision by Jewish players at New York colleges. Balter was a member of Universal's AAU basketball team, which provided half of the members of the U.S. team (along with the McPherson Oilers). Balter later said he regretted his decision to attend the Olympics. The U.S. team won the gold medal as the games were played outside on dirt courts. The final was played in the rain and the muddy surface made dribbling virtually impossible. The final score was 19-8 as the U.S. defeated Canada. On the Canadian team was Jewish player Irving Meretsky. According to Brad Herzog, Universal removed support for the team to protest the Olympics in Berlin. See Brad Herzog, "The Original Dream Team," *Basketball Digest* (Summer 2000). For additional information on Balter and Universal's lack of support for the Olympic team, see "An Olympian's Oral History," Arthur O. Mollner, 1936 Olympic Games, History (Interviewed: May 1988 by George A. Hodak).

[36] "Sports Column," *American Hebrew*, June 5, 1936. The Jewish press commented on the results, but did so with tempered enthusiasm regarding American success. American Jews relished the destruction of Aryan theories of superiority at the hands of Jesse Owens and other African-American athletes.

[37] "Parade of Events," *Jewish Examiner*, January 31, 1936, located in miscellaneous file at 92nd Street Y Archives, New York. AAU delegate Charles Ornstein publicly joined with AAU president Judge Jeremiah Mahoney in opposing American participation. See "Association

The *Jewish Examiner's* article brought negative attention to the Center movement. JWB executive director Harry Glucksman contacted the YMHA's Jack Nadel and explained the article served as a "fair notion of how people feel about direct or indirect participation in preparations for the Olympic games." Holman needed "publicly to record his views," regarding the Olympics, the AAU tournament, and the coming qualifying tournament. Holman explained that participation in "sectional tournaments" would not lead to the Olympics since, "the invitation to the City College basketball team to participate in the Metropolitan AAU championship was accepted purely as a matter of athletic competition." He explained that his players "would not participate in the Olympics" and he "would not consider the coaching of any basketball team."[38] Holman's did not address the YMHA's role in the controversy, however, forcing Nadel to publicly state in late February that the YMHA would "not enter any competition connected with Olympics."[39]

In his letter to Nadel, Glucksman explained the need for uniformity. He stated that, "we cannot afford to have confusion with resultant criticism on an issue of such widespread interest and importance." Glucksman mentioned a meeting he had following the AAU Convention with "three [non-Jewish] gentlemen," including Judge Jeremiah Mahoney, who had served as the AAU president until the boycott failed. Glucksman explained that the non-Jews "were most emphatic in their view that the cause would be practically lost if the Jews did not remain consistently aloof from all Olympic activities," and were "truly

---

Member Appointed to AAU Sports Committees," *Y Bulletin*, October 19, 1934. Holman quote, see "Speakers Attack Hitler Regime at Meeting Against Nazi Games', 1,000 Fill Kaufman Auditorium," *Y Bulletin*, December 6, 1935.

[38] Harry Glucksman to Jack Nadel, February 6, 1936; Nat Holman to Jack Nadel, February 8, 1936, Correspondence files "National Jewish Welfare Board," Executive Director records, Young Men's Hebrew Association, 92nd Street Y Archives, New York.

[39] "Jack Nadel Issues Statement Denying Charges Against the Y of Supporting Olympic Tryouts," *Y Bulletin*, February 21, 1936.

shocked that any question could even be raised about this policy by Jews."[40] The meeting illustrated the disparity between how non-Jews perceived the Jewish community and the fragmentation of American Jewish life. No single entity controlled the activities of American Jews, although the JWB hoped to become the unifying force that would make the assumptions of the "three gentlemen" a reality. At the time, however, the JWB could not control officials within its constituent institutions.

Within the larger context, the JWB's struggles reflected the transformation of the American Jewish community. The organization hoped to reach out to American Jews who did not and could not serve as athletic champions. Officials did not feel the need to produce champions, they wanted to develop the mass. Similarly, other Jewish organizations sought a more expansive role in American Jewish life by reaching out to the native-born generation. Two organizations, Workmen's Circle and Young Judaea, differed in their political ideologies, but both recognized that attracting native-born American Jews required new methods. Jewish socialists and Zionists engaged in versions of Jewish athleticism, but neither constructed a version of the champion model or seemed very interested in dispelling the stereotype of the weak Jew.

During the Depression, Jewish labor politics underwent drastic changes. Jewish labor activity had been an intimate part of the immigrant experience, although few Jewish immigrants became active members of the Socialist Party. Historian Beth Wenger found in her study of New York Jews that socialism was less a political affiliation than a "part of the social fabric of Jewish existence." The New Deal played an important role as Jews of all classes supported the Democratic Party. Since the colonial period, American Jews had fulfilled the "Stuyvesant Promise" that they would not become a burden to society. Wealthier Jews formed private philanthropic agencies, orphan asylums, and other communal

---

[40] For mention of Nadel and Holman's differences, see Glucksman to Nadel, February 11, 1936. For Glucksman's meeting with Mahoney, see Glucksman to Nadel, January 22, 1936, Correspondence files "National Jewish Welfare Board," Executive Director records, Young Men's Hebrew Association, 92nd Street Y Archives, New York.

institutions such as settlement houses to the extent that self-sufficiency became "one of the cornerstones of Jewish identity in America."[41] The Depression shook this cornerstone. All Jewish organizations felt the impact of the Depression, and mutual aid societies and charitable organizations faltered in one way or another. Although some Jews believed public aid would hinder private charity, the New Deal fulfilled the Jewish belief in communal obligation.

Affiliation with the Democratic Party negatively impacted socialist political parties. The American Labor Party (ALP), formed in 1936 by long-time labor activists including David Dubinsky and Sidney Hillman, endorsed President Franklin Roosevelt while running its own candidates locally. The *Jewish Daily Forward* also supported Roosevelt's reelection campaign in 1936. By the middle of the decade, "Jewish politics had become inexorably linked to the Democratic Party."[42] Political change also occurred due to the transformation of American Jewish communal life. *Landsmanschaftn,* immigrant hometown associations, declined during the Depression because they could not connect with the native-born Jews, who by 1930, made up a majority of the American Jewish community. Immigrant-based organizations had to adjust to post-restriction American society by attracting a new generation of members.[43]

One of the most prominent immigrant-based organizations in the early years of the twentieth century was the Workmen's Circle. Formed in 1900 as an immigrant organization, the Circle (*Arbeter Ring* in Yiddish) provided death benefits, health insurance, schooling, and other services to its members. It had broad ties to Jewish-dominated unions such as the International Ladies' Garment

---

[41] Wenger, *New York Jews and the Great Depression*, 136-165. Quote from Wenger, 137. On Jews' relationship with Peter Stuyvesant, the governor of New Amsterdam in the seventeenth century, see Eli Faber, *A Time for Planting: The First Migration, 1654-1820* (Baltimore: Johns Hopkins University, 1992), 29-33, 37.

[42] On Jewish involvement in the labor movement, see Irving Howe, *The World of Our Fathers*. Quotes from Wenger, *New York Jews and the Great Depression*, 106, 134. New York Jews had supported the Democratic Party in the 1920s and voted for both Al Smith and Irving Lehman for governor. Also see Feingold, *A Time for Searching*, 198-204; Moore, *At Home in America*, 202-230.

[43] Soyer, *Jewish Immigrant Associations and American Identity in New York*.

Workers Union (ILGWU), Amalgamated Clothing Workers, and United Hebrew Trades. The Circle expounded beliefs influenced by the Bund, the eastern European Jewish socialist organization that linked full Jewish equality and security with the wider class struggle. The use of Yiddish served as the Circle's essential Jewish identification which could not attract a younger membership within a changing Jewish community.[44]

In the early 1930's, the Circle's leadership recognized that the organization's traditional structure did not appeal to native-born Jews raised in American society. The Circle organized the Young Circle League (YCL) to attract Jewish youth since, as the Circle's official historian Maximilian Hurwitz explained, immigration restriction forced the organization "to face west, toward America." Immigration would no longer invigorate the movement. Since new members had to "come from the American or Americanized elements of the Jewish population, prudence dictated the necessity of organizing English-speaking branches of native or naturalized Americans."[45] Not all Circle members welcomed the creation of English-only branches and a general increase in the use of English. A letter to a Circle publication argued that American society pulled the Circle away from a distinct Jewish identity. "No organization can claim representation of the Jewish masses when it neglects the cultural structure and medium of…Yiddish."[46]

---

[44] Judah Joseph Shapiro, *The Friendly Society: A History of the Workmen's Circle* (New York: Media Justice, 1970), 87-99. By 1917, the Circle had approximately 59,000 members. See Tony Michels, *A Fire in their Hearts: Yiddish Socialists in New York* (Cambridge: Harvard University Press, 2003), 3. On the Circle in relation to other immigrant organizations, see Soyer, *Jewish Immigrant Associations and American Identity in New York, 1880-1939*, 66-69, 129-130.

[45] On the formation of the YCL, see Sports, *The Call of Youth*, January 1933. Maxmilian Hurwitz, "The Beginnings of the League," *The Call of Youth*, April 1936; Maxmilian Hurwitz, "The Story of the YCLA," *The Call of Youth*, May 1936. For the impact of immigration restriction on other immigrant organizations, see Soyer, *Jewish Immigrant Associations and American Identity in New York*.

[46] Report of the 39th Convention of the Workmen's Circle, *Workmen's Circle Call*, July 1939. At the 39th Convention of the Circle, an amendment to permit Yiddish at Young Circle League meetings was defeated, thus signifying a decade-long debate within the organization concerning the importance of Yiddish and the need for English to reach the next generation of potential

The Circle expressed the belief that labor sports needed to counteract the dominance of capitalist-based competitive sports. The *Call of Youth* condemned American sport for "the rape of amateur ideals," and stated that, "professional sports is crooked." In particular, because "modern business is based upon cut-throat methods, dishonesty, and crookedness," the construction of sport's "philosophy of 'honesty and fair play'" served as "false propaganda" because, "big business was then, and is now, in the saddle of American sports."[47] The worker had been deceived by the business owner, and thus misunderstood the importance of sport within the labor movement. The success of organized labor to reduce working hours and increase leisure time meant labor sport would promote socialism, fill the void produced by minimal job satisfaction, and encourage labor unity. The Circle argued that, "the philosophy of sport should in some degree effect a man's behavior at his work," and promoted a broad athletic program to "identify his [the worker's] life with his cause. ...[T]he labor organization has a definite responsibility for providing recreation."[48]

The Circle's support for the 1936 Olympic boycott focused on labor ideology, not Nazi anti-Semitism. Following the AAU Convention, an article in the *Call of Youth* declared that the slogan "transfer the 1936 Olympics – Boycott the Nazi Games" had been adopted by "every trade-unionist and labor sympathizer who knows with what brutality the Nazi fiends crushed the Labor Movement of Germany." The Circle and other socialists were not just interested in "transferring the bourgeois Olympics to a non-fascist country, but in conducting a real *workers'* Olympics – an Olympics that will be a demonstration

---

members. Also see "Yiddish Culture in the Workmen's Circle," *Workmen's Circle Call*, December 1938.

[47] "I Accuse," *The Call of Youth*, September 1935.

[48] "Sports Front," *The Call of Youth*, July 1935. The League was associated with the International Socialist Association for Workers' Sport and Physical Education. For information on leftist and labor sport, see Mark Naison, "Lefties and Righties: The Communist Party and Sports During the Great Depression," in *Sport in America: New Historical Perspectives*, ed. Donald Spivey (Westport, CT: Greenwood Press, 1985), 129-144; Wheeler, "Organized Sport and Organized Labour," 191-207; John M. Hoberman, *Sport and Political Ideology* (Austin: Texas University Press, 1984), 170-177. "Sports Reports," *Workmen's Circle Call*, August-September 1940.

of labor solidarity a demonstration against fascism and war, a demonstration for socialism!"[49] The Circle supported the World Labor Athletic Carnival, which took place in New York City as a 'counter Olympics' at the same time as the Nazi Olympics. Organized by the newly-formed Jewish Labor Committee (JLC), the Carnival attracted hundreds of individual athletes from across the country, and the "YCL received a special invitation as the only youth fraternal organization close to the trade union movement to compete."[50]

Soon after the Carnival, the Circle began to emphasize competitive athletics. In particular, the YCL concentrated "on the development of its athletic facilities and activities so that the League can successfully compete with trade union groups; also, to supply the League members with an outlet for their athletic interests."[51] Basketball became the organization's primary sport and the Circle formed one of the top amateur basketball teams in New York City. The Circle participated in the male-only ILGWU League, played against labor teams, in AAU competitions, and even against an 'All-Star' team at the 'Game of Tomorrow' at the 1939 World's Fair. Competitive sport at the Circle, however, continued to promote labor sport rather than Jewish athleticism. Spectatorship furthered the larger class struggle, since "the exultant solidarity and ringing enthusiasm which characterizes fighting players and enthusiastic fans is very close to the militancy and resolution which an inspired labor movement needs."[52]

By the late 1930s, the Circle's official English-speaking organ, the *Workmen's Circle Call* included a regular 'Sports Report' which consisted of

---

[49] "The Worker's Olympics," *The Call of Youth*, January 1936. In 1935, the YCL joined the newly formed Workers' Sport League of America.

[50] "Ends of the Triangle," *The Call of Youth*, August 1936. The Carnival was sponsored by the JLC, labor unions, and the Metropolitan AAU. On the Carnival, see Edward S. Shapiro, "The World Labor Athletic Carnival of 1936: An American Anti-Nazi Protest," *American Jewish History* 59 (March 1985): 255-273.

[51] "Ends of the Triangle," *The Call of Youth*, November 1936.

[52] "Sports Reports," *The Workmen's Circle Call*, August/September 1940. On the 'Game of Tomorrow,' see "Workmen's Circle to Play 'Game of Tomorrow' at World's Fair," *Workmen's Circle Call*, October 1939. For information on the Fair, see Susman, *Culture as History*, 212-228.

game summaries, occasional individual profiles, and the achievements of the Circle's athletic program. The *Call* also highlighted players who achieved success in college and professional basketball as Circle basketball embraced a competitive ethos. Circle teams included former or current Jewish college players such as CCNY's 'Red' Holzman, Hofstra's Nat Militzok, and others from St. John's and LIU. Coach 'Red' Sarachek also coached at Yeshiva University.[53] The presence of champion basketball players did not mean, however, that the Circle's basketball program re-focused its energies toward a champion model of Jewish athleticism.

In the new competitive culture of Circle basketball, the organization began to engage with other Jews on the court. The New York Chapter played Jewish institutions such as the Brooklyn Jewish Center and the 92nd Street YMHA. In October 1936, *The Call of Youth* published an article entitled "The Jew in Sports," which explained that unlike Europe, where "the development of athletics" occurred because of a "Jewish movement," in America, Jewish athleticism "was a phase of the Americanization of the immigrant."[54] Outside this single article, the Circle generally ignored Jewish athleticism. The competitiveness of Circle basketball and its celebrations of individual athletes reinforced historian Peter Levine's assertion that Circle basketball did not attract Jewish players for ideological reasons or as cause for racial pride. Rather, it provided elite players an additional location for competitive basketball.[55] Circle basketball reflected the transformation of a former Yiddishist organization into an American one.

The Circle's expanded use of sport coincided with efforts to present socialism as the predominant ideology in American Jewish life. At the 1935

---

[53] "Sports Report," *Workmen's Circle Call*, September 1939. Praise of various Circle players in basketball occurred in *The Workmen's Circle Call*, October 1939-January 1940. For information on Sarachek and Yeshiva, which began its basketball program in 1934, see Gurock, *Judaism's Encounter with American Sports*, 121-125.

[54] "The Jew in Sports," *The Call of Youth*, October 1936.

[55] Levine, *Ellis Island to Ebbet's Field*, 23-24. On the labor sports movement in the United States, see Wheeler, "Organized Sport and Organized Labour," 205-206.

National Convention, Leon Sosnoff stated: "Zionism, in any form, forgets the class struggle, substituting chauvinism for Socialism and associates itself with groups and classes which are inimical to the interests of the Jewish workers."[56] Sosnoff's attack on Zionism reflected the decades-long debate regarding the solution to the 'Jewish Question.' Political and ideological divisions between Jewish socialists and Zionists did not prevent their similar use of sport to attract native-born Jews. Zionists became engaged with broader aspects of Jewish athleticism even as they focused on an internal project that limited their involvement in public athletic events.

The "Zionization" of American Jews proceeded slowly after World War I. A strong anti-Zionist group believed Jews should focus on integrating into American society, not attempt to construct a new nation doomed to failure. The Balfour Declaration, however, raised hopes that a Jewish state would become a reality. Events in Palestine, riots in 1929 resulted in the deaths of hundreds of Jews, an Arab 'revolt' against the British and Jewish presence began in 1936, and the rise of Nazi Germany convinced many American Jews that they needed to actively support the development of a Jewish homeland in order to ensure the survival of European Jews. In the 1930s, however, only a little more than 1.5 percent of the approximately 4.25 million American Jews joined a Zionist organization. A small number of racial and spiritual Zionists continued to argue that Zionism should not, or could not be integrated with Americanness to construct an American Jewish identity. Most American Zionists disagreed, but tensions between political factions characterized the movement in the 1930s.[57]

During the interwar period, Labor, Revisionist (or right wing), and General Zionists, the centrists, competed to attract American Jews. Revisionist Zionists co-opted the 'New Jew' and as historian George Mosse explained, "were

---

[56] "Colonization of the 'Homeland,'" *The Call of Youth*, June 1935. As the 1930s progressed, Circle newspapers increasingly ran stories and editorials regarding the larger labor movement and decreased attention to Jewish issues.

[57] On American Zionism, see Feingold, *A Time for Searching*, 166-188; Raider, *The Emergence of American Zionism*; Urofsky, *American Zionism from Herzl to the Holocaust*.

apt to raise physical force in the service of the Jewish nation to a value in and of itself." Revisionist Zionism remained the weakest faction and splintered into ideological factions in the 1930s, although Jewish communities often welcomed leader Ze'ev Jabotinsky.[58]

Labor Zionism, according to historian Mark Raider, produced a vital political platform within a divided movement. An ideologically-driven movement, Labor Zionism promoted a pioneer movement to Palestine. The Labor Zionist magazine, *The Jewish Frontier*, criticized the Workmen's Circle as a "youth movement [that] appears to be an emasculated assimilationist variety of complete indifference to Jewish life and problems." Labor Zionist youth groups like Habonim attracted youngsters to their camps, but athleticism remained underdeveloped in the official program. In 1934, however, the Minneapolis chapter of Hashomer Hatzair, a leftist Zionist youth group, exclaimed: "we also organized a basketball team."[59]

General Zionists proved the most willing to use American popular culture to attract Jewish youth. 'Centrists' controlled the Zionist Organization of America (ZOA), which attracted prominent American Jews as a powerful fund-raising force. The ZOA never commanded the support of fervent believers and only had 9,000 members in the early 1930s. The ZOA grew during the 1930s, but found itself caught between helping European Jews and attracting young

---

[58] Quote from Mosse, *Confronting the Nation*, 172; Todd Samuel Presner, "Clear Heads, Solid Stomachs, and Hard Muscles: Max Nordau and the Aesthetics of Jewish Regeneration." *Modernism/modernity* 10, no. 2 (2003), 291-292; Eisen, "Jewish History and the Ideology of Modern Sport," 517-519. On Revisionism, see Mendelsohn, *On Modern Jewish Politics*, 73-74. For instances of Jabotinsky's visits, see "Jabotinsky to Visit Center," *The Center News*, February 22, 1935; "Vladimir Jabotinsky's Only Brooklyn Appearance," *Brooklyn Jewish Center Bulletin*, February 5, 1926.

[59] On Labor Zionism, see Raider, *The Emergence of American Zionism*. "Books," *The Jewish Frontier*, June 1937. The *Frontier* presented pictures and advertisements of young, strong Jews working the land. Organizations like Paolei Zion-Zeirai Zion (PZZZ) supported the *Frontier's* focus on the construction of Palestine. Quote from "In the Movement," *Hashomer Hatzair*, December 1934.

American Jews who confirmed Zionists' worst fear, that the Diaspora led to assimilation.[60]

In 1939, the ZOA's *New Palestine* published a letter from a "young American Jew" who considered himself "a typical assimilated Jew." He complained that despite a new consciousness regarding the threat of anti-Semitism in America and abroad, he had become "dismayed by the fact that the [Zionist] meetings were carried on in terms of Palestine and not in terms of America." He declared that most assimilated Jews "are not prepared to become crusaders in a cause," because "we are average Americans. We like to attend movies, to sit home and listen to the radio, to take our girl friends to the park, to go to a baseball game." The 'young American Jew' defined his identity through American popular culture, which muted his Jewishness. The letter concluded that most young American Jews "should like to be some sort of American Zionists, enjoying Zionism in an American way."[61]

The meetings that the 'young American Jew' found so disconcerting may have been those of Young Judaea, a General Zionist youth organization. Founded in 1909, Young Judaea provided social, physical, and educational activities for Jewish youth with the intention of strengthening their connection with Palestine. Within the Judaean structure, local clubs directed athletic activities without national guidance.[62] The movement's official publication, *Young Judaean* reported on local and regional athletic activities, mentioning in 1915, for instance, that "a basketball tournament is being arranged for Young Judaea clubs of boys in Greater New York." In 1922, "the champion team from Philadelphia" traveled to New York City to play the "senior champions" of a recent basketball tournament

---

[60] For information on the ZOA and its membership, see Urofsky, *American Zionism from Herzl to the Holocaust*, 322, 352; Raider, *The Emergence of American Zionism*, 57-60; Feingold, *A Time for Searching*, 172.

[61] "Young American Jew Puzzled," *New Palestine*, March 31, 1939.

[62] By 1919, the organization grew to over 700 clubs with more than 14,000 members.

that the *Judaean* had hailed as "the greatest achievement in athletics by Young Judaea."[63]

In the 1920s, sport became a more integral part of Young Judaea. In November 1922, the *Judaean* stated that "Jewish boys and girls are the better and healthier for taking part in sports, and they can have no better place for their athletics than right in the Young Judaean clubs." That same year, businessman Nathan Straus "contributed the sum of $250 for the purchase of prizes" for the best Judaean athletes in the country.[64] In 1925, the *Judaean* initiated a regular feature entitled 'The Younger Sportsman.' This column served as the foundation for commentary on Jewish athleticism that commonly replicated the rhetoric within the Jewish press. In October 1930, a columnist wrote in 'Sport Sidelights' that, "to my mind, the game of basketball is more typically a Jewish sport than any other. The game is played at a rather dizzy pace throughout and new situations arise at almost every moment."[65]

Judaeans used sport to unify participation and spectatorship within a healthful, recreational environment. The *American Hebrew* and the 'young American Jew' both referred to how spectatorship at sporting events reflected an individual's identity. Judaean athletic events should "arouse inter-club and inter-sectional athletic competition throughout the ranks of Young Judaea along clean, wholesome, sportsmanlike lines." The Judaean leadership supported carnival-type events and sport since "club members are normal American Jewish boys and

---

[63] "Young Judaea News," *Young Judaean*, December 1915; "New York City Athletics," *Young Judaean*, March 1922.

[64] Alfred M. Frisch, "Athletics in Young Judaea," *Young Judaean*, November 1922; "Nathan Straus," *Young Judaean*, November 1922. Straus was a wealthy businessman, who with his brother Isidore, co-owned Macy's Department store. In 1912, while traveling in Europe, the brothers and their wives visited Palestine. Isidor quickly wanted to leave, but Nathan became enamored with the country, which led to his support of Zionist organizations. Isidor and his wife Ida boarded the *Titanic* for their return to the United States, and were among those who died when the ship sank.

[65] M.S. Liben, "Sport Sidelights," *Young Judaean*, October 1930. The *Judaean* frequently focused on European sport, especially the famous Hakoah soccer club of Vienna.

girls."[66] The movement did not want to "produce 'professionals' nor to transform existing clubs into athletic groups." Young Judaean leaders expressed the belief that, "athletics is something vital and should be made an integral part of our club activity with the following understandings – that an overdose of athletics is more detrimental to the life of a club than none at all."[67]

Controlled and supervised Judaean sport would contribute to the movement's goal of preparing Jewish youth to aid Palestine. "Athletics must be more than just a filler for interest and physical development. There is a moral significance which is often overlooked." The Zionist movement would benefit from Judaean sport because "team work, cooperation, coordinated actions, a unity of purpose built by play will bring results much more swiftly than a loose program of ideologies." Team games were to be emphasized within a diversified athletic program by a "wise leader [who] will not let athletics become the main issue, but only a means to bind the individuals within his club for united action on Zionist projects."[68] Judaean leaders accepted sport as a means of attracting members in relation to Palestine, which fit into a larger project as American Zionists began to engage Europeans on the athletic front in the 1930s.

In 1931, Americans formed the Maccabi Association of America in preparation for the first Maccabiah Games, to be held the following year in Palestine. Nationalistic in form and function, the Maccabiah spectacle became the main focus of athletic achievement for Zionists and a unique form of Jewish cultural expression. The Maccabiah held great importance to Zionists as a symbol of the 'New Jew.' The health and vigor of participants served as evidence of the regeneration of the Jewish people. The 1932 Maccabiah Games received fairly wide media attention, although *Time* magazine judged the event through the lens of competitive sport: "No supremely able Jewish athletes were entered, no world's

---

[66] Benjamin Lasser, "Athletics in Young Judaea," *Young Judaean*, March 1929; "A Maccabiad for Lag B'Omer," *The Leader*, April 1938.

[67] Ibid.

[68] Meyer G. Elkins, "Athletics in Your Club," *The Leader*, December 1938.

records were broken." In contrast, the *New Palestine* proudly declared that the "small contingent" of American delegates "did splendidly at the Maccabiad." The *Young Judaean* presented the spectacle as a unifying event: "the Maccabees of the world have spoken – and the Jewish youth of the world follows."[69] The *Judaean* overstated the situation. The Maccabi movement did not serve as the predominant expression of Jewish athleticism, which remained defined by the champion model, and only a small American contingent of 12 athletes competed in individual sports.

American Jews only marginally supported the Maccabi movement during the 1930s. In 1934, the Maccabi Association created a Sports Advisory Board to expand participation, publicity and financial support. Members included prominent athletes such as Nat Holman, boxer Benny Leonard, and baseball player Hank Greenberg. This committee failed to improve the situation and financial concerns immediately before the 1935 Games meant that there remained "a doubt as to whether the American team would be able to leave."[70] Perhaps even more telling, American Jews did not enter a team into the men's basketball competition at either the 1932 and 1935 Maccabiah Games. In 1938, the former president of the Maccabi Association told the 92nd Street YMHA *Bulletin* that, "the movement in this country is dead. There are no funds to carry on the work.

---

[69] "Maccabiad," *Time*, April 11, 1932; "American at the Maccabiad," *New Palestine*, May 13, 1932; Ellis Radinsky, "The First Maccabiad," *Young Judaean*, June 1932. On the Maccabiah and the regeneration of the Jewish body, see Nina S. Spiegel, "Jewish Cultural Celebrations and Competitions in Mandatory Palestine, 1920-1947: Body, Beauty, and the Search for Authenticity" (Ph.D. Diss.: Stanford University, 2001), 81-127. The term 'Maccabi' signified the Zionist rejection of assimilation through the symbolic representation of the Hebrew resistance against Hellenic influences during antiquity. In Palestine (and then Israel), Maccabi competed primarily with Hapoel (affiliated with Labor Zionists), though both Betar (Right Wing) and Elitzur (connected to the National Religious Party) also played an important role in Israel. For information on the politics of Israeli basketball, see Yair Galily and Michael Bar-Eli, "From Tal Brody to European Champions: Early Americanization and the 'Golden Age' of Israeli Basketball, 1965-1979," *Journal of Sport History* 32, no. 3 (2005): 303-327.

[70] Paul G. Goldberg, "The Second World Maccabi Games," *Brooklyn Jewish Center Review*, June 1935; Jack Weinberg, "The Athletic Honor Roll: Sports Highlights of the Year," *American Jewish World*, September 27, 1935; Second Annual Conference of Physical Directors in Jewish Centers, October 27, 1935, Jewish Welfare Board records, 92nd Street Y Archives, New York. At the Conference, Abraham Rosenthal presented on the Maccabi in a section entitled: New Trends in Physical Education.

It is a splendid idea…[but] it no longer exists here." The following year, the *New Palestine* hailed the World Maccabi Union as "the foremost champion of Jewish culture, both physical and spiritual," but lamented that because American society "caters so much to the glamorous, this great organization has found no direct way into the heart of Jewish youth."[71]

The same year that the *New Palestine* condemned American society for being too 'glamorous,' Young Judaea expanded its athletic program by forming a National Program of Athletics and Recreation since "more boys would be drawn into the organization if such a program is arranged."[72] Basketball served as the central sport in national competitions (other activities included oratory, debates, and ping-pong), and within two years, Young Judaea clubs competed in inner-region, inter-region, and national basketball tournaments. The national committee allowed regions and clubs to determine their own standards regarding athletic contests and participations, and competition generally occurred within the organization. The Zionist need for physical bodies to construct a homeland in Palestine informed Judaean sport, and this decidedly unglamorous project limited competitive sport within Young Judaea. Young Judaea used sport as a means of attracting young American Jews and strengthening bodies, not producing Jewish athletes.

At the same time, although approaching it from a different perspective and with more internal tensions, the JWB worked to achieve the same goal. In September 1939, the 92nd Street YMHA's Athletic Council agreed to participate in a JWB national basketball tournament, hailed as the first attempt at a national sports competition. According to the *Bulletin*, officials designed the new tournament to "further the concept of the Jewish Center movement as a national

---

[71] See "Jews in Sports: Maccabi Movement is 'Dead,'" *Y Bulletin*, January 28, 1938; "World Maccabi is Held Invaluable," *New Palestine*, March 24, 1939.

[72] The initial resolution was described in a letter from Claire Aronson, 1938 National Convention Chairman in a summary of the 30th Annual Convention, Young Judaea Archives, box 30, Center for Jewish History, New York. The Athletic Committee's formation was described in the *1938-39 Young Judaea Yearbook*, Young Judaea Archives, box 30, Center for Jewish History, New York.

movement, to enable Jews to find points of contact with Jews everywhere, and to further Jewishness, generally." Officials regarded basketball as "the most popular sport of Jewish youth," and believed the tournament would serve as the catalyst for future athletic events to strengthen and coordinate American Jewry.[73]

Like the initial YMHA Athletic League, the JWB hoped to use sport to strengthen internal communal forces. Unlike the original league, however, the JWB did not intend to promote Jewish athleticism. The JWB tournament and the re-organized Metropolitan League, called the Eastern Jewish Center League, included many of the rules that had governed previous tournaments and competitions. Yet, the organizational structure and supervision had become far more extensive. Prominent officials such as Harry Henshel, Ira Streusand, Barney Ain, and others played important roles as they organized committees for referees, scheduling, and rules.[74] The rules committee stipulated that players be members of the organizations they represented and could not play for any other organization, including colleges. Officials believed this rule would "eliminate 'professionalism' from Jewish Center sports."[75] The JWB intended to drive commercialism and competitiveness out of Center basketball. Its success occurred quicker and more definitively than officials could have hoped.

During the 1937 season, the 92nd Street YMHA reached a record level in both attendance, an average of 534 fans, and income, netting an average of $104.37 per game. Two years later, the Athletic Council found itself in the midst of a budget crisis because the revenue from basketball had declined to an average

---

[73] "To Unite Jewry Aim of JWB Sports Plan, *Y Bulletin*, October 6, 1939.

[74] Minutes of the Meeting of Representatives for the Formation of Invitational Basketball Tournaments of the Jewish Welfare Board Sports Programs, October 1, 1939, Athletic Department miscellaneous file, Young Men's Hebrew Association records, 92nd Street Y Archives, New York. Some of the referees considered were prominent local officials who worked Garden doubleheaders. Among the names listed as possible officials were Lou Eisenstein, Phil Fox, Pat Kennedy, and Lou Wisner. Like previous attempts to control institutional basketball, members and institutions needed to be registered with the AAU. The scheduling committee formed three leagues and turned away applicants from Atlantic City, Albany, and Baltimore because of the distance.

[75] "To Unite Jewry Aim of JWB Sports Plan, *Y Bulletin*, October 6, 1939.

of $56.89 per game. In 1940, basketball had a one-year revival as the average net receipts increased to $85 per game, but this aberration did not change the depressed state of YMHA basketball. Attendance hovered around an average of 400 fans per game and expenses held steady at $100 per game, but receipts declined during the 1941 season when basketball netted an average of only $51.49 per game. The sudden decline in revenue surprised the athletic department, which had not requested funds from the board since the early 1920s. The lack of revenue in 1941, however, led the Athletic Council to ask for an appropriation from the board to cover the expenses of all varsity teams.[76]

Prior to the 1942 season, board members took a close look at the Athletic Council's budget and financial figures and issued a report entitled "Basketball at the 92nd Street YMHA." The board examined the structure of the team, including the coach's role in selecting players and purchasing equipment. The majority of the report focused on the commercial side: "The money realized from these games, [is] our only source of revenue." They needed this revenue "to equip and finance all other varsity teams," pay AAU dues and "for contributions" to a summer camp and charitable causes. The report blamed the lack of revenue on a number of factors, but reserved special mention for the "poor competition" of the JWB tournament since "some of the teams are not attractive to our patrons. They have no following and hence do not bring a crowd with them. Our games must necessarily be a money proposition." It recommended that the YMHA needed to play "only the best competition, get a winning team, [and] start the season against a team of stars."[77]

America's entry into World War II made it impossible for the report's recommendations to be implemented. The depletion of Association resources

---

[76] Financial figures from miscellaneous Athletic Council files, Young Men's Hebrew Association records, 92nd Street Y Archives, New York. The request from the Athletic Council was found in the Minutes of the Board of Directors, October 21, 1941, Young Men's Hebrew Association records, 92nd Street Y Archives, New York.

[77] "Basketball at the 92nd Street YMHA, 1941-1942," miscellaneous Athletic Council file, Young Men's Hebrew Association records, 92nd Street Y Archives, New York

caused the 92nd Street YMHA to cancel all varsity sports. In 1946, the Athletic Council sought to resume varsity sports and appealed for over $2,000 from the Board of Directors, half of which would be used to revitalize basketball. In 1947, the net receipts from basketball were less than $600, one-quarter of the amount raised in 1935.[78] Two years later, the YMHA played the Montreal YMHA, whose players composed half of Canada's 1948 Olympic basketball team, as part of the YMHA's 75th Anniversary celebration. This international competition aside, a *Bulletin* article the previous year indicated the true state of YMHA basketball and competitive sport in general. "Noted Sports Stars Listed Among Y's Membership" listed past athletes and possessed a tone of recollection rather than hope for future success. At the end of the decade, because of "injuries, illnesses, and players getting married, the Varsity basketball team had its poorest season in Y history."[79] Varsity teams would continue to play, but they would no longer play in front of large audiences and rarely included future or former college stars. The JWB's success in controlling Jewish center sport had impacted basketball at the 92nd Street YMHA.

During the war, the New York YWHA moved into the YMHA after giving up its building to the army. In 1945, the institution re-organized as the 92nd Street YM-YWHA. The transformation of the YMHA symbolized the emergence of a new form of Jewish community center.[80] During the interwar

---

[78] Following the war, New York fire regulations limited the attendance at games to 200 spectators. See Minutes of the Athletic Council, October 1946, Young Men's Hebrew Association records, 92nd Street Y Archives, New York. See miscellaneous Athletic Council files, Young Men's Hebrew Association records, 92nd Street Y Archives, New York.

[79] "Noted Sports Stars," *'Y' Bulletin*, December 15, 1948. "Montreal Game to Climax One of Y's Best Seasons," *Y Bulletin*, March 9, 1949; Monthly Report of the Physical Director Report, March 1950, Young Men's Hebrew Association records, 92nd Street Y Archives, New York.

[80] See Borish, "An Interest in Physical Well-Being Among the Female Membership," 92-93. In 1942, the U.S. Army appropriated the YWHA (Young Women's Hebrew Association) building, which forced the institution to move into the 92nd Street YMHA. According to the 1946 YMHA *Annual Report*, 26% of the gymnasium membership was female. Linda Borish discussed the expanded opportunities for women at Jewish Centers in the 1940s. A renewed emphasis on 'average' members along with the inclusion of a new member base helped transform the function and goal of the YMHA. The first mention of 'average' members occurred in the Board of Directors minutes on November 18, 1941 following a discussion regarding the problems of relying

period, Jewish centers had offered little Jewish content because young Jews received their 'Jewish' education in their neighborhoods, on the streets, or in the home. After the war, however, urban Jews began to migrate to suburban areas. Residential migration forced American Jews to adapt to new conditions. Voluntary Jewish identification became part of suburban life and the suburban center needed to fill a void left by the declining Jewish urban neighborhoods.[81] The cultural identity expressed at the JCC would be Zionist, ethnic, and distinctly non-racial. According to historian David Kaufman, cultural pluralism became "the rationalization for its [Jewish Center] separate existence" from denominational Judaism. The post-war Center would provide cultural activities in which an ethnic identity could be constructed.[82] It did not need competitive Jewish athleticism. Physical education at this new JCC would be recreational, although this conception of Jewish athleticism also had its detractors.

In 1948, the JWB issued the *JWB Survey*, also known as the Janowsky Report after academic Oscar Janowsky, which concluded that Jewish Centers needed to 'Judaize' their programs. Religious leaders had claimed that the Jewish Center "made only 'some' or no major contribution towards the furtherance of Judaism." JWB officials such as Louis Kraft continued to assert that Centers, as social, religious, and cultural institutions, helped "our youth live affirmatively as Jews." Janowsky believed, however, that the focus on recreational activities needed to be diminished. "It is not the gymnasium and dance hall that validate the distinctive Jewish Center, but its Jewish purpose…American Jewry is neither an athletic association, nor a health club, nor a dancing society, nor even a recreational fraternity, however, broadly one defines recreation."[83] The

---

on varsity basketball to fund the entire department. As the war effort continued to drain YMHA resources, the emphasis on 'average' members became increasingly important.

[81] Edward S. Shapiro, *A Time for Healing: American Jewry Since World War II* (Baltimore: Johns Hopkins University Press, 1992), preface. Feingold, *A Time for Searching*, 125.

[82] Kaufman, *Shul with a Pool*, 235.

[83] Both quotes from Gurock, *Judaism's Encounter with American Sports*, 103.

Janowsky Report, which went further than Kraft or other JWB officials in denouncing athletic activity in Jewish centers, reinforced the notion that competitive sport no longer had a place in the JWB. The champion model had been removed from organized American Jewish life.

As Jewish communities backed away from competitive sport during and after the war, Zionism emerged as the dominant political ideology within organized American Jewish life. In 1937, the Central Conference of American Rabbis reversed its anti-Zionist stance as events in Europe convinced many American Jews of the necessity of a Jewish homeland as a refuge. By the early 1940s, ZOA had 46,000 members, emphasized practical work in Palestine, and promoted a Zionist identity that formed the basis of an American ethnic identity. Nazi atrocities produced a "melding" of American and European thought regarding Jewish nationalism, and by the end of World War II, Zionism had become part of the American Jewish cultural identity.[84] American Jews believed Palestine had to become a state, but the war and revelations of the Holocaust did not produce a mass migration of American Jews to Israel. Rather, they provided financial support to European refugees and the State of Israel. This activity reflected American Jews' new level of security in post-war society as charges of duel loyalty vanished. In contrast, radical leftists went underground as they found themselves ostracized by other Jews after the war. The JWB did not want radicals to speak at Jewish Centers. The American Jewish Committee (AJC) published *Commentary*, which unrelentingly attacked Communism. The fear of anti-Semitism led many American Jews to become virulent anti-Communists. The majority of American Jews believed their Zionist identity reflected a tolerant American society in which they had found a safe and secure home.[85]

---

[84] Urofksy, *American Zionism from Herzl to the Holocaust*, 392-402; Mendelsohn, *On Modern Jewish Politics*, 82. According to historian Ezra Mendelsohn, American Zionism's eventual triumph occurred because the Jewish left declined in importance and Zionists were able to construct an integrated identity.

[85] Shapiro, *A Time for Healing*, 25-26, 36-38.

As Zionism became part of an integrated 'ethnic' identity, organized Jewish athleticism evolved in the post-war era. In 1948, the same year as the establishment of the State of Israel, Harry Henshel and Charles Ornstein, both prominent officials at the 92nd Street YMHA, helped organize the U.S. Committee Sports for Israel (USCSI). This organization reflected the changing direction of communal Jewish athleticism. Serving a similar purpose as the American Olympic Committee, USCSI raised money, picked the athletes who would represent the United States in the Maccabiah Games, and promoted youth sport in order to "instill a sense of pride in their heritage which links them forever to Eretz Israel."[86] Beginning in 1948, Jewish athleticism would contribute to the larger Zionist struggle for Israel's survival, not to serve a project of integration.

The JWB's transformation of Jewish Center sport effectively destroyed Jewish basketball as an interconnected network of street, school, institutional, college, and professional basketball. Educators believed that competitive sport had become a dangerous activity for modern American Jewish culture. Center officials, players, and fans participated in the unscrupulous activity that accompanied competitive sport: capitalistic and aggressive behavior. The JWB withdrew from the direction that the champion model had been taking Jewish athleticism and connected Jewish manhood with mass participation. Jewish players did not immediately stop moving from college basketball to Center basketball, but the next generation of Jewish players would find an important pathway to mainstream basketball closed.[87] If a young player wanted to play college basketball, he could no longer rely on a Jewish Center to provide a competitive outlet.

The champion model had been constructed on the basis that sport could serve a process of integration. Once Jews believed that sport had achieved this

---

[86] Levine, *Ellis Island to Ebbet's Field*, 265.

[87] As an example, former Cornell star Irwin 'Stretch' Alterson played for Union Temple during the 1948 season in the JWB's Metropolitan Section. See "In Sport Circles," *JWB Circle*, January 1948. In addition, individual institutions continued to find success in local competitions as the Cincinnati Jewish Center won the city's AAU title in 1947 and 1948.

particular end, it could be transformed into a purely recreational activity to unify American Jews. The same process of integration that the JWB attempted to control led political groups to enter the athletic world in order to attract native-born Jews. These groups did not produce a new champion model of Jewish athleticism. Their respective use of sport indicated that by the late 1930s, American Jews, although not fully accepted or integrated, focused less on sport as a reflection of Jewish normality and masculinity. Future Jewish champions would compete as individuals, not as evidence of communal athleticism or as part of a communal culture.

Chapter Six

The End of an Era: Jewish Basketball

and the Modernization of Basketball

During the late 1930s and into the 1940s, Jewish players participated in a drastically different basketball environment than their predecessors. In college basketball, the east-west regional divide diminished as standardized playing styles, important rule changes, and postseason tournaments transformed the game into a unified, national sport. The professional game emerged with similar commercial, competitive, and racial elements as college basketball as well as a new emphasis on height, which changed the nature of the game. Tall players represented a future of basketball that had no specific regional or racial characteristics, and thus did not inevitably transform Jewish basketball. By 1950, the forces of change within basketball and American Jewish life had intertwined to transform Jewish basketball into an individual pursuit among tall players.

The demise of the champion model began the decline of Jewish basketball, but did not immediately impact Jewish players at the college or professional level. The project of Jewish athleticism had produced a culture in which players could develop into individual champions in the streets and schoolyards of their Jewish neighborhoods. This neighborhood culture began to wane as Jews migrated from urban neighborhoods into suburban areas after World War II. Suburban migration reflected Jews' socio-economic mobility and acceptance within American society and did not produce a renewed culture of communal athleticism. According to historian Edward Shapiro, in post-war society, Jews faced fewer barriers to assimilation and they responded to conditions of affluence and freedom.[1] Thus, Jewish basketball's place in American Jewish life changed. Prior to the 1940s, the Jewish press defined Jewish basketball as the *collective* excellence of Jewish players at New York schools. In 1950, when a 'Jewish' team won the national championship in college basketball, the Jewish press had already stopped treating Jewish basketball as a reflection of communal athleticism.[2]

The decline of Jewish basketball occurred because of different, yet overlapping, changes to both the structure of basketball and the social position of American Jews in post-World War II American society. Jewish acceptance and upward mobility occurred amid a declining Jewish presence and an increasing African-American presence in basketball. After World War II, Americans generally identified Jews as an ethnic group. Yet, the end of this era of Jewish basketball did not occur as a simple racial transfer. Rather, the commercial and competitive pressures of Madison Square Garden led to a scandal that tarnished the image of New York college basketball and led to the decline of the city's top programs. This removed the final element of an already diminishing culture of Jewish basketball. By 1951, Jewish basketball had symbolically become part of basketball's past. Basketball continued to play an important role in the lives of individual Jews, it became less so important in their broader communities.

In 1937, college basketball made one of the most important rule changes in its history, the elimination of the center jump. Prior to the 1937-38 season, play stopped after every made basket and the teams returned to the center of the court for a jump ball. Opponents of the center jump denounced the unfairness it produced in the game. Nat Holman had declared that, "basketball as it is now is

---

[1] Edward S. Shapiro, *A Time for Healing: American Jewry Since World War II* (Baltimore: Johns Hopkins University Press, 1992), xv.

[2] Media representations of Jewish athleticism noticeably declined during World War II and did not return to their pre-war strength in the late 1940s and early 1950s. For a discussion of baseball star Hank Greenberg, see Shapiro, *A Time for Healing*, 15-20.

not 100% healthy due to the advantage held by a team with a tall center."[3] Four years later, University of Minnesota coach Dave MacMillan stated that he favored the rule change since "otherwise you have four players and a clown."[4]

MacMillan's distinction between 'players' and the center 'clown' indicated the clear bias against tall players in basketball. Prior to the 1936 Olympic qualifying tournament, the *Time* magazine described the McPherson Oilers, whose starting five ranging in height from 6'1" to 6'9", as "athletic freaks." They had perfected a "technique called 'dunking' with which they score by jumping up above the basket, dropping the ball into it." Some traditionalists believed that such activity would ruin the game. Kansas coach 'Phog' Allen spoke for many coaches and critics when he stated: "dunking is not basketball."[5]

During the early decades of the twentieth century, coaches viewed taller players as awkward, ungainly, and useful only for rebounds or the center jump. In 1934, newspapers viewed Jewish high schooler and future NYU star Irwin Witty as "a smooth player, despite his 6'3" height."[6] Coaches spent considerably more time with shorter guards and forwards who possessed the bursts of movement required in basketball. Many assumed this would continue in the post-center jump era. Ironically, the rule change produced the opposite effect. The absence of the center jump forced coaches to provide tall players with instruction,

---

[3] "Holman's No-Tap Plan Tested as Court Experts See Y Beat Collegians," *Y Bulletin*, April 7, 1933. In 1933, Holman organized a "test game" between the 92nd Street YMHA varsity and a collection of 'all-stars' from CCNY and St. John's.

[4] "On the Courts," *New York Times*, December 29, 1937. MacMillan's comments were made after the first double-header in which a record crowd of 18,148 saw Stanford defeat CCNY and Minnesota beat LIU. MacMillan was a former teammate of Holman's with the Celtics.

[5] Quote on 'freaks' from "Sport: Basketball," *Time*, April 13, 1936; Quote on 'dunking' from "Brooklyn College and McPherson Oilers Score in Garden Basketball Games," *New York Times*, March 12, 1936. Prior to the 1936 qualifying tournament, the Oilers played an All-Metropolitan team composed of the entire LIU squad and stars from NYU, CCNY, St. John's, Manhattan, Fordham, and St. Francis. MacPherson won 45-43 in "the most brilliantly played and spectacular basketball game that Madison Square Garden ever has seen." On Allen's attitude, see Harold C. Evans, "Some Notes on College Basketball in Kansas," *The Kansas Historical Quarterly* 11, no. 2 (May 1942): 199-215. Quote on 213.

[6] "Jefferson Seeks First Court Title in Facing Clinton," *New York Times*, March 24, 1934.

which increased their skill and ability on the court. Some commentators immediately recognized that a shift had occurred. In the March 1938 *YMHA Bulletin*, Stanley Frank re-issued his treatise on Barney Sedran with the additional comment that basketball "gives the big man crushing advantages over a smaller opponent." By the mid-1940s, players over 6'9" became more common in college basketball as DePaul's George Mikan, Oklahoma A&M's Bob Kurland, and St. John's Harry Boykoff changed the nature of the game.[7] Yet, tall players remained seen as "freaks." In 1943, *Newsweek* profiled the 6'9" Boykoff, New York City's first successful 'big man.' The text focused on his height, made no mention of his Jewishness and explained that, "It is rumored that the reason the 20-year-old sophomore is studying accountancy is so that he can tally his final height."[8]

In the late 1930s and early 1940s, the new generation of 'freaks' often stood under the basket to block their opponents' shot. Many commentators considered this, much like the center jump, an unfair advantage for taller players and believed that the "practice called 'goal tending' threatened to turn the game over to circus giants, whether or not they can play basketball."[9] The NCAA banned goaltending following the 1944 season, but taller players and their coaches adapted to this rule like they had the elimination of the center jump. Holman and others lamented the gradual removal of the 'small' player. Holman scoffed at Phog Allen's suggestion that the basket be raised to 12-feet, but suggested the lanes be widened to 12-feet in order to "aid the little man" by keeping taller players further from the basket. Despite opposition from

---

[7] Stanley Frank, "Jews in Sports: Barney Sedran," *Y Bulletin*, March 18, 1938.

[8] "Basketball," *Newsweek*, February 1, 1943. On Mikan as the "first" great big man, see Isaacs, *All the Moves*, 129-135; Bjarkman, *Hoopla*, 51-52.

[9] The rules committee also allowed unlimited substitutions, increased personal fouls from four to five, and provided the referee with the ability to call time out for an injured player. See "Sports," *Newsweek*, April 14, 1944.

traditionalists, however, the sport's popularity seemed to increase every year as basketball became "a sport where height pays off."[10]

An increase in frenetic activity on the court served as a derivative of the abolition of the center jump. Supporters of the center jump had claimed it positively slowed down the game so that players would not overexert themselves. According to *Time*, the results of the rule change during the first year led some "physicians and coaches" to become concerned that the pace placed "too great a strain on players' hearts." Most commentators and coaches, however, welcomed the change since the elimination of the jump: "speeds up the game, adds about seven minutes of playing time…[and] results in more spectacular tries for basketball and larger scores."[11]

The increase in scoring surpassed all expectations as teams and players adjusted to the new rules. Whereas scores in the early 1930s had often been in the teens and twenties, some teams scored in the sixties during the early 1940s. By the end of the decade, scores exploded into the seventies, eighties, and even nineties. Spectators witnessed evenly matched teams score at incredible paces and individual players became stars for scoring more than 20 points in a game. Specialization began to differentiate between positions as "playmakers" became point guards and coaches designed offenses around individual players' ability to score. In March 1947, Harry Boykoff scored 54 points, which then set a record at Madison Square Garden, in a 71-52 St. John's victory over rival St. Francis.[12]

---

[10] "Little Man: Holman Urges Changes in Cage Setup," *Los Angeles Times*, February 6, 1951; "Coach Assails Basket Ball Toss-Up as Unsportsmanlike," *Washington Post*, January 17, 1929. Sport: Basketball Pfd," *Time*, April 6, 1942.

[11] "Sport: In New Orleans," *Time*, February 7, 1938; "Sport: Point a Minute," *Time*, January 24, 1938. In 1909, Luther Gulick stated he opposed the 'cage' game "because of the excessive strain upon the heart produced by the continuous playing." See Luther Gulick, "Proposed Changes in Basket Ball," *American Physical Education Review* 14, no. 8 (October 1909): 509.

[12] Bjarkman, *Hoopla*, 47. Scoring records fell at incredible paces during the 1940s. In March 1945, NYU scored 85 points in a game against Temple and Bowling Green scored 97 points at the Garden in 1948. Boykoff scored a Garden record 45 points in 1943. That scoring mark was broken by Mikan in 1945. For Boykoff's 1947 mark, see "St. Francis Beaten By Redmen," *New York Times*, March 12, 1947. St. John's coach Joe Lapchick called Dutch Garfinkel a "playmaker" in relation to his ability to produce scoring opportunities for his teammates. See

The increased scoring also attracted spectators and intensified the commercialism of college basketball. Garden promoter Ned Irish and the Metropolitan Basketball Writers Association (MBWA) took immediate advantage of this change, and at the end of the 1938 season, they organized a postseason tournament to crown a national champion.

Described as the "Rose Bowl of Basketball," the National Invitational Tournament (NIT) invited six teams (NYU, LIU, Temple, Bradley, Oklahoma A&M, and Colorado) to Madison Square Garden in March 1938. Some basketball fans declared the NIT "will prove nothing" due to the absence of Stanford, Notre Dame, and teams from the powerful Big Ten, which did not participate in post-season games. Others asserted that bids to NYU and LIU after mediocre seasons only illustrated that the "writers are playing stooges to enrich the coffers of Ned Irish." The tournament championship game received wide media attention as Temple, with All-American Mike (Meyer) Bloom leading the way, defeated Colorado and its star, future Supreme Court Justice Byron 'Whizzer' White, 60-38 by playing "a brand of basketball that never has been surpassed in Madison Square Garden."[13] The NIT attracted fewer customers than regular season games, but its success led the NCAA to form its own postseason national tournament in 1939.

The post-season tournaments encouraged the ongoing growth and standardization of college basketball. Stanford coach John Bunn stated the Garden provided a "benefit" to all participants since "Western teams could learn about ball-handling from their Eastern opponents while...invading teams could teach the local fives a little about shooting." As more cities promoted double-headers, eastern teams sometimes traveled west and commentators declared that

---

"West's Brand of Basketball Finds Favor of Lapchick," *New York Evening Post*, December 13, 1938.

[13] "Readers' Right," *New York Evening Post*, March 4, 1938 and March 7, 1938. The *Post* was not part of the committee which organized the tournament and received 34 letters in protest of the first NIT. NYU and LIU played for the first time ever. On the final, see *New York Times*, March 17, 1938.

"basketball's provincialism is gone and the game is much healthier for it." In 1940, *Newsweek* stated that basketball was "watched annually by more paying customers than any other sport, 90,000,000 in a single season."[14] That same year, the first televised college basketball game took place, although basketball would not take full advantage of the new medium until the 1950s. Following the 1941 season, during which Nat Holman served as president of the National Association of Basketball Coaches (NABC), the organization's Coaching Committee voted to standardize the size of the ball, floor, backboards, lighting, and other equipment. Standard equipment, inter-regional double-headers, and national tournaments, helped college basketball surpass all but college football and major league baseball in national popularity by World War II.[15]

In the late 1930s and early 1940s, Jewish players had more of a presence in the NIT than in the NCAA tournament. The NCAA divided the country into eight geographic districts (four in the west and four in the east), and included only one team from each district. The NCAA's regional seeding minimized the number of Jews who would appear in that tournament. Relatively few Jews played at top Midwestern or Western colleges and only two Jewish players appeared in the NCAA tournament between 1939-1942. A New York City team did not qualify for the NCAA until 1943 or play in the championship game until 1945. In contrast, the NIT had no geographic limitations and invited the best teams in the country. It also included New York teams because of commercial

---

[14] "Activities on Basketball Courts," *New York Times*, January 4, 1938. "West Meets East and Trims It in Year-End Basketball Spurt," *Newsweek*, January 8, 1940. The NCAA formed its own tournament because it determined that it needed to control college basketball. See Applin, "From Muscular Christianity to the Marketplace," 170-171.

[15] For information on Holman's tenure as NABC president, see Nat Holman papers, City College of New York Archives, New York. On the NABC vote to standardize the game, see "Uniform Basketball and Coaches Pushed by Coaches' Committee," *New York Times*, March 25, 1941. On basketball's growth and general attendance figures, see "Sports," *Newsweek*, April 14, 1944. According to the article, Garden attendance was 249,728 at double-headers and 115,000 at the national tournaments.

concerns. The MBWA recognized the appeal of local teams and two city teams played in each NIT from 1938-1942.[16]

The high number of New York schools contributed to the success of Jewish basketball in the early years of the NIT. Eastern teams with a prominent Jewish presence won five of the first seven tournaments. Temple captured the first tournament championship, LIU won in 1939 and 1941, and St. John's became the first team to win back-to-back titles in 1943 and 1944. Yet, even as New York schools had this success, the power of college basketball briefly shifted away from the east in the mid-1940s.

World War II altered the structure of college basketball and its postseason tournaments. The war forced many schools to cancel their programs while others played freshmen to field complete teams. In 1943, the NCAA tournament joined the NIT at Madison Square Garden, which increased the Garden's importance within college basketball. Following both of St. John's' NIT victories, the team lost to the NCAA champion (Wyoming in 1943 and Utah in 1944) in Red Cross benefit games, which legitimized the NCAA tournament and provided western schools with national exposure.[17] In the minds of coaches, fans, sportswriters and players, however, the NIT remained the more prestigious tournament for the remainder of the decade. Jewish basketball thus retained its prominent presence in mainstream basketball.

During the 1946 season, Jewish players had considerable success in New York college basketball. Jews made up six of the top eight scorers in the Metropolitan district, and seven of the ten players named All-Metropolitan. They also remained well represented at the predominantly 'Jewish' schools of CCNY,

---

[16] On tournaments and results, see Mike Douchant, with special guest Jim Nantz, *Inside College Basketball*, Rev. ed. (New York: Visible Ink Press, 1997). The two Jewish players were Harry Platt of Brown University (1939) and Moe Becker of Duquesne (1940). In 1941, the NIT expanded from six to eight teams.

[17] On the Garden, see Applin, "From Muscular Christianity to the Marketplace," 246-247. "West Meets East and Trims It In Year-End Basketball Spurt," *Newsweek*, January 8, 1940. After the University of Southern California ended LIU's 42 game winning streak, Clair Bee declared "the balance of basketball power for 1940 lies west of the Mississippi."

NYU, LIU, and St. John's, although not as extensively as the previous decade. CCNY and NYU each had four Jewish starters at different times during the season, St. John's had three starters, and LIU had two Jewish starters as well as 5'8" Jackie Goldsmith, who came off the bench to lead the Metropolitan district in scoring.[18] These teams continued to headline the double-headers at Madison Square Garden and receive attention from the national press. Yet, CCNY, the school that continued to represent Jewish basketball in the minds of American Jews, had minimal success as the basketball culture changed between 1938 and 1945.

In the 1930s, Nat Holman served as the 'face' of both New York and Jewish basketball. His professional experience led the mainstream press to praise his 'scientific' coaching and his authorship of books such as *Scientific Basketball* (1922) and *Winning Basketball* (1932) solidified his reputation as a basketball expert and led to commercial and promotional opportunities. As early as 1936, he had a ten-minute radio program on WNYC and in 1934, *Time* explained his unique place in college basketball: "in his spare time, he studies sculpture."[19] Historian Peter Levine illustrated that the Jewish press often portrayed Holman as a link between the immigrant past and the native-born future. He served as the sole representative of basketball in the 1938-39 edition of *Who's Who in American Jewry*.[20]

Holman could not have represented Jewish basketball by himself. The preponderance of Jews on CCNY team, which Levine estimated at 83% of all

---

[18] On scoring, see "Individual Scoring," *New York Times*, March 11, 1946. Also see "All-Met," *New York Times*, March 10, 1946.

[19] On Holman's commercial activities, see his file at the Edward and Gena Hickox Library at the Basketball Hall of Fame, Springfield, MA. Also see the Nat Holman Papers, the City College of New York Archives, New York; "Hakoah Meets Bruins Tonight in Cage Tussle," *Chicago Tribune*, December 26, 1928. "Basketball: Mid-season Report," *Time*, February 19, 1934.

[20] Levine, *Ellis Island to Ebbets Field*, 56-59. Nat Holman in John Simons, ed., *Who's Who in American Jewry: A Biograhical Dictionary of Living Jews of the United States and Canada* (New York: National News Association Inc., 1939). See Nat Holman, *Scientific Basketball* (New York: Incra Pub. Co., 1922); Nat Holman, *Winning Basketball* (New York: Charles Scribner's Sons, 1932); Nat Holman, *Holman on Basketball* (New York: Crown Publishers, 1950).

players during Holman's tenure, meant the school continued to represent the broader success of Jewish basketball. In addition, CCNY's reputation for intellectual debate, radical thought, and tough academic admissions encouraged the general belief that Holman could not recruit star players.[21] Fans believed Holman's teams "played five-man basketball," since "talent receives no special consideration" at the school. In fact, "it is miraculous that out of the paucity of material, Holman could weld a unit able to compete at all in intercollegiate basketball."[22] The perception of Holman's teams reinforced the Progressive idea that teamwork and intelligence could overcome physical ability. Although no successful sport program existed without talent, press reports concentrated on Holman's ability to "mold" individuals into a competitive team since "outstanding individual stars are missing, and perhaps Holman would have it that way. His contention is that basketball is essentially a team game."[23]

In the early years of the national tournaments, Holman refused to acquiesce to the changing structure of college basketball. Convinced that basketball remained a "small man's game," Holman continued to produce teams that represented this ideology. Prior to the 1938-39 season, analysts declared that CCNY would have a poor season because the team, "sets an all-time high for low stature, even at City College, where a six-footer is as rare." In December 1938, CCNY had a surprising victory over the "tall firs" of Oregon, the eventual NCAA champion that year, which the New York press celebrated as "a great start in the

---

[21] According to historian Sherry Gorelick, less than one percent of the children of Jewish immigrants reached college and even fewer graduated in the first decade of the twentieth century. Even the celebrated and difficult entrance requirements into City College that caused many people to call CCNY the "Harvard of the Proletariat" only took effect in the late 1930s and before that decade, graduating classes generally numbered in the hundreds. See Shirley Gorelick, *City College and the Jewish Poor: Education in New York, 1880-1924* (New Brunswick: Rutgers University Press, 1981), 3. Also see Steinberg, *The Ethnic Myth*, 128-138. Joel Perlmann explained that in 1908, well below five percent of the Russian Jewish children in the city graduated from high school. See Joel Perlmann, *Ethnic Differences: Schooling and Social Structure among the Irish, Italians, Jews, and Blacks in an American City, 1880-1935* (New York: Cambridge University Press, 1988), 123.

[22] "Readers' Right," *New York Post*, March 12, 1936.

[23] "Holman Stresses Form at CCNY," *New York Post*, December 2, 1931.

New York vs. Rest of the World rivalry." This win only provided brief success as the team struggled during the rest of the season and then finished with a record of 8-8 in 1939-1940. CCNY earned a spot in the NIT the next two seasons, finishing in third place in 1941, but the school had a losing record in 1943 and did not play in either postseason tournament between 1943 and 1946.[24]

In 1946, CCNY returned to their previous level of success and entered its final regular season game with a record of 13-4. Few sportswriters or fans gave CCNY a chance against the No. 1 ranked NYU team, which had a record of 18-1 and had won 13 consecutive games. The build-up to the game reminded many writers of the 1934 CCNY-NYU game and "fans started camping out in front of the ticket booths" four hours before tickets went on sale at 9:00am. The ticket demand led to nine arrests for "ticket speculation" and the temporary suspension of ticket sales at 9:20am because the "line had become so long and so out of hand." Eventually, "ten mounted policemen and a detail of foot police restored order." By 3pm, "16,000 tickets" had been sold.[25]

In a surprising upset, CCNY defeated NYU by a score of 49-44 and set off a wave of celebration. According to the *New York Times*, "within fifteen minutes after the game ended, a band of about 1,000 C.C.N.Y. rooters massed near the Garden" and paraded through the streets with "a 'casket' painted in black and covered with NYU pennants and lettering." When the "marchers" reached Broadway, they "started a huge snake dance which caused a traffic tie-up and created an uproar as motorists sounded their horns in an effort to break through." The parade entered Times Square and "then headed for the Hudson [River] to dispose of the casket."[26]

---

[24] Quote on 'small man's game' and 'low stature,' from "Pessimists Ruled Out as Holman's Beavers Prepare for Opener," *New York Evening Post*, December 1, 1938; "Fury and Finesse Lead to Same Results when Beavers and Redmen Take to Court," *New York Evening Post*, December 19, 1938. In the final game of the 1939 season, CCNY defeated previously undefeated (and No. 1) NYU team to finish 8-8. CCNY also had three straight losing seasons in the mid-1940s.

[25] "Basketball Fans Stage Ticket Rush." *New York Times*, March 6, 1946.

[26] "Times Square Parade Marks C.C.N.Y. Victory," *New York Times*, March 8, 1946.

The intense celebration reflected the belief among CCNY students and fans that the victory would result in an invitation to the NIT. Considering the school's absence from post-season tournaments since 1942, many hoped this would revitalize the basketball program. Yet, the day after CCNY's victory, the NIT announced that Rhode Island State and not City College would be the tournament's final entrant. Students, furious with the decision, "assailed the tournament committee for what they termed publicity 'exploitation' in creating the impression that City would receive a berth if it defeated N.Y.U."[27] Students condemned Garden promoters and NIT officials for using the promise of a tournament berth to increase fan interest, and thus profit, in the CCNY-NYU contest. Letters of protest to Ned Irish stated that the tournament committee should have named Rhode Island State before the game. The ticket demand for the game, the celebration following the CCNY victory, and the angry response to the team's exclusion from the tournament indicated the popularity of CCNY within New York basketball and the intense passions involved in college basketball at Madison Square Garden.

Despite the disappointment of the 1946 season, CCNY had greater success in 1947. That year, Holman led the team to a regular season record of 15-4, including a 91-60 victory over NYU. CCNY then defeated Syracuse to qualify for the NCAA tournament, where it finished in fourth-place. CCNY included Holman's first African-American players, Sonny Jameson and Joe Galiber, both of whom would serve as captains in future seasons. The team, which remained predominantly Jewish with four starters and five reserves, became involved in an incident at the Garden that reflected the intensity of college basketball. The incident's aftermath indicated American Jews' growing acceptance in American society and their continued anxiety regarding the permanence of this acceptance.

On December 27, 1946, CCNY played the University of Wyoming at the Garden. A close game until the final minutes when CCNY pulled away, the "thrill packed struggle" almost turned into "bedlam" as a result of "two near-

---

[27] "C.C.N.Y. Protests Choice of R.I. State," *New York Times*, March 9, 1946.

fights, one on the court involving the players and the other on the rival benches." The *New York Times* reported that "when the players tangled on the floor, everyone knew what it was about – a lot of tense athletes, pushing each around in the heat of battle." In contrast, "no one could imagine what was behind the verbal conflict – with threatening gestures – that went on on the benches."

During the game, CCNY's Nat Holman advanced toward Wyoming coach Everett Shelton twice. Holman then refused to shake Shelton's hand at the end, which made it "apparent that something was radically wrong." After the game, Holman explained in an interview that, "I heard Shelton uttering derogatory remarks and took exception. In fact, I threatened to punch him if he repeated them."[28] *Newsweek* quoted Shelton as stating: "those New York Jews are getting away with everything." Three days after the game, Shelton apologized, although he "denied that his words…were anti-Semitic." He explained: "I am very sorry that my remarks caused such a disturbance…what I said about Jews had nothing to do with religion or anything else. The word 'Jew' was merely descriptive. I did not swear. In our section of the country, when we play against Indians we call them Indians and we call Swedes Swedes."[29]

The incident triggered an outpouring of anti-Semitic letters sent to Holman. 'Anonymous' exclaimed that Christians "hate you and your hooked-nose foreigners." A letter from Dallas differentiated "we Americans" from the "Jew" and stated that "Hitlers" will continue "springing up all over the world unless the jew changes himself…it is not the people that need changing as much as it is the jew." Another letter broached the stereotype of the weak Jew. "You people should learn to punch and not squeak and everyone would give you more credit. That is the real American way." Finally, a self-proclaimed Irishman

---

[28] "City College Tops Wyoming Quintet in Garden, 57 to 48," *New York Times*, December 28, 1946.

[29] "Basketball Coach Makes An Apology," *New York Times*, December 31, 1946; "Basketball: Heated Words," *Newsweek*, January 6, 1947. One report found in the Nat Holman archives indicated that Shelton actually stated that, "those New York Jews and Niggers are getting away with everything." However, the press focused on Shelton's use of the word 'Jew' and no other correspondence or report confirmed this account.

declared that when "we Irish" were attacked, "we simply laugh the jackass down." Jews needed to learn this skill, since, "the jockeying in sports is part of the game and this incident at the Garden was much akin to such doings."[30]

Holman also received supportive letters from both Jews and non-Jews. The Anti-Defamation League (ADL) hoped Shelton would provide a sincere apology because he "was guilty of an unsportsmanlike, an un-American and a dangerous act."[31] The CCNY faculty athletic committee passed a resolution that the school would no longer schedule games "against teams coached by Shelton." Milton Gross, the former vice president of the Metropolitan Basketball Writers Association, declared that "Shelton had forfeited his right to coach a basketball team."[32] Other individuals and organizations condemned Shelton's remarks and sent letters of support to Holman. The Labor Sports Federation, the Jewish Postal Workers Welfare League, National Negro Congress, and the American Labor Party all praised Holman for his actions. Some of Holman's former players also expressed pride in his actions as "a long step in striking against racial and religious intolerance which unfortunately prevails in our institutions of higher learning today."[33] The incident and response, from Holman's supporters and opponents, reflected the experiences of American Jews in the 1940s.

The American Jewish community experienced both exclusion and acceptance during World War II. Public indifference to the Holocaust, opposition

---

[30] Many of the correspondence held in the CCNY Archives contained vicious attacks on Holman personally and American Jews in general. See Anonymous to Nat Holman, January 2, 1947; W.B. Johnson to Nat Holman, undated; George Biltman to Nat Holman, January 6, 1947; John J. Hurley to Nat Holman (and Dan Parker of the *New York Daily Mirror*), January 3, 1947. All letters in the Nat Holman Papers, Box 2, Holman, Nat. Correspondence. Wyoming Game. 1946. CCNY Archives, New York.

[31] Meier Steinbrink to Harry Wright, December 31, 1946, Nat Holman Papers, Box 2, Holman, Nat. Correspondence. Wyoming Game. 1946. CCNY Archives, New York.

[32] "Basketball Coach Makes An Apology," *New York Times*, December 31, 1946.

[33] See Leon Slofrock to Nat Holman, December 30, 1946; Louis Brumberg to Nat Holman, December 30, 1946; Max Yergen to Nat Holman, December 30, 1946; Samuel Kaplan to Nat Holman, December 30, 1946. All letters in Nat Holman Papers, Box 2, Holman, Nat. Correspondence. Wyoming Game. 1946. CCNY Archives, New York. Quote from player Sam Liss to Nat Holman, January 7, 1947.

to Jewish immigration, and concern regarding a post-war economic recession intensified American Jews' insecurity. Polls during World War II indicated that American anti-Semitism peaked in 1944 and "approximately 30% of employment advertisements in 1942 in the *New York Times and New York Herald Tribune* expressed a preference for Christians." Yet, the fight again Nazi aggression, intolerance, and racism changed Americans' conception of Jews, and Jews' conceptions of themselves. As they had during World War I, American Jews celebrated Jewish participation in the war effort. This time, the government supported the effort. The Office of War Information produced "platoon movies" that included stock images of the "New York Jew," as well as the "southern farmer, Texas cowboy, an Ivy League intellectual, a Boston Irishman, and an Italian from Brooklyn." Historian Deborah Dash Moore explained that serving in the armed forces made native-born Jews "more American and more Jewish."[34]

The war, and Jewish soldiers' return to civilian life, helped transform the American Jewish community. The war and the Holocaust devastated European Jewish communities. American Jews experienced a religious revival from the feeling among that "assimilation appeared to be a cowardly betrayal of the six million European Jews who were murdered simply because they were Jews."[35] Internal class and ideological differences became less important as American Jews turned the fight against anti-Semitism into a crusade. Defense organizations such as the Anti-Defamation League (ADL), American Jewish Committee (AJC), and the American Jewish Congress (AJCongress) examined whether the psychological roots of anti-Semitism were pathological. Even Hollywood's

---

[34] Edward S. Shapiro, "World War II and American Jewish Identity," *Modern Judaism* 10, no. 1 (February 1990): 69- 75. Quotes on 69, 75. Deborah Dash Moore, *GI Jews: How World War II Changed a Generation* (Cambridge, MA: Belknap Press, 2004), x.

[35] Shapiro, "World War II and American Jewish Identity," 74.

Jewish 'moguls,' who had avoided any depiction of the 'Jew' after 1929's *The Jazz Singer*, produced post-war films that attacked anti-Semitism.[36]

American Jews remained aware of their religious and cultural difference from non-Jews, but they had united behind America's fight against fascism, intolerance, and hatred. In 1946, the JWB produced a two-volume work that celebrated the *multi-ethnic* make-up of the American war effort. Along with Protestantism and Catholicism, Judaism became part of an American civic religion. The Shelton-Holman incident indicated that American Jews still needed to defend against charges of foreignness or difference, although Mississippi Senator John Rankin and others found that most Americans did not accept anti-Semitic attacks after the war as they had before.[37] A book published in 1948 contained less defensive posturing than Stanley Frank's book had only 12 years earlier and indicated that Jews had joined mainstream society. Yet, it also included a sense of Jewish difference as indicated by the final prominent appearance of the basketball Jew during this era of Jewish basketball.

In 1948, author Harold Ribalow published *The Jew in American Sports*, not in response to any controversy regarding Jewish athleticism, but rather, to celebrate the achievement of a group of integrated "American athletes." The book's introduction reflected the notion that sport provided American Jews with freedom and opportunity, since "it and its followers are, in essence, democrats and tolerant Americans." Boxer Barney Ross prefaced the book, however, by explaining that even in the 1940s, Jewish athletes carried "the burden of being a Jew. It is a burden he carries in common with other minorities, which affects all of his behavior."[38] Ross indicated that Jewish athleticism no longer stood alone. Yet, Ribalow spoke to the Jewish project that had been constructed to destroy the

---

[36] On the defense work of Jewish organizations and Hollywood films, see Shapiro, "World War II and American Jewish Identity," 69-78. On an interpretation of the *Jazz Singer*'s significance, see Rogin, *Blackface, White Noise*.

[37] See Shapiro, *A Time for Healing*, 35-40. On the decline of American anti-Semitism, see Dinnerstein, *Antisemitism in America*, 150-174.

[38] Harold Ribalow, *The Jew in American Sports* (New York: Block Publishing Co., 1948), ix-x, 4.

stereotype of the weak Jew. The project may have ended, but Jews continued to face this burden. Thus, Ribalow felt the need to explain that his boxing champions retained a sense of power since they illustrated "to sports fans that Jews can fight. They don't need lengthy, scientific treatises to show them that Jews have guts; they don't need long histories revealing that Jews have an admirable war record to prove it."[39]

Ribalow celebrated the aggressive masculinity of American sport and presented Jewish athleticism as an individual pursuit. He provided brief introductory sections on specifics sports, but chapters focused on individual champions, many of whom he interviewed for the book. Ribalow provided extensive attention to baseball, amounting to eleven chapters, including those on an umpire as well as baseball's 'Clown Prince,' Al Schacht. He also featured six boxers, three football players, a bull-fighter, chess player, golfer, and a number of 'also-rans' in hockey, tennis, soccer, bowling, ice-skating, fencing, horse racing, and track and field. He explained that "close followers of sports will notice that figures in many sports are omitted." He could not write a complete history because that would include "good, but not outstanding" athletes. Nor could he include "a Jewish ping-pong star (and there are Jewish stars in this fast game)," because "too few readers are interested in reading about people they never heard of, in sports they barely know about."[40]

Despite the historical importance of Jews in basketball, Ribalow included chapters on only two basketball players. Not surprisingly, Nat Holman served as Ribalow's first basketball 'champion.' Ribalow exalted Holman whose personal "history" coincided with the "history of basketball itself." Ribalow traced Holman's career through its various stages and proudly celebrated his achievements in both the basketball and Jewish worlds. Holman succeeded at CCNY despite the school's "high scholastic requirements. Of course there is no

---

[39] Ibid., 3. Ribalow wrote *Fighting Heroes of Israel* in 1967.

[40] Ibid., 252. The bullfighter was Sidney Franklin, who was originally from Brooklyn. For information on Franklin, see Postal, Silver, and Silver, *Encyclopedia of Jews in Sports*, 181.

subsidation of athletes. And the scholastic grind is difficult." Most impressively, Holman generally had to work with "poor boys who might otherwise not get a chance to go to college," most of whom had been "unschooled in basketball" prior to arriving at CCNY.[41] For his second basketball player, Ribalow did not choose Barney Sedran or other players of the past. Rather, he featured Harry Boykoff, the 6'9" former St. John's star who had just turned professional.

Ribalow narrated Boykoff's college career at length and celebrated his burgeoning professional career, but not as evidence of Jewish athleticism in the traditional sense. Ribalow explained that Boykoff, a native-born Jew of immigrant parents, worked hard at basketball and eventually received an athletic scholarship to college. When Ribalow asked Holman how Boykoff compared against the all-time Jewish greats, the coach minimized the tall center and ranked him below many others. Ribalow noted that historically, "some of the silliest-looking basketball players have been the bean-pole athletes who were put into a game merely because of their size – and they found the little men literally ran rings around them." That began to change as coaches took "the gangling giants" and taught them how to "move around like an average-size basketball player."[42] Ribalow's text indicated that Boykoff, unlike Jews of the past, succeeded despite his size, not because of it.

Ribalow presented two contradictory opinions regarding Jews' success in basketball. He explained that "the predominance of Jews in the hoop sport is so evident that it has been the subject of learned articles and scientific treatises which attempt to prove that Jews are so built that they can best stand up under the tension, strain, and stamina [of basketball]." He noted that explanations had connected Jewish success to various characteristics: "(1) Jews are short and short men have better balance and more speed afoot; (2) they have sharper eyes and (3)

---

[41] Ibid., 230-231.

[42] Ibid., 238-249. Boykoff was coached at Jefferson High School by Mac Hodseblatt, "a CCNY man and, therefore, a Nat Holman man." Hodesblatt played for Holman at CCNY in the early 1920s.

239

they have clever minds." According to Ribalow, these explanations have "been demonstrated to be all hokum." He explained that "Jews *starred* on the basketball courts for one reason. Basketball is primarily a game for crowded cities." Holman's unquestioned expertise and skill led Ribalow to ask: "how he explained the great number of great Jewish players." Holman "pointed to the fact that Jews live in the big cities, where the game is played a great deal. He stressed that the game is a natural for Jewish boys. 'The Jew, he said, 'is fast, generally short…and alert mentally.'"[43]

Ribalow treated Jews as fully integrated individuals who had in the past used sport to become productive citizens. Outside of his focus on Boykoff, his historical narrative of basketball, which "sparkles with countless Jewish names," ended in the mid-1930s when CCNY, NYU, and LIU ruled the courts. By presenting Jewish basketball in past terms, Ribalow illustrated that it no longer served a specific Jewish project. The decline of Jewish basketball coincided with the recent "growth of the Mid-West and Far West as basketball centers," which had led the "tall blond lads of the plains and the sunny West" to take "their rightful place in the game."[44] Boykoff, as well as these 'tall blond lads,' served as the antithesis of the small and shifty basketball Jew and represented the future of basketball. Individual Jewish players had adapted to the changing structure of mainstream basketball. Yet, Ribalow provided Holman a platform in which to present his case for the basketball Jew. Ribalow's text thus included the presentation that basketball, as an urban sport, allowed the Jew to succeed because of shortness, quickness, and intelligence. The continued prominence of Jewish players in the late 1940s allowed Holman to place the basketball Jew into the present culture even as Ribalow and others viewed things from a different perspective.

Despite the reemergence of Holman's CCNY teams in 1946 and 1947, New York basketball, and its connection to Jewish basketball, seemed to have

---

[43] Ibid., 224, 232. Italics mine.

[44] Ibid., 223-224.

suffered in the post-war era. The New York and Jewish presence in the NIT declined during and immediately following the war. Three New York City teams played in the NIT in 1943 and two teams played in 1947, but only one city school appeared in 1944, 1945, 1946, and 1948. The declining number of schools inevitably impacted the success of New York and Jewish basketball. Between 1945-1948, no New York school won the NIT, and only one school, NYU in 1948, even reached the championship game.[45] In 1949, the NIT expanded its field to 12 teams in order to include more city schools. The result brought the entire culture of New York and Jewish basketball into question.

In 1949, four New York teams received invitations to the NIT because tournament officials did not want to decide between them for the eighth, and final, spot. New York sportswriters had argued prior to the tournament that "New York rated no representative in the tourney," and the result seemed to prove that "none of the local quintets justified its presence on the court." All four New York teams, CCNY, NYU, St. John's, and Manhattan, lost in the first round, which led the *New York Times* to state that, "some fans are calling it the 'New York Massacre.'"[46] The 'massacre' led commentators to conclude that New York basketball had fallen to previously unseen depths. Louis Effrat of the *New York Times* blamed a peculiarity of New York basketball for local schools' failure. The losses "proved that what New York needs, possibly even more than a good ten-cent cigar, are good big men on its college quintets. Whereas, invariably, visiting teams move in with elongated talent, the locals have to play with comparatively small athletes."[47]

Much like the condemnation of the 'Metropolitan player' after the Stanford-LIU game in 1936, negative values were attached to the New York

---

[45] Douchant, *Inside College Basketball*.

[46] "Afternoon, Night Twin Bills Today on Invitation Court Tourney Slate," *New York Times*, March 14, 1949.

[47] Louis Effrat, "Loyola Conquers City College Five in Garden 62 to 47," *New York Times*, March 13, 1949.

player. The belief that the 'Metropolitan' player could not compete with taller, more athletic players had been proven unequivocally false during the late 1930s and 1940s. The 'massacre' appeared to concretely illustrate that the city's short, speedy player no longer had a place in college basketball. Effrat did not explicitly connect the 'small' New York player to the 'Jew,' but New York basketball had long been associated with Jewish basketball and Effrat's 'small' athletes conformed to the continued perception of Jewish players. Yet, the following season, CCNY's recovered from the 'massacre' in a manner which indicated that even Nat Holman had determined the basketball Jew could no longer succeed. As Holman put together the greatest team in school history, he did so with players that bore little physical resemblance to the traditional CCNY player.

In 1950, the CCNY team included a class of sophomores that sportswriters considered the best recruiting class in school history. Jewish starters, 6'3" sophomore guard Al 'Fats' Roth, 6'6" sophomore center Ed Roman, and 6'4" senior forward Irwin Dambrot played alongside two African-American starters, sophomores 6'3" guard Floyd Layne and 6'4" forward Ed Warner. Basketball historian Neil Isaacs described the team as "taller than a typical Holman squad and more versatile." The team played well early in the year, rose to a No. 7 ranking in the Associated Press (AP) poll, and finished the season with a record of 17-5. The team went undefeated against Metropolitan opponents and earned an invitation to the NIT.[48] Many believed the team would again lose in the first round. Instead, over an 18 day span, CCNY achieved one of the greatest feats in college basketball history.

On March 12, 1950, CCNY defeated San Francisco, the twelfth ranked team in the country, in the first round of the NIT. The team then triumphed over the two-time defending NCAA champion, No. 3 Kentucky by a score of 89-50. CCNY defeated No. 6 Duquesne in the semifinals before beating No. 1 Bradley in the championship game. CCNY then played in the NCAA tournament, which began four days after the NIT final. CCNY proceeded to defeat No. 2 Ohio State

---

[48] Isaacs, *All the Moves*, 95.

and No. 5 North Carolina State to set up a rematch with Bradley in the final. The game began with Holman absent due to a 103 degree temperature and became a thrilling affair that came down to the final seconds. With a one point lead, CCNY's 'super sub' Norm Mager stole the ball from Bradley's star Gene Melchiorre and scored a final basket to complete CCNY's 71-68 victory.[49]

CCNY became the only school in basketball history to win both the NIT and NCAA tournaments in the same season, considered the 'Grand Slam.' After winning both tournaments, the school cancelled classes and parades honored the team. *Sport* magazine named Holman its "Man of the Year." According to historian Edward Shapiro, Holman also "received invitations to speak at Congregation Rodeph Shalom and the Ramaz School, an Orthodox day school" in Manhattan. New York newspapers hailed the coach and the players, who the *New York Herald Tribune* called "our boys." When asked about his players' "exceptional gifts," however, Holman downplayed their talent and "insisted that the 14 players – all of them products of a teeming city's public schools – were essentially 'just a group of intelligent boys in excellent physical condition.'"[50]

Holman did not connect his 'intelligent boys' to the basketball Jew, which belonged to a previous era. The players also had virtually no connection to the project that had produced this era of Jewish basketball, although remnants of the culture remained. The Jewish players of the post-war era did not learn the game in Jewish centers or other communal institutions. The *New York Times* described CCNY's players, both Jewish and black, as coming "from the sidewalks of New

---

[49] On the CCNY championships, see Isaacs, *All the Moves*, 97-100; Bjarkman, *Hoopla*, 63-68; Stanley Cohen, *The Game They Played* (New York: Farrar, Straus, and Giroux, 1977). Many believed Mechiorre was fouled, which was not called because the game was held in New York City.

[50] See Edward Shapiro, "The Shame of the City: CCNY Basketball, 1950-51," in Kugelmass, *Jews, Sports, and the Rites of Citizenship*, 181-183. "Basketball: Bradley Weardown," *Newsweek*, April 10, 1950. Levine, *Ellis Island to Ebbet's Field*, 78-81. In the early twentieth century, it became common to hail the coaches for their ability to turn players, including those not considered athletics, into winning teams. See Overman, *The Influence of the Protestant Ethic on Sport and Recreation*, 166-169.

York."[51] In the post-war era, the Jewish champions would be found on the streets, playgrounds, and schools of New York City's Jewish neighborhoods.

The early careers of two of the top New York players of the post-war era, Max Zasflofsky and Dolph Schayes, attested to the change in Jewish basketball. A 6'2" guard/forward, Zaslofsky played only one season at St. John's in 1946, after a two-year stint in the army, before turning professional. He remembered that as a youngster, "most of my time was spent in the schoolyards, playing basketball."[52] Likewise, the Bronx's Dolph Schayes who became an All-American as a 6'8" forward with NYU, received the majority of his basketball training on the streets and schoolyards. Schayes played basketball "because that's what you basically did in those days. The schoolyards were full of baskets, Saturdays and after school you would play ball." Both thrived in the playground culture that structured its hierarchy from the oldest and biggest players to the smallest and youngest. This culture provided opportunity for individual advancement, which helped Zaslofsky's career, since as a youth, his "one desire was to be a professional basketball player." Schayes also benefited from the playground hierarchy and he remembered that, "since I was taller, I played a lot with the older players."[53] The schoolyards indicated that Jewish basketball on the local level had moved to informal and unsupervised locations. Both players chose to spend the majority of their leisure time there rather than in organized Jewish life. This did not, however, diminish their identification with being Jewish.

Zaslofsky and Schayes chose basketball success over involvement in Jewish activities, but the Jewishness of their neighborhoods allowed them to retain a distinct Jewish identity. Growing up in Brownsville, Zaslofsky became a member of the Brownsville Boys Club as a youth. The loosely organized club

---

[51] Shapiro, "The Shame of the City," 181.

[52] Interview with Max Zaslofsky, August 27, 1980, The New York Public Library – American Jewish Committee Oral History Collection, Dorot Jewish Division, The New York Public Library.

[53] Ibid. Interview with Dolph Schayes, May 27, 1991, The New York Public Library – American Jewish Committee Oral History Collection, Dorot Jewish Division, The New York Public Library.

formed in 1940 due to a lack of facilities in which to play sports, especially basketball, and evolved into a more formal organization over time. Historian Gerald Sorin explained that the club expressed a unique American Jewish identity forged by a dense Jewish neighborhood.[54] For Zaslofsky, however, basketball and a formal Jewishness competed. He attended *cheder*, or Hebrew day school, until his Bar Mitzvah at the age of 13, but while he "would have loved to really stress the Jewish heritage as a youngster, I was pulled somewhat from it."[55] Zaslofsky overlooked his personal choice in the matter, but Schayes explained that his lack of "formal Jewish background," did not diminish his feeling that the neighborhood's "Jewishness was ever present." Schayes spoke for many of his generation when he explained that, "you just knew you were Jewish because it was obvious…everyone around you was Jewish."[56]

Zaslofsky and Schayes played in a Jewish basketball culture that began during the project of Jewish athleticism. The Jewish community center no longer existed within this culture, but Jewish basketball adapted as a neighborhood game on the local level. Schayes and Zaslofsky, as well as other Jewish basketball champions of the 1940s, retained their connection to Jewish basketball even as they succeeded on their own terms, outside of communal control. Yet, this element of Jewish basketball would not last long. Jewish urban neighborhoods like Brownsville would soon decline due to suburban migration, which restricted the ability of future generations to learn basketball in a similar informal Jewish environment. Schayes and Zaslofsky became the last great Jewish players produced within the culture of Jewish basketball.

In 1949, Jewish columnist Haskell Cohen explained in his annual that American Jews' upward economic mobility had started to have a negative impact

---

[54] Sorin, *The Nurturing Neighborhood*.

[55] Interview with Max Zaslofsky, August 27, 1980, Dorot Jewish Division, NYPL. While it is difficult to rely on the memory of Jewish players, these histories exemplified the complexities surrounding the use of basketball to form an identity. The players' closeness to the game allowed them a distinct view of the game's importance to themselves and the larger community.

[56] Interview with Dolph Schayes, May 27, 1991, The New York Public Library, NYPL.

on Jewish athleticism. Basketball remained the sport that could be "counted upon for the best report," but "the comparatively high sport dollar seemingly held little attraction for Jewish boys who prefer the stability and safety of professional and business pursuits."[57] Cohen's statement reflected American Jews' socio-economic mobility, suburban migration, and the security that Jews felt in the post-war era. It also reflected the changing economic structure of professional sports. Previous generations of Jewish players emerged from schools, centers, and colleges to earn less than $100 per game in the regional ABL, and most players had other jobs, frequently as teachers or physical educators. In contrast, St. John's center Harry Boykoff signed a professional contract in 1948 at an annual salary of $10,000.[58] Professional players in the post-war game would be taller *and* richer. They also participated in a very different environment as professional basketball moved away from its traditional culture.

Modern professional basketball emerged out of the basketball culture of World War II. During the war, armed forces teams such as the Great Lakes Naval Training Station and Mitchell Field toured the country as "morale" boosters and produced a unique basketball environment. College and professional players often played together on these teams, which existed outside of AAU or NCAA control. These teams contributed to the stylistic standardization of basketball, increased familiarity among players and coaches, and helped expand the professional game.[59] At the end of the war, many players who served in the armed forces eschewed the semi-professional leagues of the northeast and went to the Midwest, where until 1937 professional basketball had existed as an unofficial activity. That year, industrial teams formed the National Basketball League (NBL) and recruited players from local areas such as Akron and Fort Wayne. The

---

[57] Haskell Cohen, "Basketball Made Best Sports Report of Year," *American Jewish World*, September 23, 1949.

[58] Ribalow, *The Jew in American Sports*, 249.

[59] Neil D. Isaacs, *Vintage NBA: The Pioneer Era, 1946-1956* (Masters Press, 1996), xii-xiii; Vincent, *The Rise and Fall of American Sports*, 284-288.

NBL existed as a regional league until World War II when it attempted to become a 'national' league, hoping to take advantage of Americans' desire for leisure and entertainment in a post-war consumer economy.[60]

In order to provide itself with a 'national' feel, the NBL brought in two 'eastern' teams in the mid-1940s. The Rochester Royals joined in 1945 and the Syracuse Nationals joined the following year. The ABL remained a regional and semi-professional league and the full-time NBL attracted the best college talent, who turned professional as 'finished,' or ready, players. The eastern style of play remained predominant, although some teams used the fast break more often than professionals had in the past. The NBL also began attracting eastern players such as Harry Boykoff and CCNY's 'Red' Holzman. Boykoff, who made as much as $15,000 in one season, signed with the NBL's Toledo Jeeps upon graduating from St. John's in 1947. Holzman signed with the Royals in 1945 after the team's owner, Jewish entrepreneur Les Harrison, had mistakenly hired Fuzzy Levane, an Italian-American, as his 'Jewish' player. Harrison's desire for a Jewish player indicated that the model of the 1920s 'national' ABL continued to appeal to basketball owners. Harrison wanted to attract as many spectators as possible by becoming the central focus of his city's basketball culture.[61]

In 1946, the NBL, seemingly poised to dominate professional basketball in the post-war consumer society, received unwanted competition. On November 1, 1946, *New York Times* columnist Arthur Daley welcomed a "newcomer" to professional basketball. Daley focused on an important component of the league,

---

[60] On the NBL, see Peterson, *Cages to Jump Shots*, 124-138; Isaacs, *Vintage NBA*, xiii. Two Akron companies, Firestone and Goodyear as well as Fort Wayne's General Electric constructed the most powerful teams. The NBL actually started as the Midwestern Basketball League in 1935 as a quasi-amateur league. One of the teams was the Pittsburgh YMHA. According to basketball historian Robert Peterson, the league changed its name in order to avoid competition in the press with the Big Ten, which was often described as the "Midwest Conference."

[61] On Boykoff's salary, see "Harry Boykoff, 78, St. John's Star in the 1940's, Dies," *New York Times*, April 15, 2001. On Holzman's signing with Rochester, see Interview with Red Holzman, March 21, 1978, The New York Public Library – American Jewish Committee Oral History Collection, Dorot Jewish Division, The New York Public Library. Also see Isaacs, *Vintage NBA*, 81. Holzman declared that his Jewishness played little part in his basketball career, but failed to recognize its importance in Harrison's decision to sign him.

"whose franchises are held by arena owners." Considering that the "lack of adequate facilities has been the main stumbling block for all previous circuits," Daley concluded that the league "cannot help but succeed eventually."[62] That night, the first game of the Basketball Association of America (BAA) took place in Canada as the Toronto Huskies hosted the New York Knicks. Knicks owner, and Garden promoter, Ned Irish filled his team with local, and Jewish, talent. Former college stars such as Ossie Schectman, Sonny Hertzberg, Hank Rosenstein, and others had name recognition and the Knicks' home opener attracted over 17,000 fans. According to historian Robert Peterson, during half-time, the fans "saw a fur fashion show and a brief game, ending in a 1-1 tie, between a team of New York Giant football players and the old Original Celtics," including Nat Holman. The initial interest notwithstanding, the Knicks played only five more games at Madison Square Garden because of college basketball's predominance in New York and other cities. The rest of the Knicks' home games took place at the 7,000-seat 69th Regiment Armory.[63]

The BAA received only cursory attention in the mainstream press during its first season, although basketball fans paid attention when Philadelphia's Joe Fulks, a jump shooter, became the BAA's first scoring champion. The non-Jewish Fulks, a virtual unknown in professional circles before the 1946 season, had played for the Marines All-Star team during the war. While serving in the armed forces, he came to the attention of Petey Rosenberg, a former player for the

---

[62] Arthur Daley, "Sport of the Times," *New York Times*, November 1, 1946. Other professional teams and leagues recognized that the BAA may be successful and formed the National Association of Professional Basketball (NAPB) to unify the sport. The BAA refused to join. Members in the NAPB came from the NBL, ABL, Eastern League and other minor leagues. 52 teams were represented by the league in October 1946, just prior to the start of the BAA season. See "Pro Basketball Circuits form National Group," *Chicago Tribune*, October 27, 1946; Also see Applin, "From Muscular Christianity to the Marketplace," 234. For information on the post-war consumer culture, see Lizabeth Cohen, *A Consumer's Republic: The Politics of Mass Consumption in Postwar America* (New York: Knopf, 2003).

[63] Schectman scored the new league's first basket as the Knicks beat the Huskies, 68-66. The victory received a limited amount of information in the New York media. By the end of the season, the majority of the Jewish players on the Knicks had been traded or released. Rumors surfaced that it was because the league did not want to the team to be too Jewish. On the Knicks home opener, see Peterson, *Cages to Jump Shots*, 154.

Philadelphia Sphas. Rosenberg recommended Fulks to Eddie Gottlieb, the owner and coach of the Philadelphia Warriors. Rosenberg, a native-Philadelphian, became one of the three Jewish players on the Warriors, which won the league's first championship during the 1946-47 season.[64]

BAA owners attempted to transform professional basketball. The BAA instituted a draft in order to acquire college players immediately after their college eligibility had ended. A majority of the owners also had hockey backgrounds, which led them to construct an elaborate playoff system that extended the season and increased commercial possibilities. Owners agreed on an unofficial salary cap, which caused Dolph Schayes to sign with the NBL's Syracuse Nationals because it could pay him more than the BAA's Knicks. Owners did, however, provide players with signing bonuses and provided other amenities. Former LIU star Ossie Schectman, who received a $5,000 salary and a $3,000 signing bonus remembered that in the ABL, he had played for "$75 a game; the owner handed you an envelope with your money after the game. There was no contract, no training camp. Nobody taped your ankles. When we went to the Knicks' first training camp at the Nevele in the Catskills, I felt like a pioneer."[65]

Despite these moves, the BAA had to contend with the NBL, which had a better competitive reputation and attracted better talent. Competing for the services of players took a toll on both leagues. At the end of the 1947-48 season, the two leagues had reached a stalemate. The NBL had a stronger and more competitive league. The BAA had large arenas in urban areas and owners with a long-term vision. The competition proved financially disastrous for teams in both leagues as player salaries rose, but profits did not. Before the war, the market had been unable to support even one 'national' league, and the slow growth was reflected by the minimal attention paid to professional basketball in the press.[66]

---

[64] Peterson, *Cages to Jump Shots*, 156-157. The origin of the jump shot remains unclear, but Fulks's success led to its popularization. The two-handed set shot of traditional basketball was virtually eliminated within a decade.

[65] Dave Anderson, "The Start of Something Big 'n' Tall," *New York Times*, October 31, 1996.

[66] Peterson, *Cages to Jump Shots*, 150-165.

On March 12, 1947, the *New York Times* ran a banner headline regarding Harry Boykoff's breaking the Garden scoring record against St. Francis. At the bottom of the same page, the newspaper placed the BAA's standings, under "College and School Results," which included scores in baseball, hockey, and track. Next to the BAA standings, the newspaper included an AP report on the Rochester Royals' winning the regular season Eastern Division title. The entire report simply stated: "The Rochester Royals captured the National Basketball League championship for the second successive season year by defeating the Oshkosh All-Stars, western division leaders, 76-68, tonight."[67]

Stability and growth occurred after the two leagues merged. Prior to the 1948-49 season, the BAA raided the NBL and brought the four best teams into its league. A larger and unwieldy league with seventeen teams, however, did little to alleviate the commercial problems faced by many BAA teams. The influx of college talent increased interest in professional basketball, but it did not remove its marginal status in the larger sport world. One major problem remained the clear superiority of former NBL teams located in smaller cities such as Minneapolis (Lakers), Rochester (Royals), and Fort Wayne (Pistons). By the 1949 season, only three of the original BAA teams, the New York Knicks, Boston Celtics, and Philadelphia Warriors, still existed. The financial power of the BAA teams, however, led to a final merger and the re-organization of the league in 1949-50, now called the National Basketball Association (NBA).[68]

American Jews played a very different role in the NBA than they had in the 'national' ABL of the 1920s. Both leagues constructed a model of professional basketball in a prosperous economy and post-war consumer society. During ABL's brief heyday, Jews remained an 'alien' immigrant group struggling for acceptance. By the time the NBA emerged as the foremost power in

---

[67] See *New York Times*, March 12, 1947.

[68] On the early NBA, see Leonard Koppett, *24 Seconds to Shoot: An Informal History of the National Basketball Association* (New York: MacMillan, 1968); Peterson, *Cages to Jump Shots*, 166-183. In 1950, the league consolidated into 11 teams and further contracted in 1954 to eight teams as larger cities became the focus.

professional basketball, however, Jews had become part of mainstream society. Their upward mobility reflected a post-war consumer society that had encouraged the development of the NBA. Suburban Jews would become part of the league's intended audience, but as a report issued during the NBA's first season illustrated, their role on the court had diminished.

In 1950, the Anti-Defamation League (ADL) issued a report on anti-Semitism and civil rights that included a fairly in-depth examination of basketball. The report stated that basketball had long been "considered by many an easterner's game, and as often as not, a 'Jewish' game." The Jewish presence had led to "some astonishing articles seeking to prove that Jews are so constructed that they can best stand the tension and strain of the game." Paul Gallico's "absurd" conclusion that Jewish success occurred because of their "Oriental background" had been "disproved by the status of basketball today" since "men of all faiths and colors have demonstrated the ability to play the game well." The report repeated the standard non-racial reason for Jewish success. Basketball "requires little space and equipment; it is a game primarily for crowded cities" and that is why "Jewish players, in the past, were prominent." The report also provided definitive and quantifiable evidence that Jewish basketball had declined. A survey conducted between September and December 1949 found that of the 206 players in the National Basketball Association (NBA), only "eight players, less than 4 per cent, were known to be Jews."[69]

The lack of a prominent Jewish presence in the NBA reflected a change in basketball. The NBA attracted younger players like Dolph Schayes and Max Zaslofsky and required a full-time commitment. The ABL's semi-professional status remained closely tied to the traditional culture and many Jews played in the ABL until the early 1950s when the league folded. Some players, such as Ossie Schectman, who scored the first basket in NBA history, concluded their careers in the ABL after brief stints in the NBA. Yet, according to historian Peter Levine,

---

[69] Arnold Forster, *A Measure of Freedom, An Anti-Defamation League Report* (Garden City, NY: Doubleday, 1950), 171-172.

Jews made up only nine percent of the ABL in 1951.[70] The absence of a communal champion model had begun to take its toll. Jewish basketball continued to exist, but an end had neared.

By the time the NBA had become the predominant league of the professional game, the Jewish press, as reflective of American Jews' changing conception of Jewish athleticism, altered its treatment of Jewish basketball. Safe, secure, and upwardly mobile Jewish suburbanites did not need Jewish athleticism to protect them from anti-Semitic attacks. The Jewish press thus turned their attention to the business end as both players and management would represent Jewish involvement in sport. In 1950, Haskell Cohen briefly discussed the CCNY championship team in his regular "Spotlight on Sports" column before quickly moving to Abe Saperstein, whose management of the Globetrotters "is breaking every attendance and box office record with the nation-wide tour." Cohen commented on other owners such as Rochester's Les Harrison and Eddie Gottlieb of the Philadelphia Warriors, both of whom had made their names in the traditional basketball culture and managed every aspect of their respective teams, including coaching. In contrast, NBA commissioner Maurice Podoloff, a hockey man who knew very little of basketball, represented the new businessman owner that would predominate in the league. In 1951, the *American Jewish World's* annual mentioned Podoloff as well as Haskell Cohen, who had become the NBA's publicity director.[71] Their inclusion in the annual indicated Jewish basketball would no longer be exclusively defined by play on the court.

As basketball and American Jewish life changed in the post-war era, so too did the racial composition of New York college basketball. In 1950, along with CCNY's five key Jewish players, Columbia's Ivy League champion had four

---

[70] The ABL's last season was in 1953. The Philadelphia Sphas' last season in the ABL was in 1948-49, but the Jewish presence remained strong. According to Peter Levine, as late as 1946, the ABL was 45% Jewish. On the ABL and the Sphas, see Levine, *Ellis Island to Ebbet's Field*, 66-70.

[71] Haskell Cohen, "Spotlight on Sports," *American Jewish World*, April 14, 1950; Bill Wolf," Meteoric Rise of New Stars in Sports World," *American Jewish World*, September 28, 1951.

Jewish players, and NYU and LIU continued to have a distinct, although diminished, Jewish presence. Yet, the best players in New York were increasingly black, not Jewish. In 1950, the best player in New York City, and likely the country, was LIU's 6'8" African-American center Sherman White. The normative presence of New York basketball would soon be African-American to a far greater extent than the Jewish presence in the 1930s and 1940s. As this change began to occur, American Jews focused on black opportunity in society as part of their own fight against anti-Semitism.

In the post-war era, Americans began to increasingly focus on black athleticism, which reflected the broader attention paid to African-Americans. Black Americans continued to confront violence and over fifty race killings occurred in 1945 and 1946. In 1946, President Harry Truman formed the President's Committee on Civil Rights. The Committee's report, *To Secure These Rights*, condemned racial segregation and recommended the federal government take a lead role in combating social discrimination and prejudice. Athleticism became increasingly important to African-Americans, especially after the Brooklyn Dodgers' Jackie Robinson broke baseball's color barrier in 1947.[72] Brooklyn's Jews, Jewish sportswriters as well as Hank Greenberg supported Robinson during this rookie season when the young player "suffered unprecedented abuse from opposing players and fans and hostility from many of his teammates." The *American Hebrew* hailed Robinson's achievement as making the heretofore dream of equality, "a reality in the sports world."[73] The focus on black civil rights by both the federal government and American Jews reflected the reality of post-war society. Despite Everett Shelton's comments and

---

[72] Mary L. Dudziak, *Cold War Civil Rights: Race and the Image of American Democracy* (Princeton: Princeton University Press, 2000), 79-83. For civil rights in relation to sport, see Christgau, *Tricksters in the Madhouse: Lakers vs. Globetrotters, 1948* (Lincoln, NE: University of Nebraska Press, 2004), 11-14.

[73] *American Hebrew*, February 18, 1948, quoted in Levine, *Ellis Island to Ebbet's Field*, 241. Also see Stephen H. Norwood and Harold Brackman, "Going to Bat for Jackie Robinson: The Jewish Role in Breaking Baseball's Color Line," *Journal of Sport History* 26, no. 1 (Spring 1999): 115-141.

remnants of the virulent anti-Semitism of the interwar period, Jews had gained acceptance, and in comparison to African-Americans, they had integrated.

The 1950 ADL report on anti-Semitism and civil rights, *A Measure of Freedom*, included a chapter on sports entitled "May the Best Man Win." The report contrasted Harold Ribalow's faith in American tolerance by stating that, "Most people suppose that this great democratic principle is actually practiced in American sport. But there is an undercurrent of feeling that some prejudice, particularly racial prejudice, is present though carefully concealed or camouflaged." The report examined the treatment of both "Jews and Negroes" in selected sports, and indicated a sense of commonality between the two groups. Yet, the difference in discrimination they faced reflected the growing acceptance of American Jews in society.[74] The report's inclusion of Jewish participation in sports such as yachting, tennis, and golf indicated the level of socio-economic mobility achieved by Jews. Jews continued to face discrimination in elite sports but did not find themselves completely excluded. African-Americans, on the other hand, faced discrimination in all sports, including the NBA, which had no African-Americans despite the fact that "individual teams seemed to have been honest in recent attempts to hire Negro players." The report indicated that the league "did not prohibit discrimination," but if it had "created a code providing affirmatively a policy of non-prejudice, Negroes would have participated in its game."[75]

Although the ADL report did not indicate it, World War II had facilitated professional basketball's racial integration. In the late 1930s, both the Harlem Rens and Globetrotters continued their barnstorming ways. They also competed in the annual World Professional Tournament, held from 1939-1949 in Chicago. Both league and independent teams competed in the tournament, and although NBL teams generally dominated, the Rens won the first tournament (beating the Globetrotters) and the Globetrotters won in 1940. These victories did little to

---

[74] Forster, *A Measure of Freedom*, 166-167.

[75] Ibid., 171-172.

break down the unofficial racial barriers in professional basketball. The lack of . manpower during World War II led NBL owners to reevaluate their policies and in 1943, ten African-Americans entered the five-team league with the Toledo Jim White Chevrolets, owned by Sid Goldberg, and the Chicago Studebakers, fronted by the United Automobile Workers. Other NBL teams soon followed. Rochester's Les Harrison brought in former LIU star Dolly King while the Dayton Rens, made up of the former Harlem Rens, became the league's all-black team at the end of the decade.[76] The NBL integrated four years before Jackie Robinson broke the color line in baseball, but with little publicity due to professional basketball's marginal status and the war.

According to basketball historian Robert Peterson, NBA teams did not sign black players in the late 1940s because they already had a host of problems and feared losing white fans. They also did not want to alienate Globetrotters' owner Abe Saperstein, whose team remained a far bigger attraction than NBA teams. When the Globetrotters appeared in double-headers before NBA games, attendance soared. Saperstein retained a virtual monopoly on African-American talent and opposed the NBA's racial integration. In 1950, NBA owners finally voted to sign black players (they had opposed the measure the previous year) after Knicks owner Ned Irish threatened to the leave the league.[77]

Integration would eventually transform the NBA, but into the 1950s, and to some extent, the early 1960s, the league struggled for legitimacy and popularity. College basketball remained far more popular in New York and other major cities and its supremacy over the NBA, especially after CCNY's triumph in 1950, seemed substantial. The eventual success of the NBA as the commercial

---

[76] Douglas Stark, "Paving the Way: History of Integration of African-Americans into Professional Basketball," *Basketball Digest* (February 2001). The Chevrolets folded after four games. Also see Peterson, *Cages to Jump Shots*, 130-131. African-American players had competed in eastern leagues in the 1900s and 1910s. A player named Bucky Lew played in the New England League as early as 1904.

[77] Peterson, *Cages to Jump Shots*, 170-172. The teams remained the top draw in professional basketball until the early 1950s. Saperstein could pay players more than NBA teams, which had unofficial salary caps. According to Peterson, Saperstein could pay a player $10,000 whereas NBA teams paid about $7,5000 for the best players.

and competitive pinnacle of American basketball began in 1951 after a scandal virtually destroyed competitive New York City college basketball. Along with the decline of Jewish urban neighborhoods and the demise of the champion model at Jewish Centers, the scandal helped to end this era of Jewish basketball.[78]

During the early twentieth century, gambling existed at all levels of sports, including basketball. A ubiquitous presence in American sport as far back as the colonial period, gambling contributed to the popularity of horse racing, boxing, and other sports. In 1936, *Newsweek* stated that players in the ABL had been known to "throw games to opponents." Even more revealing, the *New York Times* reported a rumor in January 1929 that gamblers had offered bribes to players from Brownsville's Thomas Jefferson High School. The school principal claimed the rumors were unfounded as he attributed the "origin of the rumor to a dubious sense of humor on the part of a member of the quintet."[79] Neither shock nor outrage accompanied the *Times* report. The seriousness with which school officials and the media took the Jefferson rumors indicated that gambling and 'dumping,' or losing on purpose, may have been common in high school sport.

Gamblers found college basketball attractive before, and especially after, the advent of the Garden double-headers. In 1931, gamblers approached Mac Posnack of the 'Wonder Five' to fix a game. Three years later, the *New York World-Telegram* commented on gambling's prevalence at the first double-header in December 1934.[80] The following season, rumors about NYU players' 'dumping' swirled around New York basketball. NYU had won 45 of 46 games over a three year span before losing to the Georgetown. When the team lost three more games in a matter of weeks, the rumors spread. The players denied the allegations and complained that NYU officials did not publicly "clear them of the

---

[78] Koppett, *24 Seconds to Shoot*, 55-63.

[79] "Basketball: NYU Quins Make it More Popular than Football," *Newsweek*, January 18, 1936. "Finds Charges Unfounded," *New York Times*, January 23, 1929.

[80] Albert J. Figone, "Gambling and College Basketball: The Scandal of 1951," *Journal of Sport History* 16, no. 1 (Spring 1989): 45.

damaging whispering campaign." The Communist Party's *Daily Worker* denounced NYU authorities for not defending their players from accusations of fixing games and declared that "gambling and professionalism are attacking basketball in New York City…no one denies the Garden is full of gamblers on big game nights."[81]

Gambling generally existed beneath the surface and brief glimpses through media reports illustrated the widespread presence of gambling in basketball. Cursory mention of gambling in high school, college, and professional basketball indicated a fairly high level of activity. The introduction of the point spread, however, produced a new model of gambling by allowing gamblers to bet on whether a team would win by a certain amount of points, which meant games between unequal teams could still attract interest. This changed the dynamic of gambling as it became an activity that existed beyond winning and losing.[82] It also meant that gamblers turned Madison Square Garden, which had been hailed as the 'mecca' of college basketball, into a gambling paradise.

During the 1945 season, the national media began to pay attention to the problems associated with Garden basketball. The professional atmosphere led the Big Ten to ban schools from participating in Garden games, but the commercial rewards meant that most schools turned a blind eye to problems. In January 1945, however, a *Newsweek* column explained that fans often yelled at specific players to score based on their wagers rather than team allegiance. In response, Garden promoter Ned Irish hired detectives to banish known gamblers. He also asked fans to remain in their seats, "based on the theory that you cannot gamble without moving." That same month, Holman ordered a player not to shoot a free throw

---

[81] Stanley Frank, "NYU Dumping?" *New York Evening Post*, February 26, 1936. "Gamblers Infest Court Games," *Daily Worker*, March 1, 1936. Losses to Georgetown and Temple were surprises, but defeats by Notre Dame and Manhattan led many to believe NYU was dumping since they were too good to lose four games in such a short time period. The dumping charge was never proven.

[82] See Rosen, *Scandals of '51*, 22; Figone, "Gambling and College Basketball," 45-46.

because of the betting line.[83] The situation led Kansas coach Phog Allen to demand that all games take place on college campuses and for a basketball 'czar' to control the game. He suggested General Douglas MacArthur. Few coaches, sportswriters, or college officials took Allen seriously. Press reports indicated that his belief in a crisis and his "cries of 'fire!' were interpreted generally as cries of 'wolf.'"[84]

Gambling at Madison Square Garden intensified due to a growing familiarity of players and gamblers who often met at Jewish summer resorts in the Catskills. The 'Borsht Belt' resorts established teams and hired Jewish and non-Jewish players as busboys, waiters, life guards, and other positions so they could retain their amateur status. The Borsht Belt facilitated a familiarity between players, coaches, and fans outside of the formal setting of college basketball. When teams such as Bradley, Kentucky, and North Carolina then appeared in the Garden, players who summered in the Catskills reconnected with the Jewish fans, many of whom identified with the New York players and provided much of the commercial and popular support of Garden double-headers. The players also reconnected with gamblers who vacationed at the resorts. According to historian Peter Levine, gambling became an intimate part of the Catskill culture. Guests frequently made bets during games, although when the Tamarack owner learned of a "fixed" game, he fired the involved players (or 'staff') and kicked out the responsible guest.[85]

---

[83] John Lardner, "Sit Very Still Please," *Newsweek*, January 1, 1945; "Garden Bookies Foiled by Basketball Coach," *Los Angeles Times*, January 12, 1945.

[84] "Brooklyn Pay-Off Blows the Lid Off: Bribes Expose Basketball Gambling," *Newsweek*, February 12, 1945.

[85] Joe Dorinson, "Aint No Mountain High Enough: Borsht Belt Basketball," *In the Mountain: Newsletter of the Catskills Institute* 15 (April 2004). In reality, of course, players were there to play home and away games against other resort staffs. Dorinson quoted a *Life* article in 1950 that stated the Catskills attracted players by paying players between $500 to $1200 for a summer position. In addition, the New York Knicks had their first training camp in the Catskills. On basketball at the Catskills, see Levine, *Ellis Island to Ebbet's Field*, 84-85. For additional information on the Catskills, see Phil Brown, ed., *In the Catskills: A Century of the Jewish Experience in "The Mountains"* (New York: Columbia University Press, 2002). Though it is impossible to speculate regarding the Jewish makeup of Garden audiences, radio announcer Marty Glickman commented in a *New York Times* article that many of the fans would walk "over from

Soon after the *Newsweek* article, Garden basketball returned to the national spotlight for more than mere gambling. In February 1945, New York police arrested five players from Brooklyn College for accepting money to "fix" a game against Akron at the Garden. The school expelled the players and in the aftermath, reporters discovered that one of the players, Larry Pearlstein, had "never even been a member of the college." He ingeniously borrowed two books from the "library, walked around the campus until his face became familiar, then went out for basketball and made the team."[86]

Pearlstein's situation was not unique. At CCNY, Jack Laub had played on the 1945 varsity team "without attending classes." Laub's presence provided a hint at some of the problems within even the 'pure' CCNY basketball program. In addition to that incident, Holman quietly removed Lanny Hassman from the team after Hassman approached a teammate, All-Metropolitan forward Paul Schmones, about fixing a game. Holman did not publicize the event and he, other coaches, and the press hoped the 1945 scandal would remain an isolated event.[87]

The Brooklyn College scandal vanished from the national headlines by the end of the season, but debate over the role of the Garden's and other professional arenas in college basketball continued. In 1947, *Newsweek* wondered how "students" had time to study when schools such as Holy Cross "didn't play a single game on their own campus." The article asked coaches their opinion of the situation, especially the Garden's place in college basketball, and received

---

the garment center." The garment industry was Jewish-dominated. See Marty Glickman, "When Garden Was the Place for Basketball-wise," *New York Times*, November 25, 1984.

[86] "Sports: Sport Shorts," *Newsweek*, March 26, 1945; Albert J. Figone, "City Dump: The 1951 CCNY Basketball Scandal," *Journal of Sport History* 26, no. 1 (Spring 1999), 175-177. According to Figone, New York City Mayor Fiorello LaGuardia announced that Pealstein had never been enrolled. The involvement of Brooklyn College, a school that often played at the Garden but never attained the success of LIU, NYU, or CCNY, illustrated that the local basketball culture's involvement with Garden basketball existed at various levels and not just among the elite.

[87] Figone, "Gambling and College Basketball," 48. Figone explained that Holman reported the incident to Frank Lloyd, Chair of the Department of Hygiene, but they kept it secret due to commercial concerns.

conflicting responses. Wisconsin's "Bud" Foster reacted to fans' heavy cigarette and cigar smoking and opposed the Garden's "smoky atmosphere." Oklahoma A&M's Henry Iba believed the smoke was "a mental hazard more than anything else." Kentucky's Adolph Rupp, a presence at the Garden since the first season of double-headers, summed up the feelings of many college coaches when he argued: "Playing in the Garden was good for the boys. Playing with the best teams in the country before big crowds, they get a poise and confidence they can use later on."[88]

The Garden's "smoky atmosphere" aside, gambling remained the real danger. Rumors of fixed games occurred throughout the 1940s and Holman commented in January 1948 that he believed "another scandal similar to the previous one at Brooklyn College would break out." In 1949, police arrested four men who approached George Washington University co-captain, and Brooklyn native, David Shapiro about fixing games. At the time, officials did not believe the incident illustrated a larger conspiracy. Historian Albert Figone pointed out, however, that small-time gamblers had traveled from New York to Washington to approach a 25-year-old war veteran and law student. The incident should have alerted college coaches and officials that the problems of gambling extended far beyond the Garden.[89]

As the 1951 season began, even as New York continued to revel in CCNY's success of the previous season, Figone explained that, "the foul air of scandal hung over college basketball like a menace." By the middle of the season, it had become obvious that some teams were "fixing" games. Rumors of CCNY's involvement emerged as the team won only eleven of its first eighteen games. Many people still believed Holman had a dynasty in the making, however, and Holman even hoped the core of his 1950 championship team would

---

[88] "Basketball: Study Hour?" *Newsweek*, April 7, 1947. The article also explained that Utah only traveled "on breaks and between quarters," and CCNY "rarely makes more than one short junket a year" due to academic restrictions.

[89] Figone, "Gambling and College Basketball," 51-52.

represent the United States at the 1952 Olympics. Before that could happen, however, he, the school, and his players were disgraced by one of the biggest scandals in the history of college sports.[90]

In January 1951, former Manhattan College captain, Hank Poppe approached the school's first-ever African-American player, Junius Kellogg. Poppe offered the younger player $1,000 to fix a game against DePaul and explained: "It's easy!" Poppe told Kellogg to "miss a rebound once in a while" or "don't try to block the other guy's shot." On the offensive side: "throw the ball away when you get the chance," though it was important to "make it look like you're trying."[91] Finally, to convince his former teammate, Poppe said that professional players commonly participated in such activity, which showed that "everybody's doing it." Kellogg went to the police, who arrested Poppe. Within a matter of weeks, CCNY's Ed Warner, Ed Roman, and Al 'Fats' Roth, LIU's Sherman White and Adolf Bigos, Connie Schaff of NYU, and Eddie Gard, a former LIU player were arrested for fixing games. Soon after, police arrested CCNY's Irwin Dambrot, Norm Mager, and Herb Cohen, as well as LIU players Lou Lipman, Natie Miller, and Jackie Goldsmith. The *New York Journal-American* described the 5'8" Goldsmith, nicknamed the "Brownsville Bomber," as "responsible for the corruption of more college basketball players than any other single person."[92]

In the months following the initial arrests, the mainstream press focused on New York's corrupting influence on the youth of America. Kansas's Phog Allen stated that Midwestern basketball remained pure in contrast to the eastern game, where players "are thrown into an environment which cannot help but breed the evil which more and more is coming to light." Jews made up eight of

---

[90] Ibid., 51-52.

[91] Ibid., 51-52.

[92] Ibid., 53. Brownsville also housed Murder Incorporated, an organized crime outfit that served as the mob's killing group. See Rich Cohen, *Tough Jews: Fathers, Sons, and Gangster Dreams* (New York: Simon & Schuster, 1998).

the fifteen New York players arrested in the scandal, as well as many of the gamblers, the original arresting officer, and the judge. As historians Peter Levine and Edward Shapiro indicated, the situation "should have been a gold mine for anti-Semites." Yet, the scandal did not contain either explicit or implicit anti-Semitic rhetoric. Much like the arrests of Ethel and Julius Rosenberg for spying for the Soviet Union in the summer of 1950, any specific Jewishness connected to the basketball scandal remained muted.[93] Anti-Semitism had declined in the post-war era, as had the meanings, posited in either positive or negative respects, associated with Jewish athleticism. Perhaps most importantly, however, the scandal involved non-Jewish players outside the New York area, which reflected a larger problem in college athletics, but which nonetheless, impacted post-war Jewish basketball.

In July 1951, police questioned Toledo players regarding fixed games in 1949 and 1950. Soon after, police questioned players from Bradley, which, as Albert Figone stated, "reflected the pervasiveness and magnitude of the gambling problem." Fixing had reached small programs like Brooklyn College, private schools like Bradley, and CCNY. Kentucky coach Adolph Rupp, like many others, continued to blame New York, where newspapers "quote odds and play directly into the hands of the gamblers," and famously stated that gamblers, "couldn't reach my boys with a ten-foot pole." In October 1951, however, officials discovered that Kentucky players had thrown the team's first round NIT game in 1949. The next month, Judge Saul Streit began sentencing players and gamblers. In the end, 35 players, including almost every key player on the 1950 CCNY team, stood accused of fixing 86 games between 1947-1951.[94]

The timing of the scandal coincided with a growing concern among many Americans regarding whether the country could fight external threats without internal moral strength. In the summer of 1951, amid the escalation of the Cold War, McCarthyism and the Korean War, West Point expelled over 90 cadets,

---

[93] Levine, *Ellis Island to Ebbet's Field*, 82-86; Shapiro, "The Shame of the City," 186.

[94] Cohen, *The Game They Played*; Figone, "Gambling and College Basketball," 60-61.

including almost the entire football team, for cheating on exams, which intensified fears regarding the moral values of American youth.[95] In the basketball scandal, however, Judge Streit blamed the entire system of college athletics, especially the commercialism, recruiting, and academic fraud that accompanied 'big time' college basketball. Streit found that some of CCNY's players had been admitted after their high school transcripts had been altered. At schools like Kentucky, basketball served as the central athletic activity and the larger community supported competitive success at all costs. Streit condemned the Kentucky program as "the acme of commercialism and overemphasis." He found "evidence of covert subsidization of players, ruthless exploitation of athletes, cribbing on examinations, illegal recruiting," as well as the "matriculation of unqualified students, [and] demoralization [corruption] of the athletes by the coaches, the alumni, and the townspeople."[96]

The scandal shook college basketball, ruined the reputation of players, and virtually destroyed New York college basketball. Double-headers continued during the 1951 season, but only before a half-filled arena. The NCAA removed its national tournament from the Garden, expanded the tournament field to 16 teams, and banned duel participation in the two post-season tournament, thus making CCNY the only duel winner in history. New York barred city schools from the Garden and some of the schools, such as CCNY banned their teams from playing in non-college controlled arenas. While many sportswriters blamed the players, Judge Streit blamed coaches for turning a blind eye to the activities of their players. In New York, LIU's Claire Bee and CCNY's Holman were charged with a lack of institutional control in relation to their programs. LIU immediately deemphasized its basketball program while at CCNY a battle between the coach and administration played out during the early 1950s.

---

[95] Levine, *Ellis Island to Ebbet's Field*, 85; Thelin, *Games Colleges Play*, 105-107.

[96] Thelin, *Games Colleges Play*, 101; Andrew Zimbalist, *Unpaid Professionals: Commercialism and Conflict in Big-Time College Sports* (Princeton: Princeton University Press, 2001), 10.

In 1951, the New York City Board of Education suspended Holman for neglect of duty and "conduct unbecoming to a teacher." During the scandal, Holman had argued that it had occurred because of the "relaxation of morals in the country," and he took no responsibility for his players' actions.[97] A personal notebook indicated that Holman prepared long and hard for his reinstatement hearing, which he won in 1953, but by which time the school had de-emphasized the basketball program. He coached for the remainder of the decade with limited resources, media attention, or competitive success. In 1954, newspapers reported that although academic standards remained high, "more than a dozen basketball players" had been "admitted to the school by fraud. High School records deliberately were forged to allow unqualified athletes to enroll." Some of Holman's former players had become part of "a 'ring' of high school coaches from the PSAL" who had "received from $250 to $500 to recruit players for CCNY."[98] The final devastating result of the scandal was that basketball fans, CCNY alumni, and American Jews learned that that the mythology of CCNY basketball had been just that, a myth.

The scandal removed the final link between traditional and modern basketball. The NBA banned all guilty parties for life to ensure that college basketball's unsavory reputation did not invade the burgeoning league. The NBA's move proved vital in separating the league from the college basketball scandal and helped the continuing transformation of basketball that had little to do with the scandal. A national game with taller players had emerged. Jewish basketball had clearly adapted, as Harry Boykoff, Max Zaslofsky, Dolph Schayes, and members of the 1950 CCNY team attested. The traditional 'Jewish' schools of NYU, LIU, and CCNY, however, would no longer provide an opportunity for players to find success before moving onto the professional game. Jewish players who participated in post-scandal New York college basketball competed outside of the public eye. The mainstream press would increasingly focus on African-

---

[97] Levine, *Ellis Island to Ebbet's Field*, 85.

[98] "New Scandal Revealed in CCNY Fraud," *Los Angeles Times*, June 22, 1954.

American basketball and American Jews would not provide the same power to athletic success after 1950 as they had during the first half of the twentieth century.

The decline of Jewish basketball began long before the 1951 scandal. Socio-economic mobility and suburban migration transformed American Jewish life and American Jews entered a new stage in the post-war era. By the time of the scandal, Jewish players no longer 'dominated' New York college basketball or professional leagues. The absence of a champion model restricted the communal production of elite players and the suburban migration removed the informal basketball culture that had continued the tradition of Jewish basketball. Along with many other cultural aspects associated with the Jewish neighborhoods of the interwar period, Jewish basketball had little to do with American Jewry's future. They had achieved their dreams of economic success, social mobility, and acceptance. Jewish basketball disappeared into the immigrant and interwar past.

Epilogue

"Jews Can't Play Basketball": What happened to Jewish Basketball?

By 1951, the goal of the original project of Jewish basketball, as a vehicle to integration into mainstream society had been achieved. The champion model had succeeded in furnishing American Jews with athletic heroes at a time of anxiety and fear of exclusion. In the post-World War II era, however, the need for athletic heroes had diminished. Champions no longer served the same role they had during the interwar period. Additionally, the champion model had produced a culture that communal leaders could not accept. The dismantling of the champion model did not stop Jews from playing basketball and the sport remained popular among individuals, Jewish Centers, summer camps, and youth groups. Jewish basketball had evolved in three ways, as a recreational element in Jewish communal life, as an individual pursuit for elite athletes, and as an opportunity for financial and social success on the managerial or business side. During the previous five decades, however, Jewish basketball had played an important role in the development of basketball as it became the most popular spectator sport in America. Jewish basketball helped turn a game invented under the auspices of 'muscular Christianity' into a popular, commercialized form of entertainment that would continue to grow in the second half of the twentieth century.

From its inception, modern improvements in equipment, rules changes, player growth in height, and the development of new styles of play transformed basketball. During the early decades of the twentieth century, Jewish players from the lower East Side, the Original Celtics, the Harlem Renaissance, and other urban players established an eastern style based on speed and quickness. Not until the 1930s and 1940s did Madison Square Garden, the nationalization of the sport, Hank Luisetti's one-handed shot, and the height of players such as Harry Boykoff challenge the eastern style's traditional use of the two-handed set shot and the supremacy of shorter and quicker players. Television, which helped professional leagues dominate their respective sports, further nationalized basketball as fans became familiar with players who increasingly left their local areas for greater opportunities across the country. In 1954, the NBA invented the 24-second shot clock, which increased scoring as teams adopted an up-tempo style perfectly suited for television viewing.[1] In the latter decades of the twentieth century, the fast break would be followed by 'jumpers' and 'leapers' who continued basketball's historical progression. Yet, as basketball moved further away from its origins, Jewish basketball's role in this history became overshadowed by the 'modern' game.

In 1985, Harold Ribalow, co-authored with his son, Meir Ribalow, a new edition of *The Jew in American Sports*. In his narrative of basketball, Ribalow celebrated coaches, including Holman, Red Auerbach of the Boston Celtics, Red Holzman of the New York Knicks, and Larry and Herb Brown. Ribalow repeated his previous assertion that scientific treatises surrounding the 'Jew' had been disproved as "hokum." He omitted Holman's assertion that Jews had become successful players because of their shortness, quickness, and mentally agility. He also reduced Holman's role by giving only Harry Boykoff and Dolph Schayes individual chapters.[2] Ribalow provided the same dominant reason for Jewish success as he had in 1948: "Basketball, because it requires little space and paraphernalia, has been a popular city sport." Ribalow, however, provided a telling addendum. "As the pro game had been taken over by extremely tall young

---

[1] See Rader, *American Sports*, 242-243, 250-255. Koppett, *24 Seconds to Shoot*; Kirchberg, *Hoop Lore*. Whereas major league baseball had always served as the pinnacle of its sport (it had dominated since 1900), the minor leagues declined because of television. Potential spectators stayed home to watch the Yankees, Red Sox, and other major league teams rather than attend local games. In football, television was even more important to the NFL's rise as the predominant professional league in American society.

[2] At the time, Schayes's son, Danny Schayes, was one of only two Jewish players played in the NBA.

men from the ghettos, the game has been influenced, in style as well as personnel by black athletes. The dunk shot, the dazzling moves, the brilliance…[of black players] have led sports writers to analyze the 'white' game as against the 'black' game. Some white players play the 'black' style game of basketball and it works the other way around as well. But it no longer is, if it ever was, the 'Jewish' game."

Pete Axthelm's *The City Game*, written in 1970 after the New York Knicks won their first NBA championship, provided Ribalow's text with the dominant notions of basketball. Ribalow agreed with Axthelm belief that "basketball is the city game," which transformed the 'tall blond lads' from his 1948 text into players who "often become superb basketball players. But they do so by developing accurate shots and precise skills." In contrast, Axthelm's *African-American* city kids "simply develop 'moves.' Other young athletes may learn basketball, but city kids live it."[3] Axthelm's spatial and racial dichotomy turned basketball into a sport of distinct racial eras. Sport historian Benjamin Rader presented this idea in his important survey of American sport: "In the 1930s and 1940s, Irish, Jewish, and Italian athletes dominated the rosters of [New York] metropolitan high schools and colleges; in the 1950s, blacks began to replace the earlier ethnic groups."[4]

Within this construct, ethnic Jews became seen as *unable* to compete in the up-tempo, vertical, athletic, and 'black' game of the second half of the twentieth century. Axthelm discussed "tough" Jewish players from an earlier era, but they did not 'live' basketball in the same sense as African-Americans. Although basketball did not suddenly transform from a "Jewish" game into a "black" game, the gradual succession of black players produced what became perceived as a revolutionary 'black' style that "artistically challenged" what cultural critic Nelson George described as "the flat-footed set shots" of the pre-

---

[3] Harold U. Ribalow and Meir Z. Ribalow, *The Jew in American Sports* (New York: Hippocrene Books, 1985).

[4] Rader, *American Sports*, 272.

NBA, and pre-black, era. This 'black' style of play supposedly contained an innate blackness which had produced the expressiveness of jazz, hip-hop, and other black musical forms, and inverted the concept of 'natural' black athleticism into a positive reflection of blackness in a racist and exclusionary society.[5] A similar process within Jewish athleticism had resulted in the basketball Jew, but its legacy perpetuated the belief in a disparity between a Jewish masculinity and the American ideal.

In the early decades of the twentieth century, American Jews constructed the basketball Jew as a representative figure of Jewish difference. Facing extreme pressure to assimilate as well as resistance to assimilation, American Jews accepted the basketball Jew as reflective of their integrated identities. Success in mainstream sport did not diminish their Jewishness. The Jewish press defined Jewish athleticism as competitive success in mainstream sport and had celebrated individual athletic heroes as symbolic of Jewish normality. Yet, the decline of elite athletes in sports such as basketball impacted notions of Jewish athleticism. Jewish center officials dismantled the model when the basketball Jew, and thus some aspect of Jewish masculinity, remained rooted in the ghetto body of the early twentieth century. The Jewish mind and body remained conceptually the same, but they no longer produced an ideal within basketball. Thus, the image of the basketball Jew became rendered with negative values in which its importance to Jewish basketball has been lost.

In 2005, an episode of the cartoon, and comedy, show *South Park* included a scene in which the town's only young Jew, Kyle Broflovski, tried out for the all-state basketball team. This short Jew, although he is no shorter than his

---

[5] Nelson George, *Elevating the Game: Black Men and Basketball* (New York: HarperCollins, 1992). Quote from Hoberman, *Darwin's Athletes*, 6. Steven Pope, "De-centering 'Race' and (Re)presenting 'Black' Performance in Sport History in Phillips, ed., *Deconstructing Sport History*, 147-180; see readings in Gena Dagel Caponi, ed. *Signifyin(g), Sanctifyin', and Slam Dunking: A Reader in African American Expressive Culture* (Amherst, MA: University of Massachusetts Press, 1999); Ellis Cashmore, *The Black Culture Industry* (New York: Routledge, 1997); Pete Axthelm, *The City Game: Basketball in New York from the World Champion Knicks to the World of the Playgrounds* (New York: Harper Magazine's Press, 1970). For the continued debate over biological differences in relation to athletic achievement, see Hoberman, *Darwin's Athletes*; Entine, *Taboo*.

non-Jewish friends, served as the definitive 'other' on the court dominated by tall, thin, and athletic African-American players who towered above him. Kyle could not keep up with the superior black players and both the coach and his friend Cartman told him, "Jews can't play basketball." On a web site in which the scene can be viewed, a serious question is posed for viewers. "Is the stereotype true? Are Jews bad athletes?"[6]

The *South Park* episode indicated that the perception of Jewish athleticism had both changed and remained the same since the early 1900s. The show's creators had Cartman say that Jews 'can't' play basketball, not that they don't. They depicted Jews as willing participants in American sport, but lacking the ability to succeed. The original conception of the stereotype of the weak Jew had included an unwillingness to be physically or athletically active. Once Jews participated, Elmer Mitchell and Paul Gallico transformed Jewish athleticism to include characteristics reflected Jewish racial inferiority. Yet, the stereotype had not simply been externally imposed upon Jews. As historian Sander Gilman has explained, Jews internalized the stereotype and perpetuated the notion of Jewish superior intelligence in order to alleviate a sense of their own physical powerlessness. Thus, the belief in a physical-intellectual dichotomy within Jewish culture remains potent enough for a recent academic work to state that, "to many, an association between Jews and sports seems almost oxymoronic."[7]

It is necessary to view Jewish basketball as part of the American Jewish experience. The aggressive masculinity of American sport had been integrated into Jewish athleticism, which had been the original goal of the champion model. Players and spectators alike identified as American through participation in sport,

---

[6] South Park, "Mr. Garrison's Fancy New Vagina," episode 901, first aired March 9, 2005. The author viewed the spot on Jewlarious.com, a site connected to aish.com, a prominent Jewish content web site. On February 10, 2008, the comment board had 89 postings, among which people have condemned the spot for contributing to the stereotype of the weak Jew, have attempted to dispel the stereotype by citing examples of their own athleticism, family members, or the Jewish 'champions.' Others argued that Jews have a higher spiritual calling and have thus not lowered themselves to play sports.

[7] Gilman, *Smart Jews*. Eisen, "Jewish History and the Ideology of Modern Sport." Kugelmass, *Jews, Sports, and the Rites of Citizenship*.

capitalistic activities, and consumer culture. This participation, however, involved tensions and conflict. As immigration restriction transformed the project into community building, the need to overcome powerful internal divisions proved more important than allowing competitive Jewish athleticism to flourish. Jewish leaders and JWB officials reacted strongly to the activity on the courts and in the stands at Jewish centers, but the success of Jewish basketball in mainstream society provided American Jews with athletic heroes during a time of anxiety and unease. From its humble beginning, Jewish basketball, as played at Jewish centers, independent clubs, schools, colleges, and in the professional arena, became a daily experience in the lives of many young American Jews. Between 1900 and 1951, Jewish basketball served as an expression of Jewish racial identity, an important part of modern American Jewish culture and vital to the growth and development of America's basketball culture.

Bibliography

Primary Sources

A.   Manuscript Collections

Brooklyn Jewish Center. Records, Joseph and Miriam Ratner Center for the Study of Conservative Judaism, Jewish Theological Seminary of America, New York.
City College Athletics Collection, 1893-1970. Morris Raphael Cohen Library, City College Archives, New York.
Clara de Hirsch Home. Records, 92nd Street Y Archives, New York.
Hickox, Edward and Gena. Library at the Basketball Hall of Fame, Springfield, MA.
Holman, Nat. Papers, Morris Raphael Cohen Library, City College Archives, New York.
Jewish Community Center of St. Paul, University of Minnesota Social Welfare Archives, Minneapolis.
Jewish Welfare Board. Records, 92nd Street Y Archives, New York.
Metropolitan League. Records, 92nd Street Y Archives, New York.
Nathan and Theresa Berman Upper Midwest Jewish Archives, Minneapolis.
   Neighborhood House. Records, Minnesota Historical Society, St. Paul, MN.
Werner, William E. Oral History Library of the American Jewish Committee,
Dorot Jewish Division, New York Public Library, New York.
Young Judaea. Papers, American Jewish Historical Society.
Young Men's Hebrew Association. Records, 92nd Street Y Archives, New York.
Young Women's Hebrew Association. Records, 92nd Street Y Archives, New York.

B.   Newspapers and Periodicals

American Economic Association Publications. Ithaca, 1911.
American Hebrew. New York, 1898-1951.
American Israelite. Cincinnati, 1935-1936.
American Jewess. New York, 1895-1898.
American Jewish World. Minneapolis, 1915-1952.
American Physical Education Review. New York, 1896-1925.
American Zionist. New York,

The Arena. Boston, 1900-1908.
Atlanta Constitution. Atlanta, 1892-1924.
Atlantic Monthly. Boston, 1858.
The Athletic Journal. New York, 1921-1922.
The AZA Leader.
Baltimore Jewish Comment. Baltimore, 1908.
Baltimore Jewish Times. Baltimore, 1926.
B'nai B'rith Messenger. Los Angeles, 1903-1911.
The Bookman. New York, 1928.
Boston Jewish Advocate. Boston, 1906-1908, 1931-1935.
Brooklyn Daily Eagle. Brooklyn, 1893-1899, 1930-1934.
Brooklyn Standard Union. Brooklyn, 1931-1934.
Buffalo Jewish Review. New York, 1935.
The Call of Youth. New York.
The Campus. New York, 1907-1950.
Century Illustrated Magazine. New York, 1891-1903.
The Chatauquan. Meadville, 1892-1904.
Chicago Jewish Chronicle. Chicago, 1935.
Chicago Tribune. Chicago, 1892-1955.
Connecticut Hebrew Record. Hartford, 1920-1925.
The Crisis. New York, 1913-1935.
Current Literature. New York, 1888-1912.
Current Opinion. New York, 1914-1924.
The Daily Worker. New York, 1933-1936.
Denver Jewish Outlook. Denver, 1907-1908.
Detroit Jewish American. Detroit, 1907-08.
Detroit Jewish Chronicle. Detroit, 1926-1928.
The Eclectic Magazine of Foreign Literature. New York, 1863-1885.
Forum. New York, 1887-1928.
Forverts, New York, 1929-1931.
Godey's Magazine. New York, 1895-1896.
Hartford Courant. Hartford, 1922-1925.
Hashomer Hatzair [the Guard].
Health. New York, 1903-1911.
Hebrew Union College Journal. Cincinnati,
Hebrew Union College Monthly. Cincinnati,
Herald of Health. New York, 1866.
The Jewish Center. New York, 1922-1946.
Jewish Criterion. Pittsburgh, 1907-1908.
Jewish Exponent. Philadelphia, 1907-1908.
Jewish Frontier. New York, 1934-1945.
The Jewish Messenger. New York, 1890.
The Jewish Youth. Chicago, 1925.
JWB Circle. New York, 1946-1952.
Kansas City Jewish Chronicle. Kansas City, 1934-1935.
Kentuckian. Lexington, 1936.

Life. New York, 1935-1936.
Lippincott's Monthly Magazine. Philadelphia, 1897-1911.
The Literary Digest. , 1935-1936.
Los Angeles Times. Los Angeles, 1893-1954.
Maccabaean. New York,
McClure's Magazine. New York, 1905-1925.
Medical News. New York, 1869, 1901.
The Nation. New York, 1921-1935.
The National Police Gazette. New York, 1895-1903.
Newsweek. New York, 1933-1951.
New York Amsterdam News. New York, 1934.
New York Daily News. New York, 1931-1934.
New York Evening Post. New York, 1929-1939.
New York Herald Tribune. New York, 1931-1934.
New York Times. New York, 1881-1954.
The North American Review. Boston, 1878-1929.
Outing. New York, 1882-1911.
Outlook.
Peterson Magazine. Philadelphia, 1897.
Philadelphia Jewish Times. Philadelphia, 1925-1929.
Physical Culture. New York, 1899-1913.
Reach Official Basketball Guide. Philadelphia, 1904-1927.
The Research Quarterly of the APEA. New York, 1926-1939.
Scientific American. New York, 1876-1881.
Spalding's Official Basketball Guide and Official Rules. New York, 1897-1934.
St. Louis Jewish Voice. St. Louis, 1907-1909.
Texas Jewish Herald. Houston, 1935-1936.
Time Magazine. New York, 1932-1951.
Washington Post. Washington, D.C., 1893-1951.
Workmen's Circle Call. New York, -1950.
The Young Judaean. New York, 1912-1940.
The Youth Leader. Cincinnati, 1935-1936.
The Zeta Beta Tau Quarterly.

C.   Interviews

Norm Drucker, September 4, 2005.
Bernie Fliegel, April 2003.
Dutch Garfinkel, April 17, 2005.
Arthur Kameros, 2002.
Irwin Rothenberg, September 3, 2005.

D.   Printed Material

Addams, Jane. *Twenty Years at Hull House*. New York: MacMillan Company, 1910.

Berenson, Senda. *Line Basketball for Women*. New York: American Sport Pub. Co., 1901.

Broun, Heywood, and George Britt. *Christians Only: A Study in Prejudice* (New York: The Vanguard Press, 1986).

Cahan, Abraham. *The Rise of David Levinsky*. New York: Harper and Brothers, 1917.

Commons, John R. *Races and Immigrants*. New York: MacMillan Company, 1907.

Davenport, Charles. *Heredity in Relation to Eugenics*. New York: H. Holt and Company, 1911.

Dictionary of Races or Peoples, Reports of the Immigration Commission, 61st Congress, 3rd Session, Senate Document No. 662. Washington: Government Printing Office, 1911.

Fishberg, Maurice. *The Jews: A Study of Race and Environment*. New York: Walter Scott Publishing Co., 1911.

Forster, Arnold. *A Measure of Freedom, An Anti-Defamation League Report*. Garden City, NY: Doubleday, 1950.

Frank, Stanley. *The Jew in Sports*. New York: The Miles Publishing Co., 1936.

Grant, Madison. *The Passing of the Great Race; or the Racial Basis of European History*. New York: Charles Scribner's Sons, 1916.

Gulick, Luther Halsey. *Line Basket-Ball or Basket-Ball for Women* (New York: American Sports Publishing Co., 1901.

Holman, Nat. *Winning Basketball*. New York: Charles Scribner's Sons, 1932.

The International Jew: The World's Foremost Problem. 4 vols. Dearborn: Dearborn Publishing Co., 1922.

Jacobs, Joseph. *Studies in Jewish Statistics: Social, Vital, and Anthropometric*. London: D. Nutt, 1891.

James, Edmund J., Oscar R. Flynn, J.R. Paulding, Charlotte Kimball, Walter Scott Andrews, Charles S. Bernheimer, Henrietta Szold, and others. *The Immigrant Jew in America*. New York: B.F. Buck and Co., 1907.

Messer, Guerdon N. *How to Play Basket Ball: A Thesis on the Technique of the Game*. New York: American Sports Publishing Co., 1912.

Naismith, James. *Rules for Basket Ball*. Springfield, MA: Springfield Printing and Binding Company, 1892.

Newman, H. *The Real Jew: Some Aspects of the Jewish Contribution to Civilization*. London: A&C Black Ltd., 1925.

Paxson, Frederic L. "The Rise of Sport" *Mississippi Valley Historical Review* 4:2 (September 1917): 143-186

Postal, Bernard, Jesse Silver, and Roy Silver. *The Encyclopedia of Jews in Sports*. New York: Bloch Publishing Co., 1965.

Ribalow, Harold U. *The Jew in American Sports*. New York: Bloch Publishing Co., 1948.

Riis, Jacob A. *How the Other Half Lives: Studies Among the Tenements of New York*. New York: Hill and Wang, 1957.

Ripley, William Z. *The Race of Europe*. New York: D. Appleton and Co., 1899.

Roosevelt, Theodore. *The Strenuous Life: Essays and Addresses*. New York: The Century Company, 1900.

Samuel, Maurice. *You Gentiles!*. New York: Harcourt, Brace, and Co., 1924.

Simons, John., ed. *Who's Who in American Jewry: A Biographical Dictionary of Living Jews of the United States and Canada*. New York: National News Association Inc., 1939.

Smith, Thomas H. *Official Basket Ball Guide and the Protective Association Rules for 1906-07*. New York: Fox's Athletic Library, 1907.

Turner, Frederick Jackson. *The Frontier in American History*. New York: H. Holt and Company, 1920.

Wirth, Louis. *The Ghetto*. Chicago: University of Chicago Press, 1928.

Secondary Sources

Adelman, Melvin L. "Academicians and American Athletics." *Journal of Sport History* 10 (Spring 1983): 80-106.

———. *A Sporting Time: New York City and the Rise of Modern Athletics, 1820-1870.* Urbana: University of Illinois Press, 1986.

Alba, Richard D. *Ethnic Identity: The Transformation of White America.* New Haven: Yale University Press, 1990.

Allen. Walter R., and Angie Y. Chung. "Your Blues Ain't Like My Blues: Race, Ethnicity, and Social Inequality in America." *Contemporary Sociology* 29 (November 2000): 796-805.

Applin, Albert G. "From Muscular Christianity to the Marketplace: The History of Men's and Boys' Basketball in the United States, 1891-1957." Ph.D. Dissertation, University of Massachusetts, 1982.

Arad, Gulie Ne'eman. *America, its Jews, and the Rise of Nazism.* Bloomington: Indiana University Press, 2000.

Archdeacon, Thomas. *Becoming American: An Ethnic History.* New York: Free Press, 1983.

Axthelm, Pete. *The City Game: Basketball in New York from the World Champion Knicks to the World of the Playgrounds.* New York: Harper Magazine's Press, 1970.

Banner, Lois. *American Beauty.* New York: Knopf, 1983.

Baskin, Judith R., ed. *Jewish Women in Historical Perspective.* Detroit: Wayne State University Press, 1998.

Bederman, Gail. *Manliness and Civilization: A Cultural History of Gender and Race in the US, 1880-1917.* Chicago: University of Chicago Press, 1995.

Bellow, Adam. *The Educational Alliance: A Centennial Celebration.* New York: Educational Alliance, 1990.

Bender, Daniel E. *Sweated Work, Weak Bodies: Anti-Sweatshop Campaigns and Languages of Labor.* New Brunswick: Rutgers University Press, 2004.

Berryman, Jack. "From the Cradle to the Playing Field: America's Emphasis on

Highly Organized Competitive Sports for Preadolescent Boys." *Journal of Sport History* 2 (Fall 1975): 112-131.

Biale, David, Michael Galchinsky and Susan Heschel, ed. *Insider/Outsider: American Jewish and Multiculturalism*. Berkeley: University of California Press, 1998.

Biale, David. *Power and Powerlessness in Jewish History*. New York: Schocken Books, 1986.

Bjarkman, Peter C. *Hoopla: A Century of College Basketball*. Indianapolis: Masters Press, 1996.

Bledstein, Burton J. *The Culture of Professionalism: The Middle Class and the Development of Higher Education in America*. New York: Norton, 1976.

Bledstein, Burton, and Robert D. Johnston, ed. *The Middling Sorts: Explorations in the History of the American Middle Class*. New York: Routledge, 2000.

Blumin, Stuart M. *The Emergence of the Middle Class: Social Experience in the American City, 1760-1900*. New York: Cambridge University Press, 1989.

Bodnar, Allen. *When Boxing was a Jewish Sport*. Westport, CT.: Praeger, 1997.

Bodnar, John. *The Transplanted: A History of Immigrants in Urban America*. Bloomington: Indiana University Press, 1985.

Bogen, Hyman. *The Luckiest Orphans: A History of the Hebrew Orphan Asylum of New York*. Urbana: University of Illinois Press, 1992.

Borish. Linda J. "'Athletic Activities of Various Kinds': Physical Health and Sports Programs for Jewish-American Women." *Journal of Sport History* 21 (Summer 1995): 241-250.

———. "'An Interest in Physical Well-Being Among the Female Membership': Sporting Activities for Women the Young Men's and Young Women's Hebrew Associations." *American Jewish History* 87 (March 1999): 61-93.

———. "The Robust Woman and Muscular Christian: Catharine Beecher, Thomas Higginson, and Their Vision of American Society, Health, and Physical Activities." *International Journal of Sport History* 4 (1987): 139-154.

———. "Settlement Houses to Olympic Stadiums: Jewish American Women, Sports, and Social Change, 1880s-1930s." *Journal of Sport History* 23 (1987): 5-24.

Boyarin, Daniel. *Unheroic Conduct: The Rise of Heterosexuality and the Invention of the Jewish Man.* Berkeley: University of California Press, 1997.

Boyarin, Jonathan and Daniel Boyarin, ed. *Jews and Other Differences: The New Jewish Cultural Studies.* Minneapolis: University of Minnesota Press, 1997.

Brinkley, Alan. *Liberalism and its Discontents.* Cambridge: Harvard University Press, 1998.

Brodkin, Karen. *How Jews Became White Folks and What that Says About Race in America.* New Brunswick: Rutgers University Press, 1998.

Brown, Phil, ed. *In the Catskills: A Century of the Jewish Experience in "The Mountains"* New York: Columbia University Press, 2002.

Brumberg, Stephen. "Going to America, Going to School: The Immigrant Public School Experience in Turn of the Century New York City." *American Jewish Archives* (Spring 1984): 86-135.

Buhle, Paul. "Jews and American Communism: The Cultural Question." *Radical History Review* 23 (1980): 9-31.

———, ed. *Jews and American Popular Culture.* Westport, CT: Praeger Publishers, 2006.

Bullough, Vern L., and Bonnie Bullough. *Women and Prostitution: A Social History.* Buffalo, NY: Prometheus Books, 1987.

Butler, Judith. *Gender Trouble: Feminism and the Subversion of Identity.* New York: Routledge, 1990.

Butsch, Richard, ed. *For Fun or Profit: The Transformation of Leisure into Consumption.* Philadelphia: Temple University Press, 1990.

Cahn, Susan K. *Coming on Strong: Gender and Sexuality in 20th Century Women's Sport.* New York: Free Press, 1994.

———. "Sports Talk: Oral History and Its Uses, Problems, and Possibilities for Sport History." *The Journal of American History* 81, no. 2 (September 1994): 594-609.

Cantor, Aviva. *JewishWomen/Jewish Men: The Legacy of Patriarchy in Jewish Life.* San Francisco: HarperSanFrancisco, 1995.

Caponi, Gena Dagel, ed. *Signifyin(g), Sanctifyin', and Slam Dunking: A Reader in African American Expressive Culture*. Amherst, MA: University of Massachusetts Press, 1999.

Carson, Mina J. *Settlement Folk: Social Thought and the American Settlement Movement, 1885-1930*. Chicago: University of Chicago Press, 1990.

Carter, Dan T. *Scottsboro: A Tragedy of the American South*. Rev. ed. Baton Rouge: Louisiana State University Press, 1979.

Cashman, Sean D. *America in the Gilded Age: From the Death of Lincoln to the Rise of Theodore Roosevelt*. New York: New York University Press, 1993.

Cavallo, Dominick. *Muscles and Morals: Organized Playgrounds and Urban Reform, 1880-1920*. Philadelphia: University of Pennsylvania Press, 1981.

Christgau, John. *Tricksters in the Madhouse: Lakers vs. Globetrotters, 1948*. Lincoln, NE: University of Nebraska Press, 2004.

Cohen, Lizabeth. *A Consumer's Republic: The Politics of Mass Consumption in Postwar America*. New York: Knopf, 2003.

———. *Making a New Deal: Industrial Workers in Chicago, 1919-1939*. New York: Cambridge University Press, 1990.

Cohen, Rich. *Tough Jews: Fathers, Sons, and Gangster Dreams*. New York: Simon & Schuster, 1998.

Cohen, Stanley. *The Game They Played*. New York: Farrar, Straus, and Giroux, 1977.

Conzen, Kathleen Neils, et.al. "The Invention of Ethnicity: A Perspective from the U.S.A." *Journal of American Ethnic History* (Fall 1992): 3-43.

Cronon, William. *Nature's Metropolis: Chicago and the Great West*. New York: W.W. Norton, 1991.

Daniels, Roger. *Coming to America: A History of Immigration and Ethnicity in American Life*. New York: Perennial, 2002.

———. *Guarding the Golden Door: American Immigrant Policy and Immigrants Since 1882*. New York: Hill and Wang, 2004.

Davis, Allen F. *Spearheads for Reform: The Social Settlements and the*

Progressive Movement, 1890-1914.* New York: Oxford University Press, 1967.

Dawley, Alan. *Changing the World: American Progressives in War and Revolution.* Princeton: Princeton University Press, 2003.

de la Pena, Carolyn. *The Body Electric: How Strange Machines Built the Modern American.* New York: New York University Press, 2003.

Denning, Michael. *The Cultural Front: The Laboring of American culture in the 20th Century.* New York: Verso, 1996.

Diner, Hasia R. *In the Almost Promised Land: American Jews and Blacks, 1915-1935.* Westport, CT: Greenwood Press, 1977.

———. *A Time for Gathering: The Second Migration, 1820-1880.* Baltimore: Johns Hopkins University Press, 1992.

Diner, Hasia R. and Beryl Lieff Benderly. *Her Works Praise Her: A History of Jewish Women in America from Colonial Times to the Present.* New York: Basic Books, 2002.

Diner, Steven J. *A Very Different Age: Americans of the Progressive Age.* New York: Hill and Wang, 1998.

Dinnerstein, Leonard. *Antisemitism in America.* New York: Oxford University Press, 1994.

Dudziak, Mary L. *Cold War Civil Rights: Race and the Image of American Democracy.* Princeton: Princeton University Press, 2000.

Durham, Meenakashi Gigi, and Douglas M. Kellner. *Media and Cultural Studies: Keyworks.* Rev. ed. Malden, MA: Blackwell Publishing, 2006.

During, Simon, ed. *The Cultural Studies Reader.* New York: Routledge, 1991.

Dyreson, Mark. "American Ideas about Race and Olympic Races from the 1890s to the 1950s: Shattering Myths of Reinforcing Scientific Racism?" *Journal of Sport History* 28, no. 2 (2001): 173-215.

———. "The Emergence of Consumer Culture and the Transformation of Physical Culture: American Sports in the 1920s." *Journal of Sport History* 15, no. 4 (Winter 1989): 261-281.

———. *Making the American Team: Sport, Culture, and the Olympic Experience.* Urbana: University of Illinois Press, 1998.

———. "Marketing National Identity: The Olympic Games of 1932 and American Culture," *Olympika: The International Journal of Olympic Studies* 4 (1995): 23-43.

Efron, John M. *Defenders of the Race: Jewish Doctors and Race Science in Fin-De-Siecle Europe*. New Haven: Yale University Press, 1994.

Eisen, George. "Jewish History and the Ideology of Modern Sport: Approaches and Interpretations." *Journal of Sport History* 25, no. 3 (1998): 482-531.

———. "Olympic Ideology and Jewish Values: Conflict or Accommodation?" *Olympic Perspectives: Third International Symposium for Olympic Research*. (October 1996): 121-126.

———. "Sports, Recreation, and Gender: Jewish Immigrant Women in Turn-of-the-Century American (1880-1920)." *Journal of Sport History* 17, no. 1 (1991): 103-120.

Eisen, George, and David K. Wiggins, eds. *Ethnicity and Sport in North American History and Culture*. Westport, CT: Greenwood Press, 1994;

Entine, Jon. *Taboo: Why Black Athletes Dominate Sports and Why We Are Afraid to Talk About It*. New York: Public Affairs, 2000

Ewen, Elizabeth *Immigrant Women in the Land of Dollars: Life and Culture on the Lower East Side, 1890-1925*. New York: Monthly Review Press, 1985.

Ewen, Stuart. *PR! A Social History of Spin*. New York: Basic Books, 1996.

Faber, Eli. *A Time for Planting: The First Migration, 1654-1820*. Baltimore: Johns Hopkins University, 1992

Fass, Paula. *Outside In: Minorities and the Transformation of American Education*. New York: Oxford University Press, 1989.

Feingold, Henry L. *A Time for Searching: Entering the Mainstream, 1920-1945*. Baltimore: Johns Hopkins University Press, 1992.

Ferrante, Joan and Prince Brown, Jr., eds. *The Social Construction of Race and Ethnicity in the United States*. New York: Longman, 1998.

Figone, Albert J. "Gambling and College Basketball: The Scandal of 1951." *Journal of Sport History* 16, no. 1 (Spring 1989): 44-61.

Filene, Peter G. "The Progressive Movement." *American Quarterly* 22 (Spring 1970): 20-34.

Fishman, Robert. *Bourgeois Utopias: The Rise and Fall of Suburbia*. New York: Basic Books, 1987.

Foner, Eric. *Reconstruction: America's Unfinished Revolution, 1863-1877*. New York: Harper and Row, 1988.

Foulkes, Julia L. *Modern Bodies: Dance and American Modernism from Martha Graham to Alvin Ailey*. Chapel Hill: University of North Carolina Press, 2002.

Fox, Richard Wrightman, and T.J. Jackson Lears., eds. *The Culture of Consumption: Critical Essays in American History, 1880-1980*. New York: Pantheon Books, 1983.

Fox, Stephen. *Professional Baseball, Football, and Basketball in National Memory*. Lincoln: University of Nebraska Press, 1998.

Frankel, Jonathan, ed. *Jews and Gender: The Challenge to Hierarchy*. New York: Oxford University Press, 2000.

Frankel, Noralee, and Nancy S. Dye, eds. *Gender, Class, Race, and reform in the Progressive Era*. Lexington, KY: University Press of Kentucky, 1991.

Frey, James, and D. Stanley Eitzen. "Sport and Society," *Annual Review of Sociology* 17 (1991): 503-522.

Friedman, Reena S. *These Are Our Children: Jewish Orphanages in the United States, 1880-1925*. Hanover, NH: University Press of New England, 1994.

Fuchs, Lawrence. *The American Kaleidoscope: Race, Ethnicity, and the Civic Culture*. Middletown, CT: Wesleyan University Press, 1990.

Gabaccia, Donna R. *From the Other Side: Women, Gender, and Immigrant Life in the U.S., 1820-1990*. Bloomington: Indiana University Press, 1994.

———. "Liberty, Coercion, and the Making of Immigration Historians." *The Journal of American History* 84, no. 2 (September 1997): 570-575.

———. "*The Transplanted*: Women and Family in the Immigrant America." *Social Science History*, 12:3 (Fall 1988): 243-253.

Gabler, Neal. *An Empire of their Own: How the Jews Invented Hollywood*. New York: Crown Publishers, 1988.

Galily, Yair, and Michael Bar-Eli. "From Tal Brody to European Champions: Early Americanization and the 'Golden Age' of Israeli Basketball, 1965-1979." *Journal of Sport History* 32, no. 3 (2005): 303-327.

Gans, Herbert J. *Popular Culture and High Culture: An Analysis and Evaluation of Taste*. New York: Basic Books, 1999.

Gems, Gerald R. "Blocked Shot: The Development of Basketball in the African-American Community of Chicago." *Journal of Sport History* 23, no. 3 (Summer 1995): 135-148.

———. "Sport and the Forging of Jewish-American Culture: The Chicago Hebrew Institute." *American Jewish History* 83, no. 1 (March 1995): 15-26.

George, Nelson. *Elevating the Game: Black Men and Basketball*. New York: HarperCollins, 1992.

Gerber, David A., ed. *Anti-Semitism in American History*. Urbana: University of Illinois Press, 1986.

Gerber, Ellen. "The Controlled Development of Collegiate Sport for Women, 1923-1936." *Journal of Sport History* 2, no. 1 (1975): 1-28.

Gerlach, Larry R. "German Americans in Major League Baseball: Sport and Acculturation." in *The American Game: Baseball and Ethnicity*, edited by Lawrence Baldassaro and Richard Johnson, 27-54. Carbondale: Southern Illinois University Press, 2000.

Gerstle, Gary, "Liberty, Coercion, and the Making of Americans." *The Journal of American History* 84, no. 2 (September 1997): 524-558.

———. *Working Class Americanism: The Politics of Labor in a Textile City, 1914-1960*. New York: Cambridge University Press, 1989.

Gerstle, Gary, and Steve Fraser, eds. *The Rise and Fall of the New Deal Order, 1930-1980*. Princeton: Princeton University Press, 1989.

Gilman, Sander L. *Smart Jews: The Construction of the Image of Jewish Superior Intelligence*. Lincoln: University of Nebraska Press, 1996.

———. *The Jew's Body*. New York: Routledge, 1991.

Glenn, Susan A. *Daughters of the Shtetl: Life and Labor in the Immigrant Generation*. Ithaca: Cornell University Press, 1990

Glickman, Lawrence D., ed. *Consumer Society in American History: A Reader*. Ithaca: Cornell University Press, 1999.

Godley, Andrew. *Jewish Immigrant Entrepreneurship in New York and London, 1880-1914: Enterprise and Culture*. Basingstoke: Palgrave, 2001.

Goldbach, Erich. "Protestanism-Capitalism-Sports." *Journal of Sport History* 4, no. 1 (1977): 185-194.

Goldberg, David Theo and Michael Krausz, eds. *Jewish Identity*. Philadelphia: Temple University Press, 1993.

Goldstein, Eric L. "Contesting the Categories: Jews and Government Racial Classification in the United States." *Jewish History* 19, no. 1 (January 2005): 79-107.

———. "Different Blood Flows in Our Veins: Race and Jewish Self-Definition in late 19th Century America." *American Jewish History* 85, no. 1 (March 1997): 29-55.

———. *The Price of Whiteness: Jews, Race, and American Identity*. Princeton: Princeton University Press, 2006.

———. "The Unstable Other: Locating the Jew in Progressive-Era American Racial Discourse." *American Jewish History* 89, no. 4 (2002): 383-409.

Goodman, Cary. *Choosing Sides: Playground and Street Life On the Lower East Side*. New York: Schocken Books, 1979.

Gorelick, Sherry *City College and the Jewish Poor: Education in New York, 1880-1924*. New Brunswick: Rutgers University Press, 1981.

Goren, Arthur. *New York Jews and the Quest for Community: The Kehillah Experiment, 1908-1922*. New York: Columbia University Press, 1970.

Gorn Elliot J., and Warren Goldstein, *A Brief History of American Sports*. New York: Hill and Wang, 1993.

Gorn, Elliot J., and Michael Oriard. "Taking Sports Seriously." *Chronicle of Higher Education*, March 24, 1995.

Gosling, Francis G. *Before Freud: Neurasthenia and the American Medical Community, 1870-1910*. Urbana: University of Illinois Press, 1987.

Gossett, Thomas F. *Race: The History of an Idea in America*. Dallas: Southern

Methodist University Press, 1963.

Green, Ben. *Spinning the Globe: The Rise, Fall, and Return to Greatness of the Harlem Globetrotters*. New York: HarperCollins Publishing, 2005.

Greene, Theodore P. *America's Heroes: The Changing Models of Success in American Magazines*. New York: Oxford University Press, 1970.

Grover, Kathryn, ed. *Fitness in American Culture: Images of Health, Sport, and Body, 1840-1930*. Amherst, MA: University of Massachusetts Press, 1989.

Gruneau, Richard S. *Class, Sports, and Social Development*. Champaign, IL: Human Kinetics, 1999.

Gurock, Jeffrey S. *Judaism's Encounter with American Sports*. Bloomington: Indiana University Press, 2005.

———. *When Harlem Was Jewish, 1870-1930*. New York: Columbia University Press, 1979.

Gutman, Herbert G. *Work, Culture, and Society in Industrializing America: Essays in American Working-Class and Social History*. New York: Knopf, 1976.

Guttmann, Allen. *From Ritual to Record: The Nature of Modern Sports*. New York: Columbia University Press, 1978.

———. *Games and Empires: Modern Sports and Cultural Imperialism*. New York: Columbia University Press, 1994.

———. *Sport Spectators*. New York: Columbia University Press, 1986.

———. *A Whole New Ballgame: An Interpretation of American Sports*. Chapel Hill: University of North Carolina Press, 1988.

———. *Women's Sports: A History* (New York: Columbia University Press, 1991.

Handlin, Oscar. *The Uprooted: The Epic Story of the Great Migrations That Made the American People*. New York: Grosset and Dunlap, 1957.

Hardy, Stephen H. "Entrepeneurs, Organizations, and the Sport Marketplace: Subjects in Search of Historians." *Journal of Sport History* 13, no. 1 (Spring 1986): 14-33.

Heinze, Andrew. *Adapting to Abundance: Jewish Immigrants, Mass*

Consumption, and the Search for American Identity. New York: Columbia University Press, 1990.

Higham, John. *Send These To Me: Immigrants in Urban America*. Baltimore: Johns Hopkins University Press, 1984.

———. *Strangers in the Land: Patterns of American Nativism*. New Brunswick, NJ: Rutgers University Press, 1988.

Hoberman, John M. *Darwin's Athletes: How Sport Has Damaged Black America and Preserved the Myth of Race*. New York: Houghton Mifflin Co., 1997.

———. *Sport and Political Ideology*. Austin: Texas University Press, 1984.

———. "Why Jews Play Sports: Do Sport and Jewish Values Conflict?" *Moment* (April 1991).

Hofstadter, Richard. *The Age of Reform: From Bryan to FDR*. New York: Knopf, 1956.

———. *Social Darwinism in American Thought*. Rev. ed. Boston: Beacon Press, 1992.

Hollinger, David A. *Postethnic America: Beyond Multiculturalism*. New York: Basic Books, 1995.

Hopkins, Charles H. *The History of the YMCA in North America*. New York: Associated Press, 1951.

Horger, Marc. "Play By The Rules: The Creation of Basketball and the Progressive Era, 1891-1917." Ph.D. Dissertation, Ohio State University, 2001.

Horsman, Reginald. *Race and Manifest Destiny: The Origins of American Racial Anglo-Saxonism*. Cambridge: Harvard University Press, 1981.

Howe, Irving. *The World of Our Fathers: The Journey of the East European Jews in American and the Life They Found and Made*. New York: Harcourt Brace Jovanovich, 1976.

Hyman, Paula E. *Gender and Assimilation in Modern Jewish History: The Roles and Representations of Women*. Seattle: University of Washington Press, 1995.

———. "Gender and the Shaping of Modern Jewish Identities." *Jewish Social Studies* 8, nos., 2-3 (Winter-Spring 2002): 153-161.

———. "The Jewish Body Politic: Gendered Politics in the early 20th Century." *Nashim* 2 (Spring 1999): 37-51.

Ignatiev, Noel. *How the Irish Became White*. New York: Routledge, 1995.

Ikard, Robert W. *Just for Fun: The Story of AAU Women's Basketball*. Fayetteville, AK: University of Arkansas Press, 2005.

Ingham, A.G., B.J. Blissmer, and K. Wells-Davidson. "The Expendable Prolympic Self: Going Beyond the Boundaries of Sociology and Psychology of Sport." *Sociology of Sport Journal* 16 (1999): 236-285.

Isaacs, Neil D. *All The Moves: A History of College Basketball*. New York: Harper and Row, 1984.

———. *Vintage NBA: The Pioneer Era, 1946-1956*. Masters Press, 1996.

Jackson, Kenneth T. *Crabgrass Frontier: The Suburbanization of the United States*. New York: Oxford University Press, 1985.

Jacobson, Matthew Frye. *Special Sorrows The Diasporic Imagination of Irish, Polish, and Jewish Immigrants in the United States*. Cambridge: Harvard University Press, 1995.

———. *Whiteness of a Different Color: European Immigrants and the Alchemy of Race*. Cambridge: Harvard University Press, 1998.

Jaher, Frederic Cople. "Antisemitism in American Athletics." *Shofar* 20 (Fall 2001): 61-73.

Joselit, Jenna Weissman. "Against Ghettoism: A History of the Intercollegiate Menorah Association, 1906-1930." *American Jewish Archives* 30 (1978): 133-154.

———. *The Wonders of America: Reinventing Jewish Culture, 1880-1950*. New York: Hill and Wang, 1994.

Kammen, Michael G. *American Culture, American Tastes: Social Change and the 20th Century*. New York: Knopf, 1999.

Kaplan, Amy. *The Anarchy of Empire in the Making of U.S. Culture*. Cambridge: Harvard University Press, 2002.

Karabel, Jerome. *The Chosen: The Hidden History of Admission and Exclusion at Harvard, Yale, and Princeton*. New York: Houghton Mifflin, 2005.

Kaufman, David. *Shul with a Pool: The 'Synagogue Center' in American Jewish History*. Hanover, NH: University Press of New England, 1999.

Kaufman, Haim. "Jewish Sports in the Diaspora, Yishuv, and Israel: Between Nationalism and Politics." *Israel Studies* 10, no. 2 (2005): 147-167.

Kett, Joseph F. *Rites of Passage: Adolescence in America, 1790 to the present*. New York: Basic Books, 1977.

Kimmel, Michael S. *Manhood in America: A Cultural History*. New York: Free Press, 1996.

Kirchberg, Connie. *Hoop Lore: The History of the National Basketball Association*. Jefferson, NC: MacFarland & Company, 2007.

Kirsch, George B., Othello Harris, and Claire E. Nolte, eds. *Encyclopedia of Ethnicity and Sports in the United States*. Westport, CT: Greenwood, 2000.

Klapper, Melissa R. *Jewish Girls Coming of Age in America, 1860-1920*. New York: New York University Press, 2005.

Kline, Wendy. *Building a Better Race: Gender, Sexuality, and Eugenics from the Turn of the Century to the Baby Boom*. Berkeley: University of California Press, 2001.

Knobel, Dale T. *"America for Americans": The Nativist Movement in the United States*. New York: Twayne Publishers, 1996.

Koppett, Leonard. *24 Seconds to Shoot: An Informal History of the National Basketball Association*. New York: MacMillan, 1968.

Korelitz, Seth. "The Menorah Idea: From Religion to Culture, from Race to Ethnicity." *American Jewish History* 85, no. 1 (1997): 75-100.

Kruger, Arnd. "'Once the Olympics are through, we'll beat up the Jew' German Jewish Sport, 1898-1938 and the Anti-Semitic Discourse." *Journal of Sport History* 26, no. 2 (1999):

Kugelmass, Jack, ed. *Jews, Sports, and the Rites of Citizenship*. Urbana: University of Illinois Press, 2007.

Kurashige, Lon. *Japanese Americans Celebration and Conflict: A History of Ethnic Identity and Festival, 1934-1990*. Berkeley: University of California Press, 1994.

Kuska, Bob. *Hot Potato: How Washington and New York Gave Birth to Black Basketball and Changed America's Game Forever.* Charlottesville, VA.: University of Virginia Press, 2004.

LaFeber, Walter. *Michael Jordan and the New Global Capitalism.* New York: W.W. Norton, 1999.

Lears, T.J. Jackson. "The Concept of Cultural Hegemony: Problems and Possibilities," *The American Historical Review* 90:3 (June 1985): 567-593.

———. *Fables of Abundance: A Cultural History of Advertising in America* (New York: Basic Books, 1994.

———. *No Place of Grace: Antimodernism and the Transformation of American Culture, 1880-1920.* New York: Pantheon Books, 1981.

———. *Something for Nothing: Luck in America.* New York: Viking, 2003.

Leuchtenburg, William E. *The Perils of Prosperity, 1914-1932.* Chicago: University of Chicago Press, 1993.

Levine, Lawrence W. *Highbrow/Lowbrow: The Emergence of Cultural Hierarchy in America.* Cambridge: Harvard University Press, 1988.

Levine, Peter. *A.G. Spalding and the Rise of Baseball: The Promise of American Sport.* New York: Oxford University Press, 1985.

———. *Ellis Island to Ebbets Field: Sport and the American-Jewish Experience.* New York: Oxford University Press, 1992.

Levy, Joseph. "Maccabi Canada: Fifty Years (1950-2001) of Jewish Cultural Identity and Continuity through Sport." paper presented at the Third Maccabiah-Wingate International Congress, July 12-15, 2001.

Lim, Shirley Jennifer. *A Feeling of Belonging: Asian American Women's Public Culture, 1930-1960.* New York: New York University Press, 2006.

Lucas, John. "An Analysis of an 'Over-Crowded Worried Life': General Charles Hitchcock Sherrill's Tenure on the International Olympic Committee, 1922-1936." *Olympika: The International Journal of Olympic Studies* 11 (2002): 143-168.

Lutz, Tom. *American Nervousness, 1903: An Anecdotal History.* Ithaca: Cornell University Press, 1991.

Mandell, Richard D. *The Nazi Olympics*. New York: MacMillan, 1971.

Mangan, J.A., and Roberta Park, eds. *From 'Fair Sex' to Feminism: Sport and the Socialization of Women in Industrial and Post-Industrial Eras*. London: F. Cass, 1987.

Mangan, J.A., and James Walvin, ed. *Manliness and Morality: Middle-Class Morality in Britain and America, 1800-1940*. Manchester: Manchester University Press, 1987.

Marchand, Roland. *Creating the Corporate Soul: The Rise of Public Relations and Corporate Imagery in American Big Business*. Berkeley: University of California Press, 1998.

Margolick, David. *Beyond Glory: Joe Louis vs. Max Schmeling, and a World on the Brink*. New York: Knopf, 2005.

Matthews, Jean V. *The Rise of the New Woman: The Woman's Movement in America, 1875-1930*. Chicago: Ivan R. Dee, 2003.

May, Elaine Tyler. *Homeward Bound: American Families in the Cold War Era*. New York: Basic Books, 1991.

McCune, Mary. "Social Workers in the Muskeljudentum: 'Hadassah Ladies', 'Manly Men', and the Significance of Gender in the American Zionist Movement, 1912-1928." *American Jewish History* 86, no. 2 (June 1998): 135-164.

McGerr, Michael. *A Fierce Discontent: The Rise and Fall of the Progressive Movement in America, 1870-1920*. New York: Oxford University Press, 2005.

Medoff, Rafael." Shooting for the Jewish State: College Basketball Players and the 1947 U.S. Fundraising Campaign for the Jewish Revolt against the British in Palestine." *American Jewish History* 89, no. 3 (September 2001): 279-292.

Melosh, Barbara, ed. *Gender and American History Since 1890*. New York, Routledge, 1993.

Mendelsohn, Ezra. *On Modern Jewish Politics*. New York: Oxford University Press, 1993.

Messner, Michael *Taking the Field: Men, Women, and Sports*. Minneapolis, University of Minnesota Press, 2002.

Michels, Tony. *A Fire in their Hearts: Yiddish Socialists in New York.* Cambridge: Harvard University Press, 2003

Moore, Deborah Dash. *At Home in America: Second Generation New York Jews.* New York: Columbia University Press, 1981.

———. *B'nai B'rith and the Challenge of Ethnic Leadership.* Albany: State University of New York Press, 1981.

———. *GI Jews: How World War II Changed a Generation.* Cambridge, MA: Belknap Press, 2004.

Moran, Jeffrey T. *Teaching Sex: The Shaping of Adolescence in the 20th Century.* Boston: Harvard University Press, 2002.

Morgan, William J. *Leftist Theories of Sport: A Critique and Reconstruction.* Urbana: University of Illinois Press, 1994.

Mormino, Gary Ross. "The Playing Fields of St. Louis: Italian Immigrants and Sport." *Journal of Sport History* 9 (Summer 1982): 5-16.

Mosse, George L. *Confronting the Nation: Jewish and Western Nationalism.* Hanover: Brandeis University Press, 1993.

Mrozek, Donald J. "The Scientific Quest for Physical Culture and the Persistent Appeal of Quackery. *Journal of Sport History* 14, no. 1 (Spring 1987): 76-86.

———. *Sport and the American Mentality, 1880-1910.* Knoxville: University of Tennessee Press, 1983.

Naison, Mark. "Lefties and Righties: The Communist Party and Sports During the Great Depression." In *Sport in America: New Historical Perspectives*, ed. Donald Spivey. Westport, CT: Greenwood Press, 1985.

Nasaw, David. *Children of the City: At Work and At Play.* Garden City, NY: Anchor Press/Doubleday, 1985.

Nelson, Murry. "The Original Celtics and the 1926-27 American Basketball League." *Journal of Popular Culture.* 30, no. 2 (Fall 1996): 87-100.

———. *The Originals: The New York Celtics Invent Modern Basketball.* Bowling Green, OH.: Bowling Green University Popular Press, 1999.

Ngai, Mae. *Impossible Subjects: Illegal Aliens and the Making of Modern America.* Princeton: Princeton University Press.

Norwood, Stephen H., and Harold Brackman. "Going to Bat for Jackie Robinson: The Jewish Role in Breaking Baseball's Color Line." *Journal of Sport History* 26, no. 1 (Spring 1999): 115-141.

O'Hanlon, Timothy P. "School Sports as Social Training: The Case of Athletics and the Crisis of World War I." in *Sport in America: From Wicked Amusement to National Obsession*, ed. David K. Wiggins, 189-206. Champaign, IL: Human Kinetics, 1995.

Omi, Michael and Howard Winant. *Racial Formation in the United States: From the 1960s to the 1980s.* 2nd ed. New York: Routledge, 1994.

Oren, Dan A. *Joining the Club: A History of Jews and Yale*. New Haven: Yale University Press, 1985.

Oriard, Michael. *King Football: Sport and Spectacle in the Golden Age of Radio and Newsreels, Movies and Magazines, the Weekly and the Daily Press*. Chapel Hill: University of North Carolina Press, 2001.

———. *Reading Football: How the Popular Press Created an American Spectacle*. Chapel Hill: University of North Carolina Press, 1993.

Park, Roberta. "Physiology and Anatomy are Destiny!?: Brains, Bodies, and Exercise in 19th Century American Thought." *Journal of Sport History* 18, no. 1 (Spring 1991): 31-63.

Parratt, Catriona M. "Making Leisure Work: Women's Rational Recreation in Late Victorian and Edwardian England." *Journal of Sport History* 26, no. 3 (1999): 471-487.

Parrish, Michael E. *Anxious Decades: America in Prosperity and Depression, 1920-1941*. New York: W.W. Norton, 1992.

Pavin, Michele Helane. "Sports and Leisure of the American Jewish Community, 1848 to 1976." Ph.D. Dissertation: The Ohio State University, 1981.

Perlmann, Joel. *Ethnic Differences: Schooling and Social Structure among the Irish, Italians, Jews, and Blacks in an American City, 1880-1935*. New York: Cambridge University Press, 1988.

Peiss, Kathy L. *Cheap Amusements: Working Women and Leisure in Turn-of-the-Century New York*. Philadelphia: Temple University Press, 1986.

Peterson, Robert. *Cages to Jump Shots: Pro Basketball's Early Years*. New York: Oxford University Press, 1990.

Pfister, Gertrud, and Toni Niewerth. "Jewish Women in Gymnastics and Sport in Germany, 1898-1938." *Journal of Sport History* 26, no. 2 (Summer 1999): 287-325.

Phillips, Murray G., ed. *Deconstructing Sport History: A Postmodern Analysis*. Albany: SUNY Press, 2006.

Pluto, Terry. *Loose Balls: The Short, Wild Life of the American Basketball Association* (New York: Simon and Schuster, 1990.

Polster, Gary E. *Inside Looking Out: The Cleveland Jewish Orphan Asylum, 1868-1924*. Kent, OH: Kent State University Press, 1990.

Pope, Steven W. "American Muscles and Minds: Public Discourse and the Shaping of National Identity During Early Olympiads, 1896-1920." Proceedings. First International Symposium for Olympic Research, (February 1992): 105-124.

———. "An Army of Athletes: Playing Fields, Battlefields, and the American Military Sporting Experience, 1890-1920." *Journal of Military History* 59, no. 3 (July 1995): 435-456.

———. "Negotiating the 'Folk Highway' of the Nation: Sport, Public Culture and American Identity, 1870-1940." *Journal of Social History*. 27, no. 2 (Winter 1993): 327-340.

Pope, S.W. *Patriotic Games: Sporting Traditions in the American Imagination, 1876-1926*. New York: Oxford University Press, 1997.

Prell, Riv-Ellen. *Fighting to Become Americans: Jews, Gender, and the Anxiety of Assimilation*. Boston: Beacon Press, 1999.

Presner, Todd Samuel. "Clear Heads, Solid Stomachs, and Hard Muscles: Max Nordau and the Aesthetics of Jewish Regeneration." *Modernism/modernity* 10, no. 2 (2003): 269-292.

Putney, Clifford. *Muscular Christianity: Manhood and Sports in Protestant America, 1880-1920*. Cambridge: Harvard University Press, 2001.

Rabinowitz, Benjamin *The Young Men's Hebrew Association, 1854-1913*. New York: National Jewish Welfare Board, 1948.

Rader, Benjamin G. *American Sports: From the Age of Falk Games to the Age of Television Sport*. New Jersey: Prentice Hall, 1999.

Raider, Mark A. *The Emergence of American Zionism*. New York: New York University Press, 1998.

Ratner, Sidney. "Horace M. Kallen and Cultural Pluralism." *Modern Judaism* 4, no. 2 (May 1984): 185-200.

Reimers, David M. *Unwelcome Strangers: American Identity and the Turn Against Immigration*. New York: Columbia University Press, 1998.

Riess, Steven A. *City Games: The Evolution of American Urban Society and Rise of Sports*. Urbana and Chicago: University of Illinois Press, 1989.

———, ed. *Major Problems in American Sports History*. Boston: Houghton Mifflin, 1995.

———. *Sport in Industrial America, 1850-1920*. Wheeling, IL: Harlan Davidson, 1995.

———, ed. *Sports and the American Jew*. Syracuse: Syracuse University Press, 1997.

Rockaway, Robert and Arnon Gutfeld. "Demonic Images of the Jew in the 19th Century United States." *American Jewish History* 89, no. 4 (December 2001): 355-381.

Rodgers, Daniel T. "In Search of Progressivism." *Reviews in American History* 10 (December 1982): 113-132.

Roediger, David R. *The Wages of Whiteness: Race and the Making of the American Working Class*. New York: Verso, 1991.

———. *Working toward Whiteness: How America's Immigrants Became White. The Strange Journey from Ellis Island to the Suburbs*. New York: Basic Books, 2005.

Rogin, Michael. *Blackface, White Noise: Jewish Immigrants in the Hollywood Melting Pot*. Berkeley: University of California Press, 1996.

Rose, Elizabeth. "From Sponge Cake to Hamentashen: Jewish Identity in a Jewish Settlement House, 1885-1952." *Journal of American Ethnic History* 14, no. 3 (Spring 1994): 1-9.

Rosen, Charley. *Scandals of '51: How the Gamblers Almost Killed College Basketball*. New York: Holt, Rinehart, and Winston, 1970.

———. *The Wizard of Odds: How Jack Molinas Almost Destroyed the Game of*

Basketball. New York: Seven Stories Press, 2001.

Rosenzweig, Roy. *Eight Hours for What We Will: Workers and Leisure in an Industrial City, 1870-1920*. Cambridge: Cambridge University Press, 1983.

Rotundo, E. Anthony. *American Manhood: Transformation in Masculinity from the Revolution to the Modern Era*. New York: Basic Books, 1993.

Rumbaut, Ruben G., and Alejandro Portes. *Immigrant America: A Portrait*. Berkeley: University of California Press, 1996.

Sanchez, George. *Becoming Mexican American: Ethnicity, Culture, and Identity in Chicano Los Angeles, 1900-1945*. New York: Oxford University Press, 1993.

Sanua, Marianne. *Going Greek: Jewish College Fraternities in the United States, 1895-1945*. Detroit: Wayne State University, 2003.

Sarna, Jonathan D., and Pamela Nadell, eds. *Women and American Judaism: Historical Perspectives*. Hanover, NH: University Press of New England, 2001.

Scott, Joan. *Gender and the Politics of History*. New York: Columbia University Press, 1988.

Shapiro, Edward S. *A Time for Healing: American Jewry Since World War II*. Baltimore: Johns Hopkins University Press, 1992.

———. "The World Labor Athletic Carnival of 1936: An American Anti-Nazi Protest." *American Jewish History* 59 (March 1985): 255-273.

———. "World War II and American Jewish Identity." *Modern Judaism* 10, no. 1 (February 1990): 65-84.

Shapiro, Judah Joseph. *The Friendly Society: A History of the Workmen's Circle*. New York: Media Justice, 1970.

Silber, Irwin. *Press Box Red: The Story of Lester Rodney, the Communist Who Helped Break the Color Line in American Sports* (Philadelphia: Temple University Press, 2003.

Silberstein, Laurence J. "Others Within and Others Without: Rethinking Jewish Identity and Culture." In *The Other in Jewish Thought and History: Construction of Jewish Culture and Identity*, edited by Laurence J.

Silberstein and Robert L. Cohn, 1-34. New York: New York University Press, 1994.

Singerman, Robert. "The Jew as Racial Alien: The Genetic Component of American Anti-Semitism." In *Anti-Semitism in American History*, edited by David A. Gerber. Urbana: University of Illinois Press, 1986.

Singh, Nikhil Pal. *Black is a Country: Race and the Unfinished Struggle for Democracy*. Cambridge: Harvard University Press, 2004.

Smith, Ronald A. *Sports and Freedom: The Rise of Big-Time College Athletics*. New York: Oxford University Press, 1988.

Sollors, Werner. *Beyond Ethnicity: Consent and Descent in American Culture*. New York: Oxford University Press, 1986.

Sorin, Gerald. *A Time for Building: The Third Migration, 1880-1920*. Baltimore: Johns Hopkins University, 1992.

———. *The Nurturing Neighborhood: The Brownsville Boys Club and Jewish Community in Urban America, 1940-1990*. New York: New York University Press, 1990.

Soyer, Daniel. "Brownstones and Brownsville: Elite Philanthropists and Immigrant Constituents at the Hebrew Educational Society of Brooklyn, 1889-1929." *American Jewish History* 88, no. 2 (2000): 181-206.

———. *Jewish Immigrant Associations and American Identity in New York, 1880-1939*. Cambridge: Harvard University Press, 1997

Spiegel, Nina. S. Jewish Cultural Celebrations and Competitions in Mandatory Palestine, 1920-1947: Body, Beauty, and the Search for Authenticity." Ph.D. Dissertation, Stanford University, 2001.

Stearns, Peter N. *Fat History: Bodies and Beauty in the Modern West*. New York: New York University Press, 2002.

Sterba, Christopher M. *Good Americans: Italian and Jewish Immigrants during the First World War*. New York: Oxford University Press, 2003.

Streebny, Shelley. *American Sensations: Class, Empire, and the Production of Popular Culture*. Berkeley: University of California-Berkeley Press, 2002.

Steinberg, Stephen. *The Ethnic Myth: Race, Ethnicity, and Class in America*, 3rd ed. Boston: Beacon Press, 2001.

Storey, John. *Cultural Theory and Popular Culture: An Introduction.* 4th ed. Athens, GA: University of Georgia Press, 2006.

Susman, Warren. *Culture as History: The Transformation of American Society in the Twentieth Century.* New York: Pantheon Books, 1984.

Synnot, Marcia Graham. *The Half-Opened Door: Discrimination and Admissions at Harvard, Yale, and Princeton, 1900-1970.* Westport, CT.: Greenwood Press, 1979.

Takaki, Ronald T. *A Different Mirror: A History of Multicultural America.* Boston: Little, Brown, and Co., 1993.

———. *Iron Cages: Race and Culture in Nineteenth-Century America.* New York: Knopf, 1979.

Thelin, John R. *Games College Play: Scandal and Reform in Intercollegiate Athletics.* Baltimore: Johns Hopkins University Press, 1994.

Thomas. Ron. *They Cleared the Lane: The NBA's Black Pioneers.* Lincoln: University of Nebraska Press, 2002.

Todd, Jan. "Bernarr McFadden: Reformer of Feminine Form." *Journal of Sport History* 14, no. 1 (Spring 1987): 61-75.

Toll, William. "Horace Kallen: Pluralism and American Jewish Identity." *American Jewish History* 85, no. 1 (1997): 57-74.

Tomes, Nancy. *The Gospel of Germs: Men, Women, and the Microbe in American Life.* Cambridge: Harvard University Press, 1998.

Trachtenberg, Alan. *The Incorporation of America: Culture and Society in the Gilded Age.* New York: Hill and Wang, 1982.

Urofsky, Melvin I. *American Zionism from Herzl to the Holocaust.* Garden City, NY: Anchor Press, 1975.

Vecoli, Rudolph. "Contadini in Chicago: A Critique of The Uprooted." *Journal of American History* 1:3 (December 1964): 404-417.

Vincent, Ted. *The Rise and Fall of American Sport: Mudville's Revenge.* Lincoln, NE: University of Nebraska Press, 1994.

Ward, Geoffrey C. *Unforgivable Blackness: The Rise and Fall of Jack Johnson.* New York: A.A. Knopf, 2004.

Ware, Susan. *Beyond Suffrage: Women in the New Deal*. Cambridge, MA: Harvard University Press, 1981.

Webb, Bernice Larson. *The Basketball Man: James Naismith*. Lawrence, KS: University of Kansas Press, 1973.

Wenger, Beth S. *New York Jews and the Great Depression: Uncertain Promise*. New Haven: Yale University Press, 1996.

Wettan, Richard, and Joe Willis. "Social Stratification in New York City's Athletic Clubs, 1865-1915." *Journal of Sport History* 3, no. 1 (1976): 45-62.

Wheeler, Robert F. "Organized Sport and Organized Labour: The Workers Sports Movement." *Journal of Contemporary History* 13 (1978): 191-207.

Wiebe, Robert H. *The Search for Order*. New York: Hill and Wang, 1967.

Wiggins, David K. "'Great Speed but Little Stamina': The Historical Debate Over Black Athletic Superiority." *Journal of Sport History* 16, no. 2 (1989): 158-185.

Wiggins, David K., ed. *Sport in America: From Wicked Amusement to National Obsession*. Champaign, IL: Human Kinetics, 1995.

Wiggins, David K., and Patrick B. Miller, eds., *The Unlevel Playing Field: A Documentary History of the African-American Experience in Sport*. Urbana: University of Illinois Press, 2003.

Winter, Thomas. *Making Men, Making Class: The YMCA and Workingmen, 1877-1920*. Chicago: University of Chicago Press, 2002.

Yep, Kathleen Susan. "They Got Game: The Racial and Gender Politics of Basketball in San Francisco's Chinatown, 1932-1949." Ph.D. Dissertation, University of California, Berkeley, 2002.

Yoo, David. K. *Growing Up Nisei: Race, Generation, and Culture among Japanese Americans of California, 1924-49*. Urbana: University of Chicago Press, 2000.

Zieff, Susan G. "From Badminton to Bolero: Physical Recreations in San Francisco's Chinatown, 1895-World War II." *Journal of Sport History* 27, no. 1 (2000): 1-30.

Zimbalist, Andrew. *Unpaid Professionals: Commercialism and Conflict in Big-Time College Sports*. Princeton: Princeton University Press, 2001.

Zucker, Bat-Ami. "American Jewish Communists and Jewish Culture in the 1930s." *Modern Judaism* 14, no. 2 (May 1994): 175-185.

CPSIA information can be obtained at www.ICGtesting.com
Printed in the USA
LVOW110759090513

332978LV00005B/297/P